THE
GIRL AND THE
GAME

THE
GIRL AND THE
GAME

a history of women's sport in canada

M. ANN HALL

b
broadview press

National Library of Canada Cataloguing in Publication Data

Hall, M. Ann (Margaret Ann), 1942–
     The girl and the game : a history of women's sports in Canada

ISBN 1-55111-268-X

1. Sports for women—Canada—History. I. Title.

GV709.18.C2H338 2002   796'.082'0971   C2002-901007-1

Broadview Press Ltd. is an independent, international publishing house, incorporated in 1985.

North America
Post Office Box 1243, Peterborough, Ontario, Canada K9J 7H5
3576 California Road, Orchard Park, NY 14127
Tel: (705) 743–8990; Fax: (705) 743-8353;
E-mail: customerservice@broadviewpress.com

United Kingdom and Europe
Plymbridge North (Thomas Lyster, Ltd.)
Units 3 & 4A, Ormskirk Industrial Park, Burscough Road, Ormskirk,
Lancashire L39 2YW Tel: (1695) 575112; Fax: (1695) 570120;
E-mail: books@tlyster.co.uk

Australia
St. Clair Press, P.O. Box 287, Rozelle, NSW 2039
Tel: (02) 818-1942; Fax: (02) 418-1923

www.broadviewpress.com

Broadview Press gratefully acknowledges the financial support of the Book Publishing Industry Development Program, Ministry of Canadian Heritage, Government of Canada.

Typesetting and text design: Susan Thomas/Digital Zone

PRINTED IN CANADA

To several women physical educators whose influence upon me and others was substantial and long lasting: Judy Dunlop, Marion Ross, Anne Turnbull, Dorothy Leggett, Helen Bryans, Jean Stirling, Helen Gurney, Ruby Anderson, and Patricia Austin.

CONTENTS

Preface and Acknowledgements
IX
Introduction
I

CHAPTER 1
Early Beginnings: The "New Woman" and Athleticism
15

CHAPTER 2
Assuming Control: Women's Sport Run (Almost) By Women
41

CHAPTER 3
Girls Shouldn't Do It!: Debates over Competition and Sexuality
73

CHAPTER 4
Sweetheart Heroines: Athletic and Lovely
104

CHAPTER 5
Serious Athletes or "Oddballs"?: Transitional Years
135

CHAPTER 6
Feminist Activism: Inching Towards Gender Equity
161

CHAPTER 7
The Commodification of Physicality: 1990s and Beyond
188

Epilogue
212
Notes
217
Sources
253
Index
275

Preface and Acknowledgements

The process of writing this book goes back a long way. In the mid-1960s, I researched and wrote a history of women's sport in Canada prior to World War I as a master's degree thesis at the University of Alberta. These were the early days of sport history in Canada, and I was one of several students guided by Maxwell L. Howell, who had decided to compile, sport by sport and era by era, a Canadian history of sport. Others have described these early efforts as the "one damn fact after another" genre of descriptive history, and to some extent I agree.[1] We were all amateur historians in those days, coming to our subject with little previous training in historiography, but with a consuming passion for sport, mostly because we were athletes or physical educators or both. Even so, my story of women's sport was not told in isolation from the social and political climate of the times in that I discussed topics like female emancipation, women's fashions, higher education, and women's suffrage as a backdrop to their sport. It was, nonetheless, a beginning.

My doctoral studies in the early 1970s had little to do with history, as I was more interested in solving the immediate problems of women's sport, and, more importantly, figuring out how they could best be researched. I embarked on what turned out to be a 30-year journey of applying a feminist analysis to sport and gender, something I tried to make sense of in *Feminism and Sporting Bodies* published in 1996.

Meanwhile, gender became a category of analysis within sport history, bringing with it a burgeoning scholarship in sport and gender relations aimed at much more than simply writing women into sport history. "It seeks," wrote Patricia Vertinsky, "to forge new understandings of the historical relationship between sport and the social construction of gender by examining gender as a dynamic, relational process through which the unequal power relations between women and men have been continually constructed and contested."[2] Although there was a risk that a focus on gender and gender relations could obscure, marginalize, or even erase women, the implication was that women's sport and physical activity history needed to be more theoretically and sociologically grounded than was true of earlier work.[3] Some recent, and not so recent, historical studies have fulfilled this promise; as examples, I would point to books by Susan Cahn, Susan Cayleff, Mary Jo Festle, Jennifer Hargreaves, Helen Lenskyj, Kathleen McCrone, Marion Stell, Jan Todd, and Patricia Vertinsky.

My decision to continue researching the history of women's sport in Canada was based on several considerations. There was still no comprehensive history, which in some ways I found disappointing, but given the magnitude of the task, I now understand why. Also, what I have written is a much different history than I would have written 30 years ago. Along with many exemplary studies in women's sport history, there are several decades worth of feminist historiography, none of which was available to me in the 1960s. Finally, I was fortunate to receive a substantial research grant from the Social Sciences and Humanities Research Council, which provided the necessary funds to hire research assistants, travel to archives, conduct interviews, and much else. The project was started 10 years ago, and in the process I retired from the University of Alberta, taking with me the task of completing this book.

A good deal of the initial research, especially the arduous chore of reading old newspapers on microfilm, was done by several of my former students, whose diligence and organization saved me countless hours of searching. They are Christine Dallaire, Judith Davidson, Brenda Grace, Deborah Hambly, Erin McKee, Bethanne O'Neil, Julie Stevens, Catrin Thomas, and Vicki Thoms.

I benefited from the patience and expertise of the staffs at several public archives and sport museums across the country. Many I visited personally, and where that was not possible, I sought out information on their newly developed websites, often corresponding by e-mail. The archives visited were the Nanaimo District Museum, City of Edmonton Archives, Provincial Archives of Alberta, Toronto Port Authority Archives, Archives of Ontario, City of Toronto Archives, Vancouver City Archives, Provincial Archives of British Columbia, Western Canadian Pictorial Index (Winnipeg), Glenbow Museum Archives (Calgary), National Archives of Canada, and York University Archives. Sports halls of fame and museums visited were Canada's Sports Hall of Fame (Toronto), Northwestern Ontario Sports Hall of Fame (Thunder Bay), Royal Canadian Golf Association Hall of Fame (Oakville), Saskatchewan Sports Hall of Fame (Regina), Aquatic Hall of Fame and Museum of Canada (Winnipeg), British Columbia Sports Hall of Fame and Sports Museum (Vancouver), and the Alberta Sports Hall of Fame and Museum (Red Deer). Kathy Meagher at the New Brunswick Sports Hall of Fame (Fredericton), Tom West at the Olympic Sports Hall of Fame and Museum (Calgary), and Stephen Coutts at the Nova Scotia Hall of Fame and Museum (Halifax) immediately answered by e-mail requests for information. Finally, I spent many hours in the University of Alberta libraries, as well as the Metropolitan Toronto Reference Library, always graciously assisted by helpful staff.

I am also grateful to the following individuals for never failing to answer my questions or help me find elusive bits of information; in some cases they have done so repeatedly over several years: Marie-Claude Asselin, Nancy Bouchier, Susan Forbes, Gretchen Ghent, Bruce Kidd, Gilles Janson, Mary Jollimore, Anna Lathrop, Helen Lenskyj, Bill Mallon, Bill McNulty, Don Morrow, Susan Neill, Vicky Paraschak, Barbara Schrodt, Allan Stewart, and Nancy Theberge.

Certainly one of the most enjoyable aspects of this project was meeting and talking with women who had either competed for Canada in the past or were recognized pioneers and leaders in women's sport. Many were quite elderly, and unfortunately several have since passed away. I sat at many a kitchen table listening with admiration as these women (and some men) delighted in helping me understand what it was like in their time. I only wish it would have been possible to interview more of the many fascinating individuals who have contributed to our rich sporting heritage.

Three individuals — namely, Nancy Bouchier, Mary Jollimore, and Patricia Vertinsky — read the manuscript in draft form. Their encouragement and suggestions were most welcome and helpful, but I take full responsibility for any errors or unexplained omissions.

Finally, there are people around me who have lived with this project since its inception, always providing just the right blend of encouragement and admonition to complete it. Colleagues and friends politely listened to my endless stories about women's sporting past, often commenting or asking pertinent questions, which inevitably sharpened my thinking. Also interested and supportive were fellow members of the Beckwith Belles, marvellous women whose passions include riding horses, and forever trying to do it better. Michael Harrison at Broadview Press was unfailingly patient as one deadline passed after another. My mother, Kate Hall, invariably on the lookout for new information or individuals to interview, as well as taking on any job I requested, has been a tremendous help. Lastly, Jane Haslett, scholar and editor *extraordinaire*, was always there and understands better than anyone why projects like these take so long to complete.

INTRODUCTION

The history of modern sport is a history of cultural struggle. Privileged groups in our society — seemingly by consent — are able to establish their own cultural practices as the most valued and legitimate, whereas subordinate groups (like women) have to fight to gain and maintain control over their own experience, and at the same time have their alternative practices and activities recognized as legitimate by the dominant culture. Sport in our culture is still viewed by many as a "masculinizing project," a cultural practice in which boys learn to be men and male solidarity is forged. It remains a prime site for the maintenance of masculine or male hegemony, which refers to the ways in which male power shapes our view of the world. As an explanatory tool, hegemony allows us to conceptualize resistance and to recognize how dominant power groups seek to shape, manipulate, or control that resistance mainly by incorporating its elements into the existing hegemonic structures. For example, when women actively participate in the symbols, practices, and institutions of sport, what they do there is often not considered "real" sport, nor in some cases are they viewed as real women.[1]

What follows from this notion of sport as a site of cultural struggle is that the history of women in sport is a history of cultural resistance. In fact, the very presence of women in the male preserve of sport is evidence of "leaky hegemony."[2] How masculine hegemony in Canadian sport was resisted by women, and, in turn, how their efforts were opposed, and sometimes supported, by men is the subject of this book. It is the story of the many ordinary women (and some men) who contributed to the development of women's sport in Canada. Here, too, are the stories of outstanding women athletes of our past, many of whom have long since been forgotten.

Women continually resisted popular notions of their biologically restricted bodies through their involvement in male-defined sport, but at the same time their physical emancipation was rarely without opposition, certainly from men, and sometimes from other women. As time went on, women became more welcome on the playing fields, but they were never viewed as men's equal there.

1

As lesser athletes, they could never expect an equal portion of the athletic pie in terms of facilities, resources, coaching, training, and sponsorship, all of which provoked legal, ethical, and strategic challenges to these inequities. More recently, increasing numbers of women have gained greater access to traditionally male sports like rugby, soccer, weightlifting, body-building, and the martial arts, further challenging the gender boundaries of sport. Many of these battles are still fought today, under different terms and conditions, but resistance is never wholly successful, and it often does not result in a transformed cultural practice. Women's long history of confronting a male preserve like sport illustrates the "double movement of containment and resistance" that characterizes cultural struggles among dominant and subordinate groups. On the one hand, their presence today as physically powerful females demonstrates that sporting prowess was never naturally masculine; on the other, it continues to precipitate attempts by males to contain their resistance and aspirations.[3]

History is never linear in that events and eras do not flow seamlessly from one to another; rather, it is complicated, messy, and difficult to reassemble even a partial story from the perspective of the present. Even still, I chose to write the narrative chronologically for several reasons. Since the full story of women's sport in Canada has not been told before, it is important to pay attention to what went before and what came after a particular historical period. Students, other scholars, and those reading this book for pleasure will, I hope, find it easier going because the story flows through the decades rather than back and forth, or out of sequence, which would be the result if a thematic approach had been applied instead. Themes, of course, are developed within each chapter, and some are maintained throughout the entire book. For example, discussed throughout is the complex synergy between women's sport and gender relations in the wider Canadian society and how it has changed over the decades. Another is the changing media discourse about women's participation in sport, especially the emergence of the lesbian stereotype. I have also applied a very broad brush in writing this story for no other reason than so little has been written before. It is important to develop the big picture and leave it to others to fill in the details through more specific studies. In the end, a chronological approach makes it easier to see what is missing or what requires more in-depth study.

I follow traditional notions of historical periodization by allowing more significant events in Canadian history to shape and define the eras around which the story of women's sport is told. My decisions as to which significant events should structure the narrative are based on their historical impact upon gender relations and women's lives generally in Canada and to a lesser extent on their impact on Canadian sport. In other words, the story of women's sport, although clearly intertwined with developments in men's sport, makes more sense when we take into account the changing patterns of gender relations and their impact on cultural institutions. Although it has its roots in the nineteenth century and before, the story of women's sport in Canada takes place mostly in the twentieth century and, of course, is going on today.

According to historians, there are two major turning points in the history of women in Canada during the last century.[4] The first occurred during World War I when two major goals of the early suffrage movement were accomplished — prohibition and the right to vote — marking the end of an era. The world of the pioneer and the upper-class gentlewoman gave way to that of the "flapper" and working girl of the 1920s. Although women's sport was well established and flourishing in colleges and universities prior to the outbreak of war, there were few opportunities for the vast majority of young women unable to afford a higher education. The war changed all this. Working-class women, who flocked to the cities in search of employment, sought recreational opportunities in their spare time, and many turned to sport. They led the grass-roots movement that established women's athletic clubs, organizations, and leagues in a variety of sports, but especially basketball, ice hockey, softball, and track and field. The war was responsible for an increase in women's participation because rather than cancelling all competition, they often continued their games and tournaments to support patriotic causes or to raise money for the war effort. With so many men away, women took on more organizational responsibilities in the private sport clubs, which gave them more confidence to establish and run their own sport clubs and organizations after the war.

The second turning point occurred during World War II when married women entered the labour force in massive numbers and remained in increasing numbers over the succeeding decades. Marriage had previously transformed the lives of women, but now it was less of a transition as women worked outside the home for much of their adult lives. Again, women's sport flourished during a time of war — they used sport to raise money for a variety of war-related projects and agencies, to entertain the home-based troops, and to provide healthy recreation for girls and women. They kept their sports going, often taking over the coaching and training from absent men. Certainly the war interrupted and changed sporting careers because many national, and certainly all international, competitions were cancelled; women sportswriters disappeared from the pages of daily newspapers as they took up new assignments and responsibilities. In the immediate postwar period and into the 1950s, in a society obsessed with normalizing daily life, women's sport became increasingly characterized by a remarkable emphasis on beauty, grace, femininity, and, for some, glamour.

To these two turning points, I add a third: the resurgence of feminist activity beginning in the late 1960s, which brought about the modern women's movement.

There are some who argue that today we are in a post-feminist era, and, if this is the case, it recognizes the significance and importance of over three decades of feminist activism and organizing. It took some time for women's sport to become part of the feminist agenda, but eventually it did through, for example, legal challenges for the right of girls to play sports with boys, federal and provincial government gender equity policies and programs, and feminist advocacy organizations focussed on women's sport and physical activity.

The notion of "sport" used throughout this book is a restricted one. In a word, I mean *organized* sport, indicating that the learning of game skills becomes institutionalized through teaching and systemic preparation and that organizations evolve (clubs, schools, provincial and national sport organizations) whose purposes are to prepare competitors and regulate the competitions.[5] This does not mean I discuss activities only when the participants are training for, or competing in, organized races, because clearly, in the case of most women's sports, it took some time to reach that point; recreational activities, physical culture, and physical education all played a role in the development of women's sport. What it does mean, however, in picking a beginning point for the story, is that I chose the 1880s because that is when the first indications of organized (white) women's sport appear in Canada. They did not arise suddenly in isolation from all that went before, however, and it is important to recognize this heritage, if only briefly.

Long before the first French-speaking European women settled in Canada in the early seventeenth century, native women worked and played in the various hunting and gathering, fishing and farming cultures of early aboriginal peoples, including the Inuit groups in the north, the Iroquoian and Algonquian peoples in the east, the Plains Indians of the prairies, as well as several distinct tribes along the Pacific coast. Relatively little is known about women's lives in these early native societies, especially before the coming of Europeans, but we do know that among their amusements and leisure were many indigenous games and contests, activities we today call sports, like shinny, lacrosse, and football. Some games were restricted to men, some to women, and in a few both sexes participated, sometimes against each other.[6]

Shinny, a hockey-like ball game played on a field or on ice in winter, was often considered a women's game. The small, round ball, made of wood or stuffed buckskin, was hit along the ground (or ice) by a curved stick, the object of which was to get it through two posts or sticks at the ends of the field. Double ball, a more difficult and faster version of shinny, was also primarily a women's game. Two balls were tied together with a thong and tossed about using a long, slender stick. Baggataway (as the Ojibwa called it) or lacrosse (as the French named it) was mainly a men's game, often with religious and ceremonial significance, or it was used as a training exercise for young warriors. Among some tribes, women would run out onto the field and bestow gifts of beads or other tokens to their favourite player, causing George Beers, a Montreal dentist who in the late nineteenth century modified and organized lacrosse for white players, to comment: "... if Canada's fair daughters would revive the fashion! How it would put one on one's mettle to be a crack player!"7 Some tribes permitted women to play providing it was away from male eyes, but in a few the two sexes played together, and the women were allowed to touch the ball with their hands. Most football-type games were like modern-day soccer, where a ball (often of stuffed deer hide) was kicked between two goal posts. When men and women played together, the women could often throw the ball whereas the men had to kick it, an early example of games being modified for females.

By mid-seventeenth century, New France was comprised of merchants seeking to transform fish, lumber, and particularly fur into handsome profits; colonial administrators struggling to reproduce the political and social structures of France in the wilderness; nuns and priests devoted to imposing a particularly austere brand of French Catholicism on natives and colonists alike; and ordinary *habitants* struggling to carve farms and a new life out of the forest. The settlers' experience varied widely, depending on their social rank and where they lived. Life among the upper classes in Quebec, for instance, was marked by relative comfort and sophistication compared to the hardships and real threats to their existence suffered by the rural *habitants*. Horseback riding was considered a very salutary exercise for women, although riding for pleasure, and only side-saddle, was restricted to those in the upper classes. Travel by carriole (a sleigh) in winter and horse carriage in summer was also recommended as suitable exercise for women. Dancing schools in the larger centres taught young people the minuets, cotillions, hornpipes, and country dances in vogue at the time, despite church edicts condemning dancing, especially when it entailed mingling between the sexes.

The fall of New France in 1775 ushered in a century of extraordinary change. With the arrival of the British came the military garrisons in such major centres as Halifax, Saint John, Fredericton, Quebec, Montreal, York (Toronto), Kingston, and Niagara. The garrisons brought military officers — wealthy, well-educated, and imbued with the English private school sporting tradition. Such sports as cricket, horse racing, and fox hunting, as well as the more socially oriented regattas and sleigh, tandem, and snowshoe clubs, began to flourish. What also became apparent were increasing divisions based on class, ethnicity, and gender. Comprising the dominant class were the colonial estate-holders and landowners, the military officers, and the growing mercantile class (retailers, bankers, exporters, and the like), mainly British and certainly all male. These were the people with the greatest dedication to new sporting pastimes because they were the ones least constrained by the demands of frontier life.

On the other hand, the "underclasses" emerging in the towns and cities, and certainly the rural farmers and frontier settlers, had neither the time nor the opportunity to participate in regular games or organized physical recreation. In her famous account of pioneer life, *Roughing It in the Bush*, Susanna Moodie, a gentlewoman immigrant from Britain in the 1830s, tells how unprepared she was for manual labour on uncleared farmland near Peterborough, Ontario. Farm life was often dreary and lonely and always hard, especially for women. In the cities and towns, the taverns and inns were the chief places of public amusements, but mostly for men. They served as general meeting places and convenient locations for dances, balls, and banquets as well as travelling circuses and amateur theatricals. Numerous sporting clubs and societies were born of the tavern, such as the group of Scottish merchants who met at Gillies Tavern in Montreal on January 22, 1807, to found the Montreal Curling Club, the first sports club in Canada, restricted to men, of course.

Just as there was growing tension between the dominant class and the underclasses, so, too, was there strain between the sexes. Increasingly, women wished to escape the bonds of tradition and to experience at least a modicum of independence and adventure. Some certainly did, whether they were gentlewomen like Susanna Moodie who accompanied their husbands into the bush or common folk who settled the land and built the farms. Class cut across gender as it always does. The upper-class ladies of Kingston, Ontario, in 1812, for instance, were admonished by the opposite sex for their innocent summer amusement of swinging: "... an exercise which, allowably beneficial to the health when practised in the proper place, loses that merit when a delicate girl mounts a lofty and dangerous swing just after leaving a warm tea room, and at that hour of all others when the chilly dew is most prejudicial to even a strong constitution." The offended ladies wrote a lengthy and witty rebuttal stating that they saw neither criminality nor impropriety in swinging and that "we shall without the least hesitation recommence that favourite amusement, with the season that permits it."[8] No doubt this controversy was ridiculous to the thousands of pioneer women in the countryside whose life was a continual struggle to feed, clothe, and house their children, often alone if the husband had succumbed to disease or accident.

Many native women's traditions, certainly their earlier games and amusements, most likely continued in some modified form, but there was little space for them in the white women's world. Regardless, their games and sports did not disappear once they were gradually resettled on native reserves; it is just that we know so little about them. Unlike several native male runners and lacrosse teams, who often toured with their own shows for the entertainment of colonial settlers, nineteenth-century aboriginal women rarely participated in any form of white-organized sport. One exception appears to be water regattas where native women sometimes took part in canoeing events. On one such occasion in 1867, Montreal's *Gazette* reported that in a race for native women, two war canoes "each manned or rather womanned by six or eight squaws ... came forward to battle for aqueous supremacy." The unflattering account described them as hefty women, each dressed in "modest skirts and jacket of crimson, orange or unassuming blue, each jabbering with female loquacity."9

The final legacy of this early period in Canadian sport history is the founding and growth of the urban sports club. By 1850, Toronto boasted six such clubs: cricket (1827), turf (1828), curling (1835), lawn bowling (1837), and hunt (1843). The taverns and pubs that had originally housed many of these clubs also bred an atmosphere of drunkenness and disorderliness, which led the aristocratic elite to develop their own private club quarters. These clubs were social rather than competitive in nature. Membership was strictly controlled, as existing members proposed new members and those not deemed suitable were excluded. It went without saying that members of these early Toronto sports clubs were gentle*men*, white, relatively wealthy, probably Tory in political affiliation, and associated with the ruling Family Compact, a small group of men linked by family, patronage, and shared political and social beliefs to the professional and mercantile upper middle class.10 One of the earliest known sport clubs for women was the Montreal Ladies Archery Club, formed in 1858. It had its own practice ground on St. Catherine Street and held regular meetings and annual prize competitions. Yet, for the most part, sport at mid-nineteenth century was firmly under the governance of the male social and ruling elite, and the urban sports club was an important institution in the maintenance of this social control.

While these men-only sports clubs gradually proliferated throughout the country, particularly in major centres, regularly scheduled competitions and leagues, increasingly standardized rules, and in some sports a "national" association slowly developed. The growing mercantile middle class (businessmen, merchants, store owners, bookkeepers, clerks, and sales personnel) were interested mostly in team sports like lacrosse, baseball, hockey, and football, whereas the political and commercial elite retreated to their socially oriented curling, golf, tandem, and hunt clubs. Restricted by voluminous skirts and Victorian ideas about their physical and mental frailty, women were never welcome at these clubs, nor in most sports could they form their own. Very limited forms of physical activity were available to Canadian women in the 1860s and 1870s, and those considered appropriate were individual or family recreations, restricted mostly to those of wealth and leisure. Young women in this position were never at a loss for entertainment, with sleigh and toboggan parties, ice-boating, skating balls, and ice carnivals in winter, and the picnics, croquet, boating, and fishing excursions of summer. Ice skating was by far the most popular winter activity, especially after the advent of heated covered rinks brightened by gas lamps. Fancy skating and the ability to trace artistic patterns on the ice, the forerunner of figure skating, became popular as did the skating carnivals and fancy-dress balls. A few enthusiasts tried roller skating or "parlour" skating in summer on the floor-covered rinks. Horseback riding remained a popular outdoor diversion in summer with more women taking part in fox hunting. Riding habits were probably the first sportswear for women, as were bathing costumes, which took yards of material to make certain all flesh was appropriately covered. Lady tobogganists were advised never to wear hoops; some enthusiasts solved the problem by removing their crinolines and wrapping themselves in a sheet as they careened down the hill. A distinct improvement were the warm blanket coats with red epaulets and sashes, pointed hoods, sealskin turbans, and moccasins, which later became the favoured apparel.

Some women challenged Victorian notions of female propriety by engaging in unusual activities, more vigorous than most. In the 1870s, walking matches, or pedestrianism, became the rage, but more as spectacle than mass sport. Following their American counterparts, a few brave souls entered special women's races, like the one at Perry's Hall in Montreal early in 1879. The two contestants were Miss L.A. Warren from Philadelphia and Miss Jessie Anderson of Montreal, both 18 years old. The distance was 25 miles, monotonously round and round on a narrow track in a small hall with stifling ventilation, made worse by "smoking and expectorating." Miss Warren collapsed suddenly after 21 miles, allowing Miss Anderson to continue walking without competition, finishing in five hours and 21½ minutes amidst "great enthusiasm." Her prize was a handsome gold hunting case watch. The circus atmosphere, side-betting, and unruliness of the spectators, who one assumes were primarily male, prompted this comment in a local newspaper:

> It is to be hoped that [in] any future exhibitions of pedestrianism, some means may be taken to preserve order and to keep the track clear. It was but natural that the sympathy of the audience should be with the Canadian but when that sympathy assumed the form of attempting to trip and standing in the path of the American, it was to say the least very disgraceful.[11]

Another walking match took place later the same year, also in Montreal but this time in the roller skating rink. There were three contestants: Miss Jessie Morahan of Montreal, Miss Edwards of New York, and Miss Kilberry from Boston. The race lasted two days with the contestants walking round and round the rink, starting early in the morning and finishing late at night. Spectators came and went, and the building was filled with music to make the spectacle more attractive and to help the women accomplish their task. Each was dressed in an ankle or knee-length black satin dress, but interestingly what they wore on their feet is unknown. A newspaper report characterized Miss Morahan as a brunette, somewhat "heavy featured," decidedly Amazonian in proportions, and with the maintenance and bearing of a professional athlete. The winner (Miss Edwards) walked a total of 80 miles, and the Canadian walker came third having accomplished 60 miles — what exactly they won was not reported, although money was the likely prize.[12] The pedestrianism craze lasted not much longer than a decade due to social pressure from temperance officials, religious conservatives, and many medical doctors who branded this form of women's sporting entertainment both cruel and immoral.[13]

A leading Toronto newspaper, the *Globe*, took up the debate by condemning the long distance walking matches, but at the same time urged women to engage in more exercise especially on foot:

> In the last ten years a great many more Canadian ladies than formerly do their two or three miles a day, but the habit of taking a rapid breather habitually has not yet come into fashion, though there are encouraging indications it soon will. Wealth is not yet so great here that many women can take mounted exercise, and of those who can afford saddle horses too few indulge in the charming habit. They rather prefer lolling in carriages. Skating is not to be compared to walking — the monotony of the ice is less agreeable than the change in road and scenery, and the rink is a resort where diversion is looked for more than health.[14]

The editorial went on to suggest that "Canadian ladies" should follow the example of Princess Louise, one of Queen Victoria's daughters who at the time resided in Canada as the wife of the Marquis of Lorne, the Governor General. The royal princess apparently liked to tramp around the countryside, causing the *Globe* to suggest that "if she should do the country no other good than that of making popular a healthy and delightful exercise she should have earned a title to gratitude."

The writer of the editorial was equally keen on Ontario women taking up snow-shoeing as healthy winter exercise. Already in Quebec, he wrote, "the deep snow tempts many ladies to long tramps across country and through the silent winter forest on snowshoes."[15] A few women formed their own snowshoe clubs, such as the Ladies' Prince of Wales Club of Montreal, founded in 1861; on the odd occasion, men's clubs would arrange short tramps or races for them, but they were usually banned from the longer male-only tramps and confined to the welcoming party at the evening's social event. Similarly, short foot races for girls or "married ladies" were popular at summer picnics, but more for the amusement of spectators than for their athletic value. Most water regattas also had girls' and women's events. In 1879, for instance, at the Dominion Day Regatta at Lorne Park in Ontario, a race was listed on the program: "Ladies Race — half mile straight-away;

to be rowed in eighteen-feet inrigged lap-streak boats. Open to all ladies — prize to be a handsome gold ring."[16] Most were reluctant, many more were completely diffident, yet some young women were determined to prove that sports were for everyone, not just the few brave souls willing to risk their reputations and to endure the inevitable public criticism. They wanted to become athletes just like their brothers. Perhaps they were like the six young ladies in Ottawa who wrote to the local newspaper issuing a challenge to women in nearby Prescott to a game of football, the prize being a silver cup. The newspaper gave their request publicity, but added "we do not think there are any young ladies in Prescott who are ambitious to become champion kickers."[17] How wrong they were.

The detailed story of women's sport in Canada begins in the last decade of the nineteenth century when Victorian women rode their bicycles to physical emancipation and dress reform. Chapter 1 discusses the bicycle craze and the heated debates it provoked, illustrating the ambivalence of reformers and enthusiasts to women's sporting activity, especially the "modern mannish maidens" who took up more vigorous sports like basketball, ice hockey, baseball, and outdoor pursuits.[18] As mentioned previously, working-class women flocked to the cities before and after World War I, seeking employment. Their attempts to organize clubs, competitions, leagues, and associations, and to take control of their sport in the 1920s is the focus of Chapter 2. The 1930s (Chapter 3) saw an escalated condemnation over women's increasing involvement in vigorous sports and high-level competition, mainly from women physical educators and male sportswriters, although it had little impact on those now participating in unprecedented numbers in a host of sports or sent to compete in international events. Although World War II brought a halt to Dominion championships and an interruption to many athletic careers, women's sport at the grassroots level flourished.

Chapter 4 examines the immediate postwar period and into the 1950s when "beauty producing" sports like figure skating, synchronized swimming, and gymnastics as well as individual sports like skiing, tennis, badminton, and golf were more acceptable than the sweaty team sports, which struggled to survive. A variety of images — glamorous celebrity, girl-next-door, competing mother, and the "glamazon" — existed at the same time, each demanding both femininity and heterosexuality. The 1960s until the mid-1970s, the era discussed in Chapter 5, was a period of enormous success for Canadian women athletes, and the way they were treated in the sports media changed remarkably. Although unreserved admiration for young, successful athletes, was often patronizing and tinged with paternalism, more mature women athletes were rarely treated with the same respect. For the first time, there were explicit, sexualized descriptions of their physical appearance, and they were frequently treated as sex objects rather than the serious athletes they wished to become.

A resurgence of feminist activity beginning in the late 1960s had an impact on sport just as it did everywhere else in society. Chapter 6 examines feminist activism in Canadian sport, the issues raised, and the limited successes during the 1970s and 1980s through the efforts of individuals, government agencies, advocacy organizations, and legal challenges. Finally, as discussed in Chapter 7, the 1990s and new millennium have brought great changes to women's sport especially in North America, one of which is the valorization of team sports, especially soccer, softball, and ice hockey. With the growing professionalization of women's sport, sex is being used to sell the product, raising the persistent issue as to whether their increasing commodification and sexualization will trivialize women's athleticism.

Throughout the chapters, I have tried to mention as many outstanding individual athletes as possible, except in the last two chapters covering the period from the mid-1970s onwards, simply because their numbers and accomplishments are far too extensive. Many of the women mentioned, especially during the decades between the 1920s and 1960s, have been forgotten, and their athletic efforts insufficiently recognized. I sought out some of these very early athletes, many now in their 80s and 90s, to hear their stories firsthand. The same holds true for the sports mentioned throughout the book. Although I have tried to cover a variety of sports and activities, three sports are consistently discussed in each chapter — softball, basketball, and ice hockey — because each has a long tradition in Canada and has been played by millions of young women, many working-class. Except for ice hockey, their history remains hidden.

In a useful essay about sport history in the 1990s, Catriona Parratt reminds us that "feminist historians of sport must also continue to be sensitive to and try to correct their own imbalances, exclusions, and erasures by giving much greater consideration to women of color and ethnicity and working-class women."[19] Diversity and difference should also include disability, religion, and sexual orientation. It is these women, she argues, outside the ranks of the white upper and middle classes, who remain hidden and to whom we need listen the most. We have tended to treat sportswomen, Jennifer Hargreaves maintains, as if they were "a homogenous group with a common, shared culture," causing women from minority groups to be marginalized, and their experiences, problems, struggles, and achievements excluded from mainstream history and practice.[20] She suggests further that we need to examine how women's participation in sport is tied to their sense of difference and identity.

Although I agree with both Parratt's and Hargreaves' advice, it has not been easy to follow in this particular historical project. Aboriginal women's sport in Canada, for example, remains hidden, especially as it took (and continues to take) place on native reserves. Vicky Paraschak's historical work concerning the Six Nations Reserve in Ontario is exemplary, and we need much more like it. I have written about the few outstanding women athletes with native backgrounds who have competed for Canada. Until the 1980s, when Black women, especially those whose parents had immigrated to Canada during the 1960s and 1970s from the Caribbean and elsewhere, began to dominate Canadian women's track, there were incredibly few women of colour in Canadian sport. Again, I have made a deliberate effort to find those who were involved as early as the 1930s and talk with them. Whenever I came across evidence of early participation by women from different ethnic backgrounds or women with disabilities, it was mentioned, but the research was neither systematic nor specific, except in the case of French-speaking women in Quebec. I have also tried to ferret out as much information about working-class women's involvement in sport as possible, since I am convinced that after World War I, it was their participation, and not that of middle- and upper-class women, that was the main catalyst for the growth of organized women's sport in the following decades.

Much of this book could not have been written without the work of early Canadian women sportswriters whose columns, beginning in the late 1920s, appeared in major newspapers across the country. They were among the many aspiring women journalists in Canada brought onto the major dailies for on-the-job training, sometimes without pay, after World War I. By 1921, there were almost 250 women "editors and reporters" employed in Canadian journalism, around 13 per cent of the total, which compared favourably to the 15.5 per cent participation rate of women in the labour force generally. Women readers, although still interested in recipes and the latest fashion trends, also wished to be informed about current political and social issues within Canada and elsewhere. Besides, newspaper owners were dependent on advertising revenue, and they recognized the importance of home-makers as the primary consumers. Women journalists, expected to present a specifically feminine view of the world, were hired quite simply to attract women readers. One entirely new area for women writers was the sports page, although they were confined to reporting only about women's sports.[21]

Alexandrine Gibb and Phyllis Griffiths were two pioneers in Canadian women's sportswriting. Gibb began writing short articles for publications like *Toronto World* and the *Evening Telegram* just after the war and by 1924 was known as a "newspaper writer" and "literary light."[22] In May 1928, she began writing her "No Man's Land of Sport" column on a regular basis for the *Toronto Daily Star*, which continued until November 1940.[23] Also a pioneering leader and administrator of women's sport, Gibb wrote from her experiences as she chronicled the early days of organizing women's sport in Canada. Her column appeared prominently on the *Star*'s sports pages, often alongside "With Pick and Shovel," written by sports editor Lou Marsh, her respected and adored "chief." It was not unusual in those days for sport reporters to be actively engaged in the organizations they covered. Lou Marsh moonlighted as a hockey referee who wrote about the games he officiated; Henry Roxborough published many articles about amateur sport for *Maclean's* and other magazines while active on the Amateur Athletic Union's publicity committee; and W.A. Hewitt edited the *Toronto Star*'s sports page and at the same time ran amateur hockey.[24]

Sixteen-year-old Phyllis Griffiths, a keen basketball player, graduated from Toronto's Parkdale Collegiate in 1921 and immediately landed her first job at the *Toronto Telegram*, where she was assigned as a reporter to the city beat. By 1926, an anonymous "Girls' Sports" column appeared in the paper; it may well have been written by Griffiths. Still working full-time, she attended the University of Toronto, obtaining her degree and winning the top award for women's basketball. In May 1928, she landed her own sports column, appropriately called "The Girl and the Game," which she wrote until 1942.[25] Other women sportswriters were hired by newspapers because of their fame as international athletes, and they learned to become writers on the job. Myrtle Cook and Fanny "Bobbie" Rosenfeld, for example, were members of Canada's highly successful women's track team at the 1928 Summer Olympics. Cook began her career as a sportswriter with the *Montreal Star* in 1929, writing her column "In the Women's Sportlight" for over 40 years. In the early 1930s, Rosenfeld wrote briefly for the *Toronto Star Weekly* and the *Montreal Daily Herald* before settling in at the *Globe and Mail*, where her column, "Feminine Sports Reel," appeared from 1937 until 1958.

Similar columns began to sprout up all over the country in daily newspapers. The *Halifax Mail* employed Vaughn Mason, a local athlete, to write a "Women's Sportlight" column beginning in 1930, although it appeared sporadically and lasted only a few years. Patricia Page Hollingsworth, whose father Percy Page coached the famous Edmonton Grads, wrote briefly for the *Edmonton Journal* between 1935 and 1940. She used her column, "Feminine Flashes," to bolster publicity for the Grads when interest in the team waned (they folded in 1940 after more than 20 years). Not to be outdone, the rival *Edmonton Bulletin* began a "Spotlighting the Sport Girl" column in 1938, written by an anonymous "Susie Q." At the *Winnipeg Free Press*, Lillian "Jimmy" Coo, daughter of the news editor, and an athlete and volunteer administrator in her own right, wrote "Cherchez la Femme" for a short while before and after World War II. Also hired during wartime was Shirley Boulton, who wrote briefly for the *Winnipeg Tribune*, even though she lived mostly in eastern Canada with her soldier husband. On the west coast, the *Vancouver Sun* employed Ann Stott between 1939 and 1941 and Ruth Wilson from 1943–45 to write a column about "Femmes in Sport" (later "Femmes and Foibles in Sport").

The importance of these columns cannot be overestimated. For over 30 years, from the late 1920s until the immediate postwar period, they were a major source of information about Canadian women's sport on a daily, weekly, monthly, and yearly basis. Often several journalists wrote about the same event, or series of events, so that it was possible to cross-check the information from one source to another. Of course they were biassed, and they certainly expressed unique viewpoints, because their job was to comment on what was happening and be controversial enough to engage readers. It is doubtful that many men read these columns, except perhaps male team-owners and managers involved in the early days of softball and ice hockey, or those in Edmonton who followed the Grads, the famous basketball team. By and large, women sports columnists were writing for other women, or the "girls" as some called them, and their efforts were as much gossip and information as they were commentary. They were a little corner of the sports page, sometimes the only space, where women, their sports, and their accomplishments were duly recognized.

As mentioned earlier, the purpose of this book is to trace how male hegemony in Canadian sport was (and still is) resisted by women and how their efforts have been supported and opposed both by men and other women. It is not a book about how women have been victims of an oppressive sports structure, which is clearly not the case at all. Women as much as men have helped create the Canadian amateur sport system, and, over the years, they have become major players in developing and sometimes re-inventing this system. Completing the research and writing the book, I was continually impressed by how women through the years have been strong, active agents in creating the kind of sports world they want for their children, their daughters especially. Understanding a little of this history will, I hope, help the present and future generations do the same.

CHAPTER I

EARLY BEGINNINGS: THE "NEW WOMAN" AND ATHLETICISM

Only some six or seven years ago there were no lady cyclists in Canada. Can you fancy it, my sisters? In one short demi-decade, we have gone through the Battle of the Bloomer, taken into our lives a new pleasure, the like of which we never before experienced or even in our dreams imagined.

Grace Denison, *The Evolution of the Lady Cyclist*, 1897

As the last decade of the nineteenth century came to a close, Victorian women rode their bicycles to physical emancipation and dress reform, forever changing the look and style of women's sport in Canada. This was the era of the New Woman, the one leaving behind the fragile stereotype of her earlier, domestic sister and marching determinedly towards more education, work, service, and suffrage. As one historian observed, the bicycle extended "her sphere across the threshold, for in loosening her stays and dividing her skirts, the New Woman also took possession of her own movements and achieved a measure of self-confidence that carried her into the twentieth century."[1] Before the bicycle, more and more women in Canada, at least those who could afford the costs and had the time, began to participate in a variety of sports from skating and tobogganing in winter to swimming, equestrianism, croquet, tennis, and golf in summer. But these activities did not acquire anything resembling a mass appeal. What was needed was an easily learned, enjoyable, outdoor exercise that was robust and healthy yet did not breach late nineteenth-century standards of proper decorum.[2] Cycling met these conditions.

The bicycle itself did not bring about these changes; rather, technological advances allowed what had been the preserve of an elite few, mostly men, to become a vehicle of utility and pleasure for everyone, especially women. The first two-wheelers were patented in North America in 1866 and made their appearance in Canada soon after. Velocipedes, more popularly known as "boneshakers," were heavy, solid iron contraptions with two wooden wheels rimmed with a flattened iron band. Extremely difficult to steer, the noise they made on city streets must have been deafening. They did not last long and were replaced by the still uncomfortable and dangerous "penny farthings," which had a high front wheel, small back one, solid rubber tires, and highly perched seat. Athletic young men in military-style uniforms joined bicycle clubs, which organized race meets, riding displays, tours, and outings. The high-wheelers were impossible for women in long skirts to mount, and in any case men did not want them in their clubs. The relatively few women who rode the wheel used either single or tandem tricycles.

CYCLING TO PHYSICAL EMANCIPATION

By the mid-1880s smaller, lighter bicycles with equal-size wheels driven by a sprocket and chain began to appear on the scene. At first the tires were of hard rubber and glued to the rim, but they were quickly superseded by the pneumatic tire, at last making the bicycle safe, comfortable, and attractive to everyone, including women. The first appearance in a town or city of a "lady cyclist" was often reported in the local newspaper. The following note in the St. John's *Daily News* in Newfoundland was typical: "A spectacle of an unusual and sensational character was for the first time witnessed in the city on Gower Street last evening, a young lady bicycling with all the ease and dignity of a professional."[3] The high-wheeler soon faded from the scene to become the favourite prop of clowns and vaudevillians; at the same time, bicycle clubs of a different nature, more social than fraternal, began to sprout up all over the country. Relatively well-off women with the means to purchase a new "safety" bicycle (they sold for $50 to $110) flocked to these clubs. By 1895, there were some 10,000 "wheelmen and wheelwomen" in Toronto, and the popular Knickerbocker Club, open to both sexes, was inundated with applications for membership from those wishing to take part in summer jaunts of a "purely social character."[4] In Winnipeg, the exclusively female Tam O'Shanter Club enhanced its popularity by inviting gentlemen to accompany the members on outings, and "whatever little gathering takes place after the run is entirely at the expense of the ladies."[5] As clubs were deluged with female members, they often decided to form a branch of their own. The bicycle offered women, a least those who could afford one and had the time to enjoy it, a means to encourage exercise and good health, entertainment, transportation, and above all, freedom. They were now free to go where they wanted, when they wanted, and with whom they wanted without a chaperone. Only a horse had offered this sort of independence, but a bicycle, or "silent steed," was a good deal cheaper, travelled faster and further, and did not have to be fed, watered, and bedded down at night.[6]

Although it was possible for women in long skirts to ride a safety bicycle, especially if they put lead sinkers in their hems and guards over the back wheels to keep their skirts out of the spokes, they were more inclined to adopt shorter styles, including the controversial bloomers with tight-fitting, knee-length hose, or the more acceptable split skirt. The bloomer costume had been worn at mid-century by the prominent American writer, lecturer, and champion of women's rights, Amelia Bloomer, who wore it to defy tradition and cope with muddy streets. She had met with such vociferous criticism that the fashion soon quietly faded into obscurity only to be revived again some 40 years later with the advent of the safety bicycle, along with the controversy. The front page of *The Halifax Herald* on October 1, 1895, invited readers to "judge for yourself which costume is most becoming" by printing a large cutout of both Queen Victoria and Mrs. Cleveland (wife of the United States president) where it was possible to fold the paper and show these women wearing either a skirt or bloomer.

Not all public opinion was unfavourable. When girls and women on bicycles in small town Petrolia, Ontario took to wearing huge bloomers and hose, the local paper applauded and called the elderly ladies and gentlemen who decried the new fashion "sanctimonious hypocrites," at the same time issuing an angry blast against the "low remarks of rude and ignorant loafers."[7] As the Toronto *Globe* pointed out, "one bicyclist wearing an advanced costume does more towards furthering dress reform than a score of theorists, writers and lecturers."[8] Many women would not wear the contentious bloomers, instead adopting a daring but practical split skirt which became known appropriately as the "bicycle skirt." Three-piece "Ladies' Bicycle Suits," comprising a Norfolk jacket, skirt, and bloomers, made of navy blue all-wool serge, sold for $15.00.[9] The well turned-out cyclist, wrote one commentator, should wear a neatly cut, ankle-length skirt with spats to match, knickerbockers of the same material, a small Eton coat fitted to the waist, gloves of white chamois leather, topped by a Tam o' Shanter hat.[10] Another enthusiast suggested that black, navy, and light brown were the best colours, with the latter being the most serviceable because it did not show the dust.[11]

Unwary pedestrians soon found city streets a hazardous place to walk, and the plea went out to all cyclists, especially female ones, to "learn before you venture in the streets and so run the risk of endangering not only your own lives but ours too."[12] Special bicycle schools were opened by innovative entrepreneurs who saw the potential to make some money in empty indoor skating rinks during the spring and summer months, or by bicycle companies hoping to sell their product to newly trained graduates. In Toronto, the Remington Cycle School at McDonald & Willson's bicycle store on Yonge Street opened in March 1896 in a well lit hall with sufficient room to allow several riders to use the floor at the same time. Women riders were taught how to stay upright and, most importantly, "the correct movement of the ankle which makes all the difference between a graceful and ungraceful rider."[13] Not long after, two more large riding academies appeared in Toronto: H.A. Lozier & Co., manufacturers of the Cleveland wheel, opened their hall at the Granite rink, free from any impediments such as posts; and the Hyslop school, located on King Street, boasted a long stretch on either side so that the beginner did not have to turn.[14]

The benefits and dangers of cycling by women was the cause of much debate in the 1890s among medical practitioners, both male and female. What is important about this discussion is not that doctors approved or disapproved of cycling, but the fact that they felt compelled to speak out about a topic that seemingly had little to do with medicine.[15] For the most part their comments were directed at women cyclists, not men, evidence of a double standard towards the sexes about the advantages and hazards of physical exercise. An editorial in *The Dominion Medical Monthly and Ontario Medical Journal* laid out the grounds of the debate quite simply — either bicycle riding was good for women, or it was "injurious and should not be tolerated."[16]

There were two reasons why someone might believe the latter. One was on the grounds of "propriety," and even the writer of the editorial acknowledged that medical doctors should have little to say about matters of opinion and custom. The second reason, far more serious, was that cycling was "injurious to the rider herself and decidedly immoral in its tendencies." The saddle was not suited to female anatomy, the uterus would be seriously jolted, and "pelvic mischief" would befall the poor woman who rode during her menstrual period. Very few of these claims were supported by medical research and evidence, and Canadian medical journals often simply reprinted editorials from their British and American counterparts.[17]

What concerned some doctors far more was the potential, both real and imagined, that riding a bicycle "produces in the female a distinct orgasm." Some even claimed that the male attendants who guided "innocent maidens" around at the new bicycle schools were in the habit of intentionally raising the seat so that "at first erethism [extreme sensitivity] and then orgasm is produced."[18] More moderate medical authorities condemned these sweeping generalizations as "filthy rubbish" and instead endorsed cycling as a "healthful exercise for women, and quite free from evil as any form of recreation can possibly be."[19] Dr. P.E. Doolittle, a family physician and former president of the Canadian Wheelman's Association, wrote enthusiastically of the therapeutic benefits of cycling to all women whether they be healthy, weak, or even pregnant.[20] Others supported moderate cycling outdoors, praising the bicycle for rescuing women from their restrictive, damaging corsets, and bringing about much needed dress reform.[21]

Women doctors, far fewer in numbers then their male counterparts, also entered the cycling debates, and were usually cautiously supportive.[22] Elizabeth Mitchell and Grace Ritchie, in a lively session about the rise and merits of female athleticism at the 1896 annual meeting of the National Council of Women of Canada, praised the bicycle for its role in dress reform, and in countering negative attitudes towards women taking up exercise in general. "We should have recreation in the form of exercise, or athleticism as a duty from the good it will do us physically and morally and mentally," commented Dr. Ritchie to enthusiastic audience applause.[23] American Lucy Hall, both a physician and a cycling enthusiast, admonished male doctors who suggested that women would do as well to run a sewing machine as to ride a bicycle because the motion was precisely the same. Any woman, she argued, who is physically able to walk is capable of riding a bicycle; she also urged that "the timid as well as the more self-confident women should take it up quietly, but freely and persistently."[24] Others pointed to the inconsistency of condemning women who rode in the open air for a short time, while saying nothing about women running sewing machines in hot, stuffy rooms for hours on end.[25]

Not all women agreed with this philosophy, nor were they as supportive. At the height of the bicycle craze in the mid-1890s, the Women's Rescue League in the United States announced a national crusade against the use of bicycles by women. They circulated a strongly worded petition, aimed at Congress, linking the riding of bicycles, more so than any other medium, to the swelling ranks of "fallen" and "reckless" girls in the United States. Their circular denounced bicycle riding by young women because it produced "an immoral association in both language and dress, which have a tendency to make women not only unwomanly, but immodest as well."[26] Toronto journalist C.S. Clark, in his famous tract *Of Toronto the Good* (1898) exposing the supposed "social evil" of his beloved "Queen City," noted the Women's Rescue League petition and made his own observations: "A girl would be considered decidedly immodest did she go on long [snowshoe] tramps with boys, but on her bicycle she can at the same time gratify her taste for boys' society and satisfy the demands of propriety, which takes cognizance not so much of what you do, but how you do it, and questions your motives not at all." Clark was far more concerned about the corruption of boys and young men than he was about young women: "I assert that one girl in a bloomer costume will create far greater and more widespread corruption among boys than a city full of show bills, so will a well developed girl in short dresses."[27] Trustees of the Toronto Board of Education must have agreed with him because they instructed their inspectors to report "the names of all female teachers who have been riding bicycles in male attire, commonly called 'bloomers.'"[28]

Women's dress reform and physical culture were promoted by the suffragettes and reformers of the late nineteenth and early twentieth centuries not for feminist reasons, but for racial ones — quite simply, the race would be improved by fostering the health of mothers. Most feminists, and those who belonged to the many social reform societies, were well-to-do, educated members of an Anglo-Saxon, Protestant elite, whose major concern was the future of their race. The declining birth rate, especially among the "better sort" of people, and the pollution of the race through infectious diseases like tuberculosis and venereal disease were causes for distress. Rather than advocating eugenics, many reformers promoted a form of "environmentalism" aimed at improving the living and working conditions of the poor, which would be transmitted to the next generation. Environmentalism, therefore, "allowed women to demand a more active and freer life-style on the grounds that improvements in women's physical and mental fitness today would be transferred to her offspring tomorrow."[29] Increased opportunities for women's physical activity and exercise would result in the improved health of future mothers, but at the same time would not seriously challenge traditional gender roles, since women's reproductive and maternal functions remained her chief contribution to the world.

A woman riding a bicycle in the 1890s was the embodiment of the New Woman, those who wanted "a kingdom different from the home and a sphere of power broader than the domestic, the woman who asked for equality of education, jobs, and personal habits," but these same women were generally young, middle-class, and often did not have to work to support themselves.[30] It is misleading to imagine that all middle-class women in late Victorian Canada experienced a metamorphosis to emerge dramatically as "new" women because there were powerful forces in society making certain they were not too different from the generations who had preceded them. An ideology of separate spheres, promoted by clergymen, physicians, educators, and law-makers, meant a sharp distinction between the domestic world of women and the public world of men. The very real threat of the bicycle was that it would remove women from the home, along with its familial obligations and moral insulation.[31] "Though all women become wheelers," assured one woman cycling enthusiast, "they yet will remain women, and as wives and mothers they will preserve the order of households and by precept and example purify and elevate family life."[32]

SPORT AND THE "MODERN MANNISH MAIDEN"

While there were many who praised the healthful gains achieved by women through moderate and lady-like forms of exercise, these same enthusiasts, whether they were medical doctors, clergy, educators, or physical culturists, warned of the dangers and problems in allowing women to realize their athletic potential. The response to bicycling in the late nineteenth century illustrates the ambivalence of reformers and enthusiasts to women's sporting activity. Moderate use of the "wheel" promoted women's health and encouraged much needed dress reform, but excessive bicycling contributed to physical injury, impropriety, a loss of femininity, and worst of all, moral decline. Michael Smith, in her study of women's sport in Victorian Nova Scotia, argues that the "shift from fragile maiden to graceful womanhood" was, on the one hand, regarded as a necessary antidote to the physical deterioration of young girls, particularly those of the sedentary middle class exposed to new intellectual demands. On the other hand, the rapid emergence of a much more robust woman in the last decade of the century threatened a society uncertain of how to adapt to the New Woman and the consequent blurring of traditional gender divisions and roles.[33]

In 1890, *Blackwood's Magazine* in Edinburgh, Scotland, published a lengthy diatribe against "modern mannish maidens," a portion of which was reprinted in a Toronto newspaper.[34] The authors (presumably male) explored the meaning of "this modern craze for mannish sports and mannish ways, which has of late seized upon a certain section of young women in polite society." A particular recreation was inappropriate unless it conformed to a test: no girl or woman should be seen playing in public if "she is liable to pose therein ungracefully, clumsily, or unbecoming." Acceptable sports were horsemanship, walking, climbing, rowing, skating, lawn tennis, badminton, and golf. Cycling was "dismissed from consideration" because in 1890 the safety bicycle had not yet become popularized, and few women rode anyway. Clearly unacceptable, were the "manly" sports, team games requiring strength, speed, and sometimes physical contact, like cricket, soccer, rugby, grass hockey, rounders (a form of baseball), and their equivalents in Canada — lacrosse, football, and baseball. A news item appeared in the *Globe* that students at Wellesley, a women's college in the United States, were going to take up lacrosse because it was healthy, vigorous, and "perfectly dignified." The *Globe* editors were astonished and commented that "there must be a variety of the game that we have not seen in Canada."[35] These sports required "violent running," something it was argued that women were naturally not built to do:

> She can swim, she can dance, she can ride: all these she can do admirably and with ease herself. But to run, nature most surely did not construct her. She can do it after a fashion, just as the domestic hen will on occasions make shift to fly; but the movement is constrained and awkward — may we say it without disrespect? A kind of precipitate waddle with neither grace, fitness, nor dignity.[36]

By the last decade of the nineteenth century, Canadian women, like their middle- and upper-class counterparts in Britain, were enthusiastic participants in a variety of acceptable sports, with competitions organized in a few. Male sports clubs, mainly in tennis, golf, and curling, began admitting members' wives and daughters as "lady associates," at first for social reasons, but gradually the women themselves wished to play and compete, leading to the formation of a "ladies" club affiliated with the original men's club.

During its early days in Canada, tennis was considered a "wag's" game by the more manly and rugged team-playing male athletes, and as such, received but scant attention from any but the upper class.[37] First played on the lawns of fashionable homes in Toronto in the 1870s, it quickly spread throughout the country. Perhaps the first tournament for women was held in Montreal in 1881, and a year later players from England and Canada contested a doubles match at the Toronto Lawn Tennis Club, which inaugurated a women's Dominion championship in 1883, although there were rarely enough contestants until 1892, when the championship became firmly established. Miss Delano-Osborne from Sutton, Ontario, with an "indomitable perseverance and determination," was the undisputed Canadian champion from 1891 until 1895, when she was defeated by Mrs. Sydney Smith of Ottawa. That same year both players went to Buffalo to compete in a tournament, to be among the first Canadian women travelling to another country to compete in organized sport.[38]

Golf was also popular. Women often took part in social events at clubs to which their husbands belonged, or they organized the popular luncheons and teas, but it was not until the early 1890s that they took up the game themselves. "Ladies" clubs (actually sections of existing clubs) began to appear, the first being at the Royal Montreal Golf Club in early 1892. Later that year, the Royal Montreal Ladies' Golf Club held their first competition: 13 women took part and the winner shot 150 over 18 holes. In 1894, the Toronto Golf Club admitted women members, and within a year they numbered 100, almost half the club membership. Interclub matches began to flourish especially in Toronto, where 20 or so golf clubs were in easy reach by train or tram (by 1900 there were about 50 golf clubs across the country). A national championship began in 1901, open only to members of Canadian clubs, but golfers west of Ontario or east of Quebec were rarely able to compete because it was held at a club in central Canada. The first outstanding woman golfer in Canada was Mabel Thomson from Saint John, New Brunswick, five-time winner of the Canadian Ladies Amateur Championship between 1902 and 1908, who also represented Canada in team matches in the United States and Britain during the same period.[39]

On the golf links, as everywhere else, women were expected to act in a modest and becoming manner. A Halifax pastor complained about women golfers swearing, although the editor of the Charlottetown *Morning Guardian* came to their defence, claiming that if they did swear, it was at "the imperfections and exasperations of men."[40] What to wear was always a problem; most dressed in large hats, Norfolk jackets (often scarlet) worn over tailored shirts, and long skirts edged at the bottom with leather to protect them from wet grass. Many used a device called a "Miss Higgins," a band of elastic webbing slipped around their knees to keep their long skirts from blowing up and interfering with their shots.[41] Slip-on golf shoes with little spikes went over the toes of regular shoes; knitted sweaters and golf capes became essential for cold, wet weather.

Although the Royal Montreal Curling Club dates from 1807, it was another 87 years before women played there. The Ladies' Auxiliary Club was organized in 1894, largely through the efforts of a Mrs. E.A. Whitehead, who became its first president. This was probably the first women's curling club in the world, since the stuffy Royal Caledonian club in Scotland did not admit women, until 1895, and even then did so reluctantly.[42] A female correspondent for "The Women's Pages" of *Athletic Life* commented:

> I was much amused the other day, to see the expression of a man's face, when
> I was telling him that some women had been curling at Galt [in Ontario].
> He is a Scotchman and one pretty well known among the curling fraternity
> for his proficiency in the game, and his face was a study when he heard that
> "some of us" women were actually beginning to think that we could "curl."[43]

She went on to admit that she had never seen the game and knew nothing about it, but surely, she offered, "a woman should know better than a man how to 'sweep' and how to 'curl.'" By 1900, the Montreal Ladies' Curling Club boasted about 80 ardent members, and similar clubs had sprouted, mostly in Ontario and Quebec, whose towns were the first to build indoor rinks. A representative team of Scotsmen touring Canada in 1903, who unsuspectingly played rinks from both the Quebec and Montreal ladies' curling clubs, was "humiliated" when soundly beaten. Claiming that the women's smaller iron stone, about half the size of those used by men, was their downfall, the Scottish curlers dismissed their losses and the women's game as a "ping-pong" form of curling.[44]

By 1903, a Coronation Cup was contested by women's teams from Montreal, Lachine, Ormstown, and Quebec City with the trophy going to the team with the most wins in seven games. Some women chose to use the heavier granite stones, making it necessary to organize competitions into two classes. The Ontario Curling Association began to recognize the women's clubs officially in 1912, with the proviso that they could not be represented at meetings, and they could only participate in competitions declared open to lady members.[45] Women curlers in Kingston, Ontario, were so successful in their 1914 season that a tour of Canada was contemplated, but the onset of war interrupted their plans. Curling among women in Western Canada had a slower start. Although two rinks of girls are reported to have played in Edmonton as early as 1893, women in Winnipeg organized a club in 1908 and in Banff in 1912; the first bonspiels took place in Edmonton and Winnipeg a couple of years later.[46]

Canadian women were beginning to distinguish themselves in most other sports mentioned by the "modern mannish maidens" authors, although grace and elegance were always a necessary component. In summer, practically every town along a waterfront had a regatta, and by the 1880s most offered a "ladies race" in either single or double sculls. Sometimes, not everything went as planned. For example, at the second annual regatta at the Cartierville Boating Club in Quebec, women participated in four events — single and double skiff, lady and gentleman skiff, and the canoe tandem race for lady and gentleman. In the double skiff race, Maud and Muriel Gonne were well in the lead, when nearing the finish line they suddenly stopped rowing. Apparently a revolver discharged prematurely causing them to think they had crossed the line and won. They strongly protested, but "the judges were inexorable and awarded the race to the crew which finished first."[47] Yachting races for "ladies" were not uncommon, where the "skipper" was a woman but the one or two-man crew invariably male.

In winter, skating was a thoroughly respectable pastime: "It is as natural for Quebec girls to skate," declared a national magazine, "as it is for other women to walk." Fancy skating was becoming popular — the Rideau Skating Club in Ottawa held a women's competition as early as 1890. Mabel Davidson of Toronto, sister of the champion bicyclist and speed skater Harley Davidson, gave skating exhibitions all over Ontario and in the Maritimes.[48] In small towns, especially in southern Ontario, skating rinks were often the only existing sports facility, and, at the same time, they were also a respectable space where both middle- and working-class single women could seek fun, exercise, and male companionship. Although the cost of a season ticket ($2.50) was probably prohibitive for a working-class girl, 10 or 15 cents would allow entrance to a night's skating or sometimes a fancy carnival or masquerade. In the early to mid-1880s, commercial roller rinks began to appear in small towns, providing yet another popular and affordable space for young women to socialize and take some exercise.[49]

"Whether sleighing, skating, snow-shoeing or tobogganing, young Canada's never happy without the fair sex," wrote George Beers in 1883, "and only on the long tramps of the snow-shoe clubs are ladies suppose to be absent."[50] Ladies' nights became a feature of the snowshoe clubs, but they were allowed only on short tramps with the remainder of the evening devoted to music, dancing, and singing. The long tramps afforded an opportunity for male segregation and a particularly masochistic form of hibernal manliness: "on cross country tramps over hilly terrain under crisp, slippery snow conditions, snowshoes were broken, ankles were fractured, frostbite and blisters were common ...." Speeches at annual club dinners of the Montreal Snowshoe Club repeatedly referred to the "moral bearing, independence and manliness" of snowshoers, whereas women "could only aspire to marry a snowshoe man."[51]

Although the writers of the "modern mannish maidens" article argued fervently that women must "hold fast to their womanliness" and not aspire to be "poor imitations of men," of greater concern was the challenge these feminine athletes posed to an unwavering belief in the connection between sport, morality, and manliness. The concept of muscular or manly Christianity, which originated with the British novels of Charles Kingsley (*Westward Ho*, 1855) and Thomas Hughes (*Tom Brown's Schooldays*, 1857), had long since made its way across the Atlantic and become firmly entrenched in the curricula of boys' private schools with their emphasis on producing men of character through athleticism and team sports.[52] Among the early pioneers struggling to establish and maintain British culture in a foreign land, sports and team games like cricket, rugby football, and soccer nurtured the manly qualities of robustness, mental vigour, determination, discipline, fair play, and integrity, and were easily transplanted to reproduce the Empire.[53] Colin Howell shows how baseball in the Maritimes "defined and consolidated notions of manhood, provided a form of social bonding and brotherhood, and served to legitimate notions of male privilege."[54] The winter climate also afforded the opportunity to express a distinctly Canadian form of manliness through snowshoeing, curling, and ice hockey.

In the last decades of the nineteenth century, the notion of Christian manliness broadened considerably to encompass not only physical and moral development but success in later life, particularly in the economic sphere. R. Tait McKenzie, an early Canadian physical educator, sculptor, and orthopaedic surgeon, wrote about rugby football in 1892: it "cultivates pluck and determination in men." He continued, "the *sine qua non* of a good footballer is grit, and in after life the grit cultivated by the hard knocks will stand men in good stead in the contests of business or professional life."[55] Another doctrine in vogue at the time was social Darwinism, the belief that the concepts of natural selection, the survival of the fittest, or differentiation could be applied to both the animal and human worlds. Coupled with muscular Christianity, social Darwinism was entrenched in the private boys' schools of this period where those who survived the Spartan conditions and physically demanding activities were best "suited" to become the economic and political elite.

Aside from the obvious role of manly sports in promoting nationalism, rectitude, and later success, why was all this addressed to males, never to females? The answer lies in the strict Victorian dichotomy between *manliness* and *womanliness*. The former represented physical virility coupled with a Christian morality ensuring influence and success in the public and economic spheres. Womanliness, on the other hand, embodied a feminine ideal, no doubt stressing an equally impeccable rectitude, but also grace and beauty leading to mutual sharing and intimacy in the domestic sphere. Without sport, argued the moralists of the time, boys will become like women, which meant delicate and effeminate. "Flabby muscled boys become pliant men who only talk. Well-developed boys become men who will say and act and produce results," intoned the manual for the Canadian Standard Efficiency Tests, a program designed to promote intellectual, physical, religious, and social accomplishments among young boys.[56] On the other hand, sports made girls behave more like boys and women like men, which was not to be encouraged. Even if it was recognized that women were good, perhaps better than men at certain sports, the criticism was still there — horse riding is a good example:

> The athletic woman, riding without fear, usually of ideal weight, their perfect hands and gentle ways around horses, has put many of them in a class which seriously endangers the superiority of men, especially in the show ring. There is an old saying, however, "you cannot have everything in one horse." Likewise in women. She cannot ride, dress and look like a man and still pack along her charm as a woman, at least to the same degree. Mounted astride and often riding better than we do, with close-cropped hair, wearing our own hats, boots and breeches, we just have to take her word for it that "she is a woman."[57]

Concern that masculine sports would detract from feminine beauty, although prevalent everywhere, seemed especially strong among the middle- and upper-classes of French-Canadian society. French newspapers often ran articles to this effect, like the one in *Le Devoir* in 1912, which claimed that the best sportswomen possessed abnormal physical proportions since they were much taller, had larger shoulders, hands and feet, and were certainly more flat-chested than the young women who frequented salons and garden parties.[58]

Among some circles, sportswomen were encouraged to dress like men, and indeed behave much like them. At the annual summer camps in the Rocky Mountains run by the Alpine Club of Canada (ACC), women were instructed not to wear skirts (unless around the campfire): "No lady climbing, who wears skirts, will be allowed to take a place on a rope, as they are a distinct source of danger to the entire party."[59] Instead, women were encouraged to wear "rational" clothes, consisting of knicker-bockers with puttees or gaiters, flannel shirtwaist, stout boots with hobnails, woollen stockings, a felt hat with a brim, and sweater or short coat. From its inception in 1906, the ACC welcomed lady members, enthusiastically supported women's climbing, and officially promoted sexual equality in mountaineering. Drawing their membership primarily from middle- and upper-class urban anglophones, women made up one-third of the membership in 1907, and it remained at just over 40 per cent for the next several decades.[60] Surprisingly, the majority of these women were single and obviously had the necessary resources and time to enjoy an extended climbing holiday in the mountains.

Despite the ACC's official policy of sexual equality and enthusiastic support for women's climbing, there were unwritten codes of conduct and structure whose purpose was to perpetuate a gender-based hierarchy of skill, ability, and authority.[61] Most of the climbing at the early, annual summer camps was routine, guided, and enjoyed by both sexes, who deferred to a male (usually Swiss) guide. As more and more climbers gained experience and skill, it soon became clear that women were not considered to have the mental and physical qualities necessary to lead climbs, nor were they thought capable of making high-altitude first ascents. Although Mount Robson, the highest peak in the Canadian Rockies, was ascended first in 1913, it would be another 11 years before the first woman made the climb. This was achieved by Vancouver's Phyllis Munday, the ACC's most accomplished and celebrated early woman climber, who over a lifetime climbed some 100 peaks, nearly a third of which were first ascents.[62] Although ACC administrators never promoted the ideals of traditional femininity and, indeed, they took pleasure in praising women's climbing achievements, they did make explicit and public links between masculinity and the skills required for leading climbs and high-altitude mountaineering. Similarly, in other wilderness pursuits, such as camping and canoe-tripping, women were actively discouraged because it was considered too dangerous and unfeminine, to say nothing of the "effect that meeting adventurous women in the wilderness might have on the self-esteem of the 'summer boy' pursuing manliness in the company of his peers."[63]

Sport in Educational Institutions

It was in the schools, colleges, and universities that middle- and upper-class Victorian and Edwardian girls and young women experienced the most freedom to explore their physicality and athleticism. Private schools were more willing to introduce exercise and physical culture into the classroom than were the public schools. Not only did they often have better facilities and could charge fees for extra-curricular activities, but they were also more philosophically inclined to include some form of physical culture into the curriculum. The students who attended these colleges were the favoured mothers of tomorrow, those best able to improve the race (meaning white and Anglo-Saxon), and whose children would be healthier if, as future mothers, they were fit. An Ottawa doctor, Edward Playter, writing in an 1890 collection of essays on Canadian women, called the disregard for the physical development of young girls a disgrace, arguing that "no school for girls without proper provision for the proper culture and education, in some way, of their nerves and muscles and other bodily structures, should be regarded as complete or satisfactory."[64]

Upper- and middle-class girls were often sent to a denominational private school, where they received a Christian indoctrination and education for their roles as future mothers and moral guardians of Canadian society. A major purpose of these schools was to "mould young ladies of culture and refinement who would use their intellectual, artistic, and domestic accomplishments to enrich their own homes," although eventually they were prepared for the possibility of an independent career before marriage and motherhood.[65] Given their differing religious denominations, the approach to physical education and sport at these schools varied, with the Roman Catholic curricula the least willing to incorporate physical culture. Along with the Methodist schools, their curricula strongly reflected the idealized view of Victorian womanhood described earlier. The Anglican schools, on the other hand, such as Toronto's Bishop Strachan (opened in 1867) and especially Havergal College (1894), placed the most emphasis on the role of sports and games in building character. Prior to 1900, almost all schools emphasized only gentle walking and light calisthenics to promote good health, gracefulness, and discipline. Although outdoor recreation such as tennis, skating, horseback riding, and tobogganing was encouraged, sport was neither organized nor competitive until the end of the century.

Havergal College, founded in 1894 and located then at 354 Jarvis Street in Toronto, was the most athletically advanced of the Ontario private schools for girls. A permanent games mistress, trained at the Gymnastic School in Liverpool, England, was hired in 1901. The next year, principal Ellen Knox, keen on athletics and good at sport herself, went to Boston and personally selected a graduate of the Sargent School of Physical Education, run by Dudley A. Sargent, a medical doctor with an appointment at Harvard University, who promoted his own system of exercises based on a diagnostic and therapeutic approach. From then on, regular and detailed measurements were taken of all Havergal students, who were required to engage in calisthenic and gymnastic exercises devised to correct whatever measurements were deemed inferior. The Havergal gymnasium was equipped with parallel bars, ladders, and a box horse for gymnastics. Introduced soon after were Swedish-style gymnastics, comprising remedial and aesthetically pleasing exercises designed to promote harmonious bodily development. The proper gymnasium costume consisted of long black stockings, a knee-length, full-skirted tunic with a long-sleeved middy blouse top, and loose-fitting roped belt.[66]

Like the British schools upon which it was modelled, sports and games were important to daily life at Havergal, and Knox continually stressed the need for a "sturdy, wholesome body" to house an equally strong mind.[67] Board courts were erected first for tennis and basketball; cricket was also popular with instruction by the Cambridge graduates hired as teachers at the school. Ice hockey in the winter, golf and track in the spring were favourites, and by 1905 an Athletic Association was formed to bring the various sports clubs together under one organization. Construction began in 1902 for an addition to the school including a larger gymnasium, and — something quite unusual for schools at that time — a swimming bath, which opened in 1906. By 1909, matches against other private schools in Toronto — Branksome Hall, St. Hilda's, University College, St. Margaret's, and Bishop Strachan — were hotly but politely contested, since it was forbidden by the Havergal principal to cheer for your own team: "Let the other school clap, and you clap them." Ada MacKenzie, a 1910 Havergal graduate, who eventually became one of Canada's best golfers, captained every team on which she played; her achievements included hitting a cricket ball through the third floor window of the school building.[68]

Although games and sports had become an essential aspect of Canadian girls' private schools early in the twentieth century, athleticism never acquired anything like the same hold it had over the equivalent boys' schools. Aggressive nationalism was not a feature of female education, and girls' games were rarely used for discipline, since the maintenance of order was not a problem as it was in similar schools for boys. In most girls' schools, games were part of a "systematic and quasi-social Darwinistic program of measurement, medical inspection and physical training intended to make students healthier and so fitter for academic toil and ultimately motherhood."[69]

While physical activity in many denominational, private schools was "plentiful, pleasurable, rewarding, and increasingly vigorous," such was not the case in the public schools.[70] Where the private schools had purposely created a supportive, separate sphere, although one designed to promote "true womanhood," the public schools developed sex-differentiated curricula that segregated girls and boys, even though co-education was the norm. Girls were educated for the domestic realm and boys for wage labour, public life, and, even before war became a reality, military duty. Separate entrances and stairways, sometimes separate buildings, and certainly separate school yards and gymnasia (often none at all for girls) kept boys and girls from mingling.[71] For boys, physical training was best accomplished through military drill and cadet training; although girls' programs were not immune to militarism (until the early 1900s, physical culture was mostly taught by military men), their activities consisted primarily of light calisthenics, dumbbell exercises, and Indian-club swinging. The latter resembled a thin, wooden bowling pin and weighed one to one-and-a-half pounds. The recommended textbook on physical training contained over 50 pages devoted to Indian-club exercises: "... the splendid exercise it gives to the body, especially the upper portion, the fact of both sides being equally employed, the erect ease and freedom of carriage acquired through its practice," enthused the author, "mark it as being pre-eminently adapted as an exercise for ladies."[72]

By 1911, all provinces were eligible for funds from the Strathcona Trust, established by Lord Strathcona (Donald Smith) and the federal government to promote and teach physical training in schools and to encourage patriotism, especially among boys through the formation of cadet corps.[73] Once a provincial government entered into an agreement with the Trust, normal school students were required to take instruction on how to teach physical training. A *Syllabus of Physical Exercises,* based principally on the Swedish system of gymnastics used in Britain, was distributed to every school. Particular attention was paid in the syllabus to suitable attire for girls when engaging in the exercises: a tunic (requiring two widths of blue serge), a woollen jersey or plain blouse, and knickers (also of serge with a detachable, washable lining).[74] It is unlikely that many students were able to afford a special uniform. The overt militarism of the Strathcona Trust, together with the unequal distribution of funds, instructors, and material resources resulted, at best, in minimal benefit to girls' physical education in the public schools and, at worst, in the reduction of their physical activities to joyless, formal calisthenics.[75]

Competitive sports in both the elementary and secondary schools remained outside the regular curriculum not only because of the emphasis on military drill, but also due to a lack of facilities, especially wooden floor gymnasiums. Larger centres like Toronto were able to offer some sports earlier than most. A Public School Basketball League for both girls and boys was organized in 1900 with 18 schools participating in eastern and western sections. Beginning in 1882, outdoor public school games were held each spring at Exhibition Park. By 1900 they attracted over 3,000 boys and girls competing in a variety of track and field events, although contests for girls were still limited to a few running races for those under 12 years of age. Annual sports days became quite common among high schools, but again events for girls were either limited to novelty races like "needle threading" and "egg and spoon," or shorter distances rarely more than 100 yards.[76]

Basketball, introduced around the turn of the century, was the most popular sport for girls in high school. It was likely their first chance to participate in an active sport requiring some physical exertion. Invented in 1891 by James Naismith, a Canadian teaching physical education at the YMCA Training College in Springfield, Massachusetts, it was a vigorous indoor game designed to help keep his young male students in shape between the football and baseball seasons. It was taken up almost immediately by girls in a nearby school, although not quite so vigorously, and soon spread to women's colleges and YWCAs throughout the United States.[77] In 1899, Nora Cleary, a teacher at the Windsor Collegiate Institute in Ontario introduced the game to her students after she had sent for a basketball and rule book advertised in a booklet produced by the Spalding sporting-goods company in the United

States. The girls stood around while she read the rules, and then they tried to play, soon becoming proficient enough to travel to Detroit to play other teams.[78] Girls' ice hockey teams also begin to appear in high schools in the early 1900s, along with "paper chases," the forerunner to long cross-country runs.

Like most areas of public life, women fought for the right to gain a university education and were gradually successful. In 1875, Mount Allison in New Brunswick was the first university in the British Empire to grant a degree to a woman; Queen's University began admitting women in 1878, with the University of Toronto and McGill both following in 1884. By the turn of the century, most institutions had opened their doors to women, although their numbers remained small — 11 per cent in 1900, which had increased to 14 per cent by 1919.[79] Although women were admitted alongside men, their education was often separate and different to that of male students, who greeted their appearance with an "indefinable regret at the passing of a certain virility ... at the coming of 'the skirts.'"[80] Women students at McGill, for example, were known as "Donaldas," after Donald Smith (Lord Strathcona) whose endowment made it possible for them to be admitted into a special course.

College campuses provided middle-class women with a crucial site for athletic experimentation, a place away from home where "athletic adventures were one of the numerous ways in which young women explored their independence and charted a new generational course."[81] Physical culture, deemed important to keep women's bodies fit for the strenuous demands of intellectual activity, was often the first to appear on a campus. At McGill, gymnastic instructor Helen Barnjum, sister of long-time male instructor Frederick Barnjum, was hired in 1888 to teach club swinging and light gymnastics to women students in a dingy, damp cubby-hole that passed for a gymnasium. McGill's Director of Physical Education, R. Tait McKenzie, supported the program and bragged about the favourable relationship between the Donaldas' scholastic and athletic achievements.[82]

By the late 1890s, women attending the University of Toronto colleges were active in fencing, tennis, ice hockey, and basketball, as well as a solid favourite, the paper chase. Most Saturday mornings, the hostess team would lay an intricate trail (of torn-up paper) through woods and fields to be followed by the visiting team in the afternoon, with contestants clocked as in a race. It was, commented one observer, probably "one of the most enjoyable and health inducing sports ever indulged in by the women undergraduates," but had to be abandoned in 1914 because of the encroachment of city buildings.[83]

Basketball was the most popular team game, although finding a suitable place to play was often a problem. Before women students at McGill's Royal Victoria College got their new gymnasium, they were forced to play in dangerous surroundings: "the gymnasium pillars manifested such a tendency to knock down players that four in one week received more or less painful rebuffs, one even being confined to bed for three weeks." They solved the problem by wrapping "nice puffy coats" around the offending posts.[84] Women students at the University of Toronto were forced to conduct their activities and classes in a variety of unsuitable facilities, whereas by 1919 male students could take advantage of the fully modern facilities at Hart House, which included two gymnasia and a swimming pool. From the beginning, Hart House was restricted to men only, although money was set aside for the eventual construction of a women's building (this did not occur until 1959, and the restriction against women was not lifted until 1972).[85]

Ice hockey was also a favourite among university women. Probably the first to play were the Donaldas at McGill University who, in 1894, requested permission to use the rink and organized a series of class games. Women at Queen's University organized a team the following year, called the "Love-Me-Littles," aptly named to reflect the concern caused among campus authorities. In Toronto, the women of University and Victoria colleges competed for the first time in 1901, and games with St. Hilda's were played on an informal basis until the formation of a league in 1905. The following year St. Hilda's withdrew from the league because they disagreed with the allowance of body checking (defined then as shoving a player into the boards), which was not eliminated until 1910.[86] No doubt other universities formed ice hockey teams, but their history remains hidden.

Another kind of hockey was popular with women at some universities. Field (also known as grass or ground) hockey was introduced by games mistresses trained in England to students at Halifax Ladies College in the 1890s, later at Dalhousie University, and in 1905 to women at University and Victoria colleges in Toronto. On the west coast, the Vancouver Ladies Hockey Club was formed in 1896, and by the turn of the century the game was well established in both Vancouver and throughout Vancouver Island with teams in high schools, colleges, and communities.[87]

As more and more women took to sports in universities, associations were required to organize and promote the activities, at first on their own campuses; it would be more than a decade before intercollegiate competition took place among the major universities in Ontario and Quebec, and still later in the west. One of the earliest was the Royal Victoria College Athletic Association formed in 1901 to organize inter-class competitions in tennis, ice hockey, and fencing. The Toronto University Athletic League was formed in 1905 to promote friendly competition among the colleges. Awards were established, usually a small crest or shield worn proudly on a college sweater. Even at newer universities, it did not take long for women's athletic clubs to form. At the University of Alberta, founded in 1908, the number of co-eds grew so rapidly that, by 1913, they had formed a Women's Athletic Association with an enthusiastic basketball club. A gymnasium was secured twice a week for basketball practice, and the following year the team played in a new city league.[88]

Colleges and universities began to hire specialist teachers in physical education to teach the growing numbers of women students. At the University of Toronto in 1906, a Miss Wreyford, a graduate of the Sargent School in Boston, was appointed to instruct at both University and Victoria Colleges. Ethel Mary Cartwright emigrated to Canada from England in 1904, when she was hired to teach physical culture to the young women of Halifax Ladies College. She had completed a two-year diploma course at the South West Polytechnic in London, forerunner of the prestigious Chelsea College of Physical Education. In 1906, she moved to Montreal to become Physical Director of Royal Victoria College at McGill University, a woman-only institution also financed by Lord Strathcona, who saw to it that a well-equipped gymnasium, available only to women, was built with the facility. Affectionately dubbed "Carty" by her students, she established a required physical education program for all first-year students, and, by 1912, undergraduates needed to complete 140 hours of physical education before graduating. Her program consisted of dance, apparatus, free gymnastics, Indian-club swinging, and sports instruction, especially in tennis and basketball.[89] A strong supporter of competitive sport opportunities for her students, Cartwright helped them organize sports days, intramural events, and, most importantly, intercollegiate competition with nearby universities.

Sport for Young, Urbanized, Working Women

Only a tiny fraction of the population attended a college or university, and among these, women were a small majority. The 1911 Canadian census showed that between 5,000 to 6,000 women had graduated from university out of a total eligible population of over 2 million, yet the number of women in paid occupations was around 400,000.[90] Increasing urbanization and industrialization at the turn of the century brought thousands of young, single "working girls" into the larger Canadian cities. They left farms and small towns seeking work as seamstresses, milliners, office workers, store clerks, or as industrial workers in the expanding factories, or, if need be, domestic servants in private homes. By 1881, single women represented over 16 per cent of Toronto's population, which 10 years later had increased to 18.4 per cent. By 1891, nearly 200 factories in the city of Halifax employed over 1,200 women, most single and under 20 years old. Where daughters from middle-class families, the so-called "New Women," took up comparatively well-paying jobs in commerce, education, government, and the professions en route to marriage and a family, the vast majority of wage-earning working-class women worked because they had to.[91]

The influx to urban areas also inspired North American progressivism, with the city and its growing commercial amusements viewed as social problems, prompting middle-class secular reformers to campaign for urban parks and playgrounds and to establish agencies directed especially at girls and young, single women to provide them with "respectable" amusements. At the turn of the century, the National Council of Women, through its local councils, played a major role in the development of supervised playgrounds in larger Canadian communities, either through gaining use of school playgrounds during the summer months or initiating new areas, which were well-equipped, supervised, and offered instruction in physical culture, crafts, games, and sports. After the initial efforts of a local Council of Women, many cities formed more broadly based parks or playground associations in order to develop and maintain a network of supervised playgrounds. Among the first was Montreal, which, by 1904, had opened five playgrounds with more than 30,000 children in attendance. Ethel Mary Cartwright was instrumental in establishing a course at McGill for playground supervisors, who more often than not were women. In 1914 there were nine supervised playgrounds in Toronto, where only five years earlier there had been none. By World War I, most cities in Canada had formed a playground association and developed supervised playgrounds, with larger centres supporting inter-playground competition.[92] Although boys first benefited from the organized athletic and sports opportunities at these playgrounds, girls were eventually offered similar opportunities, and they became important early training grounds for many young athletes.

The organization most interested in young, urbanized working girls was the Young Women's Christian Association (YWCA), which first began to sprout up in major Canadian centres in the 1870s. By the mid-1880s, they strove to provide "legitimate amusements" to lure impressionable working girls away from dance halls, movie theatres, saloons, and pool halls, all deemed unhealthy and suspect.[93] Without adequate facilities, the early YWCAs could do little more than offer talks and courses. By 1900, with 14 branches established across the country, many in their own buildings with a cafeteria, gymnasium, and sometimes a swimming pool, the YWCA had effectively become a women-centred athletic club. Between 1914 and 1915, for example, the number of registrants for "physical culture" had jumped from 766 to 3,558, largely because of the new pools or the possibility of using one in the nearby YMCA.[94] The Toronto YWCA, one of the first to have a swimming pool, hired Mary Beaton, an accomplished Scottish swimmer and instructor, to conduct classes in swimming, water polo, life saving, and fancy diving. After a session, the bulky wet bathing suits were hung up in a drying room, and the swimmers dried their hair, bent over a long pipe extending from a small gas stove. By 1910, wrote one enthusiast, the YWCA had become the "axle round which all the physical culture of Toronto revolves."[95]

Privately owned schools of physical culture, catering only to girls and women, also began to develop. One was the Somers School of Physical Training, founded in 1911 by Toronto school teacher Mrs. H.B. Somers. She began by offering a class in club swinging, and gradually expanded the curriculum to include corrective exercises, interpretive dancing, and basketball, offered to a wide range of ages from young children, elementary and high school students, and young working women, to those who lived at home. By 1920 she had bought some land and raised sufficient funds to construct a separate building to house the school.[96]

Another private school of physical culture was the Margaret Eaton School, also in Toronto.[97] First known as The School of Expression, it had been founded in 1900 when Emma Scott Raff, a young widow with a child to support, opened a small studio on the corner of Yonge and Bloor streets. Here she taught elocution (voice training), physical culture, pedagogy, and literature. In 1902, Raff was appointed Director of Physical Culture for women attending Victoria College at the University of Toronto, where she gave classes in Swedish apparatus and Delsartean and aesthetic movement, while continuing to offer classes in dramatic presentation through her own school. One of her students was Margaret Beattie Eaton, wife of a young dry-goods salesman (Timothy Eaton), who convinced her husband to spend $50,000 for the construction of a new building to house Raff's growing school. Styled like a Greek temple, the new building opened in 1907, and the school became The Margaret Eaton School of Literature and Expression. Eventually, there were two distinct courses of study: one in literature and dramatic study, the other in physical culture. By 1923, physical culture students were awarded a teaching certificate in physical education, and many found employment in settlement houses, YWCAs, and private schools.[98]

There are few references to grass-roots organizing of women's team sports outside the universities and colleges before 1900, although more occurred in the decade before World War I. With only scattered clubs and teams, the task of organizing leagues and setting up competitive schedules, even locally, was a few years away. It was noteworthy when it did occur, as in an 1895 Toronto newspaper article announcing the formation of a Ladies Basketball Club. Accompanying the article, which described only the second game ever witnessed in the city, was a pen-and-ink drawing of a girl in typical bloomer dress flying through the air as she attempted to put a ball in the basket. The game, as reported in the newspaper, had been played at the Toronto Athletic Club, by some of its "lady associates":

> Although the number of players was not so large as on the previous occasion, it was generally conceded that the play was much better. The tall young kicker carried consternation and the ball, many times into the enemy's camp, while one rather diminutive member quite made up for lack of

stature in quickness of movement and certain dodging manoeuvres. The other players were in good form, the game being closely contested, and the winners being only one point ahead. A small, but very appreciative, audience took the game in from the gallery, and as usual, greeted the players with many expressions of encouragement as they chased the elusive ball. All interested in this game will be pleased to learn that the formation of a Ladies Basket-Ball Club is one of the probabilities of the near future.[99]

It was also not unusual for college basketball teams to play locally organized teams to increase their competitive opportunities. For example, the first game played in public by the Queen's University team was against a team from the local YWCA. The university's student newspaper contained this enthusiastic report:

> Mr. Bews [Queen's coach] had been boasting for some time about his team, but we thought he was simply indulging in pleasantry. However, our eyes were opened. The girls played beautiful ball. Short, fast passing, quick running, hard checking and really splendid shooting, marked the game. It was the combination that pleased us the most. Our team was much lighter than the Y's and would have been snowed under if they had not taken the ball down the floor by exceedingly clever passing. At half-time the score was 3 all, but in the second period we drew right away. The final score was 11–5 for Queen's.[100]

The women's basketball movement speedily gained momentum further east and west as well. By 1910, most towns in Nova Scotia had women's basketball teams, prompting a *Halifax Herald* sportswriter to suggest the formation of a league. "We would not," he commented, "advise the girls to form football and baseball leagues but basketball and hockey should be in line."[101] The inaugural game of the Saskatoon "Ladies Basketball League" took place on 21 October 1915 at the YMCA gymnasium.[102]

In 1912, a young teacher named Percy Page moved from Ontario to Edmonton to help organize commercial courses in Edmonton high schools. Two years later he took charge of the commercial classes at the new McDougall High School and, with his assistant Ernest Hyde, organized boys' and girls' basketball teams, even though the school had no gymnasium and home games had to be played outdoors. Hyde decided to coach the boys, leaving Page the girls. In the first year, Page guided his team to the high school championship with victories over the three other teams in the league; the next year they won the provincial championship. Since players wanted to keep playing, they formed the Commercial Athletic Society with the purpose of forming a team after they graduated. By 1917 they were known as the Edmonton Commercial Graduates (the "Grads" for short), and over the next two decades, mostly because of their phenomenal success, they had a remarkable effect on the growth of women's basketball in Canada.[103]

Another team sport with an early history of community participation among Canadian girls and women is ice hockey; the first teams appeared in the early 1890s. Just who was the first is anybody's guess, but among the earliest written accounts was of a game between two teams, simply designated as numbers one and two, in Ottawa on 11 February 1891.[104] There are also photographs of women's hockey teams dating from this period, supporting the claim that teams existed if only for social reasons and before the development of leagues and competitions. Early women's ice hockey in Quebec, for example, was very much a social affair with mostly English-speaking young women of *la meilleure société* participating. At the turn of the century, clubs existed in Montreal (anglophone Westmount), Trois-Rivières, Lachute, and Quebec City. Matches were often played for charity, or on a special occasion, such as a send-off for Canadian soldiers going to the Boer War. At the first women's hockey game ever played in Montreal, by members of the newly formed Quebec Ladies' Hockey Club, $125 was raised for the Soldiers' Wives League. The reporting of women's hockey in newspapers of this era was rare because games were played informally and infrequently. In 1902, a challenge match organized between the Ladies' Hockey Clubs of Trois-Rivières and Montreal was considered the championship of Canada since there were no organized leagues or tournaments and certainly no opportunity to travel very far.[105]

By the early 1900s and certainly by World War I, women's teams were organized in communities small and large throughout Canada, from the Maritimes to British Columbia and as far north as the Yukon. They played mostly outdoors because indoor arenas were rare. They also played mostly among themselves, although leagues made up of teams from neighbouring towns and cities began to be organized. In 1906, for example, the first Alberta provincial tournament was held at the Banff Winter Carnival with six teams competing, and, in 1914, Ontario women competed in Picton at their first provincial championship.

By the late nineteenth century, sport entrepreneurs were interested in attracting women to baseball, but only as spectators, primarily to enhance its respectability and profitability. Middle-class women had often attended the matches, dinners, dances, and other social functions associated with the game, but their patronage declined as the sport became more popular with working men, who were sometimes given to gambling, drinking, tobacco-chewing, and other forms of disreputable behaviour.[106] Clubs sought to attract women to their games by admitting them free of charge with a male escort, providing separate grandstand seating away from the riffraff, and initiating popular ladies' days one or two times a week. Baseball entrepreneurs also sponsored novelty events attractive to both men and women spectators, such as female barnstorming teams from the United States, certainly among the first attempts to market women athletes as spectacle.

One of the earliest tours was by a team from Chicago, the Blackstockings, who came to the Maritimes in the summer of 1891. Outfitted in knee-length, red and black striped dresses belted at the waist, jockey caps, black stockings, and ankle-high laced leather shoes, they arrived in Halifax with much fanfare and marched to the baseball park accompanied by flags and a brass band. Waiting there was an enthusiastic crowd of over 3,000, including more than the usual number of women spectators. They challenged a local men's team, but their skills were decidedly amateurish, and they needed assistance from the opposing team to keep the score close. The local sports press was often sarcastically critical of the Blackstockings, labelling them fakes and frauds, and in some towns they were prevented from playing by outraged clergy and reformers.[107] Still, they generated enough interest and profit that other barnstorming teams were formed in the United States, and they too eventually toured parts of Canada.

Perhaps the most famous was the Boston Bloomer Girls, formed in 1897, who toured western Canada in the summer of 1900. Over 1,200 spectators saw them play a Vancouver men's team, but the press reports were entirely uncomplimentary, complaining that the audience had been duped into seeing a few men (dressed as women) play well and the remaining women play poorly: "... it got laughable when the man on short stop would have to go out and take the ball from the right field lady because she had the women's throwing-stones-at-a-chicken style of sending in the ball, and could hardly get it more than a few feet."[108] Among the better players was Maud Nelson (who often used different last names), a legend who dominated the early years of women's baseball. She played a variety of positions from pitcher to third base with considerable skill and eventually became owner of the best teams of the era.[109] The team also travelled to other centres such as Kamloops, Moose Jaw, and Regina, often playing despite protests by conservative town fathers, who denounced them as immoral.[110] The Boston Bloomers played again in Montreal in 1902 to much interest, but when another team, the Star Bloomer Girls (also starring Maud Nelson), toured Quebec several years later, they were severely criticized by the Catholic church. In fact, one priest was so affronted he took the occasion to write a diatribe condemning all games, sports, and exercises participated in by women, insisting they should remain at home and tend the "sacred fire."[111]

Notwithstanding their limitations as ballplayers, and the controversies surrounding this bizarre form of entertainment, these early barnstorming teams provided the impetus for organizing women's baseball teams in various regions of the country. In the Maritimes, for example, the 1891 tour of the Chicago Blackstockings encouraged women's teams to sprout up in several urban centres and smaller communities.[112] However, the sport never gained much popularity among women, and it declined after World War I to be surpassed by softball, a simpler and easier game to play. Invented in Chicago in the late 1880s as an indoor game, it soon became a popular outdoor sport on the school and city playgrounds throughout North America. In Toronto, for instance, there was a playground league by 1913. Girls and women found the game especially fun because of the smaller field, larger ball, and slow, underarm pitch. In rural areas the game quickly became a popular activity at annual sports days and community picnics.[113]

WOMEN SEEKING TO CONTROL THEIR SPORTS

Golf was the first sport in which Canadian women sought to control their own affairs. In October 1900 at the Toronto Golf Club, following the first inter-provincial tournament (although only teams from Ontario, Quebec, and New Brunswick competed), those present decided to form the Ladies' Golf Association of Canada. Officers were elected, and the organization was to model itself after the Ladies' Golf Union of Britain, organized in 1893.[114] But something went wrong, and the new association did not survive. Golf historian James Barclay surmises that in 1901 the Royal Canadian Golf Association changed its constitution specifically to allow it to organize national events for women and at the same time initiated a ladies' section, making a separate women's organization super-fluous. The mystery deepens in that shortly after the constitutional change, invitations were sent out for the first national women's championship, which according to a newspaper report, would be "managed by the executive of the Canadian Ladies' Association."[115] We are left to conclude that a power struggle took place between the women of the fledgling organization and the men of the well-established Royal Canadian Golf Association, and that the women lost. It would be 13 more years before the women formed their own association.

Florence Harvey, a member of the Hamilton Golf Club and an excellent golfer, won the Canadian Ladies' championship in 1903 and 1904 (beating out Mabel Thomson). In 1912, she went to England to play in the British championship, where she became acquainted with the work of the Ladies' Golf Union, especially in establishing a uniform system of handicapping, arranging annual championships, acting as a legislative body, and promoting the game for women. It became apparent to Harvey that Canadian women golfers needed a similar organization. She seized the opportunity at a meeting on 28 September 1913 when two top British golfers came to play in the Canadian championship at the Royal Montreal Golf Club; they no doubt explained the benefits of the Ladies Golf Union and promised their support to those in attendance. The Canadian Ladies Golf Union (CLGU) was formed with Frances Campbell of Toronto as president and Florence Harvey as organizing secretary. Likely the first women's sport executive in Canada, Harvey proved to be an able administrator, quickly setting up three geographical divisions — Maritime (9 clubs), Middle (Quebec, Ontario, and the Prairies with 24 clubs), and Pacific (4 clubs) — further subdivided into districts, each with their own manager. Ladies' sections who belonged to the CLGU paid annual dues of between $10 and $20 depending on their membership, with the money going towards the cost of administering the association and for special medals purchased through the British organization.[116]

The CLGU was just hitting its stride when World War I began in 1914. All national and provincial championships were postponed (it was six years before another national championship was held), and the CLGU concentrated on raising money for the war effort, mainly through charity matches. Florence Harvey did her best to keep the CLGU together, but it became increasingly difficult, as district managers resigned to take up war work either at home or abroad. Harvey herself went off to Serbia in early 1918 as an ambulance driver, and the CLGU effectively disbanded.[117]

Although major tournaments were cancelled during the war, and Dominion and provincial championships postponed, women often competed in local and club tournaments in order to raise funds for the Red Cross, prisoners of war, or the war effort in general. Within the private sports clubs, their participation increased often to support patriotic causes; with men at war they took on more organizational responsibility, which would reap benefits for them when the war ended.[118] The war brought other changes as well, including a taste of employment in the men's world of streetcars, railways, steel and cement, munition factories, and in banks as tellers and clerks. After the war, even with the vote won, and proof that their efforts had been invaluable to the war effort, married women were sent back to their homes or into domestic service, or if they were young, single, and well-educated, into traditionally female occupations like teachers, secretaries, social workers, librarians, and the like. They could not compete for jobs with men, especially those returning from the war, and they were warned not to infringe on men's social and cultural space. Yet women, especially if they were young, energetic, working (and therefore had some money of their own) wanted to experience everything their brothers and boyfriends did including sport. Among girls and women in Vancouver, for instance, their sudden entry into this male bastion was attributed to their "new-found independence in the war."[119] From an organizational perspective, the issue was whether women would create their own clubs and associations, or whether they would try to align with men, seek their advice, and slowly move forward to autonomy. As it turns out, they chose both routes.

CHAPTER 2

ASSUMING CONTROL: WOMEN'S SPORT RUN (ALMOST) BY WOMEN

The ever-increasing tendency of girls to engage in athletic sports and pastimes has been a marked feature of the recreational activities of the present generation. The days of the restrained, genteel lawn croquet and kindred games have given way to more active varieties. The girls have encroached on the boys' fields. They go in for competitive swimming, canoeing, golf, tennis, racing, hockey, basketball, track athletics, baseball, etc. There was a significant result of a ball game at Centre Island yesterday, when the St. Michael's Parish picnickers saw the young women's team defeat the young men's team by 7 to 4 in a smartly played contest. It was not like that in the olden days.

Globe, 26 July 1928

On 12 May 1922, a little known women's basketball team left Edmonton to make the long train journey east to play the London Shamrocks for the first Dominion women's basketball championship. Before 1,500 spectators, the Edmonton Commercial Graduates beat the Shamrocks 41–8 in the first game, played under the six-player "girls" rules to the advantage of the western team. The Grads went down to defeat 21–8 in the second game, mainly because the five-player "boys" rules were used to the Shamrocks' benefit. When the Grads returned 10 days later, having won the title on overall points, a large and boisterous crowd including the mayor, city councillors, school board officials, and several hundred students were at the train station to welcome them. A triumphal parade along Jasper Avenue led to a civic reception at the Hotel MacDonald, where commemorative medals were awarded the team and their coach. Every newspaper in the country carried the story of these six young women, now Canadian champions — Dorothy and Daisy Johnson, Winnie Martin, Eleanor Mountifield, Nellie Perry, and Connie Smith, all graduates of McDougall Commercial High School — and their former teacher, J. Percy Page, who had coached them to victory.

Smartly turned out in black and gold middies with knee-length bloomers, heavy woolen socks, pads to protect their knees, and hair-bands to keep long locks out of their eyes, the Grads were fit, athletic, and feminine; fast and skilled on the court; and the very model of womanhood off it. Gregory Clark, a self-professed "old-fashioned man" and columnist at the *Toronto Star*, attended an Edmonton Grads versus Toronto Lakesides basketball game and subsequently wrote about it in a feature article for the *Toronto Star Weekly*. Although impressed by their athletic skill, he repeatedly assured his readers the athletes were women, still "essentially feminine" and "lithe, bounding, immeasurably light on their small feet." He tried to avoid condescension, although not always successfully, writing that his intent was to give the girls a boost: "For the fact of the matter is, unquestionably, that the girls are athletes of the very first rank, that their comprehension of the sport is quite as complete as any male team of any description, and the grace with which they do it is utterly and forever beyond the power of males."[1] Under Page, they trained and practised hard, sometimes with boys' teams, but, away from the basketball floor, they were expected to dress and behave like the reputable young working women they were. They helped fashion a new model of athletic womanhood, characterized by the masculine qualities of skill, strength, speed, agility, and energy, while at the same time retaining their femininity. Their very presence helped redefine the earlier contested notions of womanhood.

The period immediately following the war and throughout the 1920s was tremendously exciting for Canadian sportswomen and the fans who supported them. Certainly the media, especially daily newspapers, began to take notice. Often called the "golden age" of women's sport, it was a time when popular team sports like basketball, ice hockey, and softball became sufficiently organized to hold provincial and Dominion championships; when the best athletes, especially in track and field, began to compete internationally and eventually at the Olympic Games; and when women leaders and administrators took control of women's sport, claiming they knew what was best for girls and women, although the advice of men was still needed. It was also an era when traditionalists, mostly in the form of the male sports media, but also physical educators of both genders, issued warnings about the intensity of female competition and the wisdom of their participation in international events such as the Olympic Games.

Who controlled women's athletics in Canada in this period? Certainly it was men, particularly the Amateur Athletic Union of Canada (AAU of C) who, despite repeated requests, refused to accept female registrations. By 1914, the powerful AAU of C controlled track and field, gymnastics, handball, fencing, boxing, and wrestling, while 20 other volunteer-led governing bodies claimed "national" jurisdiction in their respective sports. Only one of these, the Canadian Ladies Golf Union (formed in 1913) had anything to do with women. Calling upon the moral physiology arguments discussed in the last chapter, most of this male ruling elite argued that highly competitive or physically demanding sports were unsuitable for girls and women. Norton Crow, AAU of C president in 1923, questioned the "wisdom and value [of] the growing tendency of women and girls to take part in public track and field."[2] Those who governed Canadian amateur sport in this era initially paid little attention to the rising tide of female participation, until they were forced to do so by the sheer numbers of girls and women wishing to compete. Innovative women sport leaders forced their hand by forging new organizations, from local to provincial to national, to look after the special interests and health of female athletes.

Working-class women, who flocked to the cities before and during the war seeking employment in factories, stores, and businesses, had little hope of attending college or university, where women's sport was well-established and flourishing. Neither could they afford to belong to the elite tennis, golf, and curling clubs, which long ago had welcomed women, albeit on the basis of restricted times to play. They sought instead to expand their sporting opportunities and athletic presence through a grass-roots movement that established women's athletic clubs, organizations, and leagues in an increasing variety of sports, although the staples were basketball, ice hockey, softball, and track and field. Individual sponsors, businesses, factories, municipalities, and sometimes women themselves, provided the necessary equipment, uniforms, and facilities to allow them to play and compete. Organizational support and leadership came from existing men's sports clubs, church and youth organizations, large and small businesses, sports entrepreneurs, and increasingly from women sports leaders determined to administer their own sports, although often with the help of men.

Among the first of these women organizers was Mabel Ray, a successful equestrian, softball and hockey player, who during World War I organized a women's softball league in Toronto, called the Commercial Girls Baseball League. With only enough players for one team, they played boys' teams during their first season, charging spectators a dollar, but by the second season, they had recruited enough women and raised sufficient money to form three teams in a league.[3] Alexandrine Gibb was another of these early leaders. After completing school in Toronto, Gibb worked as a secretary, but in her spare time was an aspiring sportswriter and an enthusiastic organizer, administrator, and promoter of women's sport. In 1919, she helped organize the Ladies Ontario Basketball Association; two years later she was a founding member (along with Mabel Ray) of the Toronto

Ladies Athletic Club and its first president. Her philosophy — "girls' sport run by girls" — was uncompromising and put into practice through the Toronto Ladies club, an exclusively women's organization with teams in several sports (basketball, softball, track and field) all coached and managed by women.[4] It never sought commercial sponsorship for its teams and maintained a summer cottage in Etobicoke for its members. In 1922, with the formation of the Canadian Amateur Basketball Association, Gibb was elected second vice-president, the only woman on the executive.

Companies employing large numbers of young, single women also recognized the need to provide for their recreational and athletic needs. In 1918, Eaton's established two clubs for its women employees, one for "senior women" and the other for those 20 and under, which in 1923 were amalgamated to form the Eaton's Girls' Club. Facilities at 415 Yonge Street in the old YMCA included a gymnasium, library, sewing room, dining room, and sitting rooms. The Club sponsored an array of activities and courses, including sports like corrective gymnastics, dancing, fencing, basketball, and badminton in the early days, and eventually bowling, volleyball, softball, and track and field. Physical educators, usually graduates of the Margaret Eaton School, provided competent instruction and supervision, in addition to a philosophy that advocated friendliness and companionship rather than athleticism and competition. A summer vacation camp at Shadow Lake in Ballantrae (about 35 miles from Toronto) provided Eaton's women workers the opportunity to experience sports like sailing, golf, and equestrianism, associated more with middle- and upper-class leisure pursuits.[5]

The Hudson's Bay Company in western Canada was also active in providing recreational sport opportunities for its employees, many of whom were young women. An athletic facility was often built near the store — in Winnipeg, for instance, five tennis and two quoits (a throwing game using a circle of rope) courts, as well as an expansive playground (opposite the Fort Garry Hotel), was opened in 1920 exclusively for store employees. During the 1920s and 1930s, news from the various store athletic associations in places like Winnipeg, Regina, Yorkton, Edmonton, Lethbridge, Kamloops, and Vancouver was reported regularly in *The Beaver* magazine ("devoted to the interests of those who serve the Hudson's Bay Company)." One of the most active groups was a women's basketball team from the Edmonton store, the Fur Trappers, who played in a ladies' mercantile basketball league, and by 1924 was the best "100% mercantile" team in the province.[6]

Local businesses, not indifferent to the added benefits of publicity, also played a role in the early development of women's sports by setting up teams and leagues for their female employees and providing the necessary sponsorship. The Western Clock Company (also known as Westclox) built a modern factory in Peterborough, Ontario, in 1923, and the majority of its employees were soon women. Although it supported the creation of industrial leagues for both men and women, the Westclox women's softball team was known throughout the community and was often the reason women went to work there.[7] In Toronto, the Supreme Ladies Athletic Club was established by William J. D'Alesandro of the R. & S. Tire and Rubber Company, who, along with M.H. McArthur of the Hinde & Dauch Paper Company, also started the famous Sunnyside softball leagues. Originally organized as a softball team, the Supreme Club, easily identified by its red and white uniforms, soon branched out into other sports like bowling and ice hockey.[8] Perhaps the most flamboyant sponsor of women athletes and teams was Fred G. "Teddy" Oke, a former hockey player, a war veteran, and self-made millionaire. When his professional hockey franchise and other interests in men's sport floundered, he turned his attention to women's sports, especially his Parkdale Ladies' Athletic Club in Toronto. He lavished money on his athletes, luring them away from other clubs with tuition fees for those who wanted to attend business college or with jobs in his mining brokerage firm, as well as clothes, perfume, travel, and other expensive gifts. When the Ladies Ontario Basketball Association fought back by establishing a strict anti-transfer rule, Oke ignored it, and they suspended his club. His largesse diminished considerably after 1929 when the stock market crashed.[9]

Although it was men who often coached and managed the growing numbers of basketball, softball, and ice hockey teams, most sportswomen felt they should administer their own activity as much as possible. Mentioned earlier was the Toronto Ladies Athletic Club, probably the first all-women's multi-sports club in Canada, with teams coached and managed by women. As we will see throughout this chapter, women administrators gradually took control of their sports, although well-meaning and often supportive men were never entirely out of the picture. These same women sport leaders, like Alexandrine Gibb and Phyllis Griffiths, also began to use the sports media, specifically newspapers and national magazines, to make the case for more attention to women athletes and their sports. They became sportswriters themselves and were among the many aspiring women journalists in Canada in the early 1920s brought onto the major dailies for on-the-job training, sometimes without pay. For the first time, there was a woman's voice on the sports pages.

FORMING THE WOMEN'S AMATEUR ATHLETIC FEDERATION

Before World War I there were only occasional references to girls' and women's track and field events and virtually none at all during the war. Walking matches (pedestrianism) were still in vogue, such as the 10-mile race sponsored by the

Toronto Star in 1907: "Thousands of spectators saw the race from start to finish, though the course was suppose to be a secret. Such expectation showed a usual confidence in the reticence of the sex, as more than a hundred ladies had entered and eight-six came to the starting point, at the corner of Dundas and Howland Avenue."[10] All but six of the starters finished the race, with a Miss Rosamund Dunn winning by nearly three minutes.

Unlike the United States, where athletics was well-established in private colleges for women, such as Vassar, Mount Holyoke, Wellesley, and Bryn Mawr, there was no such tradition in the few equivalent Canadian women's colleges.[11] One exception was the Halifax Ladies College, where the closing ceremonies in 1910 included running events and a high jump and long jump competition, along with contests like "hopping" and "circular skipping," unfortunately not explained.[12] Cross-country running in the form of a "paper chase" was also popular at some colleges, as described in the last chapter. Organized athletics for Canadian women did not originate in the college system; it began first with the informal foot races at school field days, church or company picnics, or at country-wide celebrations like Dominion Day. Novelty races, such as the egg-and-spoon or thread-the-needle, were popular among girls and women, along with more serious flat races for a prize, often a dollar or two, in special categories such as girls under 12 or 15 and married women.

After the war, it was the newly formed women's sports clubs, like the Toronto Ladies Athletic Club, which were the most active promoters of women's track and field. They provided facilities, coaches, practice time, competitions, and most significant of all, the notion that keeping records about who could run the fastest, jump the highest, or throw the farthest was important, certainly if Canadian girls were going to test themselves against the rest of the world. Not everyone was in favour of this, as noted in one of the few books on women's sport available at the time:

> In striving for records the thought and manner must necessarily become manly; and grace, that natural condition for which woman stands, be lost in an effort not naturally a woman's. The effect of the training on women who try for records is to make them sluggish, and this will be most noticed when the work is overdone. Drawn features and a white complexion will also be noticed, besides a muscular manner and appearance. Thus the point of view which aims at an increased general health and strength must necessarily become lost.[13]

Many paid little heed to this advice. In the United States, a listing of women's athletic records appeared for the first time in the 1904 edition of *Spalding's Official Athletic Almanac.* Most were from Vassar College in New York, and it is worth noting a few of the events: 100-yard run (13.2 seconds), 220-yard run (30.6 seconds), high jump (4' 3¾₀"), running broad jump (14' 6½"), and putting the 8-lb shot (29' 11½").[14] There are no equivalent Canadian records from this era, although statisticians have compiled a few scattered times from before the war. For example, in 1912 Annie Miller ran the 100-yard event in 13.2 seconds at a track meet held at Hanlon's Point in Toronto.[15]

As mentioned earlier, the all-male AAU of C paid little attention to women and did not accept female registrations. The most they had done was set up a national committee on women's athletics, comprised of five men, all prominent in the governance of amateur sport. With both the International Olympic Committee (IOC) and the powerful International Amateur Athletic Federation (IAAF) opposed to including women's track and field events in the summer Olympics, Canada's governing body took a "do nothing" position. That was the case until 1922 when French sportswoman Alice Milliat and her newly formed Fédération sportive féminine internationale (FSFI) organized a spectacular international track and field event in Paris, called the Olympiques Féminine. The IAAF finally took notice and asked its member nations to take charge of women's track and field in their respective countries. With no official body for women's track and field in Canada, the AAU of C had two options: one was to encourage women to form their own association to control the sport, and the other was to take control themselves. They chose the latter course.

Canadian women did not compete in these first women's world track and field meets because the AAU of C had little interest in promoting the sport for women, even though Canada was formally admitted to the FSFI at its third congress in Paris in 1924.[16] This did not stop Canadian athletes from competing in the United States. One of their first trips was in January 1924, when a small group of women from the Toronto Ladies Athletic Club travelled to Madison Square Gardens in New York to compete in the Millrose (indoor) Games, which had first included events for women the previous year. Surprisingly, Toronto's Rosa Grosse beat the American record holder, Marion McCartie, in the 50-yard dash, and the relay team (Grosse, Myrtle Cook, Fanny Rosenfeld, and Grace Conacher) barely lost to an American four from the New York's City Bank Club.[17] In his 1924 report to the Amateur Athletic Union of Canada, secretary Norton Crowe acknowledged that "it is no use shutting our eyes to the fact that women's competition, particularly in Track and Field, is vastly on the increase and will have to be taken into account."[18]

At the Ontario Track and Field championships at Beaverton later that summer, the AAU of C finally sanctioned two women's events (100-yards and 440-yard relay), and on a "properly measured course and timed by experienced clockers," the amazing Rosa Grosse set two world records, shaving 1.5 seconds off the time for the 100-yard event, which she ran in 11.2 seconds.[19] Her other record was in a special 75-yard race. Even male sportswriters in Canada recognized the potential: "The point is that Canadian girls, as never before, and in ever-increasing numbers, are storing up health, discipline, self-control and fine spirit of sportsmanship on the playing fields of the Dominion, and that the performances of many closely approximate those of the world's women leaders in track events."[20]

In the summer of 1925, Alexandrine Gibb was asked by the Amateur Athletic Union of Canada to conduct selection trials for a Canadian women's team, which had been invited, all expenses paid, to compete in an international track and field meet at Stamford Bridge in London, England. Gibb's appointment to select and manage the team was controversial. Apparently, the Ontario Branch of the AAU of C had received the invitation initially and immediately appointed Walter Knox of Orillia as manager and coach because of his experience with the men's team at the 1912 and 1920 Olympics, even though the invitation specified that the expenses of 10 girls and two "lady assistants" would be paid.[21] The national AAU of C stepped in and confirmed Gibb's appointment, stating that she was a "tireless and conscientious worker in the interests of women athletes."[22] However, this left Gibb precisely one week to organize the selection trials to be held at the University of Toronto stadium on 11 July since they were to sail for England on 17 July. Naturally, there was consternation in the press that athletes from outside Ontario would be unable to compete, which in the end was true. From 42 entrants, five athletes from Toronto, three from Hamilton, and one each from Montreal and St. Catharines made the team, with two reserves from Toronto. The two best sprinters in Canada, Rosa Grosse and Fanny Rosenfeld, did not try out for the team because they were previously committed to meets leading up to the Ontario track and field championships later in August.

Undeterred, Gibb and her athletes left Canada as scheduled under the watchful eye of chaperone Mrs. Gordon Finlay, sister-in-law to the AAU of C president. They were given a rousing send-off by several hundred enthusiastic friends and supporters, who showered them with gifts of chocolates and flowers. Gibb dutifully reported that the girls trained each day in the ship's well-equipped gymnasium and by walking around the decks. After dinner they were allowed to dance until 10 o'clock as long as they were in bed soon after. "What makes me so glad," she enthused, "is that everyone seems surprised at the high type of girl we have with us."[23] Upon arrival in London, the Canadians received last-minute coaching from British coaches Frederick Webster and Sam Mussabini (the personal coach of Harold Abrahams, immortalized in the film *Chariots of Fire*), both strong supporters of women's athletics. For the first time, Canadian women competed in official uniforms — scarlet socks and knickers, white jerseys edged with scarlet, and a red maple leaf on their breast — supplied by the Canadian Olympic Committee. Although they finished third overall behind Great Britain and Czechoslovakia in nine events, Webster commented on their remarkable improvement in the space of week, and that "they spared no pains to put themselves right."[24]

This first international trip had been very instructive for Alexandrine Gibb. She had observed the female-controlled British Women's Amateur Athletic Association first hand and become friends with one of its founders, Sophie Elliott-Lynn (Lady Heath), an all-round international athlete who competed in the javelin at the triangular meet in London. In fact, the two planned to write a book about women's athletics. Gibb was delighted and impressed by how seriously she and her athletes had been treated in England. Upon returning home, she immediately set out to establish a similar women's union affiliated with the AAU of C. She was determined that women should run their own sports, that girls should be coached by women, and that, although men were encouraged as advisors, they must stay in the background. Along with other prominent women's sport leaders in Toronto, Gibb wanted to create a national organization with branches in all provinces to administer and control girls' and women's sports. They formed the Canadian Ladies Athletic Club, which would provide opportunities in baseball, ice hockey, softball, and track and field across the country, and at the same time furnish the structure for a national governing body should the AAU of C oppose it.[25] Gibb became its first president.

Later that summer, the Toronto Ladies Athletic Club organized the first Ontario track and field championships for women, held at Varsity Stadium in Toronto. The star of the meet was Fanny Rosenfeld (known as "Bobbie" because she had bobbed her hair), who won four firsts and two seconds, equalling the world's record in the 100-yards and breaking it in the 220-yard event. The Russian-born daughter of Jewish immigrants, she was raised in Barrie, Ontario, but while still in high school moved with her family to Toronto, after which she found work as a stenographer at the Patterson Chocolate factory.[26] The press were effusive: "Magnificent, wonderful, splendid, sensational!"[27] Rosenfeld was representing the Patterson Athletic Club (in fact she was the only entrant for the club), which, as a result of her efforts, was the overall winner at the meet. The press also noted that practically all of the athletes had "shorn locks," and they made special mention of Rosenfeld's baggy warm-up suit, which was borrowed from her brother. At one of her first track meets she had been caught running in her father's bathing trunks and socks. Many years later, and in her inimitable style, she commented:

> We smilingly admit that our get-up wasn't exactly what fashion might decree — but what was a gal to do? With unflagging effort we tried all over town to purchase raiment in accordance with what the best-dressed sprinter was wearing, so that we could discard our modesty-preserving pup-tent bloomers, spinnaker middy and hip-length stockings. But girl athletes were

as yet in the neophyte stage, and sporting goods houses proved an absolute blank ... so we had to improvise our new and less blush-saving garments.... And anyway they got us there, even if they didn't exemplify the ultimate in art and good taste.[28]

At its annual meeting on 11 September 1925, the AAU of C approved the formation of a "women's branch," called the Women's Amateur Athletic Union of Canada, which would be governed entirely by women, but would "retain the advice and counsel" of the AAU of C's all-male women's committee. Janet Allen, President of the Ladies Ontario Hockey Association, was elected provisional president, and Marie Parkes, who taught physical education at the University of Toronto, the provisional secretary, with a temporary committee, which included Gibb, instructed to draft a constitution.[29] In one of her first articles for the *Toronto Star*, Gibb took stock of the situation across the country, suggesting that the best way to proceed would be to organize branches in each province. Ontario, she admitted, was in the optimum position with a number of already existing women's sport organizations, including those for basketball, ice hockey, and softball. Quebec (and by this she meant English Montreal) was active in basketball, ice hockey, and swimming, but there was little activity in the Maritimes. In the west, Alberta was strong in ice hockey and basketball (the Edmonton Grads were well on their way to fame); British Columbia and Manitoba were "being organized," but she made no mention of Saskatchewan.[30] She also made it clear that since women have not had the same executive experience as men, they should welcome their advice and guidance. Some years later, after a majority of women were elected to a local softball executive and the men running the league threatened to walk out, Gibb wrote:

> Men are very useful. They can help with advice and many men have done just that. Men have had years and years of experience in sport organizations and the girls have only been in the game for the past ten years. So we have lots to learn, girls. But we want a chance to learn it. If we can look after our own affairs we too will gain experience and be experts. If we keep asking the men to take all the responsible offices we will always be in the background. Don't misunderstand me in this struggle for the right of girls to sit on their own executives. Keep the men with you if you can, but impress on the men the importance of learning how these things should be done.[31]

The Women's Amateur Athletic Federation of Canada (WAAF of C) was officially formed at its first convention in Montreal, on 7 December 1926. Affiliated branches had been established in Ontario, Quebec, and the Maritimes, and the number of athletes registered in the Federation was approximately 1,200, although most of these were from the Ontario Ladies Softball Association. The convention was attended by representatives from the newly formed branches, other women's organizations, interested women athletes and physical educators, and, not surprisingly, a large number of men, including executive members of the AAU of C and the Canadian Olympic Committee. A photo in a Montreal newspaper shows almost 40 women and some 10 men. Strange as it may seem to us now, it was important that the "ladies" receive the men's blessing in their new venture, although it is doubtful any were prepared for the paternalistic remarks of AAU of C member John DeGruchy who

> expressed his personal gratification and delight at the way the ladies had thrown themselves into the work of the organization. He was amazed at the energy they had shown and wished to congratulate them upon their business-like methods.... He wished to emphasize, however, that in all these athletics for women, the womanly side must not be lost sight of, and that the women themselves must always keep in mind that the important thing is not so much athletics for women as that they are the mothers of the coming nation.[32]

The battle between the Fédération sportive féminine internationale and the International Amateur Athletic Federation over who would control women's athletics came to a truce of sorts when the IAAF offered to include several track events (as an experiment) on the 1928 Olympic program. There would be five events in total: 100-metres, 800-metres, high jump, 4x100-metre relay, and discus. Dr. A.S. Lamb, the Canadian representative on the IAAF, was one of six delegates who voted against including these events because he was personally opposed to international athletic contests for women.[33] However, it no longer mattered what Lamb thought, because now for the first time there would be a Canadian women's track team at the Olympics, and the WAAF of C set about finding the best athletes for the trip to Amsterdam.

It was clear from the outset that most of the women's Olympic team would come from Ontario. The first Canadian women's track and field championships in 1926 and again in 1927 demonstrated that, with few exceptions, the best athletes were mostly in Toronto and affiliated with the Canadian Ladies Athletic Club. One exception was high jumper Ethel Catherwood, who came from Saskatchewan. An all-round athlete, she excelled at basketball, skating, ice hockey, and baseball, as well as the sprinting and jumping events, and in 1926 at the Saskatchewan track and field championships, she set a world record (just under 5' 3") in the high jump. At the 1927 Canadian championships in Toronto, nick-named the "Saskatoon lily" because of her extraordinary beauty, she was declared the undisputed Canadian champion and a certainty to make the Olympic team. The Canadian Olympic Committee invited her to return to Toronto to train with the Parkdale Ladies Athletic Club, where the generous Teddy Oke sponsored both her and her sister Ginger by sending them to business college and then employing them in his brokerage firm. He also hired the highly experienced athlete and coach Walter Knox to help Ethel become consistent at clearing the bar at world record height.[34] Canada's other top high jumper of this era was teenager Eva Dawes of the Toronto Ladies Club. In 1926 she had set a Canadian record at the national championships, but was barred from competing in the open event the following year because the new WAAF of C constitution mandated that competitors must be 16 years old.

The 1928 Canadian track and field championships and final Olympic trials were held in Halifax in early July. The Maritime branch of the WAAF of C, headed by Elizabeth Stirling, was particularly strong, and they were keen to have at least one athlete on the Olympic team. The *Halifax Herald* and the *Evening Mail* held trials in "practically" every Nova Scotia town to find the best representative to send to Toronto for the Canadian championships in 1927. Jean McDougall of Halifax won the trip and competed in the 60-yard hurdles and running broad jump, but she was no match for the highly trained Toronto athletes.[35] Gertrude Phinney, 18 years old and running for the Ex-Dalhousie Club, was a sensation at the 1927 Maritime championships and considered to be one of Canada's foremost contenders for the Olympic team, but she opted not to compete in the 1927 Canadian championships in Toronto. She did, however, compete in the Halifax trials in 1928 to no avail.[36] In the end, the six track athletes selected to represent Canada at the Olympic Games were all Toronto-based: Ethel Smith, Myrtle Cook, Fanny "Bobbie" Rosenfeld, Jane Bell, Ethel Catherwood, and Jean Thompson.[37]

The story of the Canadian "Matchless Six" has been told and retold.[38] Twenty-one nations sent women track and field competitors to the 1928 Summer Olympics in Amsterdam, with some teams, like Germany and the United States, having as many as 19 women on their teams. The British, certainly one of the strongest teams, boycotted the event, because they were adamant that women should support and compete in the all-women FSFI world games and not in a mixed Olympics. Canada's six track entries were also joined by a swimmer, 16-year-old Dorothy Prior of the Parkdale-Dolphinet Club in Toronto, whose expenses were paid by sports promoter Teddy Oke. Unfortunately, Prior was no match for the older, "husky" European swimmers, and she failed to qualify for the final of her one race, the 200-metre breaststroke.

The Canadian story was very different on the track. Ethel Catherwood, the most photographed girl at the games, won gold and set a world record (5' 2½") in the high jump. The relay team of Myrtle Cook, Bobbie Rosenfeld, Ethel Smith, and Jane Bell beat the United States team, also in world record time (49.4 seconds). In an impossibly close 100-metre final, after Cook had been disqualified for two false starts, Rosenfeld and Smith placed second and third, even though Canadian officials — including team manager Alexandrine Gibb — thought Bobbie had beaten the American Betty Robinson. Dr. A.S. Lamb, *chef de mission* of the Canadian team, refused to support the protest, claiming that it was unsports-manlike to do so. Bobbie Rosenfeld was scratched from the discus event so that she and Jean Thompson could run in the 800-metres; they qualified for the finals and came fourth and fifth, with Rosenfeld sacrificing a possible placing by wait-ing for Thompson, who began to fade in the last 30 yards. In the unofficial stand-ings, the small Canadian team won more points than any other nation. They came home to an ecstatic welcome, both in Montreal and Toronto, and were showered with gifts, including diamond-studded wrist watches given to them by the Canadian National Exhibition.

The International Amateur Athletic Federation voted (16 to 6) to retain the women's track and field events in future Olympics, although they eliminated the 800-metres on the basis that it was too strenuous, replacing it with the 80-metre hurdles and adding the javelin throw. Alexandrine Gibb was incensed when Arthur Lamb, without consulting her or anyone else from the WAAF of C, voted against women competing in the Olympics on the premise they would be better off in the FSFI women's international games. In an article she wrote for *Maclean's*, Gibb attempted to rationalize his actions by lashing out at the negative attitude towards women athletes in Montreal:

> Dr. Lamb comes from Montreal. In Montreal, competitive athletics for women are practically a minus quantity. This biggest city of Canada never had an outstanding woman athlete in track and field. It did not have a single representative at the final Olympic trials in Halifax. Undoubtedly, this was due to the objection that exists in Montreal against competitive sports for women. Every other eastern province was well represented but Quebec was simply out in the cold.[39]

In his defence, Lamb pointed to the "many glaring inaccuracies and untruths" in the press reports including those of Gibb, although in retrospect, he admitted his error in not consulting both Gibb and Marie Parkes in the matter of future partic-ipation by women at the IOC Olympics.[40] In November 1928, just a few months after the Olympics, Gibb was elected president of the WAAF of C. Shortly after, she, along with other members of the executive, represented the Federation at the annual AAU of C meetings where Lamb's controversial vote was hotly debated.

As a result, the WAAF of C was finally given complete control over Canadian women's sports both nationally and internationally. "Only the future," Gibb wrote in her column, "will tell how fit we are to look after our own affairs."[41]

GRASSROOTS ORGANIZING OF TEAM SPORTS

The success of the Edmonton Grads on the basketball courts created more interest in the game across the country with teams, clubs, and leagues flourishing. It was the "sport of entry" for many girls, especially in schools, which slowly abandoned military drill, formal gymnastics, and club-swinging for more vigorous and competitive activities in the girls' physical education curriculum. New leagues required governance — in 1919, for example, the Ladies Ontario Basketball Association was formed, and four teams from Toronto, Hamilton, London, and Stratford entered the provincial play-downs. In Toronto alone, there were as many as 25 teams in different leagues.[42] When the Grads played the Torrid Zones in Regina in 1929, it was before 8,500 spectators, the largest turn-out for a game of any kind in Saskatchewan except for men's professional hockey. Everyone agreed that the visit of the Grads (even though they won handily at 50–12) would "give a great boost to basketball in this part of the country."[43]

Basketball, long flourishing among women students in the universities, was now ready to take another step. In the winter of 1920, Ethel Mary Cartwright, the physical director of Royal Victoria College at McGill University, invited Ruth Clark, women's physical director at Queen's University, to bring a basketball team to Montreal for a two-game match against the Royal Victoria College team, the first recorded women's intercollegiate match in Eastern Canada. The following year, the two were joined by Marie Parkes from the University of Toronto, and together they formed the Canadian Intercollegiate Women's Basketball League, although the only teams in the league were from McGill (Royal Victoria College), Queen's, Toronto, and eventually the University of Western Ontario in London. A trophy, a bronze replica of a lithe, tunic-clad, Grecian woman, was suggested by Cartwright and donated by the McGill students. The "Bronze Baby" is still one of the oldest and most proudly won awards by succeeding generations of university basketball players (as a member of the Queen's team in 1961, I fondly remember our triumph).[44]

Travel across the country was arduous and expensive, and as a result national championships featuring teams from the east and west were often challenging affairs to organize. In 1922, the cost of the Grads' first trip east was $1,500 with only $600 guaranteed by the London team. The remaining funds were raised by the Grads themselves by tapping friends, loyal Edmonton fans, and J.J. Seitz, president of the United Typewriter Company of Canada (who later donated the

Underwood International Trophy to encourage basketball among girls' teams, particularly in Canada and the United States).[45] The Grads retained their Dominion title in 1923 by inviting the London Shamrocks to a return match in Edmonton. Alexandrine Gibb played left guard on the Toronto Ladies (the "Maple Leafs") basketball team, which in September 1923 challenged the Grads for the Underwood Trophy. They were soundly trounced, as they were again the following spring when they returned to Edmonton for the Dominion championships, even though this time they brought their coach and more players.[46]

Percy Page, the enterprising Grads' coach and business manager, was determined to find more challenging competition for his ever-improving team, but to do so, he needed a means to bring in visiting teams, especially from the United States, and to meet expenses, which included the arena rental, officials' fees, advertising, and promotional costs. He also needed money to help finance the trips he planned for the Grads, especially to the United States and perhaps even to Europe. Gate receipts were the major source of funds. Ticket prices in the 4,800 seat Edmonton arena ranged from $1.00 box seats to 50 cents for general admission, and it cost school children 25 cents to sit in a special, reserved section. Advance tickets could be ordered by mail through a local newsstand. In the fall of 1923, the Grads hosted teams from Toronto, Chicago, and Ohio, winning all their games before a total of 28,000 appreciative spectators.[47]

These games and victories, in addition to some assistance from the Edmonton business community, allowed the Grads to raise over $11,000 to finance their first trip to Europe in the summer of 1924. They had wanted to participate at the Olympics in Paris, but the International Olympic Committee was not interested in having basketball, let alone women's basketball, on their program. Instead Page persuaded the FSFI to organize a series of exhibition matches for the Grads against teams in France. Eight players, along with Coach Page and Mrs. Page (as chaperone) made the long journey by train and boat to Europe, where they played six games, mostly against local pick-up teams in Paris, Strasbourg, Roubaix, and Lille, outscoring the opposition (usually by 50 points or more) with their effective short passing game. Grads player Abbie Scott, who kept a diary of the trip, commented wryly that in one game she scored 23 points — "which shows there was not much competition."[48] The FSFI granted them the first women's world title, and they returned home to much public adulation.

Unfortunately the growth of basketball across the country was hindered by the "rules" problem. By the early 1920s at least three different sets of rules were used in girls' and women's basketball. In the United States, the boy's or men's five-player, full-court game had been modified by Senda Berenson at Smith College into "girls' rules," which eventually were adopted by the Committee on Women's Athletics of the American Physical Education Association. These modified rules discouraged personal contact and tussling through stringent penalties, but most important, they limited each player to either half or one-third of the court depending on its size or the age of the girls. They argued that women's basketball was not a weak, emasculated form of men's basketball, but a different game requiring different rules *because* girls were physiologically weaker than boys:

> ... the game subjected the player to a test of physical endurance which was beyond the capacity of any but the most vigorous. The panting, gasping and calling for "time" by the player of ordinary strength, as well as the disproportionate fatigue that often accompanies a game, showed that the heart was being forced to carry an unusually heavy load. It was seen that the game which made such heavy demands on organic vitality was ill-adapted to the rank and file of girls and that its range of usefulness was much limited thereby. It was also recognized that the dangers from collision, violent contact and falling were more serious for the girl than for the boy.[49]

Published by the American Sports Publishing Company in the *Official Basketball Guide for Women*, and officially called the "Spalding Rules," they were commonly referred to as "girls' rules." Women physical educators in central Canada and the Maritimes, influenced by their American counterparts, enforced these rules in schools and universities, although the more vigorous boy's rules were often used — not without condemnation — in YWCA, community, or church leagues outside the control of physical educators. Basketball, commented a Toronto sports reporter in 1924, as played by the Toronto Ladies and the Young Women's Hebrew Association (YWHA) is "entirely too rough a game for girls."[50] This particular YWHA team (including star player Fanny Rosenfeld) went on to win the Toronto Ladies' Basketball League and, after defeating the Ottawa Alerts, travelled to Edmonton only to be beaten by the Edmonton Grads.

In 1921, with the formation of the Canadian Intercollegiate Women's Basketball League, the Spalding Rules were modified to permit each player to cover two-thirds of the floor, and these became known as the "Intercollegiate Rules." The League decided to publish its own rule book and to canvass, with some success, all high schools and universities in Eastern Canada to use these rules. By 1929, everyone agreed that the Spalding rules were the best set of "girl's rules." In western Canada, especially due to the influence of the Edmonton Grads, who switched to boy's rules in 1922, and also to the relative scarcity of women physical education teachers, most teams were coached by men and played the so-called men's game in both educational and community settings.[51] When east met west, it sometimes required the use of both sets of rules in the same match, with girls' rules being played one game, boys' the next, and both used in a final game if necessary.

By the late 1920s, the old-fashioned middy and bloomer basketball uniforms had given way to men's shorts and jerseys, sometimes with long stockings covering the knees. As more schools were built, some in close proximity, interscholastic competition developed for school girls, with more women taking on the job of coaching the teams. At the community level, it was not unusual for a town dignitary to offer a trophy for an annual competition between several nearby teams, and, as travel became easier, leagues developed. The Edmonton Grads were the undisputed champions of Canada, North America, and the "world," having travelled again to Europe for exhibition games arranged by the FSFI at the time of the 1928 Olympics in Amsterdam.

Women's ice hockey became increasingly popular, and the informal, social matches common before World War I gave way to more competitive, organized tournaments and leagues. University teams of the early 1920s competed in intervarsity leagues as well as with local clubs. The Western Canadian InterVarsity Athletic Union was formed in 1920 among Alberta, Saskatchewan, and Manitoba universities (British Columbia joined in 1923). The most outstanding player at the University of Saskatchewan was Genevra "Ginger" Catherwood, whose sister Ethel was an accomplished high jumper, as we have seen.[52] In the east, Toronto, McGill, and Queen's competed in the Women's Collegiate Ice Hockey League for the Beattie Ramsay Trophy, named after a male player on Canada's Olympic team. The University of Toronto team dominated the league, winning all but one championship in 14 years.[53]

Ice hockey was no longer a game played primarily by women in universities or from the more bourgeois sectors of society, because thousands of working-class girls in small communities and larger cities took up the sport with enormous enthusiasm. In Montreal in 1914, for example, 28 young women employed at the Bell Telephone Company formed a league with four clubs — Long Distance, Victoria, Upton, and East — although it was only to last a year. The following year, a four-club league was again formed in Montreal, including among them the Western Club, owned and operated by Len Porteous, a local entrepreneur who sought out the best players and paid them to play, therefore attracting thousands of spectators. The team was invincible, mainly due to one Agnès Vauthier, a "speedy, scientific, brilliant, and effective" player and a female Newsy Lalonde, which was high praise indeed. They won the Doran Cup in 1916 and 1917, named after its donator, P.J. Doran, who owned and managed the Jubilee arena where they played their games.[54] Their arch rivals were the Cornwall Victorias, who played teams in both Ottawa (the Alerts) and Montreal, usually demolishing the competition because of their star player, Albertine Lapensée, the "queen of all lady hockeyists," who sometimes scored as many as 15 goals in one game.[55]

The men who owned and managed these early women's hockey teams did so because they were part of the money-making efforts by commercial rinks to make a profit. Women's hockey was viewed in the same light as men's hockey, as well as the skating races, carnivals, and masquerades that attracted thousands of patrons to these rinks.[56] The women also played full contact hockey with rules designed for spectacle and entertainment, based on those of the men's new professional league, the National Hockey Association (forerunner of the National Hockey League). In the attempt to find the best players, team owners and manager sometimes allowed boys to disguise themselves as girls, only to be discovered later, not unlike the barnstorming women's baseball teams, who often had a few male players disguised as women.

It is no wonder that women's hockey was avoided sometimes by middle- and upper-class girls and women (except those who played it at university), but it had a wide following among factory workers, department store clerks, secretaries, and the like, especially in small towns, so that many more were encouraged to join existing teams or to form their own. The renewed popularity of the game towards the end of World War I saw teams pop up all across the country; they slowly began to organize themselves into leagues and organizations. In the winter of 1921, the Regent Ladies' Hockey Club of Calgary requested permission from the all-male Canadian Amateur Hockey Association to enter a tournament sponsored by the P. Burns Company, prompting the Association to consider the formation of a "ladies' section." President Sterling replied that he would take up the matter with ladies' clubs in Winnipeg, Ottawa, and elsewhere, but nothing came of it.[57] Women took matters into their own hands, forming district and provincial organizations — the Ladies Ontario Hockey Association appears to be among the first, when 20 senior clubs from all parts of Ontario were represented at an inaugural meeting in December 1922. Men were elected as honorary president and president, but the remaining executive positions were filled by women. Cognizant of the growing importance of commercial teams in their new organization, they voted to make them eligible, contrary to the rules of their male counterpart, the Ontario Hockey Association.[58] Three years later, an all-female executive was voted in, and the men were relegated to "advisors."[59]

Even in small, relatively remote towns like Fernie, nestled in British Columbia's Elk Valley along the Crowsnest railway, women's hockey thrived in the 1920s. Barely able to form two teams when they first played on New Year's Day in 1919, they emerged into a solid team able to give other teams, such as the Calgary Regents, a good contest on several occasions. By 1922 they were transformed into the Fernie Swastikas, newly outfitted in white knickers and red sweaters with a large white swastika sewn on the front. It should be noted that the swastika was one of the oldest, most widely distributed religious symbols in the world, often associated with good fortune, before its appalling use during the Third Reich in Germany. In 1923, the Fernie Swastikas won the Alpine Cup, emblematic of hockey supremacy in

Alberta and British Columbia, by defeating the Calgary Regents and the Vancouver Amazons at an annual tournament scheduled during the Banff Winter Carnival. When their train arrived home, they were greeted by cheering children let out of school for the occasion, a Royal North-West Mounted Police honour guard, and the Fernie Pipe Band, which led them on sleighs to a gala reception at city hall.[60]

By the late 1920s, there were a remarkable number of women's ice hockey teams (over 20) operating in Calgary, sponsored by community clubs, small businesses, churches, and technical and normal schools. The top team was the Calgary Hollies, who regularly battled the Edmonton Monarchs for the Alberta championship. Margaret "Prudie" Pruden was a star player with the Monarchs; she was, perhaps, not a typical player, but was representative of the new breed of women athletes. Born in Tofield in 1908, she was among the youngest of 10 children with three sisters and six brothers, all of whom played baseball and hockey. When her father died, and the family moved to Calgary, Pruden had the opportunity to play organized hockey with the Patricia Ladies Hockey Club, provincial champions in 1924–25. An aggressive player, she sharpened her skills by playing in local pick-up boys' games, not letting on she was female. In 1928, she married and moved to Edmonton, but still kept playing, this time for the Edmonton Monarchs. "Prudie" Harris helped the team win the 1927–28 provincial championship against the Calgary Hollies, when she scored on a solo rush with four minutes left in the game.[61]

Back in Ontario, all-round athlete Fanny "Bobbie" Rosenfeld, a member of the 1922 Toronto YWCA hockey team, was gaining media attention for her superb ice skills, especially the ability to put the puck in the net. By 1923, Rosenfeld was the star centre for the North Toronto AAA, who usually battled it out with the Ottawa Alerts for the Ontario title before thousands of spectators. Games were incredibly rough, players suffered cuts or more serious injury, and the male referees were unfortunately lax, prompting this editorial in the *Toronto Daily Star*:

> If ladies hockey is to be made a success, body checking must be eliminated. That is too rough a method of checking for women to employ. Games must be handled by strict referees and penalties handed out for every move that is not according to the Hoyle of hockey. Tripping, charging, shoving and holding should not be tolerated for a moment. The fans like to see the ladies perform, but they do not want to see any roughness creep into the contests.[62]

Rosenfeld's employer, the Patterson Chocolate factory, like many companies who employed large numbers of women, organized an athletic club to encourage recreation and sport among its employees. Top athletes were promised a job and the opportunity to take time off for competitions. The Patterson Athletic Club sponsored all sorts of teams, and Bobbie Rosenfeld played on them all, their perennial star player, although hockey was her favourite sport. She was not very big, perhaps five-foot-five, but wiry, quick, and above all physically aggressive: "She simply went after everything with full force.... She checked hard and she had a shot like a bullet."[63] With Rosenfeld as captain, the Patterson Pats dominated women's hockey in Ontario through the latter part of the 1920s. If there had been a Dominion championship, most likely they would have won it. In 1929, before 12,000 spectators, the Patterson Pats defeated the Quebec champions, Northern Electric Verdun, at the Montreal Forum during the popular Winter Carnival.

Turning now to softball, *Toronto Telegram* columnist Phyllis Griffiths wrote this ditty and published it in one of her early columns:

> The boys pull off smart double plays,
>> They scintillate and star;
> But where you see the thousands gaze —
>> That's where the girls' teams are.

> The boys play almost perfect ball,
>> To err they can't abide;
> But still the fans give them the wall —
>> And flock to Sunnyside.[64]

Sunnyside Beach, aptly called "Toronto's Lake Shore Playground," was a large recreational complex along Lake Ontario, off Lakeshore Boulevard. Opened in 1922, it housed a pier, children's playground, swimming pool, dining and dance pavilion, and an amusement park. At the far east corner was a rudimentary softball diamond, where the Toronto Ladies Major Soft Ball League began competing in the summer of 1923 with teams from the Toronto Ladies Athletic Club, Humber Bay Ladies Athletic Club, Karry's Recreation Club (a bowling and billiards hall), and the papermaking firm Hinde & Dauch. By 1924, both the Ladies' Major League and the Sunnyside Ladies League were attracting huge crowds of up to 9,000, and on average 5,700, for regularly scheduled games several nights each week. Park benches were set up around the field seating a few hundred patrons, but the rest jostled for a view four or five deep along the edge of the diamond or from the elevation of a nearby bridge and King Street.

The Toronto Harbour Commission, who managed Sunnyside, erected permanent bleachers for the 1925 season to accommodate some 3,000 spectators, and for this they charged a ten-cent admission fee. The Commission realized the enormous benefit of large crowds drawn to Sunnyside early in the evening, who after the game would spend money at the many concessions in the park. By 1925, gate receipts for exhibition and league games totalled $11,800, even more ($17,200) the following year, with revenues shared between the Toronto Harbour Commission and the leagues. This was good business, and a profitable one, prompting a constant stream of requests from teams seeking playing privileges at Sunnyside.[65]

Women's softball in the city exploded; by 1926 all players and leagues came under the jurisdiction of the Women's Softball Association of Toronto, headed by former player and longtime organizer, Mabel Ray. It was mandated in their constitution that "in every case the Executive of this association shall be ladies," although they appointed a three-member, all male advisory board.[66] Affiliated with the organization were 11 leagues and well over 1,000 players, who had the opportunity to play, for example, in the Major or Sunnyside Leagues at Sunnyside Park, the Danforth League at the Viaduct Park, the Beaches League in Kew Gardens, the National League at Exhibition Park, or with an inter-church or senior league. The governing association also mandated that teams sponsored by industrial firms or bearing trademark names, or having more than four signed players employed in any one firm or company, must play in an Industrial League. Presumably this was to head off criticism that some businesses were using players for commercial purposes. As a result, industrial teams playing at Sunnyside either withdrew or changed their names, and at the same time attracted players from outside their companies — Hinde & Dauch, for example, disbanded; K. & S. Tire and Rubber became the "Supremes"; and Karry's Recreation Club the "Patricias."

By the mid-1920s, women's softball in Ontario was "a mighty big thing," and it was important to create a provincial governing body. This occurred in November 1925 when principal organizer, Mabel Ray, invited Dr. Arthur S. Lamb, secretary of the AAU of C, to chair the founding meeting. Over 100 softball enthusiasts from Toronto, Hamilton, Galt, Guelph, Ottawa, St. Catharines, Peterborough, Oshawa, and several smaller places met at Toronto's Central YMCA to form the Ontario Ladies' Softball Association. The first executive was entirely female, including Fanny Rosenfeld as third vice-president and Mabel Ray as secretary, but with an advisory board composed of men. At their first annual meeting a year later, and after much debate, they decided to call themselves "women" rather than "ladies," following the lead taken by the Women's Amateur Athletic Federation. There was also considerable discussion over whether to allow men (other than the advisory board) to attend the general and annual meetings of the newly named Ontario Women's Softball Association. In the end they agreed to permit one man from each league to attend, provided he presented the proper credentials, was accompanied by a woman delegate, and took no part in the meetings.[67]

On the prairies, and particularly in Saskatchewan, softball spread like wildfire. There was already a tradition of women's baseball in the larger centres, but many switched to softball because it was easier to play and was played in less formal settings, familiar to those who had been introduced to the sport in school or on the playground. Initially sports days and picnics added "ladies' softball" to their events, but, like everywhere else, teams, leagues, and tournaments soon developed. In Regina, for example, an inter-departmental house league of employees of the Robert Simpson store on Broad Street started out on a make-shift diamond behind the store in the early 1920s, but by 1929 the Simpson's women's team was playing (and beating) eight other teams in the Regina City Softball League. Teams were sponsored by local businesses and sporting organizations. What to wear was sometimes still a problem: A women's team in Red Deer Hill was called the "Pyjama Girls" because the blue cotton pyjamas they found in Eaton's catalogue were the cheapest, most comfortable uniforms they could find. Travel throughout the province was difficult and costly, so no formal provincial competition developed in the 1920s.[68]

CREATING NEW ATHLETIC HEROINES

Often referred to as the golden age of women's sports, the 1920s were a time when women began experimenting and competing seriously in new sports, at the same time consolidating their hold on others. Nothing seemed to hold them back. There was a growing public enchantment with these new stars of the athletic world, and the sports press obliged not only by reporting their exploits, but, for the most part, treating them seriously. In her historical study of women's sport in the United States, Susan Cahn noted the 1920s produced a "kind of carnivalesque fascination with women's athletic feats as symbols of the changing gender order in American society." "The image of the female athlete," she added, "signalled a total inversion of established gender relations, an indication that female dominance might eventually replace men's traditional authority."[69]

The same was true in Canada, although the Canadian sports media were far kinder and more supportive of women athletes in this era than was true of the male-dominated media in the United States. Henry Roxborough, for example, widely known across Canada as a sportswriter and author who contributed regularly to *Maclean's*, wrote a laudatory article in 1929 entitled "Give the Girls a Hand." He profiled the recent achievements of world class athletes in speed skating, basketball, track and field, swimming, polo, and softball, commenting: "Canadian women are not just knocking at the door of the world of sport, but rather they have crashed the gate, swarmed the field and, in some cases, have driven mere man to the sidelines."[70] Still, it is true that male sportswriters often used expressions like "invaded," "captured," "crashed," and "encroached" when describing women's entrance into certain sports, and their accomplishments were almost always compared to those of male athletes.

On the organizational front, women challenged men to let them control their own sports. The Canadian Ladies Golf Union, for example, was forced to disband in 1915 due to the war, but was revived again in 1919 as a "colonial affiliate" of the Ladies Golf Union of Great Britain. Significantly, it was almost totally dependent on the Royal Canadian Golf Association for financial and organizational assistance. The men's association issued an edict in 1922 that the women must submit their constitutional changes and handicap rulings to them for approval.[71] Looking back, it is unclear whether women simply acquiesced to this paternalistic control, or took a more pragmatic view of their situation. If women wanted to play golf, they had to play in clubs controlled by men and under the rules they established. Many women who played were business or professional women, who worked at jobs during the day, and yet Saturdays and Sundays at the clubs were often reserved for men. As Alexandrine Gibb, an avid golfer and member of Toronto's Cedar Brook Golf Club, bitterly complained:

> There are still a couple of tennis courts that prohibit girls from playing during certain hours.... The same rule applies to a great number of golf courses and the same answer is readily given re the fee with the gratis remark added that "women clutter up the course."... The tragic part of it from the business woman's point of view is that she usually cannot pick up her clubs or her tennis racquet somewhere around one or two o'clock in the afternoon and say: "I'm out on business," and hie to a club — usually a golf club.[72]

During this era only one golf club was founded and run specifically for women — the Toronto Ladies' Golf and Tennis Club in Thornhill, opened in 1924 by Ada MacKenzie, Canada's outstanding female golfer of this era. She took out an option on the land, raised capital through a bond issue, sold $100 memberships to 300 women, and supervised the construction of the clubhouse and course.[73] For the most part, women had no choice but to cooperate not only with the men's association but also with their sister association in Britain. They also knew that if their game were to grow, they would have to slowly take charge of their own affairs, an end they achieved by the late 1920s. By all accounts this autonomy seems to have been won primarily through the efforts of their leader, Ella Murray, president of the Canadian Ladies Golf Union from 1919 to 1927, who "exuded a special charm which she utilized in her dealings with the male executives of the clubs whom she wished to incorporate"[74]

If the men were reluctant to give up control and their words seemed paternalistic, they believed there were good reasons to be cautious. In his 1928 presidential report to the AAU of C, Dr. Lamb reiterated his belief that women's athletics should be governed entirely by women, although he refused to recommend an

independent status for the WAAF of C until he was convinced "that the administration of their affairs will not fall into the hands of unscrupulous promoters or
those whose chief interest might be self-glorification."[75] Henry Roxborough said
much the same thing when he advised:

> ... it might also be suggested girls' sports would become even more effec-
> tive if coaching and managing "manpower" was replaced by the constant
> supervision and leadership of elder women; if executive officers discour-
> aged all attempts to use girls for personal or industrial publicity; and if the
> practice of "sports for stars" was succeeded by the ideal of developing
> wholesome play on a generous scale with the objective of contributing to
> the maintenance of a healthy, happy Canadian womanhood.[76]

Men like Lamb and Roxborough, as well as most women physical educators of
the day, were saying that women could, even should, control their sports, providing traditional gender roles went undisturbed and the gender order of society was
left intact. Many men of this era, as was true for women, had an unshakeable
belief in the Victorian notions of manliness and womanliness, masculinity and
femininity, and the clear distinction between the two. Men were willing to allow
women the right to participate in sport, even to compete at the highest levels for
the good of Canada, providing they conducted themselves with proper feminine
decorum. More importantly, they must not allow the tainted world of professionalism and commercialism to corrupt women's sport as was increasingly the
case, they believed, with men's sport of this era. Women's sport must remain pure,
and women athletes should devote themselves to the love of the game, never stray-
ing into the evil and exploited world of marketing their talents. This was an elitist view, which took no account of the fact that working-class women might wish
(or need) to earn money through their athletic talents.

In 1926, Gertrude Ederle, the 18-year-old American-born daughter of a
German butcher, became the first woman to swim across the 34-kilometre English
Channel, although several others had tried before her. She was only the sixth
person to complete the swim, and her time (14 hours, 34 minutes), temporarily
at least, was the fastest. Ederle's feat aroused pride in women, especially working-
class women, because it showed that they too could aspire to sporting greatness.[77]
It would be another 25 years before a Canadian woman (Winnie Roach Leuszler)
would successfully swim the Channel, and she too became a symbol of pride and
accomplishment among working-class women, especially in her case, mothers
with young children.

Marathon swimming was also one of the first sports in which women could
make money, sometimes big money. The earliest events do not mention money, or

prizes of any sort, which is not to say they did not exist. Then again, these races were much shorter than crossing large bodies of water like the English Channel. One of the earliest involving women was the annual across-the-bay swim of the Toronto Swimming Club, a distance of a mile and a quarter. In 1913, four women from the "old country" (Great Britain) entered the race, all finishing in good condition while some of the men were apparently near exhaustion.[78] On the west coast, an early woman competitor was Audrey Griffin, who began racing in 1915 when still a teenager. She swam (and usually won) every distance from 50 yards to three miles, but her main claim to fame was winning the annual "Through-Victoria Swim" nine times in the 12 races she entered between 1915 and 1929. Although only three miles, it was a gruelling, cold swim from the old causeway float in front of the Empress Hotel up the waterway to the Gorge Bridge. As one of Victoria's biggest sporting events in the 1920s, there were sometimes 10,000 spectators lining the course. Had money been available through a wealthy sponsor to send Griffin to Europe, she could well have won Olympic medals at Antwerp in 1920, Paris in 1924, and Amsterdam in 1928, and she might have attempted the English Channel.[79]

The most lucrative prizes in marathon swimming for both men and women were to be found in Toronto at the Canadian National Exhibition. In early 1927, a 17-year-old schoolboy from that city won the $25,000 Catalina swim off the coast of California, sponsored by chewing-gum magnate William Wrigley. George Young was instantly the toast of his hometown. The time was ripe to bring a similar event to Toronto in order to attract more people to the already popular exhibition along the shore of Lake Ontario. The first CNE/Wrigley marathon swim was held at the end of August in 1927. It was an open event over a 21–mile course (actually a seven-mile triangle completed three times) with $50,000 in prize money ($8,000 for women alone), a huge amount of money in those days. The event attracted nearly 200 swimmers, but very few women, not even the famous Gertrude Ederle. Only three brave souls survived the frigid waters to complete the race, none of them female, although prize money was awarded to the four women who swam the furthest, one being a young Toronto swimmer, Edith Hedin.[80]

The CNE marathon races continued in 1928, this time with a separate 10-mile event for women with a prize offering of $15,000. The more lucrative men's event ($35,000) was held on another day, but it was also open to the top five women finishers, which seemed eminently fair. The rules mandated that swimmers could remove their swim suits once they were in the water; these would be picked up by a following boat. Bathing suits in those days were often made of wool, a real drag in the water, and most swimmers coated themselves with axle grease to protect them from the cold. All modesty aside, women, too, must have done this — photos of competitors at the start and finish of the race show bare chests. The practice must have lasted only a few years, because by the 1930s all reports indicate that the swimmers were "suitably clothed." Canadian women rarely won the CNE marathon swims, although they sometimes placed in the prize money. In 1929, Martha Norelius of New York City, the 1924 and 1928 Olympic gold medalist in the 400-freestyle, took home $10,000 for her first-place finish.

Women were good at marathon swimming and often able to withstand freezing waters better than men. At the 1927 Halifax Harbour marathon, for example, over a five-mile course from Sleepy Cove to the Waegwoltic Club, of the 41 swimmers who started in the chilling 58 (Fahrenheit) degree waters, only 11 finished — all women. Local newspapers ran articles asking whether women were superior or whether men were in danger of developing a strong inferiority complex. One printed a cartoon headed "the weaker sex" showing a male swimmer climbing into a boat — "I'm all in" — with a smugly confident woman swimmer looking back at him as she ploughed ahead. Doris Gilfoy of the St. Mary's Club in Halifax won the race in two hours and sixteen minutes.[81]

In Quebec, an international swimming marathon took place in Montreal, with swimmers travelling east along the St. Lawrence River to Sorel, a long 39 miles. The event was open to both men and women, but prize money was small compared to the CNE swim with only $500 offered to first place, $250 to second, $150 for third, and so on. Fifteen swimmers entered the race in 1928, including several who had swum earlier at the CNE, but only two finished. One was Daisy King Shaw of Shawinigan, coached by Jack Lyons, who also looked after Toronto swimmer George Young. The "brillante nageuse" surprised everyone by doggedly completing the course in 14 hours, almost two hours after the winner.[82]

Other endurance events also attracted women, such as long-distance walking (earlier called pedestrianism). In 1921, for example, Jennie Dill and her husband joined a cross-Canada walking race, completing the distance from Halifax to Vancouver in a record 134 days. Averaging 40 miles a day, and following the Canadian Pacific Railroad, the couple were greeted along the way by admirers and well-wishers. Growing up in Halifax, Dill had a reputation as an "athlete-out-of-doors girl" who skated, hunted, and fished with her husband, although readers of the Halifax Herald who followed the couple's journey, were assured that "Mrs. Dill has not a single suggestion of the mannish in her personality."[83] She was, however, considerably thinner when they arrived in Vancouver. In 1929, 17 young women, mostly French-Canadian, took part in a 10-mile walking race in Montreal for a $500 prize, which was won by Mlle. L. Galipeau. Unfortunately, the race results were annulled due to unknown irregularities, and it is not clear whether she ever collected her prize.[84] The snowshoe marathons popular in Quebec were off limits to women, although they were allowed to race shorter distances.

Speed skating, on the other hand, attracted increasing numbers of women; two skaters who received a great deal of press attention in this era were Gladys

Robinson and Lela Brooks. Robinson learned to skate at a young age, having grown up near the Aura Lee rink in Toronto, and by 14 she was the Canadian women's speed skating champion. Her coach was Fred Robson, who before the war and at the peak of his career had held nine world records. In 1920, when she was 18, Robinson competed in the world speed skating championship at Lake Placid, New York, the first time the International Skating Union allowed women to compete, and, in a field of 18, she came third. It was unusual for a promising woman athlete to have a personal coach in those days, but Robson devised a program of skating, walking, running, skipping, and strength-building exercises for his young athlete, who trimmed a few pounds in the process. Their hard work paid off, and in the following year, again at Lake Placid, Robinson won all her events. Following her victory, she wrote a short article for *Maclean's*, offering this helpful advice to would-be champions:

> I suppose first, of course, that one should have the right type of physique. Height might seem to be an advantage in the way of length of stride, but the records of our fastest skaters contradict this idea. Practically all the world's champions have been small men. Next to having a strong, supple body a girl must have the will to discipline it if she is to make a success of skating as of any other sport. She must be willing to give up anything that will interfere with her highest possible degree of fitness. She would have to give up danc-ing, for instance, while she was in training for a skating race. Perhaps this is not so much because dancing involves a change in the use of muscles, as because it invariably means late hours and a rather enervating influence — anyway it has to be eliminated from the skater's recreations.[85]

Robinson went on to further success, often breaking a world record each time she raced, and retired undefeated when she got married. Tragically, she died in 1934 at age 32 following a lengthy illness.

Described as an "entirely unaffected, supremely modest, completely normal Canadian schoolgirl," who skates like a "lightning demon," 16-year-old Lela Brooks from the Old Orchard Skating Club in Toronto established herself as a world-class speed skater in 1925, when she won the Canadian championships in three distances as well as major competitions in various cities throughout the United States. In 1926, she broke six world records and won the world champi-onships, which were held in Saint John, New Brunswick. She came to the atten-tion of millionaire sports promoter Teddy Oke, who sponsored her early competitive forays into the United States. She married early at 18, but continued to compete under the name Lela Brooks Potter well into the 1930s.[86]

The first Canadian woman to represent Canada at an Olympic Games was Cecil

Eustace Smith, certainly an example of a "pure" athlete untainted by commercialism. In Chamonix, France, at the first official Winter Games in 1924, she competed in the ladies' figure skating competition, the only event for women on the limited program. Cecil, and her older sister Maude, were introduced to skating on the frozen ponds and backyards of a well-to-do neighbourhood close to the Toronto Skating Club, where they could practise in the new indoor arena before and after school. In 1922, Cecil was the junior ladies' champion and the following year was runner-up in the Canadian championship, beaten only by Dorothy Jenkins of the Minto Club in Ottawa. She teamed up with Melville Rogers, the men's champion, and the two were chosen to represent Canada in an official world's skating championship — the 1924 Olympics in France. Only 15, Cecil was accompanied by her mother and sister, along with the rest of the 15-member Canadian Olympic team, comprising her pairs partner Rogers, the lone speed skater Charlie Gorman, and the Granites, a hockey team. Much to her surprise, she was a hit with the British and European press, who singled out the only Canadian female competitor for her beauty and lively personality. On the day of the competition, the temperature dropped considerably, making conditions on the outdoor ice rink troublesome; to top this off, Cecil Smith was not called in time, and she had to rush over to the bitterly cold rink "benumbed and breakfastless," as one headline declared, to perform her compulsory figures.[87] She did better in the free skate, but in the end came sixth, two places ahead of 11-year-old Sonja Henie, the Norwegian sensation who was later to dominate women's skating for the next two decades. Smith and Rogers were seventh in the pairs competition, although everyone expected them to place much higher, bringing about accusations in Canadian news reports that politics influenced the judging. While abroad they gave skating exhibitions in Paris and London, reported enthusiastically by the local press. Back home, they made many appearances at colourful skating carnivals in Toronto, Hamilton, Ottawa, Winnipeg, and Quebec City, often attended by the Governor General and his wife Lady Byng. Smith went on to win the Canadian ladies championship in 1925 and 1926 and, at the Olympics in St. Moritz in 1928, came fifth (Sonja Henie won the gold). A few years later in 1930, she became the first Canadian to win a world skating championship medal, when she came second (again behind Sonja Henie) at Madison Square Garden in New York City.[88]

CONCERNS OF PHYSICAL EDUCATORS

As more girls and women engaged in active sport, with some competing at the highest levels, there was little criticism in the Canadian media, nor was there much public concern over their newfound athleticism. If anything, Canadians

Until the 1880s, women participated in very few sports. Horseback riding was a popular diversion in summer with a few women taking part in fox hunting. Riding habits were among the first sportswear for women, either in mohair or cloth for the well-dressed rider in the 1870s (from the *Canadian Illustrated News*, 28 June 1878, 413).

Golf was one of the first sports women began to play, and by the 1890s competitions were a regular event. The first outstanding woman golfer in Canada was Mabel Thomson from Saint John, New Brunswick, five-time winner of the Canadian Ladies Amateur Championship between 1902 and 1908. She also represented Canada in team matches in the United States and Britain.

Cycling was the first sporting activity for women with mass appeal. It was easily learned, enjoyable, robust, and healthy; yet it did not breach late nineteenth century standards of proper decorum. The top photo is a group of cyclists in Alymer, Quebec on the latest pneumatic tire "safeties" embarking on a summer outing circa 1898, and the bottom is of two cyclists in Nova Scotia circa 1900.

Basketball for girls was introduced to schools and communities in the early 1900s. Likely their first chance to participate in an active sport requiring some physical exertion, it became very popular. Teams and leagues were formed all across the country, such as this one in Dawson, Yukon.

(RIGHT) Very little track and field for girls and women took place before World War I. Annual sports days and company picnics were common, but contests for girls were limited to shorter distances (rarely more than 100 yards) for those under twelve years of age. Young girls in their Sunday best race at the Liberal picnic in Aurora, Ontario on 12 June 1907.

(LEFT) YWCAs were the first women-centred athletic clubs. The Toronto YWCA, one of the first to have a swimming pool, hired accomplished Scottish swimmer and instructor Mary Beaton in 1908, to conduct classes in swimming, water polo, life saving, and fancy diving.

Early in the nineteenth century, ice hockey was a favourite among university women, who sometimes played against community teams. The top photo shows women from the University of Toronto circa 1912, and the bottom shows two teams competing in Banff, Alberta circa 1911. Note the long skirts, male referee, and mostly male spectators.

(LEFT) Swimming was an acceptable sport for women, and they were good at it. One early competitor was Audrey Griffin from Vancouver, who began racing in 1915 when still a teenager. She swam (and usually won) every distance from 50 yards to three miles, but her main claim to fame was winning the annual "Through-Victoria Swim" nine times in the twelve races she entered between 1915 and 1929.

(BELOW) The Toronto Ladies Major Soft Ball League began competing in the summer of 1923 at the Sunnyside ball diamond along Lake Ontario right off Lakeshore Boulevard. The games were so popular that permanent bleachers were erected for the opening game of the 1925 season.

BRITISH COLUMBIA
SPORTS HALL OF FAME AND MUSEUM

The Edmonton Commercial Graduates ("the Grads") were Canada's most successful women's basketball team. In 1922 they won the first Dominion women's basketball championship. The team shown here travelled to France in 1924 to play in a series of exhibition matches, and was awarded the first women's world title.

Lela Brooks, Claire Eagan, Katie McCrae, and Gladys Robinson of the Old Orchard Skating Club in Toronto were Canada's top speedskaters in the early 1920s.

Pedestrianism or walking races had been popular since the 1870s, but more as spectacle than mass sport. During the 1920s, they became very popular attracting women from all backgrounds, sometimes competing for prize money or raising money for a good cause. These women were taking part in a race in Halifax circa 1920.

(BELOW) High jumper Ethel Catherwood, using the "scissors" technique, won the gold medal with a jump of 5' 2½". Here, she trains under the watchful eye of Alexandrine Gibb.

(ABOVE) The 1928 Canadian women's Olympic team before departing for Amsterdam. In the front row from left are: Ethel Smith, Jean Thompson, Myrtle Cook, Dorothy Prior, Jane Bell, and Fanny "Bobbie" Rosenfeld. Peeking through in the back row are chaperone Marie Parkes, manager Alexandrine Gibb, and Ethel Catherwood.

(BELOW) Myrtle Cook (left), one of Canada's greatest athletes in the 1920s, was disqualified in the 100-metre final, but anchored the 400-metre relay team to win the gold medal. She became a longtime sportswriter for the *Montreal Star*.

(ABOVE) The controversial finish of the women's 100-metre final. Rosenfeld (first on the left) was awarded the silver medal although Canadian officials thought she had beaten the American Betty Robinson. Dr. Arthur Lamb, *chef de mission* of the Canadian team, refused to support a protest, claiming it was unsportsmanlike.

In the 1930s, concerns were raised over "mannish women athletes" who might be males masquerading as females. Pictured here (from left) are the Polish-American Stanislawa Walasiewicz (Stella Walsh), Canada's Hilda Strike, and Wilhelmina Von Bremen of the United States, the medal winners in the 100-metre race. Although Walsh lived her entire life as a woman, upon her death in 1980, it was discovered that she had both male and female sex organs. As a result, some lobbied to award the gold medal to Strike.

CANADA'S SPORTS HALL OF FAME

The 1932 Canadian women's Olympic team in Los Angeles was called "the prettiest and most wholesome looking group of girls." Surrounding Hollywood actress Norma Shearer are (from left): Alda Wilson, Eva Dawes, Aileen Meagher, Mary Frizzell, Lillian Palmer, Betty Taylor, Mary Vandervliet, Mildred Fizzell, Myrtle Cook, and Hilda Strike.

COURTESY OF EVA DAWES SPINKS

CITY OF TORONTO ARCHIVES / SC 244, ITEM 1387 AND SC 266-14583

Marathon swimming was one of the first sports where women could make money. In 1928, the CNE introduced a 10-mile event for women with a prize offering of $15,000. Bathing suits in those days were often made of wool, very heavy when wet, so grease-coated swimmers removed their swim suits once they were in the water.

(ABOVE) Softball has always been popular among aboriginal women. A highly successful team in the 1930s was the "Caledonia Indians," who came mostly from the Six Nations Reserve along the Grand River in Ontario. The team had both white and aboriginal women, and in 1931 they were the Provincial Women's Softball Union semi-finalists.

(ABOVE) This women's basketball team, comprised entirely of women of colour except for a white coach, is unfortunately unidentified except we know they are from Nova Scotia circa 1930.

(LEFT) Vancouver sprinter Barbara Howard, the first woman of colour to compete on an international team for Canada, was a member of the 1938 British Empire Team competing in Sydney, Australia. She is seen here with high jumper Margaret Bell, also of Vancouver.

were enormously proud of these new athletic heroines, like the unbeatable Edmonton Grads, the amazing Matchless Six, and other remarkable individuals. Anxious disapproval emerged much more strongly in the 1930s, but in the period following World War I and throughout the 1920s, women's sport in Canada was a boldly exciting and new adventure, certainly for the young women who travelled across the country, below the American border, and sometimes across the ocean to compete nationally and internationally.

Early signs of criticism and disapproval were sometimes imported from elsewhere, like the brief article in *Saturday Night* magazine headed "Should Feminine Athletes Be Restrained," which reported on the growing controversy in Britain over the "girl athlete" and whether her strenuous participation in games, originally intended to be played by boys alone (for example cricket and football) was endangering her health and, by implication, the health of the nation. The article went on to quote several prominent British medical doctors, all female, some of whom were adamantly opposed to female athleticism, while others were more cautiously approving. On the negative side was Arabella Kenealy, a physician and writer with strong eugenicist ideas, who had railed against strenuous exercise for women in her articles and books since before the turn of the century.[89] In her most recent book, *Feminism and Sex-Extinction*, as well as the *Saturday Night* article, she argued that, for the good of society, women must give up all things masculine, or else they will produce weak sons:

> Women who, owing to faulty heredity or abnormal training, develop masculine instead of feminine attributes, do this at the cost of the masculine potential, which is transmitted from father to daughter, in trust as it were, from the masculine line. The result is that athletic women, or women otherwise masculine in type produce feminine offspring mainly, and seldom sons. When sons are born to them they are liable to be puny and delicate, and generally are of an inferior type.[90]

Also quoted were other women physicians with more enlightened views, and the article ended on a positive note: "In the meantime the girls are too busy with their training to answer the question themselves, but doubtless would resent bitterly having their right to play games taken away from them." Margaret Currie, a columnist writing in the *Montreal Star*, wondered why there should be any difference of opinion on the subject: "Had I a daughter, she should be taught to swim and dive, to skate and ski and dance, to play basket-ball, tennis and golf, for all games, and especially competitive games, are a process of education, morally, mentally and physically.... Don't let old-fashioned ideas keep you from allowing your daughters all the advantages that physical training and athletics can give them."[91]

Among French-Canadians in Quebec, the social upheaval brought on by the war, coupled with increasing industrialization and urbanization, provoked a new discourse on women. Although demonstrating a fresh concern for improving the health and fitness of girls and women, the underlying theme was still the importance of safe-guarding their "race" through ensuring that women, as "instruments of natural selec-tion," transmitted only the best qualities to their children. In January 1919, the *Association athlétique amateur nationale de Montréal* opened their new club, La Palestre Nationale, designed as a multi-sport centre and meeting-place for fran-cophones in Montreal. A remarkable recruitment campaign preceded its inaugura-tion, much of which took place on the pages of leading newspapers, such as *Le Devoir* and *La Presse*. Editorials in both papers stressed the importance of attracting women and girls to La Palestre Nationale because of their reproductive roles as mothers, now and in the future. As one article in the campaign stated: "... lui permettre de devenir une épouse robuste et une mère fécunde, est mieux" (permit [young girls] to become robust spouses and fertile mothers).[92] Women do not need the same vigorous sports and endurance exercises as do men, the campaign stressed, but light gymnastics, calis-thenics, and swimming for health and beauty were highly acceptable. By the early 1920s, the club was attracting hundreds of girls and young women through a special section directed by female instructors.[93]

The voices of concern in Canada came mostly from physical educators. One of the strongest opponents was the Australian-born Arthur Lamb, who had very firm, indeed dogmatic, opinions about women's participation in sport. He had studied at Springfield College of Physical Education in the United States, where he was influenced by American physical educators like Jesse Williams at Columbia University, who claimed to have biological "evidence" that women were unfit for athletics: "The width of the pelvis interferes with the running ability of the girl; in all movements of the lower extremities, either in walking or running, there is a lateral sway of the pelvis, and the extent of this oscillation determines the speed of the individual in getting over the ground. Because of this one factor of body construction the girl is unable to run as fast or as far as the boy."[94]

Lamb came to McGill University to study medicine, and, although still a student, he was appointed physical director on the basis of his training at Springfield. He obtained his medical degree in 1917, served overseas with the Canadian Army Medical Corps during the war, and was re-appointed as physi-cal director at McGill upon his return in 1919. Soon after, he was made director of physical education in a newly organized department, which controlled the men's and women's required physical education programs, intramurals, athletics, and the university's health service.

On the subject of physical education for girls, Lamb consistently voiced his opin-ion that "highly undesirable forms of competition are doing a great deal of harm, not only to the girls themselves, but to the promotion of safe and sane participation for our women of tomorrow."[95] In an address to the Ontario Educational Association, he drew attention to women's international track and field events (remember he had voted against their participation in the Olympics). As another example, Lamb also mentioned the recent tour of a British woman's football (soccer) team through parts of the United States. This same team had wanted to play teams in Canada, but the Dominion Football Association went on record "as opposed to lady soccer teams and will not permit any clubs to play against the ladies' team which proposes to tour Canada."[96] Although a strong advocate of physical education for all, rather than highly specialized programs for the talented few, male or female, Lamb prescribed special restrictions for women — no over-specialization, excessive competition, or exploitation. "All of the benefits to be secured can be had without these risks through careful supervision and selection of activities. There is no good reason why girls should not play games as much as boys, but there are many reasons why there should be very careful legislation concerning the extent of participation, safeguards against exploitation and special regulations adopted for the rules of play, which in most cases must differ from the rules of play for boys."[97]

By the 1920s there were still very few women physical educators in Canada, with the key people at universities in Ontario and Quebec. The most influential was Ethel Mary Cartwright, the physical director of Royal Victoria College at McGill University. Although she had helped found the McGill School of Physical Education and nurtured it carefully from a single summer course to a two-year diploma program that trained hundreds of students, it, too, was merged with the new Department of Physical Education headed by Arthur Lamb, and she was now completely under the authority of a man many years her junior with considerably less professional experience. Lamb did nothing to alleviate her concerns; he even chaired the committee responsible for women's physical education, denying Cartwright any recognition or position of influence. One of his stated reasons for keeping her off the executive committee of the new department was that male undergraduates would lose confidence in the committee through having "a woman with a voice concerning athletic suspensions, reinstatements, sanctions to compete, etc."[98] Cartwright fought back, and finally the intolerable situation was arbitrated by McGill's president, who sided with Lamb. Always the professional, she learned to work with Lamb, even came to admire him, but by 1927, overworked and in poor health, she resigned her position and went off to a small cottage in Magog to raise chickens. Soon after she was contacted by the president of the University of Saskatchewan, who wanted to establish a school of physical education. Since Cartwright had taught his two daughters at Halifax Ladies College, and he was aware of her accomplishments at McGill, he convinced her to resume her career. Nearing 50, she went to Saskatoon in 1929 to establish a university program identical in most respects to the one she had developed at McGill; she remained there until her retirement in 1943.

Ethel Cartwright's views on athletics and physical education for girls were typical of most women physical educators of this era, and in many ways they were similar to Lamb's. The crux of her philosophy was that girls' sports and athletics "does not strive to make them men's physical equal, but it aims at perfecting their womanhood." Good health and character, not heavy muscular development or athletic records, should be the goal of all physical activities and sports. She favoured dancing, especially folk and interpretive, basketball (played according to girls' rules), tennis, softball, field hockey, ice hockey, and lacrosse (girls' rules again), as long as they were carefully supervised and properly coached. Skating, snowshoeing, and skiing (without jumping) should be encouraged in winter, and swimming, diving, paddling, rowing, horse-back riding, and climbing in summer. She was much less enthusiastic about track and field events, fearing that most of the events were unsuitable for the "average" girl. She believed strongly that girls' sports should be organized, coached, and officiated only by women: "They are in intimate touch with the girls' health and have a wonderful opportunity to teach hygiene and healthful habits; this will be of value to the girl all her life."[99] This aspect of her philosophy became a problem when she moved to Saskatchewan, because at that time there were few women coaches and a strong tradition of men doing the organizing and officiating.

The period from the end of World War I throughout the 1920s brought significant change to Canadian women's sport: the growth of teams and leagues, especially those sponsored by industrial concerns; the beginning of international competition primarily in track and field; and the increasing control by women over the administrative affairs of their sports. Not everyone was wholeheartedly in favour of these developments. Physical educators of both sexes, and to a lesser extent the male-dominated media, issued warnings about exploitation, commercialization, and physical harm, although, as we will see in the next chapter, this was just a taste of what was to come.

CHAPTER 3

Girls Shouldn't Do It!: Debates over Competition and Sexuality

Now when the athletic girl is the rule rather than the exception she is, as you know, no longer mannish. She may be a crack golfer and yet look after her complexion. The niftiest little girl in your office may be a swift softball player. The most feminine girl you know may be a demon at basketball.

Frederick Griffin, *Toronto Star Weekly*, October 1931

There are sports, I hold, for which women are physically and temperamentally unfit, and among these I would place all those which exact too much exertion to perform expeditiously and skilfully, as well as those which bring the inevitable concomitants of fatigue and exhaustion in their wake.

Andy Lytle, *Chatelaine*, May 1933

Canadian women physical educators who travelled and studied in the United States in the 1920s and 1930s were well aware of the influential Women's Division of the National Amateur Athletic Federation and its philosophy towards women's athletics. Created in 1923, it was a large umbrella organization of state and city departments of physical education, recreation associations, colleges and universities, public and private schools, and organizations like the Girl Scouts, Camp Fire Girls, and YWCAs.[1] Although headed by Lou Hoover, leader of the Girl Scouts and wife of President Herbert Hoover, leadership came from the ranks of increasing numbers of professionally-trained, women physical educators in American colleges and universities. Greatly concerned by the rapid development of industrial and community sport now outside their control and by the takeover of women's track and field in the United States by the male Amateur Athletic Association, they decided to fight back and regain control of women's sport on decidedly different terms.

The Women's Division's platform was clear and simple. They promoted "play for play's sake," stressing the enjoyment of sport and the development of good sportsmanship and character, rather than the breaking of records and the winning of championships. They worked instead for the "promotion of physical activity for the largest portion of persons in any given group, in form suitable to individual needs and capacities, under leadership and environmental conditions that foster health, physical efficiency, and the development of good citizenship."[2] Although athletic competition for girls and women was thoroughly desirable and beneficial, totally unacceptable were intense and highly specialized contests such as interschool and intercollegiate sport and certainly the Olympics. Their philosophy was encapsulated in the creed, "a team for every girl and every girl on the team," best accomplished through a broadly-based intramural sports program, which exposed students to a variety of athletic experiences. Also popular were "play days," where girls from different institutions — whether elementary or high schools; colleges or universities; industrial, civic, or church groups — met for a day of games and athletics. Teams were mixed and formed from among those participating so that everyone, no matter how skilled or unskilled, was able to compete. Play days, they argued, would effectively eliminate spectators, publicity, gate receipts, and individual stars — indeed, all forms of commercialization and exploitation. To remove all traces of the "evils" of men's sport, they advocated a separatist philosophy whereby only women administered, coached, officiated, and controlled girls' and women's sports.

CANADIAN DEBATES OVER COMPETITION

The major proponents of this philosophy in Canada were several influential women physical educators, mainly in Toronto and Montreal, and several of whom were either from the United States or had studied there. Jessie Herriott, an American who had received her training at Columbia University in New York, was Ethel Cartwright's successor as Physical Director for Women at Montreal's McGill University. She worked directly with Arthur Lamb in the School of Physical Education at McGill. Helen Bryans had studied at the University of Toronto in the early 1920s, where she was a noted swimmer. Following graduation, she taught high school physical education in Ottawa, but also took summer courses at Columbia University before being appointed in 1929 as Director of Physical

Education at the Ontario College of Education in Toronto. By then, OCE offered a specialist certificate in physical education, which could be obtained during the winter or summer session. Enormously powerful and influential, Bryans literally placed the specialist physical education teachers throughout high schools, especially in Ontario. Not many were in a position to disagree with the one person who determined whether or not they got a teaching job.[3] Neither Bryans or Herriott wrote scholarly papers, nor gave many recorded speeches, so that it is difficult to know exactly what they thought except through their actions or by hearsay. In the case of Helen Bryans, I can confirm she was still a firm believer in the Women's Division philosophy 36 years after she arrived at OCE, because I was a member of her 1964–65 class completing the one-year specialist teacher training course following my degree in physical education from Queen's University.[4]

Florence Somers, on the other hand, did put her philosophy in writing in her influential book, *Principles of Women's Athletics,* published in 1930. Also an American, Somers was educated at Boston College, New York University, and the Sargent School of Physical Education in Boston. An experienced teacher, she was Associate Director of the Sargent School at the time she wrote her book, but in 1932 was recruited to teach at the Margaret Eaton School in Toronto and two years later succeeded Mary Hamilton as Director. The purpose of Somers' book was to lay out the principles under which girls' and women's sport should operate in educational, industrial, and recreational organizations. Although the platform put forth by the Women's Division, she argued, was the "nearest approach" to a set of principles yet available, her particular focus was to locate the "scientific" evidence from biology, physiology, sociology, and psychology that best supported these principles. Fundamental were the innate biological and physiological differences between the sexes, a doctrine with a long history. Women's anatomical structure was meant for childbearing, and her hormonal and reproductive system (specifically menstruation) interfered with athletic participation. Women's mental traits and behavioural patterns, supposedly very different to men's, were a hindrance to her success in sport: "It is an open question whether girls can ever acquire such traits as loyalty and cooperation and emotional control in the stress of close competition." Somers wholeheartedly agreed with Women's Division leaders who argued that since men fail to appreciate the limitations of girls' anatomical, physiological, mental, and emotional nature, it was essential that women, and only women, be put in charge of girls' physical activity and sport. Men had absolutely no place in the conduct of female athleticism; it was unnatural: "If women were to desire to conduct athletics for young men who have reached the age of adolescence, they would be ridiculed. If men were to attempt to organize and conduct any other social venture for girls and women, they would be ignored."[5]

The "scientific" evidence cited by Somers to support her views, even when inconclusive, was selective and representative of the highly categorical, biologically determinist thinking prevalent in this era.[6] *All* girls and women were the same (and totally different to boys and men), allowing for no individual differences, or for the fact that categories such as sex (and sex differences) overlap. Coupled with the assertion that current practices in boys' and men's sport were anything but ideal, Somers argued for girls' and women's sport adapted to their special needs and interests:

> Whether women's nature is the result of inheritance or social pressure does not alter the indisputable fact that from an early age of girlhood and throughout the span of life, her reactions to situations and many of her activities are different from those of the male. It may be possible that, in the future through the means of education and because such a condition is earnestly desired by society, man and woman will to all outward appearances be alike in their behaviour and choice of activities. People will differ on the desirability of such an outcome. Another point to be considered refers to the fact that some persons would have girls enter into athletics in the same manner as boys. These people cannot have in mind at the time of expressing this opinion that there exists more than an assumption that *boys'* athletics are not conducted in an ideal manner.[7]

The best athletic program for girls, according to Somers, was educational rather than competitive; activities should involve skill and neuromuscular control rather than strength, speed, or endurance; after puberty, girls should play only with girls especially in the more vigorous, competitive games, and all aspects of competition should be carefully controlled and monitored. "Standards measure success in athletics," she later wrote, "not in terms of scores, not in terms of pleased audience, not by winning teams or broken athletic records or championship victories, but in terms of the *welfare of the girl* who is taking part in them."[8]

It was in this context that women physical educators in Toronto, and a few other areas in Ontario, withdrew their schools from inter-school competition in the early 1930s.[9] The policy was divisive, since the majority of schools continued to compete, and some even added new sports. Of the 200 or more schools with sports facilities in Ontario, approximately 25 ceased organized inter-school competition.[10] Marian Penney was a student at the Ontario College of Education in 1930–31, and as a result was influenced by her professor Helen Bryans. Sixty-eight years later, and still with enormous pride, Penney recounted how at Oakland Collegiate in Toronto, where she taught from 1935 to 1946, she eliminated all inter-school teams and instead had 40 basketball teams and 40 volleyball teams with every one of the 500 girls in the school playing on a team. On designated "play days," the Grade Nine students played against each other, as did the Grade Ten students, and so on. Her personal philosophy — "make the unskilled skilled" — led to the belief that the athletically skilled had ample opportunity outside the school system to compete, whereas the sole purpose of school physical education and athletic programs was to instill a love of physical activity, hopefully for a lifetime, in those less athletically gifted.[11]

Of course not everyone agreed, and certainly not those outside the educational system who were trying to extend the opportunities for ordinary working girls to play and compete. Bobbie Rosenfeld, who at the time was embarking on a new career as a sportswriter, complained bitterly about the cancellation in 1931 of the girls' high school basketball league in Toronto. Not only did it strike a "distressing note" for girls' high school basketball, she protested, but it also affected intermediate and senior teams, because clubs like Lakesides, Toronto Ladies, and Parkdales relied on graduates from the high schools. She went further:

> Athletic competition teaches you the true meaning of the word "sportsmanship" and is a prime factor in giving healthy bodies and clean minds. It makes you feel that you are a strong and living creature. How much easier is one's task accomplished if our minds and bodies are in good condition and where better else to learn clean living and clean thinking than at school, and how better else then the expending of physical energy and athletic competition. It is hoped that the body responsible for the cancellation of inter-collegiate competition in basketball for girls see the error of their ways and that the girl basketeers will again have the pleasure of visiting other schools to engage them in friendly competition.[12]

At a National Recreation Association congress in Toronto in October 1931, several prominent members of the Women's Division in the United States discussed current "trends in girls' athletics" during a meeting chaired by Jessie Herriott of McGill University. Particularly outspoken was Anne Hodgkins, who until recently had been head of the Eaton's Girls Club in Toronto, but was now Field Secretary for the Women's Division. She railed against girls playing men's rules in basketball and the prevalence of male coaches, claiming that they caused over-fatigue and hysteria. Former Olympic athlete, and now sportswriter, Myrtle Cook, responded indignantly in her *Montreal Star* column:

> Why are Physical Education authorities for ever dragging up interclub contests as examples of why girls should not indulge in competitive sports? One instance of distress on the part of players is broadcast while hundreds of other keen contests which are played day after day and year after year are completed without any such occurrences and are not mentioned.

She wanted the schools to foster competitive athletics under proper direction so that "when the girls stepped out into the business world, they would not be apt to allow themselves to be exploited, such as is charged by other speakers at this congress. It is their inexperience that leads to exploitation of their individual prowess."[13] It would be some time, Cook pointed out, before there were sufficient numbers of trained women coaches to take over the thousands of girls interested in sport.

Alexandrine Gibb also attended the congress, and wrote about it in her newspaper column. Since those in the audience were predominantly physical education specialists, including students from the Margaret Eaton School or McGill, and highly unlikely to disagree with their professors, Gibb was in the minority when she spoke out against the standard Women's Division positions concerning girls' rules basketball, male coaches, or gate receipts. Not so in her column, where she attacked their views:

> It's all very well for colleges, schools, and industrial centres to talk about not taking a gate, but where would girls' clubs in Toronto be if there wasn't a gate taken to look after expenses? Who would buy the uniforms and pay the expenses of securing an amateur card and the resultant doctor's fee for physical examination? Who would pay the woman coach?
>
> And women coaches — the technically trained ones — must be paid. That is the position they have trained for and that is their life work. They are entitled to remuneration for their services. And their fees are high. And, unquestionably that is one good reason why men coaches are preferred in Toronto and other Canadian centres. The men give their services free. It is just a side line for them and they enjoy the work.[14]

Gibb's position, and that of most women's sport leaders affiliated with the WAAF of C, was that commercial or industrial sport was the only opportunity for the thousands of young women who worked in the factories, shops, and downtown businesses to play sport at all. "The girls lure the commercial firms into supporting them, so they can play ball under proper circumstances, be properly clad with clothing and have bats and balls and fun."[15] She saw this as the complete reversal of the situation in the United States, where young women athletes were sometimes enticed by industrial concerns solely for the publicity and benefits firms derived from sponsoring high-profile teams. These same working girls, members of the many softball, basketball, hockey, and track and field clubs, were the backbone of the WAAF of C, which is why Gibb lobbied constantly on their behalf for facilities, playing times, and even jobs from the same commercial firms who sponsored the teams. She also worked to ensure that top level athletes, who again were primarily young working women, were able to train and compete even though they held down full-time jobs. For those who could afford to belong to tennis and golf clubs (like Gibb herself), she frequently made a plea from the "business woman's point of view" for the same playing opportunities given men. She had no patience with the egalitarian philosophy of the American Women's Division, branding their leaders narrow and elitist:

> This association comes mostly from the aristocracy of sport ... it is made up chiefly of private school and college teachers and rigid institutions. This association believes it is perfectly all right for a girl in the colleges to take part in the sports the teachers select. The "free lancers" of sport don't fit in here. Their weakness is that they forget the masses outside their juris-diction ... the girls who never see a college except from the sidewalks. Softball is taking care of them and the commercial backers are doing a world of good in Canada.[16]

Whether they knew it or not, these women sportswriters were hitting at the heart of differences between the middle-class, university-educated, professional physical educators and the promoters of popular sports (many of whom were men) for the thousands of young Canadian working women now enjoying increasing oppor-tunities to play, recreate, and compete. These were differences not only of gender, but more importantly of social class. As historian Susan Cahn has observed for the situation in the United States: "The moderate, wholesome athlete idealized by physical educators fused appropriate female athleticism with a middle-class concept of womanhood characterized by refinement, dignity, and self-control."[17]

STRUGGLING FOR SUCCESS IN INTERNATIONAL COMPETITION

In 1929, the persistent NAAF Women's Division petitioned the International Olympic Committee to drop women's track and field from the next games sched-uled for Los Angeles in 1932. This was consistent with their earlier "Olympic Protest," whereby they objected to the participation of females in the Olympic Games because it entailed the specialized training of a few, introduced opportunities for exploita-tion, and made possible the potential for "overstrain" before and during Olympic competition. "One victory in 1932 won by a handful of American women," wrote a college physical education director, "seems too dearly bought if it involves even the partial sacrifice of the playtime of a million American girls."[18] Their appeal coincided with growing concerns of the new IOC president, Count Henri de Baillet-Latour, that the games were becoming too big; one way to trim them would be to eliminate all women's events.[19] Since the five women's track and field events included in 1928 at Amsterdam had been an experiment, they were particularly vulnerable, and in 1929 the IOC voted to withdraw them from its program of events.

Certainly not everyone in the United States agreed with the Women's Division. At the International Amateur Athletic Federation (IAAF) annual meeting in May 1930, Gustavus Kirby, president of the AAU and the United States representative to the IAAF, persuaded his colleagues to adopt the following resolution: "Unless the women are allowed to compete, the world's male and female athletes as represented in the IAAF will adopt a policy of non-cooperation in regard to the Olympics."[20] The IAAF also agreed, unfortunately, that if the IOC decided to eliminate all women's events including fencing, swimming, and platform diving, they too would go along with the decision "with regret." Elmer Ferguson, sports editor of the *Montreal Daily Herald*, and not particularly sympathetic to "strenuous" international competition for women, argued in his daily column that women should not be barred from the Olympics because their "athletic development is in full swing," but more importantly, there would be a huge outcry if they were "rudely ousted after a brief tenancy."[21] At the subsequent IOC Congress in 1931, President Baillet-Latour tried to have women's track and field eliminated, although gymnastics, swimming, tennis, and skating would stay, but he was soundly defeated. Unlike the aftermath of the 1928 Olympics, when Canadian representative Arthur Lamb voted against women's participation in further Olympics, Canada's delegate P.J. Mulqueen, much more supportive, "fought valiantly" to insure the retention of the women's events.[22]

Canadian women athletes continued to prepare for the Los Angeles games, confident they could repeat their spectacular success on the track at Amsterdam in 1928 and, as well, improve their standings in swimming and diving. At the first British Empire Games, held in Hamilton, Ontario, in August 1930, and competing for the first time against swimmers from other countries, young Canadian swimmers from the Dolphinets Club in Toronto, like 16-year-old Irene Pirie and 13-year-old Marjorie Linton, managed to place in all their races. In highboard diving, Pearl Stoneham won gold, the first Canadian woman to do so, although only Canadians competed in the event.[23]

There were no track and field events for women at these first Empire Games, because Britain preferred to send athletes to the Women's World Games in Prague, Czechoslovakia, in September; as a result other nations withdrew and the events were cancelled. Since the WAAF of C supported the movement for women to compete in the Olympics, rather than the Women's World Games run by the Fédération sportive féminine internationale, the Canadian women's track and field championships were held at the same time in Hamilton. Acclaimed as the "biggest day in the history of women's athletics in Canada," athletes arrived from nearly every province to compete. Particularly impressive were the five Vancouver athletes, including lithe, red-headed Lillian Palmer, who performed very well, prompting Alexandrine Gibb to comment that British Columbia "has steadily gone ahead with the development of girl athletes." Ethel Catherwood, competing for the first time since the 1928 Olympics, won the high jump and javelin throws (in those days, athletes threw once with the right hand and once with the left, and the two distances were added together). Count Baillet-Latour of the IOC was at the Empire Games but refused to attend the women's athletic meet. "I do not care what you people think," stated Baillet-Latour, "I do not think that women should be allowed to do boxing, wrestling, or track and field."[24]

The Edmonton Grads, now the acknowledged world basketball champions, declined an invitation to compete at the Third Women's World Games in Prague. They were saving their money for the 1932 Olympic Games in Los Angeles, where they had been invited to give a basketball demonstration. The Senior A women's team at the University of British Columbia was chosen to go in their place. They raised the necessary funds through bake sales, teas, and bridge parties, augmented by donations from the university and the good citizens of Vancouver. Nine team members, accompanied by a chaperone and their coach, left Vancouver in August to travel by CPR across Canada, ship to Hamburg, and train to Prague. They were shocked to discover that, instead of a tournament, they would play only one game before 10,000 spectators on an over-sized, outdoor cinder court, refereed by an Italian who spoke little English and barely knew the rules. Mary Campbell, a member of the team, remembers: "They crossed out all the rules in the basketball rule book they didn't like, and put in things they did like." With no substitutions (unless someone was too hurt to continue) and no time taken between the quarters or half, several players did not play, but they were useful on the sidelines, quickly attending cinder-scraped knees. The UBC women beat France, the European champions, 18–14.[25]

Jean Wilson of Toronto was the outstanding performer in women's speed skating, a demonstration sport at the 1932 Winter Olympics in Lake Placid, New York, winning a gold, silver, and narrowly missing another first because she fell before the finish line. (Tragically, Jean Wilson fell ill not long after returning from Lake Placid and died at age 23 of a degenerative muscle disease.) Still exceptional was the reigning queen of speed skating Lela Brooks Potter, who in her 1000 and 1500-metre heats broke the world records. In the medal events, Canada's figure skaters, led by Constance Wilson Samuel, did not place.

The 1932 women's Summer Olympic team was the largest yet sent into international competition with nine track athletes, nine swimmers and divers, and one lone fencer, a major accomplishment in the midst of the Depression. Even with financial help from the federal government, the Canadian Olympic Committee could not fund all its athletes; therefore, it was up to the WAAF of C, headed by

Alexandrine Gibb, to raise sufficient funds to get the women's team to California.[26] None of the original "Matchless Six," who performed so brilliantly in 1928, competed: Ethel Smith (Stewart) married, had a baby, and was no longer competing; Bobbie Rosenfeld's international career was cut short by arthritis; Myrtle Cook (McGowan) married and became a sports reporter; Jean Thompson withdrew from international competition on the advice of her coach; Jane Bell graduated from the Margaret Eaton School and was teaching; and Ethel Catherwood suffered an injury when she placed third in the high jump at the 1931 Canadian championships, never to compete again.[27]

Canada came away with a silver medal in the women's 100-metre, when "tiny" Hilda Strike, coached by Myrtle Cook McGowan in Montreal, was edged out at the tape by Stanislawa Walasiewicz (Stella Walsh) of Poland. Strike also anchored the women's 4x100-metre relay team (with Mildred Fizzell, Lillian Palmer, and Mary Frizzell), only to be beaten again at the tape by the United States, who won the gold.[28] Eva Dawes, Canada's outstanding high jumper, won the bronze medal behind Americans Jean Shiley and the yet-to-be-famous Mildred "Babe" Didrikson, disqualified from the gold for "diving" over the bar. Canada's only hope in the 80-metre hurdles, Alda Wilson, managed a sixth in a race won by the talented Didrikson. There were no entries for Canada in the women's javelin and discus events. On the swimming front, most Canadian athletes failed to survive their heats, leading team manager Gibb to observe that "there will have to be considerable improvement before our girls will be able to keep place with the world leaders in swimming."[29] The springboard diving competition was delayed when the judges sent two American entries out to change their "improper" and "over-exposed" swim suits, but they won anyway, beating Canada's Doris Ogilvie, who came fifth. In a post-mortem following the games, Henry Roxborough pointed out that, although the Canadian women had not matched the success of the 1928 team on the track, they had broken three former Olympic records in four events, but he also berated the federal government for their lack of interest in the Olympics and its failure to supply adequate funds despite the Depression.[30]

The second British Empire Games took place in London, England, in August 1934. Originally awarded to Johannesburg, South Africa, they were moved due to concerns about the treatment of Black and Asian athletes. The performance of Canada's women track athletes was disappointing, given that only Canada, England, Rhodesia, Scotland, and South Africa competed. Eva Dawes won silver in the high jump, and the relay team (Audrey Dearnley, Betty White, Aileen Meagher, and Lillian Palmer) took gold in the 660-yard relay, where two runners each completed 220 yards and the other two completed 110 yards. Again, it was Hilda Strike's fate to be runner-up when she came second in both the 100-yard sprint and, with her partners Dearnley and Meagher, in the 440-yard relay (one leg of 220 yards, and two of 110 yards). Myrtle Cook put the blame on inexperience, suggesting that track and field officials send their promising material outside the country for competition months before they are asked to step into the international field.[31]

The Empire Games in London also produced Canada's first outstanding female swimmer in international competition. She was 19-year-old Phyllis Dewar from Moose Jaw, Saskatchewan, who broke three records and returned home with four gold medals, winning the 100 and 400-yard freestyle on her own and the 4x100-yard freestyle and 300-yard medley as a member of the relay team, which also included Florence Humble, Margaret Hutton, Irene Pirie and Phyllis Haslam. Myrtle Cook called Dewar "a queen of swimmers, the greatest naiad that Canada has ever produced," who was gloriously fêted upon returning home.[32] Divers Judith Moss and Doris Ogilvie took the gold and bronze in three-metre diving. Also diving was the youngest competitor at the games, 14-year-old Lynda Adams of Vancouver.

In London, Canadian track athletes competed for the first time in the Women's World Games, following the British Empire Games. These were the fourth (and last) such games organized by the Fédération sportive féminine internationale, and, although they attracted 300 athletes from 19 nations, there was little interest or public support. Canada produced no winners in this competition, and it was now clear that Canadian athletes were falling behind their European counterparts. Again, Alex Gibb was right on the mark:

> When you see the state-conducted training of European countries for their boys and girls, you know that we are way behind the band leading in athletics. How can we expect our girls to compete against girls trained the way we find the teams of Germany, Holland, France, Russia, Italy and Japan. These athletes get extensive training with expert care. That is why the Germans are making their world marks.
>
> And yet we will send a team of girls to Berlin [site of the next Olympics] only half prepared to meet such up-to-the-moment competition. The folks at home in Canada will wonder why the Canadian girls can't come up to the mark the way the other countries can.[33]

The German-organized 1936 Winter Olympics in Garmish-Partenkirchen were a good example of how little support Canadian athletes received in this era, especially in international competition, due not only to economic restraints brought on by the Depression, but also to government apathy. According to Elizabeth Pitt Barron, who chaperoned pairs skaters Louise Bertram and Stewart Raeborn, they had no uniforms, so they bought their own white jackets on which they sewed maple leafs.[34] For the first time in the Winter Olympics, women skiers competed in a combined downhill-slalom event. Canada's entries (Marjory Miller, Edwina

Chanier, Diana Gordon Lennox, and Lois Butler) were all living in England or Europe at the time, and, after a brief training session in Grindelwald, Switzerland, before the Olympics, they went off to Germany at their own expense. Diana Gordon Lennox distinguished herself by wearing a monocle when she raced, so much so that her photo appeared in *Die Olympischen Spiele 1936*, the official German book commemorating these Olympics. No medals were won by any of the Canadian figure-skaters or skiers.

Despite uneasiness over Hitler's rise to power in Nazi Germany and increasing evidence of atrocities against Jews, there was little support in Canada for a boycott of the 1936 Olympics in Berlin. As historian Bruce Kidd has noted, those who took an anti-Olympic stance came from a narrow group outside the established sports community, namely, members of Workers' Sports Association clubs, trade unionists, progressive churchmen and educators, left-wing political groups opposed to fascism, and various Jewish organizations.[35] Canadian sportswriters were mostly opposed to a boycott and, in some cases, belittled attempts to organize one. Alexandrine Gibb, never a communist sympathizer (she openly supported the Liberal party), was indifferent to the "rabid communists" who decried living conditions among the Canadian poor, when in her view they lived much better than a good many people in the Soviet Union. She had just returned from an extensive journey through Russia; sent by her paper, the *Toronto Star*, to cover the "woman's angle."[36] As usual, she made her position on the proposed boycott crystal clear:

> It's a certainty that no matter what country drops out of the Olympics the games will be held in Germany next summer — unless a war cancels the whole show. They will not be moved to any other country.
>
> I can't help be amazed at the lack of knowledge of some of these athletes who think that if they decide not to go the games will be moved immediately somewhere else. It is your privilege not to try out for the games if you wish, but you can't move the Olympic games to any other country, and don't let anyone try to tell you it is possible.
>
> On the face of it, it is ridiculous. Naturally it will be the Olympic committee which will deal with any Olympic matters, not some outside organization which suddenly has decided they want to handle the show.[37]

One unrealistic athlete, according to Gibb, was Eve Dawes, Canada's top high jumper, who had come third in the 1932 Olympics and second in the 1934 British Empire Games. In the summer of 1935, Dawes accepted an invitation through the Workers' Sport Association of Canada to compete in Russia; when she returned, she was suspended by the AAU (Ontario Branch) for going without their permission. Rather than face continued suspension, Dawes opted to retire. Even though the WAAF of C was willing to help reinstate her so that she could compete in the 1936 Olympics, Dawes refused. Instead she accompanied a small group of athletes going to Barcelona to participate in the "People's Olympics," organized by a coalition of European socialists and labour groups and scheduled to be held at the same time as the Olympics in Berlin. However, the Spanish Civil War erupted, and the People's Olympics never took place. Eva Dawes and the other team members were suspended by the AAU when they returned to Canada.[38]

Canada's high jumper on the 1936 women's team was Margaret Bell, a member of the Vancouver Athletic Club; she was inspired by Lillian Palmer and Mary Frizzell, who had competed in the 1932 Olympics.[39] She was one of the few track and field athletes to make the team from outside the Toronto area, due to the difficulties of getting athletes to the Dominion trials in Montreal, which were held just before the team departed in mid-July. The cost to send each athlete to Berlin was about $300, a great deal of money in those days, and it was not unusual that some athletes were added to the team if they were able raise the necessary travel funds, which made the selection process suspect. The track athletes did not do particularly well in Berlin, coming eighth overall, and Margaret Bell came a disappointing ninth in her event. The best performances were by Betty Taylor, who won bronze in the 80-metre hurdles, and the 4x100-metre relay team (Dorothy Brookshaw, Hilda Cameron, Jeanette Dolson, and Aileen Meagher), which also came third. In swimming, Phyllis Dewar could not repeat her medal-winning ways because she was ill, and the others were simply outclassed. Also on the team were three fencers — Nancy Archibald of Montreal (her sister Joan competed in the same sport in 1932), Kathleen Hughes-Hallett, and Aileen Thomas, who were no match for the strong European competition. Although there was no women's basketball in the Olympics, the Edmonton Grads were also in Berlin having just completed a nine-game, undefeated European tour, in which they outscored their opponents 697 to 105.

The last major international competition of the 1930s, and as it turned out until after World War II, was the British Empire Games in February 1938, held in Sydney, Australia, a very long way by boat. Canadian athletes had to find their own way to Vancouver, the point of departure, and be prepared to be away nearly three months. According to women's team manager-chaperone Ann Clark of Vancouver, they encountered a myriad of problems in Australia, including the hot climate, inadequate living conditions, insect bites, and worst of all, the "wiseacres" back home.[40] Notable on the team was a young Vancouver sprinter, Barbara Howard, in all likelihood the first woman of colour to compete on an international team for Canada. Only 17 and still in high school, Howard was as surprised as the team selectors when she outran several well-known sprinters at the western time trials in the fall of 1937; in fact, she equalled the British Empire

Games record of 11.2 seconds. She had been running only five years and had little coaching or training beyond what she received in school. She was touted as a potential medal winner, but ended up sixth in the final of the 100-yard sprint (only Australia, Canada, England, New Zealand, and South Africa were represented in Sydney). Decades later, she still remembers someone shouting to her as she was about to take the starting position: "Run like a horse, Barbara!" "I was crushed," she recounted, "who wants to look like a horse with a big rump, and besides I was scared of horses."[41] She was more satisfied with her performance in the relays, helping Canada (along with Aileen Meagher and Jeanette Dolson) to take silver in the peculiar 440-yard relay. Canada was third in the equally bizarre 660-yard relay, where Violet Montgomery and Aileen Meagher each ran 220 yards, and Barbara Howard and Jeanette Dolson ran 110 yards apiece. Also outstanding were Robina Higgins from Winnipeg, who won the javelin; Jeanette Dolson, who came third in the 100-yard sprint; and the 4x100-yard freestyle relay swim team, anchored by Phyllis Dewar, which won a gold medal. According to the Canadian press, diver Lynda Adams was "robbed" when she placed second in both the springboard and high tower competitions.

The WAAF of C, the organization responsible for women's sport in Canada, especially track and field, was not having an easy time. Alexandrine Gibb, who had been elected president in 1928, ran the association for two years. She was followed by Toronto softball organizer Mabel Ray, who unexpectedly took over even though the presidency was due to move west to Victoria Sallis of Vancouver. Unfortunately Ray, who was also president of the Ontario Branch of the Federation and the Toronto Women's Softball Association, became embroiled in a nasty softball dispute — she was found to have mismanaged TWSA funds — which meant she should be disciplined by the very associations over which she presided. "The situation is decidedly awkward," commented Phyllis Griffiths in her *Toronto Telegram* sports column. Ray refused to back down, but in November 1931 she was ousted as head of the WAAF of C, and Gibb again took over the presidency for one year, allowing them, as one member put it, to come through a distressing year "with their colors flying so high."[42]

At the 1932 annual WAAF of C meeting in Winnipeg, Gibb was asked to remain as president for another year, but she refused, partly due to a motion put forward by the Quebec (i.e., Montreal) branch to make sportswriters ineligible for office in the Federation and to sever all association with sports while employed as journalists. Defenders of the new clause argued that sportswriters could not be loyal to the Federation while at the same time expressing their views in public, nor should the press have access to the organization's private affairs. Even though the motion was defeated by 22 against and eight for (coming from Quebec and British Columbia), it must have given Gibb pause for thought about her continued role in the organization. The vast distances separating Federation leaders, the unequal spread of athletes throughout the country (the majority were in Ontario and Quebec), and a lack of money especially in the Depression years, led to serious regional conflicts, most particularly between western and eastern Canada.[43] Since Gibb no longer had an official position, she was often outspoken about the organization in her daily column, referring to it as the "Waaflets."

By spring 1934, relations between Gibb and the Federation were such that "scrappy" secretary Ann Clark announced that both Gibb and Bobbie Rosenfeld were no longer "persona grata" with the organization.[44] The two had been appointed manager and coach respectively of the Canadian women's team competing in the British Empire Games in London that year, but the organizing committee had neglected to consult the Federation. Clark charged that Gibb no longer had any connection with the Federation and, furthermore, could not fulfill her roles as reporter and manager at the same time, despite the fact that she had done this on several occasions before. At the time Gibb was in hospital recovering from an operation; however, the AAU affirmed the appointments, and the two went to the games as scheduled.

By now, Gibb was assistant sports editor at the *Toronto Star*, and probably the most well known women's sports advocate in Canada. When she was appointed to the Ontario Athletic Commission in September 1934, the first woman then or since, her boss at the *Star*, sports editor Lou Marsh, wrote:

> Miss Gibb knows sport better than any other woman in the country and as well as any other man whose name was mentioned in the tentative line-ups of the new commission. Her experience as a writer of sport on this paper has taken her into all branches of sport, both amateur and professional, and she has an intimate knowledge of the politics and intrigues of both brands of sporting activity. Her executive ability has been frequently recognized by her appointment to important positions in connection with Olympiads and other forms of international sport, and also by her selection to represent Canada on bodies which govern amateur sport for the entire world.[45]

Gibb was particularly proud when the Ontario Athletic Commission agreed to supply free medical examinations for all girl athletes in the province — the first time, she noted in her column, "the O.A.C. has ever officially recognized that we have in Ontario a steadily growing band of feminine athletes who are in active competition in many sports."[46] As Gibb took up new challenges, she became increasingly cynical about the WAAF of C, frequently berating the leadership or dissuading them from an unpopular decision through her column. In exasperation, she wrote: "No wonder men laugh at women's meetings and associations.

This splitting of hairs and ridiculous rulings make men feel that women don't know what it is all about."[47]

INNUENDOES ABOUT FEMININITY AND SEXUALITY

While those who believed in the Women's Division philosophy, principally women physical educators in eastern Ontario and anglophone Montreal, tried to feminize sports through modification (for example, their strict adherence to girls' rules basketball), leaders in the WAAF of C, as well as the industrial promoters of women's sport, sought to feminize the athletes. Emphasizing their womanliness and beauty, perhaps even their sexual appeal, would restore the femininity of athletes potentially "masculinized" by their association with sports played by men.[48] One of Bobbie Rosenfeld's favourite sayings was that "fine athletic accomplishment often goes hand in hand with feminine pulchritude."[49] Alexandrine Gibb was forever reminding readers about the beauty of Canadian women athletes, with comments like: she is "some looker" or a "fair-haired beauty," and "just another sample of how these athletic girls rank when it comes to looks."[50] She was convinced that every international team she managed, beginning with the first one in 1925, was the most feminine crew that ever stepped on the cinder tracks. She was especially delighted when an American reporter at the 1932 Olympics in Los Angeles observed:

> The Canadian girls are undoubtedly the prettiest and most wholesome look-
> ing group of girls who have arrived for the competition. They constitute a
> denial of the general idea that a woman athlete must be built like a baby
> grand piano and have a face like a hatchet. Their ages range from 16 to 21,
> and they are here to show the world that Canada has some splendid young
> women who are good-looking and who know how to conduct themselves.[51]

When Andy Lytle (sports editor at the *Vancouver Sun* and eventually at the *Toronto Star*) called women athletes "leathery-limbed, flat-chested girls," Gibb and other women sportswriters mounted a spirited defence of female athleticism in their columns and articles. Through the Canadian Press, they distributed a photo of Olive Hinder from the Laurel Ladies Athletic Club, a "blue-eyed, lissom girl whose fair hair hangs in soft ringlets to her shoulder."[52] In a rebuttal article published in the influential women's magazine *Chatelaine*, Bobbie Rosenfeld argued that women athletes were "paragons of feminine physique, beauty and health," and not the "Amazons and ugly ducklings" depicted by Lytle.[53] She sneered at Lytle's claim that certain sports (ice hockey for one) were injurious to the health and physical development of women — "plain, ordinary, everyday tommyrot" — although she agreed that boxing and wrestling were "shouldn'ts." She also disliked being called a "muscle moll," a term never used by Lytle. It was American sportswriter Paul Gallico who first applied the label to Mildred "Babe" Didrikson, the Texas tomboy star of the 1932 Olympics, in an article he wrote for *Vanity Fair*.54 The word "moll," slang for a gangster's mistress or a prostitute, is representative of disreputable, even lawless womanhood. When applied to female athletes it was code for unfeminine, rough, mannish, and unacceptable. Texas physical education teachers, concerned that Babe Didrikson would become a role model, posted signs on school bulletin boards reading: "DON'T BE A MUSCLE MOLL."55 Why Rosenfeld would use this term is unclear; she must have picked it up from reading similar commentary from the United States, perhaps Gallico himself. Regardless, the term never gained much currency in the Canadian media.

More importantly, there was no one Canadian female athlete in this era that the sports press could use as the "very paragon of Muscle Molls." Canada did not have the equivalent of a Babe Didrikson, an immensely talented athlete, who, after her phenomenal success at the 1932 Olympics in Los Angeles, made a career in professional golf and, in the process, transformed herself from a tough, work-ing-class, Texas tomboy uninterested in marriage to a new and successful image as a happily married, feminine, domestic, heterosexual woman.56 In both talent and athleticism, Fanny Rosenfeld was Canada's "Babe," but her athletic career was prematurely interrupted in the fall of 1929 when, only in her mid-twenties, she suffered the first of many painful arthritis attacks. Although she continued to play competitive softball, basketball, and hockey for several more years, she even-tually stopped altogether and concentrated on being a sports columnist.57

In a much discussed article in *Maclean's*, Elmer Ferguson, sports editor of the *Montreal Star*, wrote that he was disgusted by the "violent, face-straining, face-dirtying, body-bouncing, sweaty, graceless, stumbling, struggling, wrenching, racking, jarring, and floundering" athletic events in which some girls engaged. Those who excel in them, ranted Ferguson, frequently look extremely unfemi-nine; his prime example was the "Galloping Ace," who in all likelihood was Helen Stephens, the American track star and gold medal winner of the 100 metres at the 1936 Olympics in Berlin — "a big, lanky, flat-chested, muscular girl, with as much sex appeal as grandmother's old sewing machine." Ferguson's point was that he, like other men, liked women athletes with "grace, sweetness, rhythm, freedom from sweat and freedom from grime" — a state achieved only by speed- and figure-skaters, high divers, swimmers, and many golf and tennis players. All the more "robust" forms of athletics, including "sprinting, jumping, hurdling, heav-ing weights, sliding into bases, struggling weakly and gracelessly around armed with hockey sticks or crashing each other at basketball in a sweat-reeking gymna-

sium," according to Ferguson, did nothing to enhance their femininity and
certainly not their sex appeal. His most trenchant criticism was that the Canadian
"beauties" who made up the 1936 Olympic track team (for example, Roxy Atkins,
Margaret Bell, Aileen Meagher, and Betty Taylor) didn't win anything, proving
that a degree of masculinity was necessary for success, but an unwanted characteristic in women: "My point is that these girls could never whip the big, masculine, flat-chested, leather-limbed, and horselike-looking stars of the game."[58]

Several letters to the editor of *Maclean's* supported Ferguson's view, but Roxy
Atkins, an accomplished hurdler, member of the 1936 Canadian Olympic team,
and secretary of the Ontario Branch of the WAAF of C, penned a lively, well-
argued defence in a subsequent issue. She astutely pointed out that most girls and
women could not afford the costs of figure skating, golf or tennis, and that swimming and diving were also out for those in small communities with no access to
pools, whereas available to both rich and poor, urban and rural, were countless
tracks, softball diamonds, hockey rinks, and gymnasiums. It was through sports
like basketball, track, softball, and hockey, argued Atkins, that "many young girls,
who were thin, scrawny, unattractive, prone to mixing with boy gangs, and
pointed for trouble ahead" were physically developed through exercise and fresh
air, disciplined by training, broadened by travel, and socially enriched through
contact with older girls and chaperones. Sports participation, she contended,
enhanced femininity; she insisted that Ferguson's innuendos about the "Galloping
Ace" (Helen Stephens) were false: "I have never known a girl, naturally beautiful,
to lose any of her good looks and charm because she became sports-minded." She
went on to recount the many athletes now married, indeed looked upon as the
"gilt-edged securities in the marriage market," including the famous Babe
Didrikson, who at that time was about to marry wrestler George Zaharias. Her
final plea was: "Girls are human beings. They want an equal chance with men to
go places, to see the world, to parade before the crowds, to win medals and cups,
to hear the cheers of spectators. They want a chance to play, to develop physically, to cultivate the spirit of sportsmanship, to meet nice people, to have an interest beyond the home and office."[59]

Alexandrine Gibb's main defence against attacks on women athletes was to
point to their obvious beauty and to implore her "girls" to conduct themselves
with appropriate feminine decorum. She wanted them well-dressed, well-behaved,
and well-spoken, and she was intolerant of anything less. Following a fracas in a
basketball game in Montreal, she admonished: "Girls will learn some of these days
that if they desire to continue in sports they must learn to control their tempers.
Mere man can get away with a fistic argument in a game, but let a feminine fist
fly or a hair pulling argument start, and it's all wrong. Curb your tempers girls or
go back to knitting."[60]

The Edmonton Grads were a good example of women athletes in this era who escaped the "mannish" label even though they played "men's rules" basketball and were highly competitive. Coach Percy Page insisted that his players be "ladies first, basketball players second," and he kept a tight rein on their behaviour both on and off the court. Whether they were travelling across Alberta or the Atlantic, the rules were the same — no going out without permission; no smoking, drinking, swearing, or chewing gum; and always be smartly dressed. On the basketball court, he demanded discipline and sportsmanship.[61]

Echoing earlier criticisms, a concern raised frequently in the popular press was whether "stressful and intense" athletic competition would harm women's reproductive capacity. Sportswriter Frederick Griffin, in an article published in the *Toronto Star Weekly*, was typical of those asking questions about whether sports were making girls "tough under the skin" or "hurting them physically." What he was really asking was whether they would make good wives and mothers by being able to reproduce the "race."[62] He surveyed a variety of experts, including a well-known gynaecologist in Toronto who agreed that fit women make healthier mothers, but patronizingly suggested that women athletes made better child-bearers because they obeyed doctors during pregnancy and labour, just as they would a coach. Griffin also gathered statistics from Percy Page about former Edmonton Grads who had married and had babies (only one married ex-Grad was so far childless). Alexandrine Gibb pointed out that "star" athletes were not neglecting motherhood by providing a list of recent examples, including Olympic medal winner and sportswriter Myrtle Cook McGowan; Rosa Grosse O'Neill, another athlete now retired from the track; and the American swimmer Martha Norelius Wright, who had married a famous Canadian athlete. Women sports columnists kept careful track of the marital status and reproductive capacity of former well-known athletes by announcing engagements, marriages, and births; if they didn't have anything concrete to announce along marital lines, they hinted at an imminent "sport romance." Most women athletes of this era retired from active competition when they married, and fewer tried to return to competition after giving birth. Some leagues made rules about married women. For example, the Toronto Women's Softball Association ruled that "a married woman cannot play intermediate softball without permission from the league."[63] Even successful athletes like Myrtle Cook McGowan were not keen on married women pursuing their athletic careers, although by 1931 she herself was not only a mother, sportswriter, coach, but was attempting to regain her running form. When American tennis player Helen Wills Moody opted out of tournaments in Europe soon after her marriage, Cook commented approvingly: "Mrs. Moody's decision not to absent herself from her husband for three months is a fine example to sportswomen who are apt to forget their protectors and rush all over the hemisphere in search of athletic honors."[64]

French-language newspapers in Quebec, if Montreal's *La Presse* is representative, paid scant attention to these issues. During the 1930s, there was very little coverage of women's sports and much more emphasis on the role of exercise and sport (walking, cycling, swimming, tennis, golf) in achieving good health and beauty. Also included was extensive fashion advice about proper sports attire, all of which appeared in the newspaper's women's section. On the sports pages, it was rarely the active athlete, but rather "la belle neige" (sport queen), who received the most coverage. These were young women, chosen for their beauty and personality, who stood at the finish line of marathon snowshoe races to greet the finishers and reward the winners. Dressed in a long white dress and fur coat, her role was to help men finish the race: "without her who knows how many men would not reach the goal?"[65] As the idea became more popular, sport queens were associated with men's sports clubs or leagues, specific sporting events, or even geographical areas. Presumably there was a good deal of prestige accorded these young women, and, in some cases, sport queens themselves were rewarded with gifts, clothes, and special trips. Usher's Green Stripe snowshoe club in Montreal, for example, used *La Presse* to list criteria for "queen" applicants to be chosen by Quebec journalists; the winner would receive a trip to Miami or Bermuda after the completion of her duties.[66]

Any discussion about the sexuality of female athletes presumed heterosexuality. No one suggested that masculine athleticism in women was indicative of homosexual love. Susan Cahn argues that the stereotype of the lesbian athlete did not emerge "full blown" until after World War II, although certainly by the 1930s, "female athletic mannishness began to connote heterosexual failure, usually couched in terms of unattractiveness to men, but also suggesting the possible absence of heterosexual interest."[67] She argues further that the lesbian connotation of mannishness was "forged primarily through indirect links of association," which is why Canadian women sports writers took great care to mention just who, among famous and even less well-known female athletes, was getting married. Not once, during this period, have I found a single reference connecting athleticism and lesbianism.

The criticism of "mannish women athletes" was not that they might be lesbians, but that they might be men. Alexandrine Gibb was particularly disparaging of athletes she suspected of being less than female, especially when the Canadian "dainty girl runners" had to compete against them. Tall and muscular athletes like "six-foot mannish in appearance girl runner from Missouri" Helen Stephens, or "huge and husky, deep-voiced" Polish-American Stanislawa Walasiewicz (Stella Walsh), all came in for particular censure, to say nothing of the women who had competed as females and were now ostensibly male: "I'd like to see a special 100 metres at the Olympic Games. In it I would put Stella Walsh, Helen Stephens, a couple of special German contestants, at least two English girls, and one or two other Europeans. Canada would not be entered." After the British Empire Games and the Women's World Games in London in 1934, Gibb called for physical examinations of all athletes wishing to compete as female: "I had a dressing room full of Canadian girls weeping because they had to toe the mark against girls who shaved and spoke in mannish tones!"[68] Whether any of these athletes were men is not known, but several well-known athletes changed their designated sex from female to male. One documented case was Czechoslovakian Zdenka Koubkova (known later as Zdenek Koubka), who in 1934 held the women's world record for the 800-metres and could, according to medical authorities, make a choice of sex.[69] The Fédération sportive féminine internationale eventually erased her record and times from their books. When Stella Walsh, one of the most successful women track athletes of the 1930s, died in 1980, it was discovered that she suffered from mosaicism, a condition producing an unusual chromosomal pattern and ambiguous genitalia. Several decades later, Roxy Atkins Andersen, a Canadian who had competed against Walsh, lobbied to have her titles taken away (including her gold medal in the 100-metres at the 1932 Olympics, where Canadian Hilda Strike came second). "There's a thin dividing line between a mannish woman and a womanish man," argued Andersen, "and those who aren't completely woman should be disbarred."[70] However, testing to determine if athletes wishing to compete as women in international competition were in fact female was not put in place until the 1960s.

UNPRECEDENTED PARTICIPATION

Debates over strenuous competition or innuendoes about certain "mannish" athletes were of little concern to the thousands of girls and young women now participating in unprecedented numbers in softball, basketball, hockey, track and field, swimming, and a host of new sports, such as bowling, badminton, alpine skiing, competitive cycling, even cricket. Development did not take place evenly across the country, with some sports struggling in some regions, while thriving in others. Other sports saw a definite decline, especially those dependent on public interest. The 10-mile women's marathon swim at the Canadian National Exhibition, for example, was gradually reduced to five, then three miles, and cancelled altogether due to the war between 1938 and 1946. The Depression also made it difficult for professional swimmers to obtain sponsorship. Ann (Mundigel) Meraw, a successful distance swimmer from Vancouver, who competed in the CNE swims in 1934 and 1935, always had to pay her own way. Meraw "advertised" for various companies — for example, Ginger Ale and Beehive Corn Syrup — but all she ever received were a few cases of their product.[71]

On the prairies, during the terrible drought-laden years of the Depression, many considered softball a "godsend." Ball diamonds were everywhere; the game was cheap to play, since it required a minimum of equipment; and it was fun and exciting, providing a much-needed distraction. Almost every rural Saskatchewan community had a "ladies" softball team, who travelled by horseback, foot, or truck to practise on a rough diamond laid out in a nearby farmer's field. One player from the small community of Watrous remembers playing barefoot in the rain and mud: "In my young days, it was just plain old fastball, no gloves. Now I hate to think about it, your hand swelled up, but it didn't seem to bother us. We seemed to get along pretty good that way, that's all we knew." In Saskatoon, a ladies league consisted of teams like Quaker Oats, Arthur Rose, What Nots, BA Oil, Mercantiles, and Wood-Valence, attesting to the local firms most interested in sponsoring women's softball. By 1935, the senior women's league was playing regularly at Cairns Field, softball's "castle" in the city's heart, where for 10 cents you could see a first-class men's or women's double-header. The Regina's Ladies' League, with Simpson's, Woolworth's, Orange Caps, Pilsners, and others, drew larger crowds then the men's league, as was the case in other centres like Moose Jaw, Swift Current, and Lloydminster.[72] These leagues produced a host of talented ballplayers, and some ended up playing in the United States for the All-American Girls Professional Baseball League of the 1940s and 1950s. Nearly half of the 60-odd Canadians who played in the All-American came from Saskatchewan, because, as one player joked, there was nothing else to do there "except play ball and chase grasshoppers."[73]

Softball was also popular among aboriginal women, especially those who lived on reserves, although references are fleeting and not well-documented. The "Caledonia Indians," for instance, came mostly from the Six Nations Reserve along the Grand River in Ontario. The team had both white and aboriginal women; off the reserve they played exhibition games in southern Ontario, including the Toronto leagues. Dorothy Wilson, an aboriginal from the Six Nations Reserve, played on the team in the early 1930s and remembers: "we'd come home from school, do our homework, eat dinner, do the dishes, and practice until you couldn't see for the dark. I lived for ball. I started getting excited the day before the game."[74] When her team came to Toronto to play, it was treated as an exciting novelty, as witnessed by sportswriter Phyllis Griffith's comment: "INDIANS ARE COMING: Beaches Girls Softball League fans have a real attraction arranged for them at Kew Gardens Saturday evening when the Caledonia Indians will play one of the Beaches teams. The Indians have several honest-to-goodness Indians in their line-up, and are a good team into the bargain."[75] By today's standards this was a racist remark, but it does point to how unusual it was for aboriginal women to be seen playing sport in the 1930s. The Beachettes, whose Chinese pitcher was also noted, beat the Caledonia Indians that time.

By 1930, over 200 teams were affiliated with the Ontario Women's Softball Association, five times more than was the case in 1925; by 1937, there were so many club applications that numbers were restricted to prevent it from becoming too unmanageable.[76] Women's softball in Toronto was the envy of other large centres across the country. By the mid-1930s, there were numerous intermediate and senior leagues in the city, although the most well-known and prestigious was still Sunnyside's Olympic League, with perennial favourites including the Supremes, Langley's Lakesides, Toronto Ladies, and Sunday Morning Class. Many teams were commercially sponsored; although firms like Simpson's and Rexall's also employed quite a few of their players, most had no connection with their sponsors. Sunnyside's gate receipts were sufficiently large, with revenue shared between the clubs and the Toronto Harbour Commission, that commercial backing was not always necessary. In 1929, each club received somewhere between $300 and $400; a decade later with revenues still on the increase, the share for each was nearly $700, more in some cases. Toronto Ladies, a multi-sport club, financed other non-paying activities (track and field, basketball, hockey) out of their softball "take." No wonder the Edmonton players, struggling in their Boyle Street league, were envious, because after passing around a milk bottle at games during the season, total donations were barely enough to give each team between $30 and $40.[77]

With jobs at a premium in the Depression, some players were lured away from Toronto to play softball in Montreal, a practice that understandably angered unemployed players in Quebec. Bobbie Rosenfeld was a good example. In April 1932, she left Toronto, where she did not have full-time employment, to take up a position writing a sports column for the *Montreal Daily Herald*. She also played softball for Muncy's Ladies in the Montreal Major Ladies League, was president of the newly formed Provincial Women's Softball Union of Quebec, and played basketball for a women's team at the local Young Men's Hebrew Association (YMHA). However, three months later, for reasons that remain unclear, she left the *Herald*, and, despite efforts by her basketball team to find her another job in Montreal, she returned to Toronto to work for an insurance company. The practice of enticing softball players from Toronto to Montreal became so common that the Quebec Branch of the WAAF of C called for an investigation, charging that jobs, most only temporary, were given to the imported players to camouflage professionalism. On the other hand, Bobbie Rosenfeld and others were critical of commercial softball's "slavery system," which bound a player to one team when she wanted to play for another, because this, too, had all the earmarks of professionalism. Most leagues had an iron-clad rule stating that "players playing for a club must remain with that club until properly released by same"; disputed cases went before the local or provincial softball association for resolution.[78]

Despite the fact that softball was booming in Ontario, played extensively on the prairies, and enthusiastically in Montreal and the Maritimes, it was difficult to organize a Dominion-wide championship. Although the Canadian Women's Softball Association was formed in 1928, it never seems to have held an annual meeting, and by 1939, it no longer existed. There were serious difficulties in the early 1930s when controversy and acrimony erupted within the Women's Ontario Softball Association over allegations of money mismanagement at Toronto's Sunnyside park against Mabel Ray and William D'Alesandro. They also ran the Toronto and Ontario governing bodies, according to Alex Gibb, with "Mussolini-like control of the family compact."[79] Despite being censured by the Ontario Athletic Commission, Ray and her supporters refused to resign, causing a break-away group to form the Provincial Women's Softball Union, which eventually took control of the game in Ontario. Although Ray and D'Alesandro continued to maintain the Canadian Women's Softball Association, it lost all support and was eventually disbanded; by then it was extremely difficult to hold a Dominion championship due to financial constraints of the Depression.

Softball was a tough game, and players frequently got hurt. Women sports columnists, especially in Toronto and Montreal, dutifully reported the various league injuries, which ranged from minor cuts, bruises, and dislocations to seriously broken bones and concussions. Injured players were assisted through the league's emergency fund with exhibition games held periodically to raise money for this purpose. Until well into the 1930s at Sunnyside, only the catcher and player on first base could use mitts, and shoes with spikes were never allowed. Players wore rolled up stockings with no skin showing between their shorts and leg, although teams from the United States playing at Sunnyside kept their socks rolled down, prompting Alex Gibb to joke that if the Canadians wanted to attract more spectators, they too should bare their legs. International contests with teams like the Cleveland Erin Brews, Chicago Down Drafts, and Detroit Rainbows played to capacity crowds of 3,000 crammed into Sunnyside; in comparison, 14,000 fans in the spring of 1939 watched Langley's Lakesides (managed by Bobbie Rosenfeld) play exhibition softball at Madison Square Gardens in New York.

While softball flourished in the decade preceding World War II, ice hockey struggled to maintain its earlier dominance. Although the Dominion Women's Amateur Hockey Association was formed in 1933 to oversee national championships, the game was organized and played unevenly across the country. According to a survey by Alex Gibb, strong hockey teams existed in the Maritimes, such as the Crystal Sisters of Summerside, PEI, but with no provincial association. There had been a significant decline in Quebec, which Myrtle Cook in Montreal hoped to remedy with a provincial league. The nine-year-old Ladies Ontario Hockey Association had yet to solve the problem of teams scattered throughout the province, which made a provincial play-down difficult, although that "smart Preston team" (the Rivulettes) was an inspiration, and the game thrived in northern Ontario. In the west, Manitoba and especially Winnipeg were strong; Alberta was probably the best organized of all the provinces with terrific fan support, but Saskatchewan had few teams and no organization, and British Columbia was coming along due to the efforts of hard-working Doris Parkes. Gibb also commented that smaller centres could more successfully operate a girls' hockey team than larger ones, because girls need to be trained from a young age, preferably on an icy pond with the neighbourhood boys. When older girls step out onto the ice, she argued, no matter how proficient their skating, wielding a hockey stick was something else again. "Taking the entire country, you see that girls' hockey is really with us. It is widespread and rather thin in parts, but it is here. The west has the edge so far as opportunity and natural ice is concerned."[80]

Like the Edmonton Grads in basketball, Ontario's Preston Rivulettes dominated Canadian women's hockey in the 1930s by winning 350 games, tying three, and losing only two. Originally a softball team, by 1932 they ruled the Ontario intermediate league, and the next year, after a solid win in an exhibition game over the University of Toronto, they entered the senior league, never to look back. Their only defeat came in 1933 when they travelled to Edmonton to challenge the Western Canadian champions, the Edmonton Rustlers, for the first Dominion title, and lost in two games. After that, they won the Ontario title and the Canadian championship (in the years it was played), until they disbanded in 1941.[81] Although strong teams existed — like, for instance, the Winnipeg Olympics in the west, who challenged the Rivulettes later in the decade for the national title, while in the east the Montreal Maroons were their strongest rivals — there was little opposition for the Preston team, which made for lopsided games. Myrtle Cook, president of the Canadian Women's Hockey Association, was unsuccessful in finding suitable opponents and the necessary funds, for the Preston Rivulettes to play exhibition games in Europe. Without balanced competition, interest in hockey waned; as well, the cost of equipment and lack of ice time posed insurmountable problems for some teams, with many completely disappearing during the war. By 1941, in Toronto, for instance, there was not a single women's hockey league remaining; in Winnipeg there were no teams at all. Unlike softball, which had a huge following in the United States and many highly skilled players, there was little interest in hockey, with few sufficiently experienced teams to bring to Canada for exciting matches. A women's hockey league based in New York, possibly playing Canadian teams, was discussed at one point, but nothing came of it.[82]

Canadian women's basketball in the 1930s was dominated by the unbeatable Edmonton Grads, still coached by Percy Page, who worked incessantly to promote his team and find them suitable competition. Although the Grads played a major

role in establishing and promoting women's basketball nationally, even internationally, their supremacy over all contenders became a hindrance to developing
worthy opponents across the country. In 1938, the Canadian Basketball
Association set up a special "Senior A" series, to which the Grads automatically
qualified, with other clubs entering on a volunteer basis when they felt they had
sufficient strength to play against them. Other teams entered the normal "Senior"
series, where the competition was more even, in an attempt to develop serious
opposition for the Grads.[83] On the other hand, whenever the Grads travelled
across the country, they played numerous exhibition games along the way to help
promote the sport. On a trip to Germany in 1936 to participate in the Summer
Olympics, for example, they stopped to play teams in Regina, Winnipeg, St. Paul,
Peterborough, Ottawa, and Montreal before heading across the Atlantic, where
they played nine straight games against various British and European clubs, beating one team, the London Pioneers, by an amazing 100–2 score.[84] According to
most observers, the single most significant factor in the success of the Grads was
their coach, Percy Page, who controlled every aspect of the team from its inception in 1915 until it disbanded in 1940. His dedication, along with a sensible feeder
system, community support, and the devotion of his players, brought an unprecedented record of 502 wins and only 20 losses.[85]

One problem in promoting girls' basketball across the country was the continuing problem of differing rules. Dorothy Jackson, a physical educator at the
University of Toronto, conducted a national survey in 1941 to ascertain what rules
were being used across the country. She discovered there was still an even east-
west split with British Columbia, Alberta, Saskatchewan, and Manitoba governed
almost entirely by men's rules, whereas Ontario, Quebec, New Brunswick, and
Nova Scotia accounted for most of the 53 per cent using girls' rules. She also noted
that a handful of women physical education teachers in private schools, a few
high schools, and also YWCAs had introduced the girls' game in the west with
limited success. Similarly, there were organized leagues using men's rules in eastern Canada, but they were almost entirely outside the schools, universities, and
teacher training colleges.[86]

Although there was a dramatic increase in the number of girls and young
women participating in a variety of sports, both individual and team, not everyone wishing to exercise chose sport. Earlier physical culture movements gave way
in the mid-1930s to mass health movements, in which women were encouraged
to exercise for attractiveness, fun, pleasure, and fitness. The first and most successful of these was the Women's League of Health and Beauty, founded in London,
England, by Mary Bagot Stack in 1930.[87] Its purpose was to promote healthy
motherhood and universal peace by encouraging women to incorporate fitness
into their daily lives: good health, it was argued, led to peace, not war. In

September 1935, Prunella Stack, daughter of the League's founder and known as the "most perfect girl," came to Toronto for the official launch of the League in Canada. An enthusiastic audience packed the Eaton's auditorium where 130 new Canadian League members, dressed in uniforms of black shorts and white tops, gave a demonstration of rhythmic exercises. "Our system is for women and planned for women," stated Stack, "we don't want to develop the muscles of ball players; such a system would be wrong for us."[88] By 1936, the League had attracted over 1000 members in Toronto; two years later this had grown to over 5000, with branches in other Ontario centres as well as Montreal. Unfortunately, the war severely curtailed the activities of the League, many of its branches closed, and it never recovered to the level of its heyday in the 1930s.[89]

At about the same time on Canada's west coast, another mass physical recreation movement was developed to help combat the effects of the Depression, and in particular the enforced idleness of unemployed young men. Popularly known as "Pro-Rec," the program was the brainchild of Jan Eisenhardt, supervisor of playgrounds in Vancouver, and inaugurated in November 1934. The BC government, who administered the free program, established Pro-Rec classes at rented facilities (church and community halls, school gymnasia, armouries) throughout the province and trained instructors at a special summer school. The primary activity was European gymnastics, supplemented by sports activities, and, although originally designed for young men, women were immediately attracted, especially to the Swedish gymnastics and dancing. By 1939, the program had attracted some 30,000 participants in 155 centres, with women outnumbering men by two to one. At the end of each winter season, mass displays of fitness and gymnastic activities helped to publicize the program and attract more members. Wrote one observer at this event, referring to the women:

> The majority of the women were between eighteen and thirty, with a scattering of older ones with greying or white hair and considerable weight. Tall rangy girls were not much in evidence; most of them were of medium height or even shorter, and fairly plump in general build. Black hair was absent except in the case of a half dozen Chinese and Japanese girls.... Make-up, if used at all, was not conspicuous, in so far as a mere male observer was aware.... The average of good looks was indeed very high. An aura of health, buoyancy, cheerfulness, confidence, and courage was the predominant impression.[90]

Pro-Rec was exceedingly popular, and, through the encouragement and financial support of the federal government, it became a model for similar public recreation programs in other provinces. During wartime, the federal government developed a fitness program, primarily to improve the health of future armed forces recruits, which followed closely the ideas developed through the Pro-Rec program.[91]

EFFECTS OF WORLD WAR II

On 26 November 1940, *Toronto Star* sportswriter Alexandrine Gibb wrote in her women's sport column: "So long until the summertime. Keep your chin up but not out. I'll be seeing you. C'est la guerre! C'est la vie and au revoir to sports!" She was given responsibility for editing the *Star*'s section on women's war work in Toronto, mostly about their efforts to raise money, sew and mend uniforms, operate canteens and "hostess houses" for the troops, and the like. Whether Gibb liked her new role at the paper is difficult to tell; she probably had little choice, and she never returned to her daily sports column.[92] The paper tried to maintain news of "Feminine Sports" by having someone else write her column, but by 1944 it, too, had disappeared. Other women's sport columns suffered a similar fate. *Winnipeg Free Press* sportswriter Lillian "Jimmy" Coo signed off her column, "Cherchez la Femme," in early 1942 because she was about to join the Canadian Woman's Auxiliary Air Force and move to Toronto.[93] In October 1942, when the *Toronto Telegram* appointed Phyllis Griffiths as the first woman photo editor of a Canadian newspaper, she turned over her longstanding column "The Girl and the Game" to someone else, but by 1949 it was gone.

The loss of influential women commentators in the daily sports media, especially those like Alexandrine Gibb and Phyllis Griffiths, was one consequence of World War II. Another was that facilities were taken over by the forces, making practices and competitions difficult, especially indoor track and field that relied on existing armouries. By 1940, the Edmonton Arena, home to the Edmonton Grads, had been taken over by the RCAF, forcing the Grads to practice and play elsewhere — that summer they disbanded. The war also brought annoying equipment shortages: "Give softball bats loving care because they're as hard to get as a waiter's eye," advised Bobbie Rosenfeld.[94] Male coaches disappeared as more and more young men joined the forces and went overseas, with women taking over the coaching and training or whatever else they had to do to keep their sports going. Unable to find a greenskeeper, the women of Toronto's Kew Beach Lawn Bowling Club, some over 60, rolled up their sleeves, pushed around the heavy roller and lawn mower, and manicured their own greens.[95] Well-known women athletes and officials joined the many voluntary service corps, or were recruited into the armed forces, and became too busy to continue with sport.

Competitions, especially Dominion tournaments, were routinely cancelled, as were all European and world championships, including the 1940 and 1944

Olympics. Not everyone agreed with this policy, arguing that championships were important in keeping up morale and maintaining fitness. Myrtle Cook, for example, felt strongly that the WAAF of C should continue to sponsor major events: "young women should have their opportunity of championship whirls, some compensation for long months of training and keeping themselves in top physical shape. Perhaps it escapes the championship isolationists that it is vitally important that the womanhood of Canada should be physically fit in these times."[96] Early in the war, Phyllis Griffiths used her column in the *Toronto Telegram* to make a plea for carrying on as usual, but admitting that changes were inevitable:

> While we're gasping and gaping over the new war news, let's remember — those of us who have anything to do with girls' sport — that the less we talk about withdrawing from this, and abandoning the other, the better for the morale of all concerned.
>
> Certainly, to meet conditions, we'll have to make changes in the set-ups of the various sports. Long and expensive trips are out; teams have got to be allowed to sign extra players so that games can go on when some girls are detained by night war work; fancy equipment must be forgotten, and we'll be using softballs until the covers are off and basketballs till they're bulged and battered.
>
> But we've got to have sport and athletic recreation, both for participants and spectators, and with more young men going on active service all the time, the girls are going to have to shoulder more of the playing field task.[97]

Although many women entered the armed forces during the war, and thousands more laboured in the war industries, the vast majority of Canadian women contributed to the war effort through unpaid labour in the home or volunteer work in their community, and sportswomen were no exception. They did this in several ways: One was to raise money for the war effort, another was to entertain the troops through sport, and yet another was to provide healthful recreation for girls and women. Across the country there were countless examples of local women's sport groups raising money for a variety of war-related projects and agencies. The Canadian Ladies Golf Union, for instance, postponed all national and provincial championships and used golf as a means to raise money for war charities such as the Red Cross. Through tournaments, individual club donations, and by selling a poster with the word "Spitfire" spelled out in golf tees, the CLGU sent $40,000 to the Wings for Britain Fund. In all, the CLGU raised more than $81,000 during the war years, enough for two aeroplanes, and CLGU sewing rooms turned out thousands of clothes for war-stricken victims.[98] Similarly, the WAAF of C, especially the Ontario branch, organized its registered athletes to collect and make clothing for British children through its "Bundles for Britain" fund.

With large numbers of soldiers, sailors, and airmen based or training in Toronto, the Sports Service League was created to provide equipment and entertainment for the troops. Roxy Atkins Campbell, an international track athlete and able sports official, chaired the League's women's section, helping to organize women's softball and basketball games, as well as multi-sport carnivals at the Coliseum in Exhibition Park, where many armed forces personnel were billeted. Sometimes only troops were admitted to the event; at other times, admission was 10 cents for anyone in uniform and 25 cents for everyone else. On 17 December 1941, for instance, some 10,000 spectators were "packed to the rafters" in the Coliseum to watch the Simpson's Volunteers, an all-star basketball team from Toronto, battle the Iowa-state champion Stenos to a 37–27 loss.[99] Sport-military carnivals at the Coliseum, with local women athletes taking tickets and selling programs, were enormously popular and highly successful at raising money for the *Toronto Evening Telegram*'s British War Victims Fund. They featured a variety of sport demonstrations, a competitive game of women's basketball, band music and military displays, and sometimes a special attraction, creating a circus-like atmosphere. At one carnival, the American world-class runner Stella Walsh was pitted against a male competitor, losing by a fraction to the appropriately-named RCAF champion, Flight-Sergeant Lightfoot.[100]

In order to promote health, fitness, and readiness among Canadians, and to remove the stigma of "playing in time of war," the federal government encouraged the expansion of sport and recreation programs for industries, churches, athletic clubs, and leisure time agencies like the YWCA and YMCA.[101] Industrial sport, especially in the expanding wartime production sector, became an essential aspect of national defence and was regarded as a wartime necessity especially for women. With the reserve pool of male civilian workers fast depleting, thousands of women were recruited and placed in the industrial plants that manufactured guns, ammunition, tanks, ships, planes, and other equipment of war. In September 1939, for example, only 119 women worked in aircraft plants, but by February 1944 the number had risen to over 25,000, nearly one-third of the workforce.[102] Since increased production was key to the war effort, industrial plants began to concern themselves with the health and welfare of their new, principally female, employees.

The General Engineering Company (GECO) was a huge wartime plant built in 1941 in Scarborough, Ontario. More than three-quarters of its employees were women, the majority of whom were married. It soon established its own recreation department with a male sports director and three full-time female assistants and built indoor facilities to accommodate shuffleboard, badminton, volleyball, deck tennis, darts, and practice golf, with outdoor facilities for volleyball, badminton, tennis, horseshoes, softball, and hockey. Arrangements were also made for employees to swim, ride, and ski at convenient locations. New employees were asked to specify their recreational or athletic training and interests, and every effort was made to encourage them to participate in a comprehensive array of recreational offerings. Swimming and riding were the most popular activities, followed by health and beauty classes, bowling, and badminton.[103] Smaller industrial plants like the John Inglis Company in Toronto and the Westclox factory in Peterborough, whose wartime employees were mostly women, also increased their emphasis on sports and developed innovative recreation programs for their employees.[104]

Shirley Boulton, who wrote a "Women in Sport" column for the *Winnipeg Tribune* in the early 1940s, asked: "Will girls' sport ever take the place of men's as a crowd drawer in wartime?"[105] She concluded that it might only be in places like Toronto, bulging with troops, where women's basketball was providing first-rate entertainment to capacity crowds. Winnipeg, she argued was also populated with airforce blue and khaki, and she saw no reason why girls' softball, especially assisted by a peppy military band, could not attract the crowds. In many ways, women's sport benefited from increased wartime interest, especially among male members of the armed forces who were treated to highly competitive basketball and softball games, and skilful displays of other sports like figure skating and badminton. Although major tournaments and championships were cancelled, competitions at the local, provincial, and sometimes national level continued, especially if there was an opportunity to raise money for the many war funds.

Like millions of ordinary Canadians, women athletes and sport organizations contributed to the overall war effort. Although sport suffered, it recovered quickly in the immediate postwar era, but with a different emphasis and perspective. Like all areas of social life in postwar Canada, change was inevitable.

CHAPTER 4

SWEETHEART HEROINES: ATHLETIC AND LOVELY

Dear Barbara Ann: Your public would
Prefer to show its gratitude
With tributes rare and wonderful,
And, preferably, tangible.
A rope of pearls, a wrap of mink
A private indoor skating rink,
A larger Buick, still, and creamier,
With testimonials from the Premier.
But since such gifts are out of line
We send this simple Valentine —
A license, issue to your art,
To skate school figures on our heart.

Mary Lowrey Ross, *Saturday Night*, 1948

The Valentine tribute to Canada's most loved sweetheart of the postwar era, figure-skater Barbara Ann Scott, ran in the normally staid national magazine *Saturday Night*. The full-page coverage featured a stunning photo of the skater taken by famous Ottawa photographer Yousuf Karsh. Dressed in an off-the-shoulder, white ruffled frock, and exquisite necklace, with a crown of tiny flowers in her hair, she was the epitome of loveliness and femininity. Surrounding the picture were hearts, stars, frilly lace, and a line drawing of a costumed skater performing a graceful skating pose. Her athleticism erased, Scott's physical beauty was the centrepiece of this tribute to her artistry and success.

Barbara Ann Scott was the first Canadian to win a figure skating world championship (in 1947) and Olympic gold medal (in 1948), after these events had been cancelled for several years due to the war in Europe. She touched the souls of Canadians in a way that no athlete has before or after. Her place in sporting history, magnificent accomplishments aside, had a great deal to do with timing, something she recognizes herself: "I think it was because after the war, when everything was down and gloomy and it was the first time a world or Olympic figure skating title came to Canada." At age 18, after a group of her late father's friends raised $10,000 to finance her trip, Scott was sent to Davos, Switzerland, in February 1947 for the European championships and then on to Stockholm, Sweden, for the world competition. She remembers going "with the blessings of Canada, with lucky charms and telegrams. When I won ... it was something that was cheerful, something they could be happy about. I was kind of adopted as everybody's little girl, which was very sweet and kind."[1]

Scott first learned to skate during the late 1930s at the prestigious Minto Skating Club in Ottawa, where she soon caught the attention of coach Otto Gold.[2] Still very young (she was 11 in 1940), there was no need for her to turn professional during the war, unlike other top Canadian skaters of this time, who were forced to pursue their careers with shows like the Ice Follies and Ice Capades if they wanted to skate at all. As a "little bundle of cuteness," she captured the Canadian junior ladies' title in 1940, having competed in the event for the first time the previous year, and became the youngest skater ever to win a national title. She moved up to the senior championship the next year, still diminutive and only 12, but it would be three more years before she won the senior title a few months before D-Day in 1944 (no competition took place in 1943 due to the war). Interestingly, the junior championship that year was won by Suzanne Thouin of Montreal, the first time a French-Canadian had done so.[3] By 1947, Scott had won four national senior titles and was ready to test her performance against the best skaters in Europe and the world, which would mean skating outdoors in frigid temperatures and unpredictable ice. Against 21 competitors from seven countries and before 15,000 spectators, she won both the compulsory school figures and the colourful free-skating competition with a display "unparalleled since Sonja Henie flashed into prominence as the 'Norwegian Doll' in 1936."[4]

Scott returned home a national heroine and was royally fêted, especially in Ottawa, her hometown, which showed its gratitude with the gift of a canary yellow Buick convertible. Two months later, she was forced to give it back, when Avery Brundage, then vice-president of the International Olympic Committee charged that acceptance of the car violated the amateur code.[5] In Prague next winter Scott successfully defended her European title, and then on terrible, slushy outdoor ice in St. Moritz, her event postponed and almost moved elsewhere because of the melting conditions, she won the Olympic gold medal, affirming not only her superior skating ability, but also her grit and determination. She capped off that incredible European trip of 1948 by again winning the world title in Davos, Switzerland. "She is a thoroughbred," gushed a Montreal sportswriter, "the sort of person who comes along once in a life time to enable and glorify sport, erasing much of the dross that surrounds it."[6]

A tumultuous reception awaited Scott upon her return to Canada's capital, where children were let out of school, and she toured the main streets in a car strewn with spring daffodils. My family lived in Ottawa, and I remember seeing her as she passed by, but was too young to understand who she was or what she represented. I had, however, no desire to acquire a Barbara Ann Scott doll, complete with skates, fur-trimmed dress and tiara, because to do so would seriously damage my tomboy image. Like millions of other young girls of my generation, I took up figure skating, but secretly longed for black hockey skates, hoping one day to play with my real heroes, the stars of the Toronto Maple Leafs or the Montreal Canadiens, knowing full well that I could never be, in fact did not want to be, like Barbara Ann Scott. She was, as one commentator has observed, "a female role model that not only said all there was to say about femaleness at that time, but a model that implied being female meant being perfect."[7] Her name, spoken only with the utmost respect and admiration, was a social reprimand to those girls and women, less feminine, less perfect, who balked at dressing, speaking, and behaving like "ladies."

THE OTHER BARBARA ANN SCOTTS

If you ask Canadians to name a female figure-skater before Barbara Ann Scott, most cannot do so, such is the hold she has on our memories and knowledge. It is understandable that few remember skaters in the 1920s and 1930s like Cecil Eustace Smith or Constance (Wilson) Samuel, but immediately prior to Scott's reign in the mid-1940s, there were several skaters — Mary Rose Thacker, Norah McCarthy, Eleanor O'Meara, and sisters Dorothy and Hazel Caley, among them — whose careers would have been very different had the war not intervened. I tell their stories, if only briefly, because it is important to understand that Scott's phenomenal success was due in part to timing, to the fact that she was a young girl growing up during the war, and that, when it came to an end in 1945, making travel to Europe again possible, she was ready to compete at the world level. Had the war not necessarily changed the aspirations of older skaters at a similar stage in their amateur careers, perhaps any one would have become as famous and as admired as Barbara Ann Scott. They possessed similar qualities — beauty, charm, talent, and determination — and each was fortunate to grow up under privileged circumstances.

Mary Rose Thacker, from the Winnipeg Winter Club, won the Canadian senior ladies' title in 1939, 1941, and 1942, and was North American champion in

1940 and 1941. Trained by the best coaches in New York and London, skating and performing since she was four years old, she was also an expert swimmer and horsewoman, had studied ballet, dancing, and fencing, and spoke several languages. A "pretty girl, sweet and shy" with brown hair and hazel eyes — quite small in stature at five feet four inches and 115 pounds — she was portrayed as a "symphony on skates," a "will o' the wisp," and "graceful as a melody." Many predicted Thacker would capture the world titles; in fact, she was named to the 1940 Olympic team, but this event, along with all European and world skating championships, were cancelled. She had no choice but to turn professional and, after a brief stint performing in ice shows, applied her talents to coaching, becoming the first "pro" at the Vancouver Skating Club in 1945 and opening the first summer skating school in British Columbia two years later.[8]

At 19, Norah McCarthy, a "beautiful black-haired skating cutie," was a star in the famous Ice Follies, touring all over North America, and making a great deal of money. She had become a professional in 1942, having won the Canadian senior ladies' amateur championship in 1940, the pairs title (with Ralph McCreath) in 1939 and 1940, and the same North American championship in 1941. Norah and her younger sister Tasie had been skating since childhood. They were devastated when their father, a railway official, was transferred to North Bay, Ontario, because that city lacked a skating coach, but their mother brought them to Ottawa each winter to skate and train at the Minto Club. In summertime, the McCarthy sisters trained in the United States at the skating school in Lake Placid, often starring in the glitzy carnivals put on especially for tourists. Skating for eight months a year meant they were tutored privately. It all paid off. In 1938, Norah won the Canadian junior ladies' title, as did Tasie the following year. After winning the senior championship two years later, Norah was named to the 1940 Olympic team, but went nowhere abroad because of the war. Like Mary Rose Thacker before her, she was forced to become a professional in order to pursue a skating career. Before her rise to stardom with the Ice Follies, she often made weekend trips to Callander (outside of North Bay) to teach the growing Dionne quintuplets how to skate. With "hazel eyes, a tilted nose, an unaffected smile, and a slim, five-foot-six figure," combined with an all-round, but acceptable, athleticism (she played tennis, rode horses, swam, sailed, canoed, fished, and hunted), Norah McCarthy was everyone's ideal of the healthy Canadian outdoor girl.[9]

As a gangling teenager Eleanor O'Meara won her first singles skating title at the Toronto Granite Club in 1931. Five years later she vaulted into the senior ranks, stealing the senior Canadian title away from Constance (Wilson) Samuel, the perpetual winner for over a decade. She did it again in 1938, but lost out to Mary Rose Thacker and Norah McCarthy in the next few years. In 1941, she teamed up with husky six-foot Ralph McCreath (as did McCarthy before her), and together they won both the Canadian and North American senior pairs title. Described by a journalist as the "pretty, long-legged Canadian girl, with the flashing smile and freckled brow," she turned down many offers to skate professionally until the spring of 1943, when she signed with the Ice Capades. The war had dashed her hopes to compete in Europe, especially at the 1940 Olympics. She chose instead to perform throughout Canada and the United States at benefits and entertainment shows for the troops, until she learned that the big ice shows sold millions of war bonds by giving special performances to which admission could only be obtained by buying a victory bond. An immediate success, O'Meara was considered by some enthusiasts as the "greatest natural skating ballerina," greater even, according to a California columnist, than the legendary Sonja Henie. "Call it o-oomph, showmanship, or whatever you like," observed the Ice Capades press agent, "Eleanor O'Meara has learned to combine her great natural skating ability with her refreshing beauty and personality." She was, they said, a thoroughbred, and a skater with sparkle.[10]

Dorothy and Hazel Caley first learned to skate in their Toronto backyard, which their father flooded each winter for his five daughters. Their serious training and coaching took place at the Granite Club, where by the mid-1930s, the teen-aged Caley sisters were the women's pair champions of Toronto and district. This unique event was soon abolished, and the two sisters had to compete separately, with Dorothy winning the Canadian junior singles title in 1936 and the senior championship the following year. They much preferred to perform as a pair, or in the "fours" (two women and two men), winning the North American fours title (with Montgomery Wilson and the ubiquitous Ralph McCreath) in 1937. They, too, set their sights on the 1940 Olympics and an Australian tour, but of course were foiled by the war. Sonja Henie had seen the sisters perform as a pair and in 1940 persuaded them to join her touring ice revue as professionals. Their first show opened at the Rockefeller's brand new ice theatre at Radio City, New York. Soon they were stars, travelling all over North America, and second only to Henie herself in billing. They were, enthused one observer, "internationally known as daring improvisers, whose split second timing is a miracle of grace." The Calleys remained unaffected by their success, refusing to have a manager, spurning all movie offers, and skating only when they pleased. Hazel married in 1941 and took the next year off to have a child, while Dorothy skated by herself. By 1943, they were performing together again, "the greatest sister act in the business."[11] Another highly successful skating team was French-Canadian sisters Denise and Francine Benoit, who paired up after older brother Pierre and then his replacement, Elton Adair, went off to war, leaving Denise on the sidelines. She persuaded the Ice Capades producer to give her younger sister Francine a chance, and the two became a vivacious, fast skating tandem in high demand.[12]

Figure skating, and the possibility of stardom in an ice show represented a dream for many young Canadian girls, especially those whose parents could afford the skating lessons, special coaches, and travel to competitions. The most promising were taken out of school and tutored at home or on the road, in search of the best opportunities and training, also requiring considerable financial resources. The father of Megan Taylor, a British figure skater who in 1942 was world champion, estimated it cost at least $50,000 to make his daughter a star.[13] By 1946, 20 per cent of the Ice Capades' cast was Canadian, and many more were considered in the frequent auditions seeking new talent.[14] Soon after her Olympic glory, Barbara Ann Scott turned professional, a glamorous if not somewhat reluctant celebrity, eventually replacing her own idol, Sonja Henie, in the Hollywood Ice Revue. At her peak, she earned over $100,000 a year, not just from skating, but also from lucrative product endorsements of skates, clothing, dolls, and other products like Canada Dry ginger ale, making her the first woman athlete in Canada to be transformed from a celebrity to a commodity.[15]

SPORT AND THE POSTWAR SOCIAL-SEXUAL ORDER

The immediate postwar period of women's sport in Canada was characterized by a remarkable emphasis on beauty, grace, femininity, and, for some athletes, glamour. Gone for the most part were debates about whether or not sport would masculinize women competitors, because the proof was there for all to see: so long as women participated in "beauty producing" sports like figure skating, synchronized swimming, or gymnastics, and as long as they looked feminine on the tennis or badminton courts, golf courses, and ski hills, they would not be criticized. For example, the Wurtele twins, noted skiing stars of the 1940s, were described in a *Maclean's* article as follows:

> What are they like these sisters of the skis? First of all, they are good-looking girls. When they sit together on a chesterfield under a standing lamp in the living room of their home, you notice they have the kind of healthy, bright hair that looks as though it has been slightly bleached from long hours in the sun. They have clear skin, good color and merry brown eyes. They are not Amazons; neither are they will-o-the-wisps. They stand five feet six and have identical weights.[16]

But athletes sweating on the basketball courts, softball pitches, ice hockey rinks, and the cinder tracks were suspect, their femininity (although rarely their sexuality) continually questioned. The public was assured, over and over again, that those who achieved success were feminine and womanly, and when their competitive days were over, they would glide happily into married domesticity and fulfill their natural responsibility to have children. The exceptions were unusual and few.

The long wartime period had disrupted the entire society, especially the gender order — the pattern of relations between men and women and what it means to be masculine or feminine. The loss of hundreds of thousands of young men, many permanently, to the battlefields in Europe and elsewhere and the mobilization of equally large numbers of women into the war effort at home sharply challenged long-held social conventions of men as breadwinners and women as wives and mothers. The entrance of women into the army, navy, and airforce, as well as into the non-traditional trades required by the munitions factories, aircraft plants, shipyards, and war industries in general brought about societal disapproval including "jitters over femininity."[17] There was considerable ambivalence over women joining the armed forces; consequently, various efforts were directed at assuring their femininity and heterosexual attractiveness. These included fashionably designed, well-fitting uniforms, beauty culture classes, glamour shots of especially attractive servicewomen, and, most important of all, the insistence that women's employment in the forces was only temporary, after which they would return to their homes and normal jobs. Recruitment propaganda stressed that women would not become less marriageable once they joined the forces; indeed, the announcement of military weddings became a regular feature on the women's war effort sections of daily newspapers. Although the war provided many Canadian women with opportunities for travel, work, and responsibility, and temporarily caused a destabilization in the traditional sexual division of labour, it also reinforced traditional notions of womanhood and femininity.

With the Allied victory in Europe in the spring of 1945, weary veterans returned home to be greeted with admiration and gratitude by their government and the general public alike. Men, and especially male veterans, were given preference in employment; women were encouraged by both government and industry to return home and stay there. Wartime incentives to draw women into the labour force were cancelled, and there were few opportunities for them to retain the skilled jobs and high wages of the war years. Working mothers were considered a serious threat to the idealized image of the nuclear family, especially as the numbers of married women in the workforce continued to increase.[18] In the federal public service, for example, married women were immediately discharged (and barred from employment until 1955). Working-class women were redirected from lucrative employment in manufacturing to uninteresting and poorly paid jobs in domestic service. The idealized women's life changed dramatically from one of employment and productivity during the war (while at the same time taking care of the home front) to an emphasis immediately after the war on domesticity and raising their children (of the postwar baby boom). Media portrayals of married women suggested stereotypical "happy homemakers, winsome wives, and magnanimous mothers."[19]

The heterosexual nuclear family, as the primary stabilizing influence on both individuals and the nation as a whole and as the only site of legitimate sexual behaviour, was the cornerstone of the social-sexual order in the postwar era. Having a family, and being part of a family, were important markers of social belonging and conformity to prevailing standards: "the formation of families and the raising of children was, at root, a patriotic obligation." The state of the family, maintains sociologist Mary Louise Adams, was *the* central concern of postwar life in Canada. The ideal Canadian family was urban, white, Anglo-Saxon, and middle or upper class; the fact that many Canadians, by choice or circumstance, lived in families very different from this image was conveniently ignored. In her study of postwar youth and the making of heterosexuality, Adams argues that the postwar social-sexual order in Canada was constructed and maintained through a variety of sites including schools, courtrooms, social-work agencies, municipal bureaucracies, popular advice literature, and mainstream social comment.[20] To this list, I would add sport, especially women's sport.

High-profile women athletes in the postwar period contributed to and strengthened the prevailing social-sexual order in several ways. Several images were present at the same time, each based in reality, but also idealized and often contradictory. One was of beauty and glamour, of well-known celebrities earning money through talent and hard work, like Barbara Ann Scott and other professional figure-skaters in the travelling ice shows. Another image was that of the "glamazon," like Jackie Macdonald, a tall, beautiful, statuesque bleached-blonde, who in the 1950s was Canada's best shot putter and among the top discus throwers. Strength, muscles, and beauty were strangely incompatible, and, when present, femininity and womanliness needed to be constantly reasserted. The *Canadian Sport Monthly*, which in the 1950s was the official magazine for golf, skiing, tennis, and badminton, frequently ran photos of comely women athletes in bathing suits (sand-skiing for instance), which prompted one male reader to compliment them for their "cheesecake."[21]

Yet another image was that of anybody's daughter, the girl-next-door with special talent, whom all would be proud to claim, providing she was white, Anglo-Saxon, and preferably from English Canada; swimmers Marilyn Bell and Helen Stewart, golfer Marlene Stewart, and skiers Lucile Wheeler and Anne Heggtveit fit this role. These were wholesome, normal girls, the sort parents liked their sons to date and eventually marry. Indeed, they did get married, sometimes in the middle of successful athletic careers, which frequently brought an end to competition, but in some cases only a brief hiatus while they produced several children.

Thus, another image became firmly established in this era, that of the competing mother, although as we will see shortly through the life stories of several such
women, medical and public opinion were rarely on their side.

It is also no accident that the high profile Canadian women athletes who
emerged in the postwar era and throughout the 1950s were from individual sports
like figure skating, golf, skiing, badminton, diving, swimming, speed skating, and
gymnastics. Figure-skaters Barbara Ann Scott, Marilyn Ruth Take, Suzanne
Morrow, Frances Dafoe, and, later in the 1950s, Barbara Wagner and Marie
Jelinek, were often in the sports news. Such was also the case with golfing
phenomenon Marlene Stewart (later Streit), who probably received more
sustained press coverage than any other Canadian woman athlete of this era.
Skiing twins Rhona and Rhoda Wurtele, whose sporting careers were affected by
the war, were media favourites, as were the highly successful Lucile Wheeler and
Anne Heggtveit, two of Canada's best skiers. No event received as much media
attention as 16-year-old Marilyn Bell's astonishing swim across Lake Ontario in
1954, although her subsequent conquests of the English Channel and the Straits
of Juan de Fuca were also highly publicized. Often in the news was her older,
more audacious contemporary, Winnie Roach Leuszler, unique because she was
a mother and sometimes pregnant (eventually she had five children) when she
swam those exhausting marathons. Many a courageous young woman in this era
sought fame (and money) by attempting to swim across a large body of water.
Less well-known athletes in other sports, but no less successful, were diver Irene
MacDonald, gymnast Ernestine Russell, water-skier Carol Anne Duthie, and
badminton experts Claire Lovett and Marjory Shedd.

Some sports were non-Olympic ones, and therefore outside the jurisdiction of
official control, such as the Canadian Olympic Association. Athletes who excelled
and sought international competition often did so on their own, which meant
they came from privileged backgrounds and could afford the costs of training,
coaching, equipment, and competitive experience. As such, sports like figure skating, golf, skiing, gymnastics, synchronized swimming, badminton, and tennis
were more attractive and acceptable to girls from white, middle-, and upper-class
families, but overall participation was low. Sports more accessible to those less
privileged — track and field and speed skating are good examples — suffered
from a lack of official support and organization, with few ways to identify talent
and to coach and train those with potential.[22] After the war and during the 1950s,
track and field athletes, as well as swimmers, were able to compete in several international venues, among them the Summer Olympics, the British Empire and
Commonwealth Games, and the Pan-American Games, but they received little
media attention except during these special events. Certainly many more women
played the usual team sports — softball, basketball, volleyball, and less often field

and ice hockey — but their outstanding players were rarely identified, and the sports themselves relegated to the back pages of the sporting news, dominated more so than ever by men's professional sport.

"Coloured" athletes (sometimes referred to as "dusky") were still very unusual in this era, even though in 1945, Myrtle Cook wondered what all the fuss was about when baseball player Jackie Robinson, the first Black in the major leagues, signed with the Montreal Royals. As she pointed out in her column, women athletes of colour had long since made their mark on the Canadian scene. She mentioned Barbara Howard, the first visible minority athlete to compete for Canada internationally, as well as Jean Lowe, the current Ontario track champion, and several others.[23] The most accomplished Black athlete of this decade was Rosella Thorne of the Montreal Olympic Club, an outstanding track athlete who was a member of several international teams. Born in 1930, she attended Commercial High School in Montreal and first came to prominence at an international indoor track meet in Hamilton in 1949. She was also a good basketball player and, with Violet McKenzie, was one of two Black members of the Montreal Meteors, Canadian intermediate champions in 1950. With money tight, the 1950 British Empire Games team was drastically reduced, but Thorne made the team and went to Auckland, New Zealand, where she competed in the 80-metre hurdles, broad jump, and relay. As a result of her achievements that year, she was awarded both the Velma Springstead Trophy and the Montreal *Daily Star* Trophy. The Black community in Montreal were proud of her accomplishments, and she remembers several events where she was honoured and given gifts. She was a member of the 1952 Summer Olympics team in Helsinki and the 1954 British Empire and Commonwealth Games team in Vancouver, after which she retired from competition. Reflecting on whether she encountered any racism during her career, Thorne told the story about being on board ship on the way to New Zealand and a little girl called her a "nigger." She wanted to ignore it, but her teammates "went into orbit," complained to the girl's mother, and thereafter trained early in the morning so Thorne would not be further embarrassed.[24]

GIRLS NEXT DOOR AND COMPETING MOTHERS

Seventeen-year-old golfer Marlene Stewart from Fonthill, rated the top athlete in Ontario in 1951, was frequently described as a pert teenager, a bright-eyed miss with a ready smile, or the freckled-faced Little Miss Stewart.[25] Barely over five feet tall, she was often called a child, making her achievements all the more notable given her diminutive stature. Sportswriter Trent Frayne described her as the "chattiest, cheeriest, chirpiest kid-next-door who ever snapped her bubblegum in the high-school gymnasium."[26] She had astounded the experts by winning the Ontario Ladies' championship, as well as both the Canadian Ladies' Closed and Open amateur championships against older, more experienced competition. Portrayed in the popular media as a normal, teenage "bobby-soxer," also a "natural-born tomboy," Stewart went from obscurity to adulation in just a few years, her normality repeatedly stressed:

> She wears sweaters and skirts and two-tone saddle shoes and white ankle socks, lives with her mother and dad and thirteen-year-old sister Dolly in Fonthill, a rolling pleasant little town of fourteen hundred on the south side of a hill twelves miles northwest of Niagara Falls. She prepares the family meal every evening, looks puzzled if anyone asks whether she has favorite exotic dishes. "Heck, no," she says, "just lots of meat and potatoes."[27]

By 1957, Marlene Stewart had twice been awarded the Lou Marsh Trophy as Canada's outstanding athlete, as well as the Velma Springstead Trophy, and in four years (1952, 1953, 1956, 1957) she was voted the top women athlete by the Canadian sports press. She won four Canadian Open and six Canadian Closed championships, plus the British and the United States titles, all in the space of six years. According to the pundits, her future choices were simple — marriage or professional golf — and if the former, it "would see the end of her winning stature."[28] Canada's favourite daughter was married in April 1957, but she continued to play tournament golf for a year or so, at which point she took three years off to have two children. When she returned to competition in 1963, she again won the Canadian Closed and Open championships against the new crop of women golfers, including Gail Harvey, Betty Stanhope Cole, Judy Darling, and Gayle Hitchens, dispelling any doubts about whether she could have succeeded professionally had she chosen that route. That same year she was awarded the Bobbie Rosenfeld Trophy for the fifth time as Canada's outstanding woman athlete.[29]

Although three years younger, marathon swimmer Marilyn Bell had much in common with Marlene Stewart. Only teenagers when they first came to prominence, both were from middle-class families. Marlene's father owned an electrical appliance store on Fonthill's main street, and the family lived behind the store. Marilyn's father was a grocery store buyer, and due to the shortage of postwar housing in Toronto, his family lived in an apartment over the store; her mother had been a stenographer before their marriage. Both athletes had one younger sister. When Marlene was 12, like the boys with whom she skated, skied, and played ball, she started caddying at the Lookout Point golf club near her home, saving up enough money to buy her own clubs. Gordon McInnes, the club's pro, rewarded his tireless caddie by showing her how to hit a golf ball and patiently correcting her faults. She entered her first tournament in 1949. That same year, 12-year-old Marilyn came second in the CNE junior one-mile swim. Her mother enjoyed swimming and had prompted her young daughter to take lessons, first at Oakwood pool. When it became clear that Marilyn preferred distance swimming over sprints, she came under the tutelage of Gus Ryder at the Lakeshore Swimming Club, where some of the best marathon swimmers in Canada trained. At 14, Marilyn turned professional in order to earn money for university, winning $300 in 1952 when she came fourth in the women's three-mile CNE swim. The following year she came third and added $500 to her bank account.[30] But in the end, Marlene and Marilyn differed in that the golfer remained an amateur and competed all her life — still today in senior tournaments — whereas the swimmer became a professional at an early age, ending her career after just a few years, so that she is remembered as she was in the mid-1950s: a "sweet, normal Canadian girl" who did something truly remarkable.

Marilyn Bell was all set to compete in the 1954 CNE marathon swim, when both the women's and men's events were cancelled. The CNE signed a highly publicized $10,000 agreement with 34-year-old American marathoner Florence Chadwick, giving her $2,500 in advance, with the rest to be awarded if she completed a swim across Lake Ontario. Earlier in July, Marilyn had competed (and won $1,150) in her first major marathon swim, coming seventh overall as the first woman to finish in the 26-mile Atlantic City ocean marathon around Absecon Island. More determined than ever to tackle both Lake Ontario and the famous Chadwick, Marilyn sought sponsorship (through Alexandrine Gibb) from the *Toronto Star* after its rival, the *Telegram*, turned her down. CNE officials relented on the condition she swim "for the glory of Canada," refusing to guarantee any prize money if she was successful. Winnie Roach Leuszler, the first Canadian to swim the English Channel three years before, now 28 and the mother of three children, also decided to try her luck, although she was not sponsored in any way.

In an article for *Maclean's* about the swim, June Callwood suggested that no other Canadian human interest event had stirred the reading and listening public so deeply, except possibly the Moose River mining disaster in Nova Scotia in 1936.[31] This may still be the case. Nearly 50 years later, I am astounded at the extended press coverage the swim received, especially in the Toronto dailies, although, as Callwood pointed out, the event provoked a bizarre newspaper war between the *Toronto Star* and *Telegram*. With no live television to record the swim itself, begun late at night on September 3 from Youngstown in New York, and no way to keep track of the swimmers except through sporadic press reports, the focus shifted to the young schoolgirl, who the next night, after swimming 40 miles in 21 hours, touched the concrete breakwater at Toronto's Sunnyside.

Florence Chadwick, exhausted and sick from the rolling swells, had been pulled out several hours earlier. Winnie Roach Leuszler suffered enormous bad luck. In the dark and confusion at the start, she soon lost contact with her guide boat, turned back, and was picked up by a fisherman who returned her to shore. She started again the following morning, but with the water churning and suffering cramps after swimming nearly two-thirds of the way, she too was pulled out.[32]

Canada's "little lady of the Lake" was fêted and honoured unlike any woman athlete who had gone before. In his book *Swim to Glory*, published barely two months afterwards, Ron McAllister says she was the "subject of more rumours and conjecture, more speculation, imagination, more madness and frantic adulation than any other Canadian girl of any era."[33] There was a ticker-tape parade and celebration in Toronto; interviews with *Time, Life*, and numerous other magazines; and 25,000 requests to the *Toronto Star* for a free photo of Marilyn. She accumulated gifts, prizes, and contracts worth $50,000, and made countless radio, television, and personal appearances throughout Ontario. As a 12-year-old teenager, thoroughly smitten by Marilyn and her magnificent feat, I excitedly sought (and got) her autograph when she came to an Ottawa shopping mall. There was talk of movie stardom, but in the end, Marilyn decided to return to her studies at Loretto College School, train for future swims, and continue to teach swimming at the Lakeshore Swimming Club. On 31 July 1955 she became the youngest person (at 17) to swim the English Channel. The following summer she attempted to cross the Juan de Fuca Strait from Victoria on Vancouver Island to Port Angeles on the United States side, regarded as the Mount Everest of marathon swimming, but failed. Barely conscious after battling the cold, rough waters for nearly 10 hours, she was pulled out. She tried again in a few weeks, this time swimming from Port Angeles to Victoria, and succeeded in 11 hours 35 minutes, becoming only the fifth swimmer and second woman to swim the strait.[34] In 1957, like Marlene Stewart Streit a few months before her, Canada's other favourite daughter got married. But unlike her contemporary, Marilyn moved to the United States, giving up swimming and her university studies to devote her energies to marriage, domesticity, and starting a family.[35]

While professional swimmers grabbed most of the headlines during the 1950s, Canada's amateur swimmers, especially the women, were equally as talented and successful, due mostly to the establishment of proper training and coaching regimes. Competitive swimming had not been allowed to advance, especially during wartime when most competition was halted, so that the team representing Canada at the 1948 Olympics was very much outclassed. Kaye McNamee, one of Canada's top freestyle specialists at the time and a member of the team (with Irene Strong, Vivian King, and Joyce Court) explained that it was impossible to be world class if you only trained twice a week.[36] They were expected to be ambassadors for Canada, rather than potential medal winners. McNamee was also a member of the 1952 Helsinki team (with Irene Strong, Lenore Fisher, and Gladys Priestly) where, although the Canadians improved their performance, they still lagged far behind the well-trained Americans, Australians, and East Europeans. However, at the 1955 Pan-American Games in Mexico (it was the first time Canada entered this competition), Beth Whitall from Montreal was the star performer, winning both the 400-metre freestyle and 100-metre butterfly; Helen Stewart from Vancouver won the gold medal in the 100-metre freestyle; and Lenore Fisher of Ocean Falls, BC, took the 100-metre backstroke. These victories were particularly sweet, because, without a world championship, it was one of their few opportunities to go against swimmers from the United States. At the 1956 Melbourne Olympics, several swimmers reached the finals of their events, including Virginia Grant from Toronto, Sara Barber of Brantford, Ontario, and Montreal's Beth Whitall. The 400-metre relay team finished fifth, and diver Irene MacDonald came third in the 3-metre event. Canada was at last approaching a "world power" in women's swimming.

Helen Stewart's competitive career is a good example of how Canadian swimmers in this era benefited from a much improved approach to coaching and training, yet at the same time was disadvantaged by insufficient technical and scientific knowledge; she was, in fact, on the cusp of the changes that made Canada into an international swimming force. She began swimming as a youngster in the mid-1940s at the Vancouver Amateur Swim Club under the legendary Percy Norman. As she improved she began to take part in small, inter-club competitive meets, then the Canadian championships; when she was 16, she made the 400-metre medley relay team at the 1954 British Empire and Commonwealth Games in Vancouver. Prior to this, she trained once a day, usually a couple of times a week, although a month before the Commonwealth event, she trained twice a day, every day. Coach Norman's assistant was Howard Firby, who was much more interested in the science of swimming, and by the mid-1950s Stewart was training with him exclusively at his new club, the Dolphins. Under Firby, her training in the water increased substantially; she was tested regularly for fitness, given advice on diet, and provided with dryland training exercises. Often described in the media as pert, wee, dainty, petite, and, on one occasion, "fresh-as-dew little mermaid," Stewart was in reality five feet seven inches in height, a solid 135 pounds, and still growing. Her best year was in 1955 when in March at the Pan-Am Games, she won a gold medal. Later that same year, she shattered several national records at the provincial and national championships and swam in the United States Nationals, doing very well. All of this earned her the BC Athlete of the Year Award and the Beatrice Pines Trophy (Canada's outstanding woman swimmer of the year). Although she broke the world record in the 100-yard freestyle in October

1956, just a few weeks later at the Olympics in Australia, she did not do as well as expected because she was tired and very much overtrained. "No one," she explained, "knew very much about tapering off." She married in 1958 and competed in swimming for the last time at the Pan-Am Games in Chicago the following year.37

As much as the media lauded the achievements of Canada's women athletes, the notion persisted that, because they were not under the same pressures as male athletes to train themselves for a career, they could have their "fling" with no thought to the future. Women athletes were able to enjoy their brief period of freedom before marriage and children; this, according to the pundits, explained why as a group they did better internationally in amateur sport than their male counterparts. It was not always recognized that Canada's most celebrated athletic daughters often came from relatively well-off families, who could afford to support their training and send them to competitions. This was particularly true for downhill skiing, which emerged as a sport for Canadian women in the mid-1930s with the formation of the first women's ski club, Montreal's Penguin Ski Club, whose members soon took up ski racing. In 1935, the Seigniory Club at Montebello instituted the first Dominion championships for women.38 During the 1940s, Canada's best hopes in skiing were the Wurtele twins, Rhona and Rhoda, but their competitive careers were severely curtailed by the war when most national and all international competitions were cancelled. Both were members of the 1948 Winter Olympics team competing in St. Moritz, but, due to a disastrous training accident, Rhoda did not compete, and Rhona fell twice during her downhill race, coming last. Both married in 1949, continuing to compete, which was unusual. Rhoda competed well into the 1950s and was a member of the 1952 Olympics team, earning a ninth place in the giant slalom.

Lucile Wheeler, the first Canadian ever to win a skiing medal at an Olympics (in 1956), gives credit to the Wurtele twins: "I learned a lot from them about sport and determination."39 Wheeler, whose family owned a resort lodge in the Laurentians in Quebec, learned to ski at an early age. At 12 she won the Canadian junior championships, at 14 she was a member of the Canadian team competing at the world championships, and at 16 was the youngest Olympian on the 1952 Canadian team. Winters spent in Europe under the tutelage of Pepi Salvenmoser in Kitzbühel, Austria, and her own talent and determination made her a world-class skier, culminating in the giant slalom and downhill titles at the world championships in 1958. "She might have been anyone's daughter" wrote the editors of *Canadian Sport Monthly* in their tribute, failing to note Wheeler's privileged background and the unique opportunities she had been afforded. In fact, her father estimated that her training and travel had cost him at least $30,000 over the years, which seems like a pittance now, although it was a good deal of money then. She retired the next year, acknowledging that the arduous career of a world champion skier would not mix with marriage and children.⁴⁰

I am not certain who came up with the term — perhaps Myrtle Cook — but Canada's top women skiers in the 1950s were often called "skierinas." It was meant as a compliment, but it also signalled that women skied differently than men, like ballerinas on snow with speed and grace. Aside from the Wurtele twins and Lucile Wheeler, top skiers, like Joanne Hewson, Rosemarie Schutz, Monique Langlais, Carlyn Kruger, Gigi Sequin, Nancy and Janet Holland, Faye Pitt, Claire Monaghan, and the incomparable Anne Heggtveit enjoyed considerable media attention and public support. Brought up in a skiing family in Ottawa, Heggtveit was just a shy youngster when, at 15, she surprised everyone by winning the prestigious 1954 Holmenkollen giant slalom in Norway over a field of world-class skiers. A broken leg the next year meant that her performance at the 1956 Cortina Olympics was respectable, but not what it should have been had she been fully recovered. She made up for it at the next Olympics in Squaw Valley by winning a gold medal in the slalom, a first for Canada. Her victory was no accident, since she was a perfect "case history of the arduous and expensive process by which world skiing champions are made," which included "nineteen years of skiing, the most careful grooming, and personal qualities of determination, courage and determination."⁴¹ Heggtveit retired after her Olympic victory, marrying a few years later.

In the period before the war, motherhood and competition were often seen as incompatible. There were few high-profile women who were both competitive athletes and mothers, although there could well have been many more at the recreational level, competing away from the public eye. Married women were mainly predominant in sports like golf and curling, presumably because it was unusual for single women to belong to the many mixed clubs where these sports took place (on the assumption they were seen as a threat). Although golf was certainly competitive and longstanding women's champion, Ada MacKenzie (who never married) was very much in the news, curling was considered more of a social sport. Whatever the sport, motherhood was thought to make a woman less competitive. When badminton player Kae Otten Grant, the Canadian champion in 1951, returned to competition three years after marriage and the birth of twins, the *Canadian Sport Monthly* asked: "Will Kae, now a devoted mother and wife, be the relentless competitor that she was?"⁴²

The old arguments about strenuous exercise making women unfit for motherhood continued to circulate, especially in sports like track and field, still dogged by claims of reproductive damage, physical masculinization, and lack of heterosexual appeal. Swimming, on the other hand, did not involve the high impact or jarring effects of running, jumping, hurdling, and throwing thought to damage female reproductive organs. Whereas track and field was an "ugly, muscle-bunch-ing sport," swimming was considered an "attractive, muscle-stretching one."[43] Most sports and physical activity, done moderately, were acceptable to prepare women for motherhood by making them strong and fit, but actual mothers (and worse still, those pregnant) competing, especially at a very high level, was a very different matter. Even the war and the role women played in it, either working in jobs usually reserved for men or facing physical dangers in war-ravaged Britain and Europe, did little to change attitudes towards mothers competing. After the war, these attitudes became more entrenched, but more women were willing to defy them and prove that motherhood, at least physically, had little to do with athletic competition. In fact, it might be an asset.

At the first Summer Olympics following the war, which were held in London in 1948, the most spectacular and successful athlete was a 30-year-old housewife and mother of two, who was also in the early stages of her third pregnancy. Fanny Blankers-Koen of the Netherlands, nicknamed the "Flying Dutchwoman," won four gold medals — in the 80, 100, 200-metre hurdles, and 4x100-metre relay — and perhaps would have won more had she not been prevented from competing in the high jump, long jump, and javelin by IOC rules limiting her to three individual events. She demonstrated to the world that pregnancy and motherhood had not diminished her athletic ability; she became a role model for women athletes refusing to let childbearing and raising children prevent them from fulfilling their potential. Two Canadian exemplars, although not nearly as well known as Blankers-Koen, but no doubt as gutsy and determined, were marathon swimmer Winnie Roach Leuszler and speed skater Doreen Ryan.

Born in 1926, Winnie Roach was the third oldest of 12 children. She honed her athletic skills on Toronto playgrounds, but it was swimming that attracted her the most and where she excelled. Her railway-worker father coached some of the professional marathon swimmers who swam at the CNE; he also started the Maple Leaf Swim Club in Port Credit to teach younger swimmers, including his daughter. Surprisingly, Eddie Roach was a non-swimmer, and his daughter claims never to have seen him in the water. Winnie began competing as a young child, and she would regularly race in the annual Port Credit River swims, a distance of a mile and a half. In 1937, at age 11, she competed in the one-mile senior women's championship swim at the CNE, placing seventh. After completing some high school, Winnie went to work at a variety of jobs, serving in the Canadian Women's Army Corp for a brief spell during the war. She married Morris Leuszler, a career soldier, in 1946 and soon started a family.

Winnie Roach Leuszler (the name she always used) made her professional swimming debut in 1947, when, just two months after the birth of her first child, she competed in the women's five-mile swim at the CNE. A photo in the Toronto *Telegram* shows Winnie, in bathing suit attire and holding her young baby, alongside her parents and a much younger sister, with the heading: "Mother of Two Months Old Baby Hopes to Win 5-Mile Swim." According to Winnie, she needed the prize money, did not have to pay her father to train her, and besides, she trained very little anyway. She placed second, winning $1,000 in prize money. She repeated the feat again in 1948, coming third, although this time she was three months pregnant with her second child, something her father revealed after she climbed from the water, very tired and suffering from severe stomach cramps. Several decades later, Winnie recalled that she was constantly told by race officials she should not be swimming, but she ignored them, got a doctor's approval, and went ahead anyway.[44]

By the early 1950s, Winnie was rated as one of the top marathon swimmers in the world through a poll conducted by a British newspaper, the *London Daily Mail*, which in 1950 sponsored the first, international cross-channel race. It was limited to 20 swimmers, who paid their way to England, although sponsors covered their living expenses and supplied the guide boats. Winnie, who had long dreamed of swimming the channel, convinced Toronto's *Telegram* to sponsor her trip (one-way) across the Atlantic for the second international race in 1951. By now, she was 25 and the mother of three children, the youngest being nine months. She asked a friend to care for the baby, entrusted the older two to nuns at the Carmelite orphanage, and off she went. Bad weather delayed the swim for several days, but on August 16 a flotilla of small ships accompanied the swimmers across the waters from Cap Griz Nez in France to the Dover port on the English side. With her father in the boat, Winnie did extremely well for the first 15 miles, but then leg cramps slowed her down, forcing her to swim against the strong tide: "You are ready to touch the cliffs and the next thing you know, they're fading away." She vividly remembers everything about the swim, including her father's constant encouragement: "Come on Winnie, you better hurry up — the kids want their ice cream — come on get going!" She finished the swim in 13 hours, 45 minutes, the second woman in the race and the seventh overall, and, most significant of all, the first Canadian ever to swim the English Channel. A *Toronto Star* reporter, in Winnie's boat for the entire swim, commented: "It was the greatest display of doggedness and self punishment that I for one have ever seen and anyone who underrates the ordeal of a channel swim doesn't know what he's talking about." Her prize money amounted to about $1,400, out of which she paid her own and her father's way home. They arrived back to a ticker-tape parade up Bay Street in Toronto, where at city hall, she was presented with a silver tea service. "Winnie is a real champion," declared the mayor.[45]

Now a celebrity, Winnie toured for a few weeks with a water show that travelled to various cities in Canada and the United States. When asked what she did in this show, her response was "look good!" Apparently, she would waterski and then be dropped off near shore, where she would swim in. While she was away, her mother looked after her children. She also announced she would attempt the 22-mile Catalina swim, but unfortunately encountered boat problems, and the swim never took place. The decision to swim Lake Ontario in 1954 came more by chance then planning, as explained earlier, and it was one of the few times she did not complete an endurance swim. She made two more attempts to cross that lake, once in July 1956, when she was pulled out after 18 hours, and again a few weeks later as an unofficial entry in a CNE-sponsored swim; this time she lasted only three hours. Winnie continued to swim and coach wherever she found herself, which was a good many places as she followed her husband to his military postings. She taught her children how to swim, and, when her eldest daughter touched the wall first in a race they swam together, she knew it was time to quit. She continued to give countless hours back to the sport through her work with the Red Cross Water Safety Program and the Royal Life Saving Society, as well as many aquatic clubs.[46]

By the time Doreen Mcleod Ryan was married in 1952 at age 21, she was the best woman speed skater in Canada, indeed in North America. She had come to prominence in 1947 by winning the national junior title, and followed this with winning the intermediate title in 1949 and finally the senior women's Canadian championship first in 1951 and again the following year, when she also won the North American title. Traditionally a working-class sport, competitive speed skating suffered during the Depression, when there was little money for the upkeep of skating ovals and the hosting of major championships. During the war, it saw further decline because, unlike other sports, speed skating could not be used to raise money for the war effort. The sport was still struggling to recover after the war, and there were several years in which national championships were not held because no city could afford to host them. Doreen Ryan remembers selling raffle tickets (three for a quarter) to raise money for the train trip from Edmonton to Sudbury in the winter of 1947 for the national championships. Along the way, competitors were picked up in Saskatoon and Winnipeg; when the train reached Sudbury, it was put on a siding and became the skaters' home during the competition.[47]

Between 1951 and 1964, Ryan won 10 senior titles and competed in both the 1960 Winter Olympics (the first time women's speed skating was an official event) in Squaw Valley, California, and the 1964 Olympics in Innsbruck, Austria, while at the same time giving birth to three children, the first in 1953 and the others in 1955 and 1960. Admonished by family and friends that strenuous athletic activity would negatively affect her ability to have children, Ryan ignored this advice, and her first two children "just happened." In order to keep training, she would squeeze in an early morning run before her husband and children awoke, get the family going for the day, often go to a part-time job, do her weight training over the noon hour, and, during the skating season, take her children to the oval while she trained, sometimes going out for an additional skate after they were in bed. She remembers no other contemporary speed skater who trained and competed under similar circumstances, but she was encouraged when she learned that the Russian women skaters, who dominated world competitions, were convinced that having children made them stronger.[48] Called "Canada's Mrs. Doreen Ryan — Edmonton housewife" by both male and female sportswriters of the day, Ryan resented the descriptor, pointing out that male athletes were never described in relation to their marital or domestic status (and for the most part are not today). Like Winnie Roach Leuszler, she was signalled out as being different, and, without saying it overtly, there were many commentators who wondered if as housewives and mothers they should be in the cold waters and on the skating ovals in the first place. Yet, at the end of the decade, when two married tennis players decided to withdraw for unexplained domestic reasons from the Canadian playoffs, they were chastised and threatened with suspension.[49]

One clear advantage of the competing mother was that her heterosexuality and womanliness were assured; her children were proof that not only was she attractive to the opposite sex, but she had suffered no damage to her reproductive organs through strenuous exercise. It was further confirmation that the childish "tomboy," one characteristic of which was an interest in sports and outdoor activities, had grown up and become a woman. To be a successful heterosexual required bringing one's gender into line with the prevailing norms, and for girls and teenagers this meant learning to be feminine, acquiring the skills of domesticity, and enjoying the company of men. Rarely was any direct connection made, or even insinuated, between tomboyism and eventual lesbianism.[50] There was also no media discourse — not even a hint — making the connection between being a women athlete and a lesbian.[51] Of course, this does not mean there were no lesbians in sport, which would be a ridiculous conclusion. It is likely that there was a lesbian presence in sport, just as there was anywhere else in society, but the extreme homophobia and the gender conservatism of the postwar era prevented lesbians, athletic or otherwise, from making their sexual preference known. An article in *Canadian Home Journal* in 1951, certainly one of the first on the topic, argued that lesbianism was not rare and that "we need to have more than a vague and horrified notion of what it is if we are to understand and help to solve the social problem it presents."[52] The size of the problem, suggested the author, was hidden behind a wall of secrecy and silence. He went on to recount the story of two fictional lesbians, one of whom had been a "hard-bitten tomboy," but the other shy and pretty, which provided little evidence that tomboyism was a predictor of lesbianism. Athletes I have interviewed, who were active in this time, indicate a range of opinions from acknowledging that lesbians existed, especially in team sports, to total denial of their presence. On one point they all agree — no one talked about it.

CONFRONTING THE "MANNISH" IMAGE

Softball continued to flourish in North America in the 1940s. By mid-decade it was estimated that some 10,000 girls and women were playing on organized soft-ball teams in Canada, from tiny communities to much larger ones, especially those with wartime industrial plants employing large numbers of women.[53] Although no team could claim to be Canadian champions, as there was still no Dominion tournament, several teams had ventured to the United States to play in the "world championships." Teams like Toronto's Lakeside Langleys, Sunday Morning Class, and Volunteer Simpsons had all played there, as had the Moose Jaw Royals from Saskatchewan and the Vancouver Western Mutuals. The Canadian teams, wrote one observer, "show more of the girlish side of the picture when it comes to the style of their play. Their actions in throwing and batting do not have the tinge of masculine play like the United States girls. They do not go in for boyish bobs and do not have the fire and fight of the average American team."[54] This may explain why the Canadian teams were regularly beaten by their American counterparts, in addition to the fact that by 1943 women's softball in the United States had become big business with the formation of the professional All-American Girls Softball League (AAGPBL, later called the All-American Girls Professional Baseball League) by chewing-gum magnate Philip K. Wrigley, owner of the Chicago Cubs major league baseball franchise. Concerned that the war would deplete men's major league baseball, Wrigley looked to women players to temporarily replace the men's game, a concern that did not materialize, and he soon sold his share in the AAGPBL to Arthur Meyerhoff, a close associate and advertising agent who ran the league until 1950.[55] Teams were initially located in four mid-western cities: the Kenosha Comets and the Racine Belles in Wisconsin, the South Bend Blue Sox in Indiana, and the Rockford Peaches in Illinois. At its peak, the AAGPBL had expanded to 10 cities, and drew hundreds of thousands of fans. A rival league, the National Girls Baseball League (also known as the Chicago Glamour League), was formed among a half dozen semi-pro teams in the Chicago area in 1944, leading to salary wars, talent raiding, and a nasty lawsuit.[56]

Players were needed for these teams, and in the case of the All-American league, the Chicago Cubs scouting network hunted for them throughout the United States and Canada. Of more than 600 women who played in the AAGPBL, even for just a few games or only one season, 64 were Canadian. The majority came from the prairie provinces, especially Saskatchewan, and the remainder from Ontario or British Columbia, with one lone player from Quebec.[57] Some became stars like Eleanor "Squirt" Callow from Winnipeg, a solid fielder who played for the Rockford Peaches from 1948 to 1954, becoming the Babe Ruth of the league with more home runs and triples than any other player in the league's history. Others had their moment of glory, like Olive "Ollie" (Bend) Little of the Moose Jaw Royals, an original member of the Rockford Peaches, who pitched the first no-hitter in league history. Some showed great promise, which unfortunately did not materialize when they joined the All-American. Thelma Golden, perhaps the best pitcher ever seen at Toronto's Sunnyside, was assigned to the Rockford Peaches in the first season, but quit before the end of spring training. Past her prime, she was expected to pitch to much younger power hitters in a gruelling summer schedule. A few players, like Helen (Sandiford) Nelson from Toronto played one season with the All-American, and then joined the rival National Girls Baseball League in Chicago, where softball rather than baseball was played, the pay was as good but the travel less, and there was little concern about the player's "femininity." Faye Burnham, who played softball in Vancouver for the Western Mutuals, was offered a weekly salary of $91 to play in the Chicago league, but chose not to because she was teaching and had no interest in working in the summer months. "Besides," she commented many years later, "some of them were pretty tough-looking specimens."[58]

One Canadian All-American player stands out above the rest for her skill, longevity, and enthusiasm. Following in the tradition of her eight brothers and sisters, Mary "Bonnie" Baker began playing softball in a Regina city league at age 12 as a catcher. Married at 17, she worked in the Army and Navy department store during the day and played ball for the company-sponsored team a couple of times a week. A Regina-based hockey scout named Hub Bishop told the Wrigley operation about Baker, and she was signed in 1943 to play for South Bend; she promised her soldier husband, who was on active duty overseas, that she would quit the moment the war ended. She also identified other top-ranked, promising players especially in the Regina area, including her sister Gene George, which partially explains why so many Canadian players in the AAGPBL came from Saskatchewan. Baker herself was an excellent fielding catcher and was named to the all-star team several times. She did not stop playing when her husband returned from the fighting, prolonging her career by switching to second base, and eventually becoming a player-manager, the first and only player to do so, for the struggling Kalamazoo Lassies in Michigan. She skipped the 1951 season to have a child, returning for one last season in 1952 as the league was winding down.

Mary Baker's "well-groomed style and dark good looks established her as the embodiment of the All-American virtues," and she was often chosen by the league to pose for publicity shots and act as a spokesperson.[59] Wrigley and Meyerhoff's genius in promoting the All-American was to distance it from the tarnished, "mannish" image of women's softball by insisting that players adopt the rules of men's baseball (the league soon lengthened the base paths, went to a smaller ball, abandoned underarm pitching for sidearm, and later switched entirely to overhand pitching). His theory was that fans, a good percentage being male, would be drawn to feminine and attractive women playing a man's game. "The more feminine the appearance of the performer, the more dramatic the performance," intoned the league handbook, which unequivocally stipulated how the players were to dress off the field (no shorts, slacks, jeans or anything "masculine"), wear their hair (off the shoulder, but no boyish bobs), apply cosmetics (always use lipstick), and how they were to behave in public (no smoking, drinking, obscene language, or "moral lapses").[60] Their playing uniform consisted of a belted tunic dress with short sleeves that buttoned up the front left side, coloured in pastel shades of either green, blue, yellow, or peach. Players accepted these rigid restrictions on dress and decorum simply as rules that had to be followed, especially if they wanted to keep their jobs. Manitoban Evelyn "Evie" Wawryshyn, who played for several teams in the league between 1946 and 1951, was never bothered by the emphasis on femininity, nor did she think the necessity to look attractive inhibited her play:

> I had no trouble with it at all, really and truly. It was just a rule, and I figured I had to adhere to the rules. So you wore skirts in public; you got used to it. It just came naturally to put on your skirts and blouses and saddle shoes; it's a nice, comfortable look.
>
> You mean, would you not perform as well because you had that feeling you should look feminine? You must perform daintily? No, I didn't do it that way, and I'm sure the other girls didn't put something on or pretend to be something they weren't; they played just the way God intended them to play.[61]

The AAGPBL came to an end in 1954. The war had delivered a captive audience eager for entertainment in bleak times, but postwar prosperity brought a renewed interest in men's professional sport enhanced by television's ability to bring live games into millions of homes. The league became more out of step with the times, especially with regard to the domestic role of women in the 1950s. Coupled with poor financial management, teams began to fold, and the league was finished. Softball, however, continued to grow and expand. In Canada, the first Dominion women's championship was held during the 1951 Canadian National Exhibition, with Edmonton Mortons beating Toronto Ace Bowling in a best-of-three series.[62] The CNE was also responsible for bringing the women's "world" championship, sponsored by the Amateur Softball Association of America, to Toronto in both 1952 and 1953. Several Canadian teams entered the tournament each year, but they were eventually eliminated by the stronger American teams.[63] On a sad note, Toronto's Sunnyside stadium and ball park were demolished in 1956 to make way for an expressway, thus ending over 30 years of some of the best women's softball ever played in Canada.[64]

Unlike softball, women's ice hockey did not flourish in the immediate post-war period nor into the 1950s. It was already on the wane in the late 1930s, and it had a very tough time surviving wartime conditions. After the war, male leagues were given priority on the public and community ice arenas, especially with the growth of minor league hockey for boys. When nine-year-old Abby Hoffman begged her parents to let her play organized hockey in the mid-1950s, she was (unknown to the league) the only girl among 400 boys. When it was discovered that "Ab," the 73-pound defence stalwart for the St. Catharines Tee Pees, was a girl, everyone was taken totally by surprise. "She certainly doesn't play like a girl," said her coach. Growing up with two older brothers, Hoffman had honed her hockey skills on the streets and rink near her home, and she desperately wanted to play in a proper league. Her parents went along with the deception so she could play, taking her to the hockey rinks fully dressed. Hoffman, who later went on to have a stellar athletic career as a middle distance runner, was a media celebrity for a short while, and there were hopes that a girls' league could be organized in Toronto, but the interest was simply not there.[65]

With little public or media interest in women's hockey, teams had increasing difficulty finding sponsors. Often it was softball players looking for an exciting winter sport who tried to generate interest in the game. In the early 1950s, for example, the East York Girls' Hockey Club sponsored by Gord's Snack Bar, travelled to several nearby communities in Ontario to play exhibition games and to campaign vigorously for the revival of women's hockey, with little success.[66] Even in universities, where women's hockey had a long and distinguished past, interest dwindled, and so did the finances to support the teams. In Ontario universities, for instance, competition had been cancelled between 1936 and 1948 due to lack of interest and the war; there was a brief revival for a few years, but for almost all the 1950s there was no women's intercollegiate ice hockey competition. Dominion championships were held at least during the early part of the decade, but the teams competing were those who could find sponsorship to travel. The strongest team in the west was the Moose Jaw Wildcats, who captured the senior women's title first in 1951, defeating the Port Arthur Bearcats, and again the following year against the Winnipeg Canadianettes, but they, too, ran out of women's teams to play and ended up competing against men's teams.[67]

Women's basketball was also struggling, although it was much stronger in some areas of the country than others. At mid-decade, Bobbie Rosenfeld commented that "women's senior basketball in Canada hit its lowest ebb in championship play when only 425 fans attended the three-game series in Vancouver to see the Eilers retain the Dominion title, defeating Saskatoon."[68]

She was referring to the Vancouver Eilers, who like the west coast Hedlunds before them, dominated senior women's basketball in Canada throughout the

1950s. With the demise of the Edmonton Grads in 1940, a new Vancouver team sponsored by Hedlunds Meat Packers became the team to beat when they won the Canadian senior women's basketball championships between 1942 and 1946, although, due to wartime travel restrictions, it was challenged only by other teams in the west. Even after the war, without air travel in Canada, national champions in basketball were declared after a series of eastern and western play-offs with the Manitoba-Ontario border serving as the national divide. The provincial champions from the two furthest provinces would travel east or west to the next province, play the champion there, and then move on to the next province if they won, or return home if they lost. In 1950, for example, in the first postwar playdown series to cross the country, the British Columbia champions, the Eilers, travelled east through Cardston, then to Saskatoon and Winnipeg, and finally on to Toronto, where they met the winners of the Eastern Canadian championships, the Montgomery Maids from Toronto. The Eilers were away three weeks, travelled over 4,000 miles by train, and played nine games without a loss.[69] Since this system required substantial time and financial commitments on the part of players, teams from the east were not always able to fulfill their obligations, causing them to default. It was sometimes easier for eastern teams to play American teams just below the border, as was the case in 1955 when the Toronto Bridgmans defaulted, although they were able to play in the first Canadian-American Girls' Basketball League championship in Hamilton.[70]

Western teams dominated Canadian women's basketball because they had always played men's rules and were used to a faster, more complex game, whereas players in eastern Canada were brought up on girls' rules in the schools and universities and were more comfortable with a slower, less demanding, and aggressive game. Although the commercial leagues in Ontario used the rules of the Canadian Amateur Basketball Association (the men's rules), they were seldom a match for the more skilful teams from the west, especially Vancouver.[71] After 1958, with air travel more common, the Canadian championship was determined by a round-robin tournament to which all provincial championship teams were invited. In 1959, at the Pan-American Games in Chicago, Canada was represented for the first time in women's basketball by a team chosen mostly from the Vancouver Eilers and Saskatoon Aces with a couple of additional players. The Canadians lost all but one of their games and were no match for teams from the United States and South America. "The Canadian players," reported manager Ruth Wilson, "are slow and awkward in comparison."[72]

"Canada has never entered a woman in the Olympic field events, for the simple reason that she has never had a competitor that could pitch a javelin or discus further than you could toss a country boy," remarked Bobbie Rosenfeld in one of her columns in early 1952.[73] She was touting the prospects of Mary Lawrence, a local softballer, who at five feet eleven inches and 185 pounds certainly had the size necessary for the throwing events. She was coached by Lloyd Percival, an all-round athlete himself, who in the early 1940s started the Sports College in Toronto and was well-known throughout the country for his Saturday morning radio show providing training and fitness tips. Lawrence held the Canadian shot put record in 1952, but again Canada chose not to send any women to compete in the field events (javelin, discus, shot put) at the 1952 Helsinki Olympics. She would have been no match for the powerful Soviet bloc athletes, some of whom aroused suspicion as to whether they were actually women. And, if they were women, were they the kind of women Canadians wanted their girls to become?[74] Sports that demanded sheer strength, like tossing a heavy object into space, were incommensurate with femininity, unless the person doing the tossing was extremely feminine.

Jackie MacDonald — tall, statuesque, glamorous, and frequently compared to actress Marilyn Monroe — certainly fit the bill. As a 20-year-old elementary school teacher, having been a good athlete in high school, she had begun working with Lloyd Percival. He was impressed by this vivacious, bleach-blonde, who regularly arrived at practice on a Harley Davidson motorcycle and was determined to be the best shot put and discus thrower in the world. She started by winning the Canadian shot put title in 1953 and was named to the 1954 British Empire and Commonwealth Games team. She did well in the shot put competition, coming second and establishing a new Canadian record, and was all set to compete in the discus when suddenly just before her event she was withdrawn by the Canadian officials for alleged "professionalism." Her picture had appeared in a soft drink advertisement in a Vancouver paper, although MacDonald herself gained nothing financially from the appearance. She contends that the stodgy Canadian track and field officials, intent on upholding the "amateur" ideal, were upset over the fact that Percival made his living from coaching and that his leading-edge techniques were gaining attention; this was a way to damage his credibility.[75] She was cleared a few days after the games ended and competed several months later at the 1955 Pan-American Games in Mexico, coming fifth in the discus (there was no shot put event).

Far more crucial to MacDonald in the 1950s was her image as the best woman shot putter this side of the Iron Curtain, obviously muscular and strong, yet at the same time claiming fragility and femininity. Coach Percival wanted her to bulk up significantly, to become even more muscular, and MacDonald not only had reservations, but also was more concerned about becoming some sort of "freak." Writer June Callwood wrote a feature article for *Maclean's*, which stressed MacDonald's many attempts to confront her "Amazon in shorts and spikes" image:

> ... by dressing with delicacy, she vigorously combats the effects of being able to lift a hundred-and-fifty-pound bell bar. She lightens her hair to

honey blonde, wears sooty mascara and flowerlike perfumes, favors slen-
der-heeled pumps, pastel sweaters, pearls and dangling earrings. As her
muscles grow stronger, she fights back with an angora beret, sewn with
sequins. Though she is tall — five feet ten and weighing a hundred and sixty
pounds — Jackie is determined never to be picked out of a crowd as the girl
most likely to move a piano.[76]

Callwood's article was accompanied by a series of photos showing MacDonald
weight training and competing, but also as a grade-school teacher, preparing for a
date, sewing curtains, and "aproned, domestic and very, very feminine." Her view
now of the article is that it reflected how she felt at the time, and it showed other
aspects of her life that she enjoyed. The fact that she was engaging in so-called "feminine apologetic" behaviour in order to refute the perception that being an athlete
(especially one of size and strength) and a woman are incongruous was not something she was aware of at the time.[77] MacDonald went on to compete at the 1956
Melbourne Olympics, where her tenth place in the shot put was a personal best.
The following year she was the only Canadian representative at the World Youth
Games in Moscow, where she gained a credible fifth in the shot put, especially
against the consistently better Soviets and East Europeans. The trip also opened her
eyes to the vastly superior training, coaching, and competitive opportunities available to these athletes, and just how far behind we were in Canada. She was married
in 1958 and competed one more time at the British Empire and Commonwealth
Games that summer in Cardiff, Wales, earning a third place in the shot put event.

Obviously attractive and feminine athletes did not always challenge the belief
that women should compete primarily in "beauty-producing" sports like swimming, gymnastics, and figure skating, even though these too demanded strength,
endurance, and intensity.[78] Synchronized swimming was, and still is, a happy
meeting ground between athleticism and femininity. It is a physically demanding sport that encourages athleticism and competitiveness (judged against an
ideal, numerical standard), but, at the same time, reinforces stereotypes of traditional femininity (graceful, flowing, splashless).[79] Originally called ornamental,
fancy, or scientific swimming, its origins in Canada date back to World War I
when women began to earn Royal Life Saving Society awards, which in addition
to competent swimming and life saving techniques included tricks and figures.
Swimming clubs, especially in Montreal and Toronto, held annual galas featuring competitive swimming, diving, water polo, and fancy swimming. The first
provincial competition took place in 1924 at the Montreal Amateur Athletic
Association pool, won by Margaret Shearer (later Peg Seller, she became a coach,
administrator, and promoter of the sport for many years) of the Montreal YWCA
swimming club. A Dominion championship was held as early as 1926 in "grace-

ful and scientific swimming," with the winner receiving the Gale Trophy, donated by Frances C. Gale, a Montreal enthusiast of the new sport."[80]

Water ballets or pageants, performed almost exclusively by young women, became popular in university physical education programs, at summer camps, and in public and private pools. In the 1930s, water shows starring Olympic swimming celebrities, like Eleanor Holm, Buster Crabbe, and Johnny "Tarzan" Weismuller, toured North America, attracting some Canadian performers. The Hollywood film industry recognized their entertainment value when, in the 1940s, it transformed the athletic and voluptuous Esther Williams, a former competitive swimmer and performer in the San Francisco world fair Aquacade, into a movie star through her blockbuster "aqua-musicals" (*Bathing Beauty*, for example, appeared in 1944). The increased postwar interest in synchronized swimming in Canada can be partially attributed to public enthusiasm for these glitzy Hollywood water pageants and glamorous stars like Williams. As cultural historians have suggested, her success was due to the brilliant way she merged femininity and athleticism into an "aesthetically pleasing yet politically innocuous form."[81] Synchronized swimming (the name change occurred in 1949) became the perfect vehicle for young female swimmers to display their athleticism, yet still retain their femininity, and perhaps even an unrealistic dream of movie stardom in their future. After all, Canadian-born Norma Shearer, a top swimmer at the Montreal Amateur Athletic Club, *had* become a famous Hollywood actress more than a generation earlier.[82] Beyond Toronto and Montreal, clubs began to sprout up across the country in schools, colleges, and YWCAs lucky enough to have swimming pools, or at the few public indoor pools in major cities.[83]

The Regina YWCA Splashers (later the Synchronettes) formed in 1941 and performed in local water shows. The Winnipeg Synchronized Swimming Club, organized in 1947 surprisingly with both boys and girls, held water shows to pay for pool time, suits, and equipment; the boys did comedy, and the girls provided the glamour. The first British Columbia Ornamental Swimming championships took place in 1949 at the Crystal Pool, the only indoor pool in Vancouver at the time.[84] In the cool Atlantic waters by Halifax's Waegwoltic Club on the Northwest Arm, nightly water shows with lights, music, and costumed swimmers entertained hundreds of spectators on warm summer evenings in the late 1940s. The shows were carefully planned to coincide with a sufficiently high tide for the deepwater tricks, although just what the audience was able to see is unclear. *Maclean's* ran an article promoting "ornamental swimming," claiming it was the finest hobby a woman could have, providing them with grace, poise, and body control: "It's smooth and swanlike, yet at the same time has a vivacity about it that makes it fascinating both to perform and watch."[85]

The Canadian Amateur Synchronized Swimming Association was established in 1950, having split off from the larger swimming body. By then, the highlights at national championships were the solo, pairs, and group routines (with music), rather than the tedious figures and strokes. There were several synchronized clubs in Alberta by 1957, including the Edmonton Aquadettes, with enough interest to form a provincial association. At this time I was a high school student in Ottawa, at Glebe Collegiate Institute, one of the few schools in the city with a swimming pool. A strong swimmer, I eagerly tried out for the synchronized swimming team, but suffered immediate rejection, because above the waterline my skinny, slightly bowed legs and non-pointing, crooked toes were hardly "smooth and swanlike." The next summer I did succeed in becoming a member of the short-lived Brighton Beach (long since closed due to pollution in the Rideau River) aquatic group, smartly outfitted in our red Jantzen swim suits and sequin-decorated bathing caps, performing so far from shore no one noticed my physical inadequacies.

Swimmers from Canada and the United States gave demonstrations of synchronized swimming at the 1948 London Olympics, at the first Pan-American Games in 1951, and again at the 1952 Olympics in Helsinki. The 1950s marked the beginning of synchronized swimming as we know it today with more emphasis on solo, duet, and team routines accompanied to music and less importance given to strokes and compulsory figures. June Taylor of Toronto was Canada's first international champion, and the Peterborough Ornamental Swim Club was the top team in the early 1950s, although competition was just with the United States. The first truly international competition took place at the 1955 Pan-American Games in Mexico when a group of five Canadian swimmers, mostly from Ontario and Quebec, achieved two seconds and a third against two other nations, Mexico and the United States. The competition was dropped in 1959 due to an insufficient number of teams willing to compete. On the home front, Quebec swimmers (like Joan Orser, Marjorie Bradshaw, Eila Lindell, Barbara Monoghan, and Barbara Malenfant) dominated national solo and duet competition, while the Peterborough club was also a successful team competitor. English-speaking universities, particularly in Ontario, Quebec, Alberta, and British Columbia, played a significant role in the development of the sport by providing a training base and offering competitions.[86] It would take several more decades, however, before synchronized swimming was accepted as an official Olympic sport (in 1984).

PHYSICAL EDUCATORS SEEKING CONTROL

The pre-war problems of the WAAF of C became much more serious during wartime. Although it continued to operate, dissension erupted over whether or not to hold the Canadian women's track and field championships (cancelled in 1940 for the duration of the war). Annual meetings were discontinued, and its activities were reduced mostly to fund-raising for the war effort. In 1942, the national president, Edith McKenzie of Winnipeg, took a job in Washington, DC, leaving the organization without an official leader, although Ann Clark in Vancouver and Irene Wall in Montreal worked hard to keep the organization running. After the war, a few leaders tried to regroup, but with no money and few new faces, they decided the best route was to amalgamate with the men's AAU of C.[87] Of the six provincial women's branches, only three favoured the move, Alberta disagreed, and the two others expressed no opinion. The amalgamation formally took place in March 1954, with the assurance that women would continue to have a direct voice in sports in which they participated, as well as a say in the selection of women athletes for teams competing internationally. It was agreed that each provincial branch of the AAU of C would have a woman on a national women's committee, chaired by Margaret Lord of Hamilton, who became the only woman on the executive of the male-controlled AAU of C. Ann Clark and Irene Wall bitterly opposed the amalgamation, with Wall refusing to surrender the Federation's records and eventually burning them.[88]

The collapse of the WAAF of C meant there was no longer a woman-controlled organization to speak on behalf of the athletic interests of girls and women in Canada. However, since their voice had been muted for some time, and since the organization did not necessarily represent the opinion of all women sport leaders in Canada, its demise left the door open for another group to try to fill the vacuum. Women physical educators, especially in eastern Canada, wished to convince everyone connected with women's sports that national standards and desirable practices were essential. These would be very different from the WAAF of C constitution, which laid out the rules and regulations for women competing, especially in track and field.[89] Rather, they were almost identical to those laid out by the National Section on Women's Athletics (NSWA) of the American Physical Education Association in the United States, which had worked with the NAAF Women's Division to forge a united front against all forms of highly competitive sports for girls and women. Dorothy Jackson, a graduate of the Margaret Eaton School, who had also done post-graduate work at Columbia University, returned to her former school to teach in the late 1930s. In 1941, when the Margaret Eaton School became part of the University of Toronto, Jackson was appointed to the new School of Physical Education.[90] She was impressed with the philosophy of women physical educators in the United States, so she set about to create a Women's Athletic Committee (WAC) through the Canadian Physical Education Association, which would replicate the aims and purposes of its American counterpart. With few resources, she convinced other like-minded physical educators across the country to join the WAC; she undertook a basketball rules survey; and she circulated the NSWA "Desirable Practices in Athletics for Girls and Women," which ultimately became the cornerstone of the policies and practices of the WAC.[91]

During the late 1940s and early 1950s, the WAC's principal concern was encouraging the use of girls' rules in basketball and improving the standard of basketball officiating by establishing local rating boards, exactly as had been done in the United States. Leadership came mostly from university-based physical educators, such as Gladys Bean and Iveagh Munro at McGill, Dorothy Jackson at Toronto, and Marion Ross at Queen's, as well as individuals like May Brown in Vancouver, Freda Wales and Dorothy Walker in Nova Scotia, Helen Gurney in Ontario, and Dorothy Nichol in Montreal, all of whom worked in schools or recreational agencies. What they had in common was the belief that women, and only qualified women, should teach, coach, and officiate girls' and women's sports according to a set of standards that placed the social benefits of participation ahead of individual glory and the winning of championships. Most had been trained either at the Margaret Eaton School, McGill University, or the University of Toronto, and in some cases they had completed graduate work in the United States where they observed first-hand this philosophy in action. They had little or nothing to do with the WAAF of C; in fact, they were generally opposed to its policies and practices. After the demise of the WAAF of C in 1954, women physical educators became more convinced than ever that they could transform the WAC into a national organization, which would be the controlling body for all women's sport in Canada.

Another pioneer in women's physical education in this era was Cécile Grenier, who in 1939 founded l'Institut d'éducation physique in Montreal. She was attracted to European gymnastics through her studies in France, Denmark, and England, although like many of her English-speaking counterparts, she had also studied at Columbia University. The purpose of the institute was to prepare instructors to teach gymnastics and physical education in schools, playgrounds, and holiday camps throughout Quebec.[92] In 1949, Grenier led a delegation of women physical educators from Quebec to Copenhagen, Denmark, to attend the founding congress of the International Association of Physical Education and Sport for Girls and Women (IAPESGW).[93] Another influential woman physical educator at this time was Doris Plewes, head of the federal government's Division of Fitness in the Department of Health and Welfare. She was also at the inaugural IAPESGW conference and played a significant role in helping to establish the organization. It was clear that Canadian women physical educators and sports administrators were not only making a significant contribution within the country, but were also seeking to expand their influence within the nascent international women's sport and physical education movement.

CHAPTER 5

Serious Athletes or "Oddballs"?: Transitional Years

There's been a tendency over the years on the part of the Canadian sports public, which is by definition overwhelmingly male, to lump female athletes into a category of womankind that also includes topless masseuses, female Members of Parliament, radical feminists and lady presidents of large corporations. Oddballs, in other words. Minority figures. Women who are out of the ordinary and who are, anyway, not to be taken seriously.

Jack Batten, *Homemaker's Magazine*, September 1973

Jack Batten went on to say that sport fans in Canada "have been forced to make some radical adjustments in their outlook on the country's women athletes." Why? It was because they were winning more world-class championships and capturing more individual titles than Canada's male athletes had done in the same time period. Taking into account that the number of events for men was approximately twice that for women at major international games, they outperformed their male counterparts at nearly all these games in the 1960s and 1970s. Canadian women consistently won a greater proportion of medals at these competitions than would be expected given their much smaller numbers on teams. For instance, at the Summer Olympics, women on average constituted only 20 per cent of the Canadian team, but won 30 per cent of the medals; at the Winter Olympics the ratio was only 16 per cent of team membership, yet they also brought back 30 per cent of the medals.[1]

Athletes like Anne Heggtveit, Barb Wagner, Petra Burka, Debbi Wilkes, Nancy Greene, Karen Magnussen, Mary Stewart, Elaine Tanner, Angela Coughlan, Marilyn Corson, Marion Lay, Leslie Cliff, Donna-Marie Gurr, Abby Hoffman, Debbie Brill, and Nancy McCredie all won medals at major international games.

Some became more famous than others. Despite these accomplishments, the male sports media tended to excuse the relatively lesser performance of Canada's male amateur athletes either because their talent pool had been depleted through the attraction of professional sport, or because they needed to put childish pursuits aside and get on with the serious business of training for a career and supporting a family. For example, Jim Coleman, a nationally syndicated sportswriter, commented: "At the level of amateur competitive sports, Canada is dominated by the Female of the Species ... the implications are that Canadian girls excel Canadian boys in their dedication to the rigorous training schedules which are demanded of their individual sports."[2] He went on to refute the idea that girls are more willing to make personal sacrifices than boys, but also suggested they were more able to do so. His thesis was that Canadian parents, particularly those with few financial worries, still subscribed to the "Daddy's Little Girl" theory of raising children. Where boys were expected to rush through their schooling and become financially independent as soon as possible, with professional sport as an option if they have talent, there was no great rush to push Canadian girls to independence; besides, there were few opportunities for them in professional sport. Daddy's Little Girl could indulge herself and finish her schooling later if necessary. Writing in *Maclean's*, Lionel Wilson argued that one reason Canada was short of top athletes (he ignored the women's accomplishments) was that too many of our best athletes were "psychologically driven" toward football: "It is the rare boy who can ignore the glamour of football and concentrate on some less well-publicized sport."[3]

In some respects, these commentators were right. With the exception of golf and tennis, there were no professional sports for women in this era; thus, the only avenue for them to reach the highest pinnacle of their sport was through a medal at a world championship or major international games such as the Olympics, the Pan-American Games, or the British Empire and Commonwealth Games. Certainly in the late 1950s and early 1960s, they got to these international events and trained for them because they had supportive families who could afford to pay. All this changed quite dramatically in a relatively short period of time. State involvement (some prefer to call it intervention) in amateur sport from the 1960s onwards resulted in the rationalization, restructuring, and professionalization of the Canadian sport system, as well as radically altering the experience of being a high performance athlete. Some athletes experienced this transition during their competitive careers, whereas others competing in the 1970s benefited more from the changes made a decade earlier. Basically, the intensity of training and coaching of young athletes increased markedly, a nascent sports science was applied more rationally, and there were substantially more resources available to bring in top level coaches (often from Europe) and also to provide international competitive opportunities.[4]

The fact that Canada's women athletes were doing better internationally than males seemed irrelevant. Issues around equity, such as the lack of competitive opportunities for females, the discriminate use of resources to provide more recreational and competitive privileges for males, and the sexist and stereotypical portrayals of female athletes in the media were completely ignored in this era. They would have to wait for the appearance of second-wave feminism and its application to women's sport in the mid-1970s before much of this would slowly change.

The 1960s and early 1970s were a transitional, somewhat difficult, period for women's sport in Canada (and amateur sport generally) for a variety of reasons: the changing political and administrative structure of the sport system, changes in the significance and meaning of sport in Canada, the role of sport in the wider goals of government, and the increasing professionalization and commercialization of men's sport. Women, both as athletes and leaders, were often left out of the decision-making processes, and they were divided among themselves, more so than in the past, about the best way to chart their future.

WOMEN AND THE GOVERNANCE OF AMATEUR SPORT

Canada's international athletic successes were at an all-time low in the late 1950s and early 1960s. Canadians were shocked when the Soviet Union, now a rising athletic power, beat them at the 1954 World Hockey championships and again at the 1956 Winter Olympics when they took the gold medal in hockey. Our worst Olympic performance was in 1960 in Rome with only one medal, a silver, won by the men's rowing eight. After decades of mediocrity, *Canadian Sport Monthly* declared the 1961 Canadian track and field championships "little better than a rural community sports-day" citing poor planning, insufficient preparation, and inadequate facilities:

> If that is the best that Canada can put forth in 1961, after a disastrous decline on the international fields of competition over the past twenty-five years, after having seen what other countries are doing, after reading official reports for years on what is lacking, after pleading for federal aid to all and sundry, then heaven help us indeed since we seem utterly incapable of helping ourselves.[5]

The advent of television in 1952 and its spectacular growth in a few short years meant that most Canadians could see for themselves the disastrous decline in our athletes' performances abroad. At the same time, television brought sport into the lives of millions of Canadians, although it was also blamed for an increasingly sedentary lifestyle. Live sports coverage was a staple of the Canadian Broadcasting Corporation

(CBC) in the early years of television. I spent many an afternoon or evening with my family watching Canadian football and "Hockey Night in Canada," even boxing from Madison Square Gardens, and of course baseball's World Series. The athletes featured on television were almost always professional and male; we rarely saw women athletes, except perhaps during the Olympics. For those interested in participating in sport, the economic prosperity and growth of the postwar era put money into people's pockets, allowing more choices for leisure activities. The federal government had also benefited substantially during the war from increased taxation, allowing it to grow in size, funnel new money into health and social-welfare programs, and initiate federal/provincial cost-sharing agreements.[6]

Prime Minister John Diefenbaker, whose Conservative government came to power in 1957, was a strong nationalist who believed that national pride could be enhanced if Canada did better in international sport, and he was aware that many countries were using success in sport as a measure of their global strength and power.[7] Therefore, given a more favourable political climate, sport and fitness leaders as well as interested politicians lobbied the government to become more involved financially and administratively in sport. With impetus from the Duke of Edinburgh's 1959 speech to the Canadian Medical Association, in which he rebuked Canadians for their low fitness levels, and Diefenbaker's successful visit to the Pan-American Games in Chicago the same year, everything was set for the passage of Bill C-131, the Fitness and Amateur Sport Act in 1961.

Bill C-131 officially committed the federal government "to encourage, promote, and develop fitness and amateur sport in Canada." It was intended to encourage mass participation as well as to improve international sport performances. It provided $5 million annually for an administrative structure and personnel, federal/provincial cost-sharing agreements, grants to sports governing bodies, the initiation of the Canada Games, and scholarships and research grants to physical education specialists.[8] Established sport leaders were prepared to accept government financial assistance at the risk of losing some autonomy so they could build a better sport system for Canada. To some extent it worked. At the 1966 British Empire and Commonwealth Games in Jamaica, for example, almost every Canadian athlete reached the finals of their event, and the medal totals were higher than ever before, with the most improvement in swimming and on the track. Elaine Tanner, the 15-year-old Canadian swimming sensation, accounted for one silver and three gold medals on her own, along with a first and second in the relays, one of which set a world record. It was the best Canadian team showing since the 1930s. An explosion of information about sport had produced more sophisticated Canadian athletes and coaches. They knew what to expect from international competition, and they prepared themselves on that basis. Nationwide clinics, part of the Fitness and Amateur Sport program, where world-class coaches and athletes lectured and gave training sessions, contributed a great deal to this new knowledge and poise, especially among coaches. With more money available to send them abroad, Canadian athletes benefited enormously from valuable international competition.[9]

Nancy Greene, Canada's pre-eminent skier in the 1960s, acknowledged in her autobiography that she never had a "private" coach, or paid her way anywhere, because someone always helped: "I am totally a product of organized skiing in Canada."[10] In 1961, her first year on the European circuit, skiers on the national team were not necessarily the best racers in Canada, but rather those with wealthy parents or from well-to-do ski clubs who could afford to send them abroad. In Greene's case, it was the citizens of Rossland, her hometown in British Columbia, who raised sufficient capital to send her and another skier to Europe. She and other western-based skiers fought hard to establish a proper program where the national team, comprised of only the best skiers chosen through selection trials, was centralized, and skiers could coordinate their schooling and skiing. By the time her future husband, Al Raine, took over the program in 1968, it included a large coaching staff and a $600,000 annual budget, of which $150,000 was designated for the national team.[11]

Greene was also a member of the three-person Task Force on Sport established by Pierre Trudeau in 1968 when his Liberal government came to power. Although the focus of the task force was mostly on ice hockey, specifically examining Canada's poor performances at the world championships and why some Canadian cities had no National Hockey League (NHL) franchise, it recommended a more interventionist approach by the federal government to amateur sport in general. In 1970, the federal government put forward *A Proposed Sports Policy for Canadians*, which established the basis for their involvement in sport in the 1970s. It clearly signalled their intention to put more effort and resources into the improvement of Canadian performance in international competition and the development of elite athletes, as well as the encouragement of mass participation for fitness and enjoyment.[12] Women, however, nor any other group under-represented in sport and physical activity, were not singled out for special attention.

Who was speaking on behalf of women athletes at this point? Aside from several women's sport governing bodies (e.g., golf, curling, lawn bowling, field hockey), the Women's Athletic Committee (WAC) of the Canadian Association for Health, Physical Education and Recreation (CAHPER) was the only organization with a relatively broad focus on women's sport. Unfortunately, its members were never able to meet face-to-face, due to a lack of funding, and they had to rely on the work of dedicated volunteers to continue their struggle. In fact, it was not until 1964, after WAC had brought substantial revenue to CAHPER by printing and selling a basketball rule book (also translated into French) of the girls' rules game played in Canada, that they were provided with the necessary resources to meet. At this point, WAC decided to expand its activities beyond basketball to volleyball and synchronized swimming, requesting money through the National Advisory Council on Fitness and Amateur Sport to host a series of clinics for women coaches. The request was granted, and several well-attended clinics took place in late 1964 and early 1965, marking the first time the federal government had provided money specifically for women's sport. Taking the lead from their American counterparts, the Division for Girls' and Women's Sports (DGWS), the Canadian group also encouraged advanced competition outside of educational institutions, provided it was "sound, carefully planned, and well directed" and run by "qualified women, ... whenever and wherever possible." This was a remarkable change from the past, when former leaders had strenuously objected to high level competition. Although WAC's leaders wanted to expand their influence, most sports were turning to Fitness and Amateur Sport for funding and showed little interest in liaising with the Women's Athletic Committee. More problematic was that WAC's eastern-based leaders had little understanding of realities in western Canada, where males often taught, coached, and officiated girls' and women's sport simply because there were too few qualified women physical educators. They could not adhere to WAC's stringent policies, leading to such antagonism and misunderstanding that few leaders in western Canada supported the group, and most ignored it.[13]

Something that helped bring east and west together was the 1966 decision by WAC to abandon girls' rules basketball and switch to the five-player, full court, unlimited dribble game that had been played in western Canada for decades. Therefore, one of the most divisive issues in girls' and women's sport in Canada was finally resolved. The second biennial conference of WAC, under the guidance of chair Helen Gurney, also brought together for the first time representatives from the four Canadian women's intercollegiate sport conferences with several national sport governing bodies involved in women's sport.

Along with the historic basketball decision, the meeting also resulted in the formation of the University Women's Physical Education Committee (UPEC), chaired by Patricia Austin at the University of Alberta, whose dual purpose was to examine the recruitment of women into the profession of physical education and to set standards for university women's athletic programs. With the formation of the Canadian Women's Intercollegiate Athletic Union (CWIAU) in 1969, there were simply not enough people to do the work of three committees — WAC, UPEC, and CWIAU — and, since the federally-funded sport governing bodies were becoming more relevant to women's sport, WAC was dissolved in 1973.[14] Sadly, most sport governing bodies involved very few women, and they had little understanding of the issues and concerns that had driven WAC, and the WAAF of C before it, for so many years. Regional differences and a lack of money, in addition to their inability to adapt to changes in the governance of Canadian amateur sport, were contributing factors to the demise of both these organizations.

Although university women had participated in broadly-based athletic programs since the 1920s, there were not yet national women's championships at the intercollegiate level. Many of the older, more established eastern universities were opposed to national competition, whereas in the west, especially among the younger physical educators (including myself) involved with women's sport in the newer universities, there was a clear demand for change. The CWIAU was formed as a separate organization because the women were initially rebuffed by the men's CIAU. Despite financial problems and no clear consensus across the country, they went ahead with national championships initially in three sports — swimming and diving, gymnastics, and volleyball — with basketball added soon after. At the 1973 championships, staged in Montreal, Winnipeg, Calgary, and Wolfville, more than 200 women athletes competed from five regional conferences. However, by 1978 it was recognized that having two separate organizations was administratively awkward and financially wasteful, so the CWIAU and CIAU agreed to amalgamate, forming the Canadian Interuniversity Athletic Union.[15] The problem of who spoke specifically for women athletes in Canada was still not resolved, since there was no longer any central, multi-sport organization with the mandate to do so.

MEDIA PORTRAYAL OF WOMEN ATHLETES

The tone and tenor of how high profile women athletes were portrayed by Canadian sportswriters also changed considerably. The athletes featured and discussed were invariably from individual sports, because, for the most part, international competition for females was still restricted to competitive and synchronized swimming, track and field, skiing, figure skating, gymnastics, and fencing. Limited international competition was available in volleyball and basketball, but team athletes were generally ignored by the media. Athletes in individual sports were consistently younger than the international-level athletes of earlier decades, making their accomplishments all the more remarkable. True, Marlene Stewart, Lucile Wheeler, Anne Heggtveit, Marilyn Bell, Helen Stewart, and others had achieved international success as teenagers in the 1950s, sometimes unexpectedly, but the pressures on young Canadian athletes in the 1960s and early 1970s were more demanding, and their successes and failures more public. They went off to international competitions carrying the hopes and expectations of an entire nation. In an article for *Maclean's* assessing Canada's track and swimming potential at the upcoming Commonwealth Games in Perth in 1962, Peter Gzowski labelled them "young and fast," pointing out that "the kids have done it themselves with the help of very few coaches and officials who are as amateur as the youngsters they coach and officiate."[16]

This was especially true for Canadian women athletes, who at the international level often performed better than their male counterparts despite the lack of training and preparation. Swimmer Mary Stewart (sister of Helen Stewart) was only 13 when she was named to the 1959 Pan American Games team in Chicago, winning a silver medal as a member of the 4x100-metre free style relay team. The next year at the Olympics in Rome, where overall Canada had a dismal performance, Stewart qualified for the final in the 100-metre freestyle; two years later, and still only 16, she won a gold and silver at the Commonwealth Games in Perth. At 15, and with only a year's running experience, Abby Hoffman was sent to the 1962 Commonwealth Games to compete in the 880 yards. She finished last in the final, but the experience motivated her to become one of the most dedicated and enduring Canadian track athletes of this era. Between 1962 and 1975, she competed at four Olympics, four Pan American Games, two Commonwealth Games, three Fédération Internationale du Sport Universitaire (FISU) Universiades, and at one Maccabiah Games.[17]

Dubbed "Mighty Mouse" by her Vancouver Dolphin teammates because of her compact build and tenacious approach, 15-year-old Elaine Tanner was the most successful swimmer at the 1966 Commonwealth Games in Kingston, Jamaica, where she won four gold and three silver medals, and established two world records. Two years later at the Mexico City Olympics, and under enormous pressure to bring back gold, Tanner came second in her best events, the 100 and 200-metre backstroke, and also picked up a bronze as a member of the 4x100-metre freestyle relay team. Even though this was the best-ever performance at an Olympics by a Canadian swimming team, the 17-year-old Tanner was devastated by what she, and some members of the Canadian press, viewed as failure, prompting her to retire from competition the following year.[18]

By the mid-1970s, some questioned whether it was reasonable to expect such young teenagers to withstand the pressures of their own dreams, often unrealistic given the rising standards of international competition, let alone those of an entire nation. For example, Halifax swimmer Nancy Garapick set a world record in 1975 when she was only 13 and was expected to bring back gold at the 1976 Olympics in Montreal. "To Canada," observed sportswriter Alan Edmonds, "Nancy is one of those Great White Hopes that every nation seizes upon in the year before the Olympics."[19] Fortunately, Garapick herself did not see it that way, as she explained to me several years later:

I enjoyed the experience for sure; I didn't feel the pressure because you're in that situation and I think it helped being young. You didn't really understand what was going on. Again, it was another meet where you were swimming and you had trained and it was fun. You were meeting people that you had seen at other meets and there wasn't anything laying on the line. Nobody was making any big expectations of you; and also since I had such a crummy year, the press had really laid off a bit and Nigel [Kemp, her coach at the Halifax Trojan Aquatic Club] had backed off too. I didn't know that myself at the time, but later on we talked about it and he just said no to interviews and that sort of thing just to make you feel like you are away from that. Being in the training camp situation for a month previously, you really were away from it and you don't see any papers or they just let you see what is good. Not that they control it, but they have it in your best interest not to read stuff.[20]

Nancy Garapick, the 14-year-old swimming sensation from Halifax did not win gold in Montreal, but she finished with a bronze in both the 100 and 200-metre backstroke and an Olympic record set in one of the heats for the 100-metre.[21] Still, she remembered being grilled by the media immediately after her races about why she hadn't won. "They would just throw questions at you," she recalled, "and they can be very, very personal questions. When you are young, you wonder why adults are asking you these questions, and why they don't just stop."[22]

Male sports journalists in Canada, writing about these young athletes in newspapers and magazines, generally treated them with respect, although often paternalistically, like proud fathers beaming over their children's accomplishments. As young, mostly pre-pubescent teenagers, they were portrayed as androgynous, sometimes boyish, and often impish; their sexuality, established or developing, was never discussed. Alan Edmonds, for example, described Garapick as "neither tomboyish, nor overtly feminine; she admits to liking boys, dancing, movies and her 10-speed bike."[23] A few years earlier, Trent Frayne, writing in *Maclean's*, depicted 16-year-old swimmer Mary Stewart, who a few months before had set a world record in the 110-yard butterfly event, as "a lissome, bubbling youngster with braids in her hair, bands on her teeth and pure magic in her water style."[24] Peter Gzowski wrote of track star Abby Hoffman, who was 15 at the time: "Although in track suit and spikes she walks a little like a second baseman and she runs with the fury of a man, she may not be quite so tomboyish as this may sound, but a shy and pleasant teenage girl."[25]

Skier Nancy Greene received continuous press coverage beginning in 1958 with her introduction on the national scene at the Canadian Junior Championships, where at 14 she finished third in the slalom and second in the downhill, behind her older sister Elizabeth, who came first in both events. By 1960, she and her sister were on the Canadian Olympic team, competing at Squaw Valley. Finishing well back in their events, they saw Anne Heggtveit finish first in the slalom, Canada's first-ever Olympic skiing gold medal. Myrtle Cook, still writing her sports column for the *Montreal Star*, compared them to the skiing Wurtele twins, Rhona and Rhoda, who dominated Canadian women's skiing in the 1950s. For the first time, incidentally, the women's team was not accompanied by an "official" chaperone, although no doubt Cook, by then 58 years old and primarily responsible for clothing the Canadian Olympians, acted as such.[26]

As a member of the women's national team from 1959 until she retired in 1968, Nancy Greene came of age under public scrutiny, competing in three Olympics and several world championships. For part of each year, she and other members of the Canadian ski team were in Europe either training or competing, well away from the unnecessarily intrusive daily Canadian sports press, who anyway cared little about skiing. By the late 1960s, according to Greene, many Canadian papers belatedly discovered that she had become a celebrity, and they would dispatch any available writer — most knew almost nothing about skiing — just to get a story. In her autobiography she complained about the way sportswriters, and by inference the general public, viewed women's skiing and the "girls" who were her friends:

> They seem to think it's all a jet-set existence, full of glamorous people, fabulous settings, everyone doing the boogaloo or something, and now and then coasting down a hill. That is about as far as you can get from reality. The ski racing world is actually a lonely, isolated kind of place, cut off from almost everyone except other competitors, ski officials and a few press people. And within that tight little world, you encounter girls who are, at least in my view, as complex and fascinating as any teenagers you'll ever meet. They are hardly simple-minded teenyboppers.[27]

The *Canadian Sport Monthly*, where Greene received the most press coverage, called her Vancouver's "happy-go-lucky little speedball." She was given the nickname "Tiger" because of her attacking, aggressive style on the ski slopes. Hilles Pickens, publisher of *Canadian Sport Monthly*, referred to the 1963 women's national team (comprised of Linda Crutchfield, Vicki Rutledge, Nancy Greene, Nancy Holland, Shelagh Pike, and Karen Dokka) as "skierettes," admitting that the fancy (and patronizing) label did not fit the "lithe, whipcord, cool-eyed young female characters." Pickens assured his readers they were girls — "normal healthy, I emphasize the word, Canadian girls" — and he went on:

> Regardless of dedication which must be a part of any effort by youngsters such as our girls, the strain shows. But minds are glued to the final effort....

> Then each girl will know what all this has been worth and it is that impend-
> ing sense of responsibility to oneself and one's country that can make nice,
> quiet normal young Canadian ladies into tawny, agile athletes.[28]

Although admiration for the youngsters was sometimes patronizing and often tinged with paternalism, more mature women athletes were not always treated with the same respect. A whole new way of writing about high profile women athletes, mostly in their 20s, emerged in the 1960s. In-depth articles, again mostly about outstanding athletes in individual sports, appeared in national magazines, like *Maclean's* and *Saturday Night*, and in weekend supplements to daily newspapers, like *The Star Weekly*, *The Canadian Magazine*, and *Weekend Magazine*, although rarely in women's magazines such as *Chatelaine*. Writers like Peter Gzowski, Jack Batten, Trent Frayne, Alan Edmonds, and Paul Grescoe were responsible for many of these articles. It was not until the mid-1970s that women writers began to publish features on women athletes and women's sport in national magazines.

Women sports journalists had disappeared from the daily newspapers along with their columns. Bobbie Rosenfeld was still at the *Globe and Mail*, but she was not in good health. Robert Fulford, who joined the *Globe's* sports department in 1950 as a young reporter, remembers that even then she walked with great difficulty, due to the painful arthritis she suffered throughout most of her life. She relied less and less on attending actual sporting events; as a result, her column became less factual and more gossipy, written from other newspapers, conversations, and her own memories.[29] In fact, she gave up her daily "Sports Reel" column in 1958 to become a member of the *Globe's* promotion department; she retired in 1966 but died, sadly, three years later at age 65. The last of the original women sports journalists, Myrtle Cook McGowan, continued writing for the *Montreal Star* until her retirement in 1969. As the 1960s progressed, her "Women's Sportlight" column appeared much less frequently, as she wrote more about amateur sport in general, although her passion was still women's sport.

Women sports writers did not show up again in the sports departments of major Canadian newspapers, and then only in a select few, until well into the 1970s, and they were certainly not employed to write exclusively about women's sport. Christie Blatchford, for example, was fresh out of journalism school in 1973 when she was hired by the *Globe and Mail*. Two years later she took over the most prestigious column in Canadian sports — one written over the years by the likes of Ralph Allen, Jim Coleman, Scott Young, and Dick Beddoes. Blatchford rarely wrote about women's sport, except at the Olympics, concentrating instead on men's professional sport. She positioned herself as "one of the guys," establishing her persona as "tough-talking, hard boiled, sentimental — but a great lover of contact sports, from the thud of the puck to the thud of [male] bodies smashing against each other."[30]

In 1974, the *Globe and Mail* hired two other women journalists to write about sports, although neither had any previous experience as sportswriters. One was Mary Trueman, who had been working for a paper in Windsor, Ontario, writing a religion column, and the other was Nora McCabe, who was writing a social column for the *Toronto Star* and jumped at the chance to work at the *Globe and Mail,* known more as a "writer's paper." McCabe had no journalism training, although previously she had been living in political Ottawa and, as a single mother, was looking for an interesting job where she could learn to write. She wrote about a variety of sports, male and female, amateur and professional, and now admits to being unaware (or concerned) about how women athletes were portrayed in the print media, nor had she any knowledge of her journalist predecessors like Alex Gibb and Bobbie Rosenfeld.[31] Similarly, Jane O'Hara was in her early 20s when she was hired at the *Toronto Sun* in 1975. The sports editor at the time was interested in having athletes write about their sports, and O'Hara had spent seven years on the women's professional tennis circuit. After three years of writing for the *Sun,* she moved to *Maclean's* for ten years, but in 1988 she became the sports editor of the *Ottawa Sun.*[32]

Alison Gordon, a freelance writer who had lucked into some baseball features, was approached in early 1979 to share the professional baseball beat at the *Toronto Star.* She spent the next five years covering the Blue Jays in the American League. As a "socialist, feminist, hedonist with roots in the sixties, a woman who had marched against the bomb, done drugs, and never, ever even wanted to date the head jock at school," she cherished the time she spent in their world and wrote an entertaining book about her experiences. "The real challenge of the job," she noted, "was having to do it better than anyone else or risk failure on behalf of the whole female sex."[33]

During the 1960s and early 1970s, the two most obvious changes in how women athletes were represented in the print media were the explicit, sexualized descriptions of their physical appearance and their treatment as sex objects. What was only hinted at in the immediate postwar period became far more conspicuous, the language more candid, and the innuendo over sexuality more daring. Male sports journalists rarely refrained from commenting upon the "womanliness" of their subjects, as if to confirm their own manhood and heterosexuality. Lawyer-turned-writer Jack Batten, for example, who penned a number of articles on Canadian women athletes in the 1960s and 1970s, wrote this about swimmer Merrily Stratten: "The motion of her body, swiveling gently in the water, had a grace and beauty to it, even a hint of erotic attraction."[34] It was as if male sportswriters had suddenly discovered the connection between athleticism and femininity.

Certainly since the 1920s, both male and female sportswriters had enthused about the physical beauty of many Canadian track and field athletes. For instance,

Ethel Catherwood, the "Saskatoon Lily," and winner of the high jumping gold medal at the 1928 Olympics, was perpetually cited as a prime example of "beauteous" Canadian girl athletes, but in those days her physical appearance was rarely described in much detail, nor was she depicted as a sexual being. Similarly, Barbara Ann Scott, the most glamorous celebrity athlete of the 1940s and 1950s, was treated with the utmost respect and deference by the Canadian press. Where earlier sportswriters often maintained that athleticism and femininity were mutually exclusive, the 1960s saw a deliberate attempt to link the two in ways not seen before. The downside was that more often than not an athlete's physical appearance was the focus rather than her accomplishments, and female athletes who were not feminine in a conventional sense, nor especially attractive, were cruelly singled out and criticized, also in ways not seen before.

Writing about 21-year-old Jenny Wingerson, one of Canada's first pentathletes (80-metre hurdles, shot put, high jump, long jump, and 200-metre sprint), Jack Batten focussed on her good looks, making it clear she was the "loveliest" entrant in the women's pentathlon at the 1964 Tokyo Olympics, even more so than her "vivacious" rival, Diane Gerace, who earlier in 1964 set a world indoor high jump record. About Jenny Wingerson (later Meldrum), he wrote:

> [She] is twenty-one, has sunny blonde hair, long shapely legs and honey skin and competes in the world's least likely sport, apart from free-style wrestling, for beautiful girls who want to keep their good looks.... Russian girls are best at the pentathlon — with their blunt, muscular bodies, they *look* like pentathlon winners.[35]

A few years later, Paul Grescoe wrote this about another pentathlete, Debbie Van Kiekebelt, who competed internationally for Canada in the early 1970s:

> She is a striking woman, and very tall. Except for her thighs, which are athlete-thick, she has the body of a fashion model and, in fact, has dabbled in modelling from time to time since she was 13, including a Miss Chatelaine magazine cover. She has fountaining brunette hair held fast this morning by a gold bandana. A clear oval face that erupts into lopsided smiles. A modest bosom under her white Olympic T-shirt with its red stripes and maple leaf. And those legs — they seem to go on forever — lithe and shapely in red shorts that keep hiking up.[36]

Debbie Brill, Canada's top high jumper in 1970 (she had cleared six feet, which was nine inches higher than Catherwood's 1928 gold medal jump), maintains that the Canadian sports media "discovered" women's track and field at this time because suddenly "there was a bunch of us young, talented and, by and large, quite good-looking." She elaborated:

> There was Diane Jones, blonde, confident and so well-stacked that she could walk around the dressing room with a towel knotted under an arm and comfortably supported; there were the sprinters Stephanie Berto and Patty Loverock; long jumper Brenda Eisler, and pentathlete Debbie van Kiekebelt, a particular darling of the Toronto media. There had been a general understanding that track and field women tended to be homely; now, suddenly there was a crop that passed certain tests, both on the track and in front of the cameras.[37]

Being in front of the cameras, and being viewed by millions on their television sets was becoming important especially in women's golf. Twenty-year-old Sandra Post from Oakville, Ontario, stunned the golf world when she defeated the number one American player Kathy Whitworth at the LPGA championship on 24 June 1968 at the Pleasant Valley Country Club in Sutton, Massachusetts. The Ladies Professional Golf Association, better known as the LPGA, traces its roots back to efforts in the 1940s by a handful of talented women golfers in the United States, including Mildred "Babe" Didrikson Zaharias, to create an association for women professionals. After several aborted attempts, the LPGA was founded in 1950 to develop tournaments, seek prize money, and generally promote women's golf. In its first year, the LPGA sponsored a 14-event schedule with nearly $50,000 in prize money, but by the end of the decade it could boast of $200,000 over 26 tournament stops. Televised golf coverage brought the LPGA Tour and its players to millions more spectators and fans. The first televised women's professional golf tournament was the final round of the 1963 United States Women's Open Championship. By the end of the 1960s, LPGA prize money had grown to $600,000 for 34 tournaments, and women's professional golf was now big business.[38]

Sandra Post was the first Canadian to play on the LPGA Tour.[39] A child prodigy, who had her sights on a professional golf career at an early age, she was by the late 1960s a seasoned player with a strong record in United States tournaments. She is still the only Canadian ever to win a professional major. She went on to win eight more LPGA tournaments, but never another major.[40] In an article about how Post (along with skier Nancy Greene and swimmer Elaine Tanner) were putting Canada back into the prestigious world of international sport, Alan Edmonds wrote:

> ... little Sandra Post, who is five-foot-four, 125 pounds and pretty, pugnacious and confident ("cocky" her manager calls it) and as concerned with

finding Mr. Right as she is with becoming the world's greatest lady golfer, tied up her sun-bleached hair in green plastic rollers, chose a blue miniskirt for the morning and went to sleep dreaming about the treachery of that dogleg, par-five 12th hole and her boyfriend Dave, whose golf career has been interrupted by the US Vietnam draft.[41]

The focus of the article was less on Post's success and more about how the LPGA was fending off charges that "women athletes are either not women, or at least not womanly" by their determined "miniskirted effort to glamorize girl golfers." We learn more about the LPGA's femininity campaign, and Sandra Post's efforts in that respect, then we do about women's golf. In fact, Edmonds could not even get the name of her boyfriend correct. His name was not Dave, but John Elliott, a young American professional golfer whom Post married in 1970 and unhappily divorced a couple of years later.[42] Jack Batten described women on the LPGA Tour as "tousle-haired, sunshiny, more muscular and perhaps more 'masculine' than most woman, like a gang of phys-ed teachers, but fresh and appealing in an Anne Murray kind of way."[43] Contrast this sexist and patronizing tone with that of Marci McDonald, a senior writer for *Maclean's*, writing about Sandra Post and other LPGA members several years later:

Other women straggled in around her — big, square-jawed, rawboned women, freckled and rangy. Not your ordinary women, it was clear at a glance. Their faces were confidently naked of makeup, skin etched in squint lines and leathered by the unrelenting sun. Their haircuts were styled with one eye to the wind, and they walked with a lope from the hip in long, easy strides.[44]

Another top golfer during this era was Jocelyne Bourassa from Shawinigan, Quebec, the second Canadian to play with the LPGA. Always a crowd pleaser, she was well into a stellar amateur career when a wealthy Montreal businessman, Jean-Louis Levesque, became her sponsor, which allowed her to play on the 1972 LPGA Tour. He also organized a Canadian Ladies' Professional Golf Association, and brought the LPGA Tour to Montreal by sponsoring the $50,000 La Canadienne, held in June 1973. Although everyone hoped Bourassa would win, very few thought she could — but win she did after a sudden death play-off with two other players. Jocelyne was the toast of Shawinigan and the rest of Canada; she went on to play until 1979 when a bad knee forced her to leave the Tour.[45] In an article for *Maclean's*, the prolific (at least in 1973) Jack Batten focussed on Bourassa, who according to him "radiated an approachable tomboy charm." Here is a brief excerpt:

In fact, Jocelyne cuts a vaguely comic figure even when she isn't trying. She's a husky woman, a little broad in the beam, and her face seems slightly smallish for the torso. Her face can't make up its mind whether it belongs to the cute kid next door or to a determined pug, someone with a tough style. It lets you know, anyway, that it is the face of someone independent, aggressive, a woman who can — what the hell — play touch football or baseball with men. When she plays golf, the tail of her blouse tends to come out of her skirt, and the elastic bandage she wears on her bad knee stretches loose and droops around her ankle without her caring or even noticing.[46]

It is difficult to tell that this is the same Jocelyne Bourassa described by James Barclay in his superb history of golf in Canada:

> ... a jaunty, dark-haired beauty of five feet five-and-a-half inches, with determined blue eyes and an engaging smile, captured the hearts of many Canadians golfers or not. Very much a product of Quebec — and oh! How it was proud of her — she had the Trevino-like quality of making golf seem fun while playing it with deadly earnestness.[47]

Diver Bev Boys's weight was constantly discussed in the media. A native of Pickering, Ontario, Boys won every major diving competition in the world in the late 1960s — gold medals at the Commonwealth Games, the Pan American Games, and at the US Nationals — yet, at the 1972 Olympics, she finished fifth in springboard diving "in the face of enormous obstacles." As her coach Don Webb explained in an article published in *Maclean's*, Boys was 20 pounds too heavy: "She's been under terrific pressure during her winning years, and she started to balloon."[48] Constant prodding by her coach and publically in the media, as well as her own efforts at dieting, actually made her gain more pounds in the period before the 1976 Olympics in Montreal, where again she came fifth. Although in later years Boys recognized she was a little overweight, she feels strongly that the media were extremely unfair, especially as she received little or no assistance (such as a nutritionist) from the Canadian amateur sport system.[49]

Despite the blatant sexism, most Canadian sportswriters of this era treated women's sport and women athletes seriously, especially those who achieved international success. In fact, they admired them, even if it was in a begrudging fashion. For instance, Peter Gzowski admitted:

> As a man who gets most of his enjoyment of sports from watching them these days, I can't help applaud the ... uh, prominence of these athletes. For one thing, I'm just nationalistic enough to get hopped up about *any*

group of Canadian athletes doing well in world competition, and if they're girls, well, it couldn't bother me less.[50]

A few years later, *Homemaker's Magazine* ran a salute to Canada's best women athletes of the day: figure skater Karen Magnussen; equestrian Barbara Simpson Kerr; skier Judy Crawford; divers Bev Boys and Cindy Shatto; track stars Glenda Reiser, Debbie Van Kiekebelt, and Abby Hoffman; golfers Sandra Post and Jocelyne Bourassa; tennis player Andrée Martin; badminton expert Nancy McKinley; table tennis star Violetta Nesukaitis; and Olympic swimmer and national team volleyball player Helen (Stewart) Hunt.[51] Mini-biographies and a suitably feminine photo of each athlete preceded an article by the ubiquitous Jack Batten. After an unfortunate (for Canada) Olympics in 1972, where Karen Magnussen's silver in Sapporo was the only medal of the Winter Games, and swimmers Leslie Cliff (silver) and Donna-Marie Gurr (bronze) accounted for two of the five medals Canada won in Munich, Batten argued that most of the country's best athletes were women: " ... Canadian women have been winning more world-class championships, capturing more individual titles and generally displaying more style than Canada's men have come close to managing in the same time period."[52] He went on:

> The point is that women are at last finding the opportunities to make their mark in Canadian sports. Not in all of them, mind you, not in the highly publicized and highly muscular games like football and hockey (though even that day may come, considering the present accelerated rate of development). It is in the athletic activities that call for some subtlety, plenty of grace and generous doses of courage, that women are grabbing the championships and, grudgingly, the crowd's cheers.[53]

Batten also argued that not only were Canada's women athletes accomplishing more, they were doing so in the face of hardships rarely, if ever, confronted by male athletes. Sport was a man's world, meaning that Canada's sport apparatus, from neighbourhood to national levels, from amateur to professional, was never geared to deal with female athletes. He provided no remedies as to how to fix this problem. Like other commentators before him, he suggested that women athletes have an advantage over their male counterparts. Where society expected men to achieve in three fields — business, marriage, and sport — there was no such pressure on female athletes, and (until marriage and children) they were free to concentrate on sport. In an era before second-wave feminism provided women with a reason to question this perspective, many women athletes were supportive of Batten's view. For example, Abby Hoffman remarked about her own athletic career: "As a girl athlete, I haven't had all the pressure to get married and have kids, and being a girl, I haven't had the pressures to be the breadwinner for some silly bitch, three children, and a house in Don Mills."[54]

SPORTS IGNORED BY THE MEDIA

One athlete featured in the 1973 *Homemaker's Magazine* article was Helen (Stewart) Hunt, a world-class swimmer mentioned in the previous chapter. By now she was in her late 20s and embarking on a second international career in a different sport — volleyball. Hunt retired from swimming in 1959, then trained as a physical education teacher and began playing volleyball with her students. She joined the Vancouver Alums, a local team that eventually became a perpetual winner of the Canadian championship (their name changed many times, and in the early 1970s, they were the Vancouver Chimos). The game had become a fast-growing sport since World War II, when it was a favourite pastime of the troops, and afterwards was included in most school sport programs. It also continued to have a strong following in the services as well as in the YMCAs and many ethnic clubs, such as the Toronto V-Club Latvians and the Montreal Estonians, two top women's teams during this era.[55]

Although women's volleyball had been introduced to the Pan American Games in 1959, Canada did not send a team until the 1967 Pan-Ams in Winnipeg. The team drew players mostly from Vancouver (including Helen Hunt) and Toronto, but they were hopelessly outclassed by stronger teams from South America and the United States. In those days, before much specialization in team sports, a few top volleyball players chose to play on the Pan-Am women's basketball team in Winnipeg instead (it did a little better).[56] The notion of being an all-round athlete in several team sports was still very much in vogue; this was certainly good for the athletes, but where other countries were specializing and centralizing their women's teams, Canada was being left behind at the international level. Helen Hunt was also a member of the Canadian women's volleyball team that competed in the 1971 Pan-Ams in Cali, Columbia, with her team, the Vancouver Calonas (later called the Chimos), supplying most of the players. In Canada, however, the Chimos had little or no competition, and they were forced to raise funds to pay for team trips to other countries or to help bring better competition to Canada. "Like lionesses in heat," wrote one sportswriter, "the Chimos chase after as many challenges as they can find, and they're willing to travel wherever they may be."[57] In 1974, in preparation for the 1976 Montreal Olympics, where women's volleyball would be on the official program for the first time, Moo Park from South Korea was hired to coach the national women's team. Although Hunt was initially named to the team, Park decided he did not want any "married ladies with children" on the team, especially those considered too "old" (she was 35).[58] Much to her disappointment, she did not compete in Montreal, where the Canadian team, incidentally, came eighth out of eight teams, not an encouraging result.

Women's team sports, like volleyball, basketball, ice hockey, softball, field hockey, and others were flourishing in the 1960s and 1970s, but you would never know it from the almost total lack of press coverage. Aside from men's professional sports, the sports media were rivetted on individual athletes, especially those who performed well or better still who brought glory to themselves and to Canada by winning an Olympic medal or world championship. In less prestigious events, and certainly in team sports, top athletes were generally ignored. Marjory Shedd of Toronto was a good example of one such athlete. In the 1940s, she played junior basketball and in 1950 led the Toronto Montgomery Maids to the national senior title. She switched to badminton and volleyball, winning six national singles titles and 14 ladies' doubles titles in the former. She played on volleyball teams like the champion University Settlement Blacks and was a member of the 1967 Pan-Am volleyball team. In 1970, when she was in her early 40s, she was a member of the Commonwealth Games badminton team.[59]

Other talented athletes laboured in obscurity, although occasionally the public would hear about them through brief media attention, and among them were several accomplished native athletes. Martha Benjamin, from Old Crow in the Yukon was one of Canada's top women cross-country skiers in the early 1960s. Inspired and trained by Father Jean Marie Mouchet, an Oblate priest who served with the French ski troops during the war, Benjamin won the Canadian women's championship in 1963, but there was no money to send her to the 1964 Winter Olympics in Innsbruck, Austria. Although the women's Nordic events had been part of the Olympic program since 1952, it was not until 1972 at the Sapporo Olympics in Japan that Canada (and the United States) sent a women's team. By then, the Territorial Experimental Ski Training (TEST) program had been established, assisted by funds from the federal government, and based on Father Mouchet's original project of training skiers in the MacKenzie Delta.[60]

Identical twins Sharon and Shirley Firth emerged from this program to become Canada's top female cross-country skiers in the 1970s and early 1980s. They grew up in a traditional native family, living off the land, first in Aklavik and then relocated to Inuvik in the North West Territories. Although introduced to skiing as young teenagers in 1965 by Father Mouchet, they were soon coached by a Norwegian, Bjorger Pettersen, who was hired by the Canadian Amateur Ski Association to work with the TEST program and find the best skiers. The Firth sisters — along with Roseann Allen, also of Inuvik, and Helen Sander from Ontario — competed as the first Canadians to do so in the cross-country events in the Olympics in Japan. Allen and the Firths were also the first Canadian aboriginal women to compete in an Olympic Games. Lacking the experience especially of the Nordic and other European skiers, Sharon did very well to finish twenty-sixth in the 5-kilometre event and twenty-fourth in the 10-kilometres. Unfortunately Shirley had just recovered from a severe bout of hepatitis prior to the Olympics and was not up to her usual form. Still, in the 3x5-kilometre relay event, the Firths with anchor Allen came tenth, less than five minutes behind the winning Soviets. Sharon and Shirley went on to win a combined 48 Canadian championships and to compete in three more consecutive Olympics.[61]

Bev Beaver and Phyllis Bomberry were from the Six Nations Reserve in south-western Ontario near Brantford, the largest aboriginal community in Canada, where women's softball had been a tradition since the 1930s. The successful Oshweken Mohawk Ladies Softball team, formed in the 1940s, had won three Ontario women's intermediate championships in the 1950s and 1960s. The team disbanded in the mid-1960s to be replaced by a new generation led by outstanding pitcher Bev Beaver, and they went on to win many native and non-native championships. In 1968, Phyllis Bomberry was the first female recipient of the Tom Longboat Award, given annually (since 1951) to the most outstanding aboriginal athlete of the year. As the all-star catcher for the Toronto Carpetland Senior A softball team, she lead them to victory at the 1967 and 1968 Canadian women's championships, and she was also a member of the Ontario gold-medal winning team at the Canada Games in 1969.[62]

Jenni Mortin, in her history of softball in Saskatchewan, writes that the 1960s were softball's golden age: "skilled players showed those skills in good parks, audiences came back, topnotch pitchers became household names."[63] This may well have been true on the prairies and even elsewhere — for example, in 1961, 51 teams were affiliated with the (Ontario) Provincial Women's Softball Union, and 15 years later their numbers had grown to 260[64] — however, as a sport, softball was almost invisible on the sports pages of daily newspapers. In some circles there was a name change to "fastball," not only in hopes of attracting additional fans, but also to distinguish it from the more recreational game of slow-pitch, where the pitched ball is tossed in a high arc. The most exciting development, and certainly the most important one for the game's future, was the explosion of interest in minor league softball, where *both* boys and girls — squirts, pee wees, bantams, and midgets — learned the game and developed their skills. In Saskatchewan, as was probably true elsewhere, Mortin documents the growth of these minor leagues, especially for girls, throughout many prairie centres.[65] Unfortunately, not everyone across the country was as keen on the development of girls' softball. Enthusiastic and talented girls, faced with the prospect of not playing at all unless they played on a boy's team, were often denied that opportunity due to unrelenting attitudes that girls and boys should not compete together.

Until 1966, basketball was still hindered by the lack of one set of rules played across the country and the mind-set, at least among some physical educators, that the participation of women in highly competitive sport was harmful. In an article on women and competitive basketball, Helen Eckert at the University of British Columbia summarized the scientific literature, which by and large showed no ill effects among women participating at a high level. What was more interesting were the results of a questionnaire she had distributed to former members of the Edmonton Grads basketball team, most of whom were now married and having children. Twenty-five former Grads (31 had been contacted) replied to Eckert's questionnaire, which suggests that they were as keen as anyone to assure the world that no reproductive damage had occurred through their participation in international basketball. The results were entirely predictable: the children totalled 49, an average of 2.13 per married Grad (all but one who replied was married).[66]

During most of the 1960s, the Vancouver Eilers (now called the Richmond Merchants) were still the dominant force in Canadian women's basketball, although teams from Saskatoon and Hamilton also won the Canadian championship.[67] High level international competition was still restricted mostly to the Pan American Games where Canada was rarely among the winners. Without a centralized national squad, as was the case with other nations, they could not be as competitive. In 1967, for example, in preparation for the Pan-Ams in Winnipeg and just a few weeks before the competition was to begin, some 20 participants were invited (at their own expense) to a training camp in Vancouver from which 12 would be chosen for the team.[68] The team did quite well, coming third among five teams. In colleges and universities, basketball was growing steadily, but it was not until 1974 that a national intercollegiate championship was established, providing a much needed incentive to develop sophisticated training programs and hire qualified coaches.

It was also in the universities in the 1960s, as well as at the community level, where women's ice hockey saw a revival of sorts. In Ontario, for example, a few hotbeds of hockey could be found in smaller communities, but team names often reflected the notion of being an imitation of a men's team as opposed to teams in their own right — for example, the Burlington Buffaloettes, the Kapuskasing Kookettes, the Preston Golden Trianglettes, the Brampton Canadettes, and the Wallaceburg Hornettes. Most of the players donned full hockey equipment, usually hand-me-downs from brothers and boy friends, but figure skates were still frequently worn. Much more of a problem was the lack of media attention, virtually all of which focussed on men's professional hockey, so that many were unaware that women's hockey even existed. The first Dominion Ladies Hockey Tournament, in which 22 teams took part, was organized in 1967 as a centennial project by the Brampton Canadettes club.[69]

At the same time women's hockey was being revived at the community level, it was also making a comeback in the universities, at least in Ontario. Led by Katherine "Cookie" Cartwright, a student at Queen's University, a small group of students (I was among them) started their own team in 1961, eventually winning approval to set up a varsity women's hockey league for a two-year trial period. Western, McGill, Queen's, and McMaster universities as well as the Ontario Agricultural College (now the University of Guelph) all joined the league. I remember with great disappointment not being able to play on the Queen's team because I was already playing intercollegiate basketball, and it was decreed that we could not play both sports. Despite our enthusiasm, women's university hockey struggled in this period because of indifferent support from the university community, specifically athletic departments.

Female ice hockey at the community level also faced a different challenge in the 1960s in the form of a new sport — ringette — a game invented by Sam Jacks, a director of parks and recreation in North Bay, Ontario, to provide girls with a viable alternative to hockey, especially in competing for ice time on crowded rinks. Invented in 1963, the game was a cross between lacrosse and hockey, where players skate using a straight stick to pass, carry, and shoot a rubber ring to score goals. It was easier than hockey and designed to be played exclusively by girls. The game caught on very quickly both among girls and their parents, who considered hockey too violent for their daughters. Ringette was viewed as a gentler sport with a suitably feminine image played in a safe, all-female environment. The fact that most of the coaches were male did not seem to be an issue because, inevitably, they were fathers interested in contributing to the sport. The game's feminine image was solidified by the names given to different age categories — Petites, Tweens, Belles, Juniors, and Debs. By 1969 there were sufficient teams and leagues to found the first provincial ringette association in Ontario, and during the next decade organizers established other provincial associations, a national office, and launched Canadian championships. The first international competition was in 1979, when a Canadian team travelled to Finland.[70]

By 1975, women's community hockey had grown in Ontario to the point where a new Ontario Women's Hockey Association was founded; rather, it was re-founded (remember that the original Ladies Ontario Hockey Association was established in 1922). Katherine Cartwright, now a Kingston lawyer and former player for the Kingston Red Barons, was its first president. This was a critical step for women's hockey in Ontario, allowing them to battle a male bureaucracy that refused to take the women's game seriously. In other provinces, specifically Alberta, Prince Edward Island, and British Columbia, women's sections were launched within the male associations, but it was Ontario who was instrumental in driving the women's game forward nationally.[71] The privately run Dominion Ladies' Hockey Tournament, now staged annually in Toronto, had nearly 70 teams wishing to participate, but most were from Ontario, Quebec, and the northeastern United States because there was no money for teams to travel from further away. Nonetheless, the sports equipment manufacture CCM was busy marketing a "Jill Strap," a chest protector with cups to accommodate breasts, and most important of all, hockey skates made for a narrower women's foot.[72] As well, the intrepid Cartwright demonstrated considerable vision in 1974 when she wrote to the American Hockey Association supporting a bid for women's hockey to be included in the Olympics.[73]

Also making their mark in this era were an increasing number of adventurous women athletes who challenged, and sometimes transgressed, gender roles. In 1960, Toronto secretary Elaine McCrossan was the first Canadian woman, and among the first in North America, to achieve a black belt in judo, symbol of the highest degree of accomplishment.[74] Stephane Ruys de Perez, a Toronto mother of two whose husband also raced, was one of six serious female sports car racers in Canada in the early 1970s.[75] Male sportswriters often did not know what to make of them:

> Their involvement is the more surprising because there's something oppressively masculine about a racing car. It's sleek, but that's because it has to be — a sort of auto-dynamic sensuality — but there's still an arrogant *maleness* about the fat, muscular tires, the squat body shell and the uninhibited exhaust that produces a primeval cross between a bellow and a call to arms. It's a shock to see a driver remove the helmet — and shake out a tumble of women's hair.[76]

Women also took up dangerous sports like scuba diving and parachute jumping, but they were still sometimes thwarted in their efforts to cross gender boundaries, even in sports with little risk. In 1966, Abby Hoffman, then a University of Toronto student and aspiring Olympian, attempted on three separate occasions to use the large indoor track in the male-only athletic facilities at Hart House and was refused each time.[77] Yet, despite the criticism and negative publicity, some women pursued their sporting interests in so-called men's sports. The Canadian Belles, for example, were a group of "rough-and-tough ladies," who were the only team from Canada playing in a four-team women's professional football league in the early 1970s. Originally created as entertainment ("a comedy sport") to be hired out by groups wishing to raise money, the league became highly competitive, but did not last long.[78] Professional roller derby, racing at breakneck speed on roller skates around a track while trying to upend your opponents, was popular in the United States during the 1960s and 1970s. One star on the circuit was Francine Cochu from Montreal, who played for the Oakland Bay Bombers, earning about $10,000 playing four or five times a week 10 months of the year.[79]

SEX TESTS AND SEXUALITY

In 1966, female contestants at the European track and field championships in Budapest had to take part in an extraordinary private parade — partially nude before the inquisitive stares of three female women doctors. The International Amateur Athletic Federation (IAAF) had adopted the new rule in order to quell persistent rumours that some athletes competing as females were actually men.[80] Despite the humiliation, women athletes had to undergo visual genital inspections at the 1966 British Empire and Commonwealth Games in Jamaica, at the 1967 Pan American Games in Winnipeg, and again at the 1967 European track and field championships in Kiev, where a chromosome sex test was also introduced for the first time. One athlete, Ewa Klobukowska of Poland, co-holder of the world 100-metre record, passed the visual inspection, but after the sex test was disqualified on the basis that she had "one chromosome too many" to qualify as a woman.[81] The IAAF also stripped her of the two medals she had won in the 1964 Olympics and annulled her other records. The buccal smear analysis, where a small scraping of cells is taken from inside the cheek, made its Olympic debut in 1968 to assess whether or not the athlete was a genetic female or male.[82] Only one in five women athletes were given the sex test at the Winter Olympics in Grenoble, but in the summer in Mexico City, all 781 were tested and issued with certificates indicating a "positive sex-chromatin" result.[83]

The introduction of sex tests coincided with significant advances for women in terms of their participation at the Olympic Games, with the number of their events increasing dramatically throughout the 1960s and 1970s. For example, at the Summer Olympics, the 800-metre running event was reintroduced in 1960. Women's volleyball, the first team event for women, was introduced in 1964, along with the pentathlon and 400-metre event in track and the 400-metre individual medley swimming event. The 1968 Olympics in Mexico City saw the inception of six more swimming events, and in 1972 at Munich, the 1500-metre run, 4x400-metre track relay, and kayak slalom were introduced as well as the reintroduction of archery.[84] Consequently, the number of women on Canada's Olympic teams increased from 11.3 to 22.6 per cent for the Summer Olympics between 1960 and 1972, and from 21.4 to 38.3 per cent for the Winter Olympics during the same period.[85] The introduction of sex testing at the Olympics, originally called "femininity control," not only tried to determine who was a genetic female, but was also a means to combat the media's insinuations over the masculinity of women athletes. Sex testing arose out of a contradiction: Olympic competition for women was becoming more rigorous, requiring athletes to be stronger, faster, and increasingly competitive; yet, at the same time they must *look* like women, and, most important of all, their femaleness had to be "scientifically" assured. The fact that no man was ever caught masquerading as a woman after sex tests were introduced merely bolstered the International Olympic Committee's contention they were doing the right thing.[86]

With women athletes becoming more "masculine," at least in appearance and attributes, the longstanding insinuations about their sexuality finally came into the open. Often hidden through silence, certainly in the Canadian popular press, lesbianism was beginning to receive more attention. In fact, sex in all aspects, including homosexuality, was more openly discussed than in previous decades. An article in *Chatelaine*, for example, attempted to sort fact from myth about the causes and frequency of this "sexual deviation" among females. The article made no mention of female athleticism nor any potential connection to lesbianism except to suggest that girls' roles were less rigidly defined than those of males. "Girls swing back and forth between masculine and feminine as they grow up: a tomboy, a girl scholastic or athletic achiever is more acceptable *as a girl* than a sissy or passive nonachieving boy is *as a boy*."[87] The article went on to state, however, that psychiatrists could distinguish groups of lesbians, one of which was biological females who have a decidedly masculine build — "look at one of their arms without the rest of the figure, and you'd swear it was a boy's." Although athletes were not mentioned specifically, it would not have been too big a jump to make the connection. With so little information available, articles like this were important in shaping the public discourse about homosexuality in Canadian culture during the 1960s.[88]

Within the media discourse on women athletes, a direct connection between athleticism and lesbianism was beginning to be more than just vaguely implied. For example, in a 1973 article on the Vancouver Chimos, the best volleyball team in Canada at the time, Paul Grescoe wrote:

> They are not the big, butch girls the male chauvinist might expect. Under their loose sweaters — "Up Your Volleyball," the back of one reads — their baggy sweatpants and shorts, the protective pads on their knees, lurk some women who'd be whistled at in their civvies. Only thick thighs and the occasional masculine-muscled arm reflect their training.[89]

The term "butch" could simply imply a mannish athlete, replacing the earlier attribute "amazon." On the other hand, it can be read as an obvious code for lesbian, often an assertive and strong-minded one at that. Regardless, Grescoe makes clear that the athletes' masculine bodies, interests, and attributes could be mistaken for a visible representation of homosexuality were it not for the fact that most of them either had sex appeal or were self-declared heterosexuals. Later on in the article, he refers to Carole Bishop, 23 and single: "I date but most of the guys resent my training. We tell our girls that they better get married before they join the team because they're not going to after." Although speculative, it could be argued that "mannishness, once primarily a sign of gender crossing, assumed a specifically lesbian-sexual connotation."[90]

Physical education majors and teachers were so vulnerable to accusations of being masculine, butch (the label "lesbian" was rarely used), and the like, that the profession's leaders went to great lengths to dispel the image, as they had for many decades in the past. I was a physical education student at Queen's in the early 1960s, and my memories include many lectures on how to behave, dress, and conduct ourselves as "proper" young women. One of our textbooks said it all:

> First, each major should be *very* careful of her own hair styling, her sports clothes, and her campus clothes. No jeans, slacks, or leotards for street and campus wear. Her sports clothes should be uniform, *clean*, and worn only for sports. Careful grooming is a rule. Hats, "heels 'n hose," and gloves worn to church. Every major should study movement, in dance, sports, body mechanics or movement exploration classes, to try and develop fine carriage and a smooth walk (avoiding both the athlete's swagger and the model's hip-switch).[91]

Most of us thought this sort of advice to be silly and stupid in the extreme, and, except where official policy dictated we ignored it. Besides, we were much too busy with our studies and athletic pursuits to think about it very much. Although many of us had been designated as "tomboys" in our youth, except for the fact that we were all white and likely middle-class, we were as different from each other as any other group of young women. Whatever accusations and insinuations came our way, we took them in stride, rarely discussed them, and got on with the business of becoming PE teachers, recreation directors, YWCA personnel, and other professionals.

CHAPTER 6

FEMINIST ACTIVISM: INCHING
TOWARDS GENDER EQUITY

At my old school two years ago, the girls boycotted the usual male-dominated awards' assembly and staged their own instead to recognize the outstanding *female* athletes in the school. The unfortunate fact, though, is that the schools still do not succeed either in enhancing the fitness levels of students or in providing good competitive opportunities. Most girls leave school in a physically autistic state and haven't the faintest idea how to get any pleasure out of sport.

Abby Hoffman, *Maclean's*, February 1975

By the mid-1970s, Abby Hoffman's long and distinguished track career was coming to an end. She competed in one more Olympics (her fourth) in Montreal in 1976, where she was chosen to carry the Canadian flag in the opening ceremonies. Always political, articulate, and independent, she was increasingly an outspoken voice for the plight of amateur athletes in Canada, especially women. Through newspaper and magazine articles, radio commentaries, and public speaking, like Bobbie Rosenfeld, Alexandrine Gibb, Myrtle Cook, and Phyllis Griffiths before her, she took on the male sports media by challenging their sexist and stereotypical portrayals of female athletes; she chastised school systems for neglecting girls' sports and physical education; she raged against the lack of professional opportunities for women athletes; and she condemned the sex inequities of the sports world, especially the lack of recreation programs, facilities, training opportunities, and prize money. She marvelled that Canadian women athletes had done so well over the years "despite the apparent conspiracy amongst the schools, the media, the recreation authorities and the Canadian culture itself to turn girls away from sport."[1]

161

Beginning in the late 1960s, after lying dormant for decades, there was a resurgence of feminist activity in North America and elsewhere in what we now call "second-wave feminism." I remember an international conference in 1969, where I gave one of my first academic presentations, about the role of the safety bicycle in the emancipation of women. After my session, an American colleague asked if I was a "women's libber" whereupon he told me about the new women's liberation movement in the United States. I listened in amazement, later learning that much the same was happening in Canada. In both countries the grassroots women's movement was an outgrowth of the leftist student movement of the mid-1960s, as female student activists met in informal groups and shared their dissatisfaction with the treatment of women not only in the student movement, but also in the larger society. These leftist women's caucuses gradually broke away to form their own women's liberation groups, taking with them socialist values and a belief in revolutionary change to be brought about through consciousness-raising, demonstrations, and counter-culture literature.[2] It was highly unlikely, however, that sport and physical activity were on the agenda of these first women's movement groups.

At the same time, long-established women's groups in both Quebec and English Canada began to regroup and reorganize. Among the first (in 1966) were the Fédération des femmes du Québec, a coalition of existing women's groups with a focus on urban women, and the Association féminine d'éducation et d'action sociale, whose concern was primarily rural women. Similarly in English Canada, representatives from some 30 reform-minded organizations (like the National Council of Women, the YWCA, the Women's Christian Temperance Union, the National Council of Jewish Women, the Canadian Federation of University Women, the Imperial Order Daughters of the Empire, the Voice of Women, the Federated Women's Institutes, and the Canadian Federation of Business and Professional Women) came together to form the Committee on Equality for Women. Their principal objective was to obtain a royal commission to examine the status of women, a goal achieved in early 1967, marking the beginning of the organized (second-wave) feminist movement in Canada. Through public sessions and media promotion, the commission did its work, consulting widely throughout the country. *The Report of the Royal Commission on the Status of Women in Canada,* published in 1970, covered women's role in the economy, education, family, public life, law, and poverty. It contained 167 carefully worded recommendations, giving second-wave feminism in Canada a badly needed agenda, one with the potential to transform Canadian society.[3] It would take a little time for women's sport and physical activity to become part of this new feminist agenda, but, eventually, like most areas of social life, it did.

SEX DISCRIMINATION IN RECREATION AND SPORT

By the mid-1970s, parents all across the country were waking up to the fact that their daughters were not being treated in the same way as their sons when it came to recreational and sporting opportunities. More importantly, recreation agencies and sport organizations, most of whom were dependent on public facilities and funds, could no longer sustain the argument that they had no moral or legal obligation to provide equal opportunities to both sexes. Until the institution of provincial human rights commissions in the mid-1970s, there was little or no recourse for Canadian girls and women who complained of sex discrimination in sport. In the United States, there was great excitement over Title IX, an educational amendment legislated in 1972. Designed to prevent sex discrimination against students and employees in federally funded education programs, it had an almost immediate impact in some areas. For example, women athletes wishing to attend an American college or university now had access to more athletic scholarships. In Canada, there was no Title IX, nor the legislative mechanism to put it in place; more importantly, athletics were not as integral to our education system as they were in the United States.[4]

By the late 1970s, sport-related complaints of sex discrimination began to come to the attention of provincial human rights commissions. The majority of cases involved young girls wishing to play on all-male sports teams, usually at the all-star level. Some human rights commissions refused to accept such complaints, arguing that they did not consider sport and recreation to be within their jurisdiction. In the cases that did go through the full judicial process, the issues they raised were often lost in the legal wrangling over interpretation of the law. The main value of these sport-related human rights cases was to bring public interest, concern, and pressure to bear on eliminating unequal, sex-discriminatory sport and recreation programs.

Increasing government involvement brought more attention to the role of sport and physical activity in the lifestyle of Canadians. The first national survey of leisure time activities was conducted by Statistics Canada in the spring of 1972; in it, sports included activities like bowling, curling, hockey, and badminton, while jogging, cycling, and exercise programs were considered among the physical activities. Approximately 22 per cent of the adult population engaged in some form of sport or physical activity at least once a week in the three-month period under investigation, but the percentage of adults who devoted more than seven hours per week to sport or physical activity was very small (approximately 5 to 6 per cent). Also interesting was the finding that, although males were more involved in sports than females, gender differences were not marked. For instance, 17.7 per cent of the male population between 20 and 44 years engaged in sport activities at least one to three hours per week in contrast to 13.9 per cent of the female population in the same age category. The differences between the sexes was minimal as age increased — for example, in the 45 to 54 age group, 88.4 per cent of females reported that they engaged in *no* sport activity as opposed to 82.4 per cent of the males. There were virtually no gender differences in physical activity participation no matter what the age. While married women tended to participate most with their families or spouses, researchers speculated that "Canadian society probably provides limited opportunities for involvement by unattached females or groups of females" with community organizations and exercise and keep-fit groups being the exceptions.[5]

Recreational opportunities provided for girls by municipal agencies and the like were often very narrow and highly stereotyped. An Ontario survey revealed that males were involved in a greater number of recreational activities than females with the greatest difference occurring during the school years.[6] The Toronto Parks and Recreation Department, for example, showed a dismal sex bias in favour of males. In the 10 city-operated recreation centres, boys were offered approximately 260 hours a week of physical recreation, while girls had only 130 hours with arts and crafts, cooking, choir, theatre arts, cheerleading, and baton twirling taking up the rest.[7] In the summer of 1977, a community school in Etobicoke, a suburb of Toronto, offered two recreation programs, one called "just for the guys" and the other "girls and things." Included in the boys' program were activities like hiking, baseball, and a trip to the stadium to see a Toronto Blue Jays' baseball game. The girls' program featured sewing, cooking, modelling, hair styling, and skin care. After a mother tried to register her two daughters, aged seven and nine, in the program designated for boys only and was refused, a complaint was lodged with the Ontario Human Rights Commission. In the investigation that followed, the Etobicoke Parks and Recreation Commissioner defended the program, saying: "What's wrong with girls taking cooking lessons, some of them really need it.... We're not going back to the traditional stereotyped roles, but this unisex thing is going too far, in some respects — we've got to the point where boys don't even know if they're boys anymore."[8]

School athletic programs were also found to be biassed in favour of boys. In a 1977 survey of Ontario high school competition, males comprised almost three-fifths of the interschool athletes, and the discrepancy was even larger in metropolitan and large schools. Sports like football and wrestling, not open to girls, usually accounted for most of the gender differences. Yet, the majority of high school girls (over 60 per cent) simply did not participate at all in interschool or out-of-school competitive sports.[9] The situation was not much better at Canadian universities with competitive athletic programs: only 28 per cent of the athletes participating in competitions sanctioned by the Canadian Interuniversity Athletic Union in 1978–79 were female, mostly because they had fewer sports in which to compete.[10]

Companies employing large numbers of young, single women played a role in the early development of women's sports by setting up teams and leagues for their female employees and providing sponsorship. Woodward's, a large Western-based department store, sponsored this 1938 basketball team.

TORONTO STAR

Alexandrine Gibb (1891–1958) was an athlete, pioneering leader and administrator of women's sport, manager of several international teams, and Canada's most pre-eminent woman sports journalist in the 1920s and 1930s.

Ada MacKenzie (1891–1973) was Canada's most outstanding golfer throughout the 1920s and 1930s. In 1924, she founded one of the few golf clubs run specifically for women—the Toronto Ladies' Golf and Tennis Club.

CANADA'S SPORTS HALL OF FAME

National Archives of Canada / PA-116105

During the Second World War, the federal government encouraged the expansion of sport and recreation programs for industries, churches, athletic clubs, and leisure time agencies like the YWCA and YMCA. Wartime industrial plants employed mostly women, and since greater production was key to the war effort, there was increased concern for their fitness and health.

Barbara Ann Scott was the first Canadian to win a figure skating world championship (in 1947) and Olympic gold medal (in 1948), after these events had been cancelled for several years due to the war. As a professional, she made over $100,000 a year from skating and lucrative product endorsements, becoming the first woman athlete in Canada to be transformed from a celebrity to a commodity.

National Archives of Canada / PA-500868

Canada's Sports Hall of Farne

In 1950, Fanny "Bobbie" Rosenfeld (1903–1969) was voted Canada's women athlete of the half-century. An all-round athlete in softball, ice-hockey, track basketball, and tennis, her competitive career was cut short by arthritis. She switched to coaching and managing, and became a popular and successful sportswriter.

No event in the 1950s received as much public and media attention as sixteen-year-old Marilyn Bell's astonishing swim across Lake Ontario in 1954. Greeted by some 350,000 well-wishers in Toronto, she was feted with a ticker tape parade along Bay Street and reception at city hall. She is shown here thirty years after that famous event.

Another marathon swimmer of this era was Winnie Roach Leuszler, unique because she was a mother, and sometimes pregnant when she swam in marathons. In 1951, she became the first Canadian to swim the English Channel.

Golfer Marlene Stewart (later Streit) received more sustained press coverage than any other Canadian woman athlete in the 1950s. Portrayed in the popular media as a normal, teenage "bobby-soxer," she went from obscurity to adulation in 1951 by winning the Ontario Ladies' championship, as well as both the Canadian Ladies' Closed and Open amateur championships against older, more experienced competition.

Skiers Anne Heggtveit, Ginette Sequin, and Lucile Wheeler of Canada's Olympic alpine ski team discuss the downhill course at Cortina, Italy in 1956. Wheeler won a bronze medal at these Olympics, and Heggtveit won gold in 1960 at Squaw Valley.

With more attention paid to high-profile, individual athletes in the 1950s, women's team sports were neglected. Softball was still popular, and the first Dominion women's softball championship was held during the 1951 Canadian National Exhibition. Women's ice hockey lost ground because male leagues dominated the public and community ice arenas.

The Oshweken Mohawk Ladies Softball team from the Six Nations Reserve in southwestern Ontario won three Ontario women's intermediate championships in the fifties and sixties. Phyllis Bomberry (front row, third from left) was the first female recipient of the Tom Longboat Award, given annually (since 1951) to the most outstanding aboriginal athlete of the year.

(ABOVE) In the 1960s, Canadian women athletes often performed better than their male counterparts, especially in tough international competition. Here are the 1968 bronze medal winning 4 x 100-metre freestyle relay swim team (from left): Marion Lay, Angela Coughlan, Elaine Tanner, and Marilyn Corson. Tanner also won silver medals in the 100 and 200-metre backstroke.

(LEFT) Canada's preeminent skier in the 1960s was Nancy Greene, nicknamed "Tiger" because of her attacking, aggressive style on the ski slopes. Competing in three Olympics, she won gold and silver medals in 1968 in Grenoble, France. At the end of the millennium, she was voted the twentieth century's top Canadian female athlete.

(LEFT) Abby Hoffman, shown here at the 1972 Olympics in Munich, had a long and distinguished track career. Competing in her fourth Olympics in 1976 in Montreal, she was chosen to carry the Canadian flag in the opening ceremonies. Always political, articulate, and independent, she increasingly became an outspoken voice for the plight of amateur athletes in Canada, especially women. In 1981, she was appointed Director General of Sport Canada, a position she held for ten years.

(ABOVE) Concerned about how they might be perceived, particularly in male-dominated sports, female athletes sometimes made considerable effort to project a feminine, non-threatening image. Trapshooter Susan Nattrass was the first (and only) woman to compete in Olympic trapshooting in Montreal in 1976, and by 1983, had won six world championships. She competed in her fourth Olympics in 2000 in Sydney, Australia.

(ABOVE) During the 1960s and 1970s, athletes in individual sports were consistently younger than international-level athletes of earlier decades, making their accomplishments all the more remarkable. Halifax swimming sensation Nancy Garapick was only thirteen when she set a world record in 1975. Expected to win a gold medal in Montreal in 1976, she was beaten by two swimmers from the former East Germany. Much later it became known they were steroid users.

(BELOW) Founding members of the Canadian Association for the Advancement of Women and Sport (20 March 1981). For the past twenty years, as the leading organization for girls and women in sport and physical activity, CAAWS encourages girls and women to get out of the bleachers, off the sidelines, onto the fields and rinks, and into the pools.

Team sports for girls, especially soccer and ice hockey, saw a remarkable growth in the 1990s. In soccer, females account for over one-third of the new registrations each year, and the growth in girls' and women's hockey has been steady since the mid-1980s. In the photos are a soccer player on the Alberta under-16 girls' team and a hockey competitor from the Northmemorial Athletic Sports Association in Calgary.

REAL TIME MEMORIES

DIGITAL D'S PHOTOGRAPHY

The Canadian Women's Wheelchair Basketball Team has not lost an international game in over a decade of play, having accumulated an astonishing 43-0 win/loss record. Below they are playing Australia in the gold medal game at the 2000 Paralympic Games in Sydney Australia. Left is Albertan Lori Radke, a member of the national team since 1994.

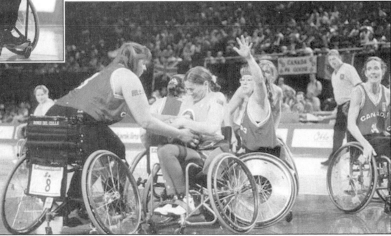

COURTESY OF THE CANADIAN PARALYMPIC COMMITTEE

FREESTYLE PHOTOGRAPHY

Today, there are increasing opportunities for women to play professional team sports. Soccer player Charmaine Hooper (centre of photo) is one of several Canadian players now competing in the new Women's United Soccer Association, featuring top players from the United States as well as the best internationals from twenty different countries.

ANDRE RENNER

High-profile women athletes today use their bodies to market their sports, and themselves. The Canadian women's cross-country ski team sold calendars featuring nude pictures of themselves to raise their profile and funds for their team. Pictured here, from left, are: Sara Renner, Amanda Fortier, Milaine Theriault, and Jamie Fortier.

One notion still prevalent in this era was that girls and young women were not drawn to sport because of certain "myths." For instance, an otherwise positive article in *Homemaker's Magazine* claimed that these myths were the greatest handicap to women's progress in sport. They cited four examples: it's unfeminine to be athletic; hockey and such sports make women too aggressive; a girl can't do strenuous sports during her period; nor should she do them during pregnancy.[11] In the mid-1970s, the long-held view that females were handicapped in sport because of their biology and that they might do irreparable damage to their reproductive system through strenuous activity was still one of the principal explanations as to why fewer girls than boys chose sport. Along with the persistent belief that athleticism and femininity were incompatible, these myths were seen as the main barriers to improving the situation. In preparing the book *Fair Ball: Towards Sex Equality in Canadian Sport* for the Canadian Advisory Council on the Status of Women in 1982, we were specifically instructed to include a section on myths, and of course, provide the evidence to dispel them.[12] We chose to focus on these "myths": female athletes are limited by their biology; women don't have men's endurance; exercise and sports are harmful to the reproductive system and cycle; and girls and women are more susceptible to injuries. Also included was a section on "myths that are not really myths," in which we addressed the so-called conflict between femininity and sport. We took to task researchers who insisted on "proving" that women athletes were still psychologically feminine even though they participate in a culturally acknowledged masculine activity. To study these stereotypes, we argued, was to perpetuate them. Finally, we acknowledged the presence of male homosexuals and lesbians in sport, just as they were everywhere else in society: "They are there, they will continue to be there, and to either ignore them or exaggerate their presence is to uphold a very false image of sport."[13]

What was missing from an analysis of why fewer girls and women participated in sport, why most of the coaches were male, why far fewer women than men were running sport, and why more resources went to males was any notion that the problems and barriers were built into the Canadian amateur sport system. Certainly, the barriers to equality were slowly being identified, mostly through the work of government and government-sponsored agencies, such as the Women's Program in the Fitness and Amateur Sport Branch of the federal government and the Canadian Association for the Advancement of Women and Sport. Yet, the obstacles preventing equality were not simply removed through a process of identification; inequitable conditions were often not perceived as problematic by the very individuals and organizations perpetuating them; and rarely did it seem possible to confront the power relations that constituted sexism (and racism). The mid-1970s to the end of the 1980s was a period of struggle for (and sometimes among) the many individuals and groups working to bring about real change for the betterment of girls and women in sport.

On 20 September 1973, before 30,000 people in the Houston Astrodome and millions more on television, North America's top women tennis player, Billie Jean King, decisively beat a 55-year-old male player named Bobbie Riggs in three straight sets. Touted as the "Battle of the Sexes," some have called it a watershed for women's sport especially in the United States; others claimed it as a victory for women's liberation. Whatever it was, it signalled that women's sport was now a part of the feminist agenda, or as one analyst put it, "Women's Lib met Women's Lob."[14]

EFFECTING CHANGE

Federal government involvement in Canadian amateur sport began officially in 1961 with the passing of Bill C-131, the Fitness and Amateur Sport Act. Even so, government involvement in sport remained indirect and consisted mainly of distributing funds to national sport governing bodies and to the provinces in the form of federal/provincial cost-sharing agreements. Although sport governing bodies were accountable for the use of these funds, there was no accountability in terms of whether the monies were used for both male and female athletes. The federal government's 1968 Task Force on Sport was focussed mostly on professional ice hockey and Canada's success (or lack of) in international sport and made no mention of women as a special group. Quite simply, governments at all levels in Canada were unconcerned about the plight of women's sport throughout the 1960s.

Along came the *Report of the Royal Commission on the Status of Women in Canada* in 1970. Among its many recommendations, only two related to sport and were directed at the lack of equal opportunity for girls in school sport programs.[15] Since what happened in schools fell under provincial jurisdiction, the federal government initially did little to respond. Under pressure, they finally hired a consultant within the Fitness and Amateur Sport Branch (FAS) in 1972. This person was former Olympic swimmer Marion Lay, and her duties, among other things, included "defining the problems facing women in sport and designing programs to alleviate these problems."[16] Lay immediately went to work building networks among athletes, coaches, physical educators, recreation practitioners, and academics in the universities. She proposed research studies to gather information, conferences and symposia to focus the issues, and promotional films and resource material to generate interest. Although it was an immense task for one person to accomplish, she made some progress in these early days of feminist activism in sport.

A highlight was the first national conference on women and sport held in Toronto in 1974, which brought together athletes, coaches, educators, administrators, and researchers interested in furthering the development of women's sport. Laura Sabia, a well known feminist and one of the leaders who had provoked the federal government into calling a royal commission on the status of women, gave the opening keynote address. Calling for the development of a relationship between the women's movement and women's sport, as well as continued pressure on governments to initiate change, she assured those in attendance that "Women's Lib" was "nothing more than equality of opportunity, responsibility, and choice." In her summary comments at the conclusion of the conference, Abby Hoffman spoke for many delegates when she said, "I think some of us were perhaps too self-conscious and a little too ambiguous and ambivalent about our role as women in sport to take on an additional burden of becoming part of the women's movement." The outcome of the conference was a series of sensible recommendations directed toward governments, sport and recreation agencies, educational authorities, status of women groups, and the media.[17]

FAS also initiated several promotional projects aimed at increasing the participation of women in sport and physical activity, including the film *Your Move*, a photographic display, posters, and a family allowance cheque insert. National sports governing bodies were encouraged to pay more attention to programming for their female members, and two sports designed specifically for women (netball and ringette) were given special funding.

Along with others (including Abby Hoffman and myself) hired on contract, Lay attempted to convince senior officials that the needs of women in sport were inadequately met through existing government policies, programs, and structures. However, there was strong resistance to the suggestion that the administration of Canadian sport should be restructured to accommodate the needs of women.[18] FAS personnel did not view women in sport as a particularly significant issue; they maintained that their policies were not discriminatory and their programs were open to everyone. Besides, if it was an issue, national sport governing bodies could submit appropriate proposals.[19] As activists, we were trying to find solutions to what we believed were relatively simple problems, not realizing that the changes we naively "demanded" attacked the system at its core and that men do not give up power willingly.

Another development that pushed women and sport issues even further to the background was the federal government's rush in the 1970s to promote high performance sport. In 1976, FAS was assigned its own minister, Iona Campagnola, a neophyte member of Parliament from Prince Rupert, British Columbia. She had "a keen sense of the political potential of elite sport and the capacity to capitalise on the publicity inherent in international sport events."[20] For the next three years, her major concern was to define the branch's mandate more clearly and to develop an effective national sports policy. After much public input, policy clearly shifted towards federal support for excellence in sport, leaving the primary responsibility for recreational programs to the provinces and territories, but there was still no recognition of women as a target group for special attention. On some issues (abortion for example) Campagnola was a strong feminist, but for most of her tenure as the minister responsible for fitness and amateur sport, she stead-fastly stuck to her position that "the needs of women in sport could adequately be met through existing Branch policies and programs."[21] Her influence was substantial. In 1977, she was named as one of the 50 "makers and breakers in Canadian sport," along with only three other women — Abby Hoffman, Christie Blatchford (sports columnist for the *Globe and Mail*), and Colleen Howe, wife of hockey player Gordie Howe (presumably because she looked after his interests).[22]

Campagnola lost her cabinet position in the spring of 1979 when the Liberal government was defeated. During the brief, one-year Conservative government, she was replaced by Steve Paproski, a former professional football player, who had little time to become familiar with his job. When the Liberals regained power in 1980, Gerald Regan, the former premier of Nova Scotia, took over as minister.

Two events occurred in 1980 to make it a watershed year for feminist activism in Canadian sport. The first was a second national conference on women's sport held in Vancouver in March. The Female Athlete Conference, co-sponsored by FAS and Simon Fraser University, brought together many of the same people who had attended the first national conference in 1974. Very little had changed in the inter-vening six years, and it was realized that simply talking about change was no longer adequate. Action was clearly needed. Most also recognized that although their indi-vidual efforts had increased the opportunities for girls and women to participate, they still lacked power and resources within the Canadian sports system; until struc-tural inequalities in the system were attacked, little of substance would change.[23]

The second important event was the establishment of an official Women's Program within FAS. Since 1974, Marion Lay (eventually assisted by Sport Canada consultant Sue Vail) had submitted proposals annually for a special women's program. There was no reaction until 1980 when FAS officials, sufficiently concerned about an inadequate response to the 10-year review of the Royal Commission on the Status of Women recommendations, finally relented. The Women's Program, jointly responsible to Sport Canada and Fitness Canada, was initiated in the fall of 1980 with a one-time budget of $250,000 (from lottery monies); Sue Vail was appointed to oversee it.[24] The program's mandate was "to develop and promote ways of involv-ing more women in sport and fitness activities" by removing some of the "traditional barriers" that inhibited full and equal participation by women.[25] There were four key areas of activity: financial contributions to national sport and recreation organ-izations for projects related to the participation of females in sport and fitness; an internship program for retired women athletes seeking jobs in national sports organ-izations; liaisons and information exchange with other relevant federal agencies; and policy development related to women and physical activity.

One of the Women's Program's early projects was a national survey on women in sport leadership in Canada, the first time such a study had been conducted. At this point there were some 75 national amateur sports organizations receiving a total of over $25 million annually from the federal treasury, most with full-time paid professionals and an office in Ottawa. These sport associations or governing bodies were (and still are) administered by a mix of volunteers and paid staff. Similar structures, although not nearly as extensive, had also been established in the provinces and territories. Employment in these sports organizations reflected the same pattern as in other sectors of society — men in management and the higher level positions, and women segregated in the clerical, office administrator, and program coordinator positions. At the national level, only 30 per cent of the paid coaches and administrators and 26 per cent of the volunteers were women.[26]

It was clear from this survey and others that not only did women coach far less than men, their percentage decreased further as the level of competition increased. For instance, a survey of coaches in Ontario high schools showed that only 26 per cent were female, and that co-ed teams in the schools were often coached by males. In Canadian universities, the number of full-time coaching positions held by women had actually decreased, despite the increase in female athletes, so that approximately 60 per cent of the women playing on a university team were being coached by a male. At the very highest level of expertise, the coaches of national teams, only 13 per cent (or less than a dozen) were women. A comprehensive National Coaching Certification Program, which provided coaches at all levels the opportunity to improve their knowledge and skill in the theoretical, technical, and practical aspects of coaching had been in place for a few years. In many sports, the levels of certification (five in all) were still in the developmental stage. There were, however, twice as many males in the program as females, whose progression through the various levels was less successful.[27]

Still, there were hundreds and sometimes thousands of women, primarily volunteers, coaching in every conceivable sport. Their numbers were impressive in sports such as gymnastics, synchronized swimming, volleyball, basketball, field hockey, and figure skating, but they were found primarily in schools, clubs, and community leagues, rather than coaching college, university, provincial and territorial, or national teams. The arguments about whether only women should coach females were as alive in the 1980s as they were 40 years before when the Women's Athletic Committee of the Canadian Physical Education Association tried to impose their women-only philosophy across the country. Throughout the years, the issue had been a divisive one among those holding conflicting philosophies: hire a woman coach regardless of her skill or hire the best qualified regardless of gender. It was the latter philosophy that had won out in the end.

Women were virtually absent from positions of higher responsibility in Canadian sport and, thus, of power in the decision-making process. For example, there were only two women among the 38 members of the Board of Directors of the Canadian Olympic Association. Women made up less than one-fifth of the board members of national sport organizations, although in some associations, females comprised at least half, if not more, of the registered membership. On the professional level, women occupied only a small proportion (less than 20 per cent) of the full-time executive director and technical director positions in these same organizations. At the university level, the vast majority of athletic administrators were male (75 per cent). Things had looked promising in 1973, when Patricia Jackson was made athletic director at the University of Saskatchewan, the only woman to hold such a position at a major North American university, but clearly this was an anomaly.[28] The only university conference to have retained separate governing organizations for men's and women's athletics was in Ontario where there were many more female athletic directors, which simply affirmed the argument made by physical educators and others that women were better off running their own sports.

From the mid-1970s and throughout the 1980s, there was increasing concern over the continued under-representation of women leaders in the Canadian amateur sport system, especially at the national level. On every front, the numbers of women with power and authority in the sport system remained much the same as they had when the first studies were conducted in the late 1970s, and in some cases their numbers had actually declined (for example, women physical education teachers employed in secondary schools). Study upon study documented the problem, some going beyond description to understand the processes and dynamics that structured gender, in other words, the relations of power between women and men in these organizations.[29]

It was clear that women faced stereotypical notions about their competence despite their formal qualifications, organizational resources, and technical expertise. They were assumed (in actuality or in the perception of themselves and others) to lack the proper training, motivation, and skills to succeed, when in fact they were often in every way as qualified as men. Where women had to prove themselves and work their way up the sport hierarchy, the competence of men, whether or not it was true, was taken for granted. Working or volunteering in primarily a masculine sports world, women had to learn the language, symbols, myths, beliefs, and values of that very male culture, sometimes turning themselves into "honorary" men to be successful. One of the reasons often cited for women's under-representation was that their family responsibilities were a "given" and beyond the control of the organization; for example, child-care facilities and arrangements were routinely of no interest to the organization. Where a strong and informal male network existed to enhance men's opportunities, a much weaker female network provided little support. Male (white) elites ensured the maintenance of the status quo, and their own power, by selecting individuals most like themselves. Although women perceived and experienced discrimination in greater numbers than did men, most organizations saw no need to initiate any sort of affirmative action program or structure to address the needs of women.

Some national sport organizations, more aware and concerned about the problem of women's under-representation than others, initiated "women's committees" to address issues pertinent to females. Among the earliest committees were those in the rowing association, which held its first meeting in 1981, and Women's Bicycling Voice in cycling, officially recognized a year later.[30] The women's cycling committee was the most successful, due in part to the organizational culture of cycling, which attracts older, alternative lifestyle participants because of its strong recreational and transportation sections. Their main accomplishment was the adoption of a "Policy on Equal Opportunity" by the Canadian Cycling Association that outlined the issues, goals, policy statements, and implementation strategies for attaining equality for females in cycling. Very few national sport associations followed their lead by creating special women's committees, and most ignored the importance of developing women leaders or addressing issues of concern to girls and women.[31]

In 1981 Abby Hoffman was appointed the Director General of Sport Canada. Obviously a strong advocate of women's sport, she encouraged the Women's Program to assist national sport organizations to realize the importance of gender equitable programs and policies, and she provided some funding. Taking the lead, Sport Canada formulated and adopted a *Policy on Women's Sport*, which on the surface was a strongly worded statement seeking equality:

> To attain equality for women in sport. Equality implies that women at all levels of the sport system should have an equal opportunity to participate. Equality is not necessarily meant to imply women wish to participate in the same activities as men, but rather to indicate that activities of their choice should be provided and administered in a fair and unbiased environment. At all levels of the sport system, equal opportunities must exist for women and men to compete, coach, officiate or administer sport. The purpose of this goal is to create an environment in which no one is forced into a predetermined role or status because of gender.[32]

There was, however, widespread resistance among national sport organizations to implement gender-based affirmative action programs when they did not contribute to their more important goals of preparing elite Canadian athletes to compete successfully in international sport. More importantly, the policy had little "teeth" in that funds were not withheld from national sport bodies even if they made little effort to comply.[33]

By the end of the 1980s, Sport Canada took direct action by pressing national sport organizations to include strategies for the development of women coaches and administrators in their high performance planning. It had earlier initiated an internship program to encourage young women with appropriate sport backgrounds to enter careers as sport professionals, and at the same time, it subsidized national sport organizations willing to provide interns with suitable kinds of work experience. The internship program was a success in that most interns went on to full-time positions, although mostly at the entry or junior level, in the Canadian amateur sport system. It was, however, very difficult for women to move up or even be hired into the senior positions (like executive directors, technical directors, and national coaches), especially in high profile and big budget sports. In response, the Women in Sport and Fitness Leadership program was revamped to help selected women prepare themselves for leadership roles so they would be better qualified and ready for these senior jobs.[34]

The Women's Program in Fitness and Amateur Sport, which by 1986 had a manager in both Sport Canada and Fitness Canada, sought to work directly with a new women's sport advocacy organization, the Canadian Association for the Advancement of Women and Sport, which was formed in 1981. It provided it with funding and support, but as we will see in the next section, there were problems with government involvement in a private organization, whose purpose was to critique and push the state into doing much more for women in sport in Canada.

CANADIAN ASSOCIATION FOR THE ADVANCEMENT OF WOMEN AND SPORT

In 1974 the American professional tennis player Billie Jean King took the prize money she had won as the year's best female athlete and donated it to start the Women's Sports Foundation. King and other top women athletes sketched out their ideas of what a foundation advocating women's sports in the United States might hope to achieve. The Women's Sports Foundation was the first advocacy organization established during second-wave feminism explicitly to achieve a better deal for girls and women in sport. As a non-profit, membership-based organization, its goal was to get women of all ages and skills involved in sport activities for their health, enjoyment, and personal development. The Foundation's first executive director, handpicked by King, was Eva Auchincloss, who at the time was assistant publisher of King's magazine, *womenSports*.[35]

Canadian sportswomen were envious of this new organization, but, since there was no philanthropist like King on the horizon, they looked to the state for the necessary funding to establish a similar advocacy organization. Besides, unlike the United States, there was already a high degree of government involvement and funding in the Canadian sport system.

Although the idea of a national organization was discussed informally for several years, it was not until the Female Athlete Conference in Vancouver in 1980 that delegates first recommended the establishment of a "National Women's Sport Foundation to serve as a communication network and advocacy group across the country."[36] Funded by the Women's Program in FAS, and attended by a small group of sport administrators, federal government representatives, athletes, coaches, university-based physical educators, and representatives from the major national feminist organizations, a two-day workshop to discuss the idea was organized and held at McMaster University. Out of these discussions came the Canadian Association for the Advancement of Women and Sport (CAAWS), formerly established on 20 March 1981.[37]

The workshop was probably the first time that leaders within the Canadian women's sport community discussed the relationship between sport and feminism.[38] Some delegates were actively involved in the women's movement and readily saw its relevance to sport, whereas others were uneasy at the very mention of feminism. After considerable discussion, the group endorsed a series of statements asserting that "there is inequality in sport based on sex, the sport system is sexist, and an understanding of sex roles and sexism in sport is the starting point for an analysis of sport."[39] These statements were labelled a "feminist perspective on sport," which was a significant step for those who had formerly shunned any identification with feminism. Another controversial decision was taken over the merits and meaning of the phrase women *and* sport as opposed to women *in* sport. Delegates chose the former for two reasons: the advancement of women in sport would only be achieved if the condition of women in general was improved, and sport itself was in need of reform to reduce its emphasis on commercialism, violence, and performance rather than participation.

The founders of CAAWS formulated a clear statement of the organization's purpose: "to advance the position of women by defining, promoting, and supporting a feminist perspective on sport and to improve the status of women in sport." Toward this end, four activity areas were identified: advocacy, research, leadership development, and communication both within and outside the organization. Its goals were: to eradicate sexism in sport; to design new models for sport and strategies for change; to develop and maintain a network to promote participation and lobby for change; to provide a support system for individual and collective initiatives to help women function in the sport system; to develop a feminist analysis of sport; to facilitate greater involvement of women in all aspects of sport; and to contribute to the women's movement and social change in favour of women generally.[40] The fact that CAAWS was at the same time openly feminist and government-funded was not at all unusual given the politics of the state and the Canadian women's movement at the time. As political scientist Jill Vickers has pointed out, an operational code of the second-wave women's movement in Canada was the belief that change was possible and that state action was an acceptable way of achieving it. "Most Canadian feminists," she argued, "perceive the state more as a provider of services, including the service of regulation, than a reinforcer of patriarchal norms, and most seem to believe that services, whether child care or medicare, will help."[41]

In its early years, CAAWS was funded through grants from the FAS Women's Program as well as the Secretary of State Women's Program, which eventually allowed it to acquire office space and a staff person; produce a newsletter; fund local research and action projects; and provide travel and accommodation expenses for board meetings, annual conferences, and general meetings. By 1985, it had a membership of 300, with enthusiastic chapters in Vancouver and Ottawa, and other groups springing up across the country. Like most national feminist organizations in this era, it was almost totally dependent on government largesse, causing some to question whether it was vulnerable to co-optation. Many active members were employed in the sport delivery system either at the national, provincial, or municipal level, and it was not unusual for managers of the FAS Women's Program to play a leadership role in CAAWS through its board of directors. In theory, it was hoped that CAAWS and the Women's Program could work in partnership, but government personnel often faced unrealistic expectations or were accused of not being radical enough by their counterparts in CAAWS.[42]

For many women active in CAAWS, this was their first and perhaps only affiliation with a feminist organization, and it was these women who sometimes raised questions about the association's commitment to explicitly feminist principles. The sort of feminism expressed by organizations like CAAWS was liberal reformism, in the sense that it was seeking to provide girls and women with the same opportunities and resources as boys and men and to remove the barriers and constraints to their participation. Girls and women tended to be treated as homogeneous categories with little recognition that differences in background, class, race, ethnicity, age, disability, and sexual preference led to very different expectations and experiences of sport. What also went unchallenged was the fundamental nature of male-defined sport with its emphasis on hierarchy, competitiveness, and aggression. Those pushing for a more radical agenda adopted an unequivocal women-centred perspective, which recognized and celebrated differences among women and at the same time seriously questioned male-dominated and male-defined sport.[43]

Throughout the 1980s, these ideologically differing perspectives within CAAWS were often played out in the struggles over sexual politics. In the early days of the organization, lesbian issues were certainly discussed, but there was little public debate and no open recognition to suggest that CAAWS was anti-homophobic or lesbian-positive. The membership and leadership were split between those who viewed sexuality as a private and personal concern versus those who saw it as a political issue. For some, the organization was perceived to have an "image problem," as expressed through letters of concern to the CAAWS newsletter whenever the lesbians in CAAWS became too visible. For example, the first newsletter of the association (Fall 1982), called "Kick-off," showed on its cover a line drawing of a strong, powerful woman kicking a soccer ball, and inside there was a review of the film *Personal Best*, about a lesbian athlete. The first public debate about sport and sexuality did not take place until the 1985 annual conference, where those in support of more political activity around the issues stressed the importance of solidarity and the need to recognize that homophobia hurt all women in sport. From this point onwards, resolutions were passed at various annual general meetings such as: "CAAWS endorses the inclusion of sexual orientation in the Canadian Human Rights Code"; "CAAWS is opposed to discrimination against lesbians in sport and physical activity, and that CAAWS undertakes to support advocacy efforts to ensure lesbian equality of rights"; and "Given that there are lesbians with CAAWS, and homophobia within CAAWS, the Association needs to address these internal concerns."[44]

For those who took a more radical stance, these human rights and education strategies were insufficient because they were too liberal and they depoliticized sexuality, even though they were recognized as gradual steps toward a politicization of lesbian issues. Neither side made much progress, and, despite these well-meaning resolutions and the workshops that produced them, lesbians in CAAWS experienced difficulty in keeping lesbian visibility and homophobia issues on the agenda. The resulting divisiveness took its toll on association members' time and energy, and it was easier to focus more on the important work of lobbying governments to make women's sport a priority. To some extent the state played a role in enforcing silence on these issues when the Secretary of State Women's Program (at the time a major source of funding for CAAWS) directed in 1987 that it would no longer fund groups or project proposals whose primary purpose was "to promote a view on sexual orientation" or "to support advocacy efforts to ensure lesbian equality of rights." Although this was not the primary purpose of CAAWS, the government directive had implications for the association, which by then had taken sufficient steps to become unequivocally lesbian-positive and anti-homophobic.[45]

Like many Canadian feminist organizations of this era, the leaders of CAAWS constantly worried over the lack of funding and how to bridge huge geographical distances, as well as cultural and linguistic differences, to fashion a truly national organization. Internal struggles over vision (advocacy versus service to members), structure (hierarchical versus consensus-building), jurisdiction (strong central organization versus local chapters), and over their constituency (recreational versus elite athletes) were frequently on the agenda. By 1987, the organization had become more overtly feminist with a clear focus on advocacy. In her keynote address at the annual conference, Acadia University professor Wendy Bedingfield put it succinctly: "I have heard and read much regarding current issues in Canadian sport and one of the constants is that *women* are themselves an issue. I am here to tell you that *I* am *not* an issue in sport. Neither my hair style, my dress, my language nor my sexuality are issues in sport. Neither are yours."[46] Their mission statement was now: "CAAWS defines, promotes and supports a feminist perspective to advance the position of girls and women and to improve the quality of sport and physical activity." They also put forth five position statements to make it clearer:

1. CAAWS believes that systemic inequalities result in unfavourable resource allocation, programming and leadership development for girls and women in sport and physical activity.
2. CAAWS promotes actions which place and support women in decision-making positions in sport and physical activity.
3. CAAWS believes that the survival and advancement of women and sport and physical activity is dependent upon feminist empowerment and the feminist community.
4. CAAWS believes that any representation of girls and women in sport and physical activity should eliminate stereotypes and promote participation as a positive force in their lives.
5. CAAWS believes that feminist values must be validated and entrenched in the management and delivery of sport and physical activity.[47]

Feminist processes were also incorporated into daily operations such as sharing power between staff and board members, consensus decision-making, rotating chairpersons, and ensuring inclusiveness. One of two major successes to come out of this period was the National Coaching School for Women, the brainchild of CAAWS member Betty Baxter, which took a women-centred and athlete-centred approach to coaching, specifically in basketball and volleyball. The other was the Breakthrough Awards, which celebrated the achievements of individuals and groups who through sport and physical activity broke societal barriers and inspired participation.

In 1990, CAAWS was one of several national women's organizations to lose its operational funding from the Secretary of State Women's Program, and, although it had some project money from the Women's Program in Sport Canada, it was forced to downsize drastically and rely on volunteer assistance. The organization struggled to survive, only to be saved a year later by an agreement to move it into the mainstream of sport by establishing an office in the Canadian Sport, Fitness and Administration Centre in Ottawa, where all national and multi-sport organizations were located, and to provide it with substantial core and project funding through Sport Canada's Women's Program. As a result, it became less a women's (feminist) organization that promoted its aims through sport, and more one that sought to improve the lot of women already in sport through a sports organization for women.

LEGAL CHALLENGES TO INEQUALITY

In the summer of 1976, Bruce Bannerman, manager of the Waterford Squirt All-Star Softball team, registered his team with the Ontario Rural Softball Association (ORSA).[48] One of the players was Debbie Bazso, nine years old. The Association returned Debbie's application and her 50 cent registration fee with the comment "cannot play." Bannerman complained in writing to the president of the ORSA, claiming its constitution did not prohibit girls from playing, to which the association responded: "no girls are allowed to play with boys teams in our league or any other organized league that is a member of the Ontario Softball Council."[49] Despite the ORSA's objection, Bannerman took his team, including Debbie Bazso, to the first playdowns against a team from Caledonia. A protest was lodged by the coach (ironically a woman) of the Caledonian team on the grounds that Waterford was using an unsigned player not qualified to play because of her sex. The ORSA disqualified the Waterford team from further competition. Subsequently, Bannerman filed a complaint, on behalf of Debbie Bazso, with the Ontario Human Rights Commission, the first time such a case had been brought forward.

From the Commission's viewpoint, the Bannerman/Bazso case presented clear and compelling evidence of sex discrimination. It had accepted the case on the basis of what was believed to be a denial, on the grounds of sex, of "services and facilities available in any place to which the public is customarily admitted." The interesting aspect of this case, and others like it, was the principal legal question being addressed. It was not whether a girl should be allowed to play on a boys' sports team, but whether an amateur sports organization, like ORSA, fell within the definition of public services and facilities in provincial human rights legislation. The ORSA contended, among other things, that it was sufficiently "private" and did not have to abide by this provision. A Board of Inquiry, however, found that it did: "The public nature of the services is further emphasized by the fact that the ORSA receives government funding for its work and that the Regional Municipalities make available public facilities for the ORSA playdowns."[50]

Two other fundamental issues were raised by this case. The ORSA, in defence of its action, claimed that integrated softball would provide occasions for a breach of bodily privacy. Again the Board of Inquiry disagreed, since the changing of clothing for play invariably took place at home and the children were driven to and from the games in their baseball attire. In the event a mixed team wished to avail itself of a locker room for dressing and showering, the Board found no reason why boys and girls could not dress and shower sequentially, thereby avoiding any risk of bodily exposure of one sex to the other. The second issue centred around the question of whether separate but equal athletic programs were justifiable. The ORSA claimed, of course, that they were, and stated further that fairness and competition would be effectively destroyed if mixed competition were permitted at all age levels. However, in this case, the Board found that, although separate but equal athletic programs may afford some advantages, they also tend to hold back the very able and qualified females from competing at the upper level of a particular sport where no equivalent girls' team is available. As a result, the ORSA was ordered to cease holding sex-segregated divisional softball playoffs for children 11 years and younger.

The case, however, did not end there. The ORSA appealed the decision to the Supreme Court of Ontario Divisional Court, which overturned the Board's decision on the grounds that the ORSA, established to provide an organized system of softball playoffs among Ontario communities, offered a facility open to teams composed of either boys or girls, but did not offer a facility for integrated softball. Therefore, the refusal to grant Debbie Baszo a playing card did not contravene the Ontario Human Rights Code. For its part, the Ontario Human Rights Commission appealed the ruling to the next judicial level, which was split as to whether or not the Board's original decision should be upheld. Although the majority decision was upheld, and the appeal was dismissed, the one judge (a woman) with a minority opinion said something very telling: "Indeed, there is no suggestion that Debbie Bazso did not meet all the tests of eligibility for the play-offs. Her case seems to me therefore to be on exactly the same footing under the section as the case of a boy denied registration by the ORSA because he is black."[51] In the final chapter of this case, the Ontario Human Rights Commission tried to appeal the decision to the Supreme Court of Canada, but their application was denied.

Around this time, three other similar high-profile cases were making their way through the judicial system with varying degrees of success. In northern Ontario, 10-year-old Gail Cummings applied to join the Huntsville Minor Hockey Association in October 1976 and was accepted. However, after she was selected for the under-11 Huntsville All-Star team and played in several games, she was informed that the Ontario Minor Hockey Association (OMHA) would not accept her registration, because its constitution forbade girls to play on teams under its jurisdiction. The OMHA was governed by the rules of the Canadian Amateur Hockey

Association, which in turn restricted membership to "every male person." Gail Cumming's mother filed a complaint with the Ontario Human Rights Commission, and, like the previous Bannerman case, a Board of Inquiry ordered the OMHA to allow registrations from girls. They, too, appealed the ruling, arguing that they should be exempted from the Human Rights Code on the grounds of public decency. The association claimed that the pile-ups and physical contact characteristic of hockey would constitute an "invasion of bodily privacy" if girls were allowed to play with boys. They also argued that psychological harm would be done to boys if they lost to girls, boys would play "softer" when playing with girls, and future family stability was in danger if boys learned in hockey to roughhouse with girls instead of treating them with respect.[52] In the end, after appeals and counter-appeals, the Ontario Minor Hockey Association won the case. Bruce Kidd, former Olympian and by now a well-known educator, was appalled by the decision. In a letter to the provincial minister of Culture and Recreation, he commented: "If sports governing bodies are legally considered 'private' associations — despite the complete monopoly over opportunities they enjoy in most sports — then no athlete can have recourse to human and civil rights legislation and common law precedents to redress a grievance."[53] For her part, Gail Cummings, an all-round athlete, who ran, skated, and played lacrosse as well, earned a spot on the Huntsville All-Star lacrosse team, who cared little that she was a girl. She eventually earned an athletic scholarship (in lacrosse) to Temple University in Philadelphia.[54]

Other cases involving minor league hockey were brought forward in Nova Scotia and Quebec, and interestingly, with more success than had occurred in Ontario. Tina Marie Forbes was an 11-year-old girl in Hebron, Nova Scotia, who liked to play hockey. In the fall of 1977, Tina's father tried to register her with the Yarmouth Minor Hockey Association (YMHA) so she could play in house league hockey. After repeated attempts, each time being told that Tina could not play because she was a girl, the Forbes complained to the Nova Scotia Human Rights Commission. Since Tina only wanted to play in a house league, and not in all-star, inter-zone, or inter-provincial hockey, all of which would have come under the jurisdiction of the Canadian Amateur Hockey Association, the Board of Inquiry ordered the YMHA to allow her to play. A similar case in Montreal, involving Françoise Turbide, who wanted to play bantam (age 13 and 14) hockey eventually went to the Quebec Superior Court. Here the judge ruled that the local league and the Fédération québécoise de hockey sur glace must allow girls to play; more importantly, the Canadian Amateur Hockey Association ruling prohibiting girls from playing would no longer affect residents of Quebec.[55] While the Turbide case was in litigation, the ensuing publicity and threat of legal action persuaded officials in the Fédération québécoise de hockey sur glace to allow seven-year-old Sarah Sniderman to join one of their novice teams.[56] The ramifications of the decision in Quebec also extended to 11-year-old Manon Rhéaume, who in 1983 was the first girl to play in the Quebec International Peewee Hockey Tournament. Growing up in Lac Beauport, just north of Quebec City, Rhéaume played goal alongside her two brothers on a team coached by her father. Her team also played in the tournament the next year, after which, in a media interview, Rhéaume predicted: "One day, a woman will make the National Hockey League. If no one prevents her."[57]

By the early 1980s, there had been some 50 sport-related cases brought before provincial human rights commissions. They ranged from young girls complaining of being forbidden to play on boys' teams in sports like baseball and hockey, to women objecting to restricted hours at private golf and curling clubs, to a senior high school student wishing to train with a boys' wrestling team in order to improve her judo skills. Many cases were resolved informally; yet some human rights commissions refused to accept cases involving sex discrimination in sport. Ontario had by far the most cases, many of which remained unresolved. In 1981, under pressure to clarify its legislation, the Ontario government amended its Human Rights Code to include a section that specifically exempted membership in athletic organizations, participation in athletic activities, and access to the services and facilities of recreational clubs from its sex equality provisions. This effectively legalized sex discrimination in sport, leaving no legal recourse, and certainly nullified the 20 or so sport-related cases before the Ontario Human Rights Commission at the time.

The resulting public outcry prompted the Ontario government to set up a Task Force on Sex Equality in Athletics in 1982, headed by Toronto lawyer John Sopinka. Its mandate was to determine which changes, if any, were needed in the area of legislation or elsewhere to provide equal opportunity for both sexes. Local chapters of CAAWS, community groups, and boards of education mobilized to provide the task force with data on sex inequality in sport participation and programs. Unfortunately Sopinka recommended no changes to the Ontario Human Rights Code, opting instead for the "gentle approach of administrative persuasion" (he suggested funds be withheld from sports groups that do not provide equal opportunity) rather than the litigation route to equality.[58] Sopinka's rationale for not recommending a repeal of the offending section was because not everyone in the women's sport community was in favour of complete integration, especially if they could have parallel opportunities for both girls and boys.[59] Others argued that the discriminatory clause in the Code flagrantly violated the Canadian Charter of Rights and Freedoms and would not stand up to a legal challenge. All that was needed was a test case to see if this was correct, and groups like the Women's Legal Education and Action Fund (LEAF) promised to help shepherd the challenge through the judicial process.

Along came 12-year-old Justine Blainey, who in 1985 was chosen to play on a boys' hockey team in the Metro Toronto Hockey League, but was barred from playing by the Ontario Hockey Association. She wanted to play boys' hockey because of the bodychecking and slapshot, neither of which were allowed in the equivalent girls' league administered by the Ontario Women's Hockey Association. LEAF took up her case, providing a lawyer to argue the Charter points. The case itself generated tremendous publicity, and the media responded with in-depth reports, not just about Justine Blainey's legal troubles, but also about sex inequality generally in amateur sport.[60] At the appeal stage of the process, LEAF sponsored an intervention by CAAWS in order to file American case authorities, which had adopted the view that both separate girls' teams and access to boys' teams were necessary to advance women in sport. In April 1986, the Ontario Court of Appeal struck down subsection 19(2) of the Ontario Human Rights Code, ruling that it contravened the equality provisions (section 15) in the Canadian Charter of Rights and Freedoms. In the majority decision, Justice Charles Dubin said it all: "In substance, it permits the posting of a 'no females allowed' sign by every athletic organization in this province."[61] Blainey then took her original complaint against the Ontario Hockey Association back to an Ontario Board of Inquiry, which eventually ordered that the OHA be prohibited from refusing any female the opportunity to compete for a position on a hockey team on the same basis as males.

The Blainey saga was important because it helped focus debate around an issue that split the women's sport community: sex-separated versus sex-integrated sports and organizations. On one side were those who argued that only through separate (but equal) programs for girls and boys would equality be achieved, and if girls were allowed to integrate on boys' teams, so must boys be allowed to play on girls' teams. This would, in their view, be extremely harmful to girls' and women's sport. The integrationists, on the other hand, argued that ability and not sex should be the criterion for forming athletic teams. Girls who did not have the opportunity to participate in a particular sport, except through an all-male team or league, should be permitted to play with boys if they have the necessary skills. They also argued that the "disadvantaged" individual (in this case girls) be allowed to move up to boys' competition; whereas boys, who were considered "advantaged" should not be allowed to move down. Finally, they maintained that, because resources were often not available for a parallel girls' structure, one league would be more efficient and less costly.

Although feminists saw the Blainey case as a victory for human rights, there were some in the women's sport community who argued vehemently against her right to play boys' hockey, notably those involved with girls' and women's hockey. They did so primarily for two reasons: first, the admission of girls to boys' hockey would spell the end of girls' hockey; second, they rejected the assertion that the developmental and competitive needs of girls and women could not be met through their own programs. They challenged the notion that boys' hockey was a better and more legitimate version of their own game.[62] The women's game did not (and still does not) permit intentional body checking, and there was virtually no fighting, both of which were the mainstay of the men's professional game, although some boys' minor hockey programs and men's recreational leagues banned them too. Women's hockey, as well as ringette (played almost exclusively by girls and women), were kept fervently "separate" by their leaders and organizers because they were convinced the real question was not the ability of females to play with males, but the legitimacy and recognition of women's sports.

For integrationists, the issues surrounding the separate-versus-integrated debate were complex, and they argued that a single approach would not serve the interests of all girls and women in all sport contexts. In a comprehensive discussion paper on the subject, sport sociologist and activist Helen Lenskyj pointed out that certain factors must be taken into consideration before policies and programs intended to address the problem of sex inequality in sport would achieve their goal. These were: the age of the female athlete (pre- or post-pubertal); the context of the sport (school, community, university); the level of competition (from recreational to highly competitive); the history of the sport (traditionally male, female, or both); and the nature of the sport (team, individual, contact).[63] The Canadian women's magazine, *Chatelaine*, took up the prickly debate, with Helen Lenskyj from CAAWS representing the integrationists and Fran Rider, president of the Ontario Women's Hockey Association, expressing the opposite view.[64] Aside from the usual arguments on both sides, Rider spoke of "ill-informed feminists," to which Lenskyj retorted that, as a result of feminist lobbying, the opportunities for girls and women to become involved in organized sport had increased substantially, and the jump in female participation rates bore this out. The readers of *Chatelaine* voted 60 per cent for and 29 per cent against girls playing on boys' teams, with the remainder undecided.

In the meantime, the one female player destined to make it to the big leagues of men's hockey was slowly making her way up the hockey ladder despite a good deal of negativity along the way. "Why waste time on a girl? ... She's taking my boy's place — he could make it to the NHL, and she never will" was the general sentiment. At age 17, and in the absence of Olympic hockey for women, Manon Rhéaume had more or less hit the wall with regard to her hockey career. She had moved from peewee to bantam, but was refused entry into the midget AAA level, a necessary step if she was ever to make it to the professional ranks. She quit until persuaded to play for a Sherbrooke women's team headed for the Quebec provincial championship; they also came second to Ontario in the 1991 Canadian championships. In order to gain more experience and playing time, Rhéaume was offered a chance to practice and play with the Trois-Rivières Draveurs of the Quebec Major Junior Hockey League as a back-up goalie, the first woman ever to play at this level.[65]

ATHLETES AND FEMINISM

So far, this chapter has been about government policies and strategies, feminist lobbying, and the legal challenges undertaken to counter sex discrimination and inequities in the Canadian amateur sport system during the mid-1970s until the late 1980s. At the same time, quietly and often with little media attention, hundreds of Canada's top women athletes were defying the myths about women's physical inferiority and gloriously making their mark on the world stage as many others had done before. There were so many of them that it is possible to tell just a few of their stories and then only briefly. It is safe to say, however, that hardly any of these athletes saw themselves as feminist activists. Some tried to distance themselves from the women's movement and, although supportive, disliked being seen as a feminist role model expected to push the cause of women's rights. For example, Debbie Brill, Canada's best high jumper throughout the 1970s and 1980s, wrote in her autobiography:

> I was also, overnight, a champion of the feminist movement, which made me very uneasy. In some ways I could see how the idea would work: I had had a child without marrying the father; I had snapped right back into my career, and through the years my image had been that of someone who said her piece and wasn't able to be pushed around by authority.[66]

As someone who often defied authority and went her own way, Brill was an exception in a state-subsidized amateur sport system not likely to produce many individuals with a radical critique willing to bite the hand that fed them. Besides, most sports had (and many still do have) an authoritarian power structure that demands discipline and obedience, which works against political awareness — in short, you did what the system or coach said. On the other hand, many feminists saw sport as too trivial, much less important than other causes, and failed to see it as a site of cultural struggle where gender relations were reproduced and sometimes resisted.

Despite the fact that, as the host nation, Canada won no gold medals at the 1976 Summer Olympics in Montreal, it did improve its overall standing from twenty-first in Munich in 1972 to eleventh. Funding for amateur sport had increased substantially in the period prior to the 1976 Olympics; at the same time, the federal government took over the support program and monitored the preparation of elite athletes in the push to improve Canada's performance in international amateur sport.[67] For the first time in the history of the Commonwealth Games, in Edmonton in 1978, Canada placed first in the unofficial standings, ahead of the traditional front runners, Australia and England. In the women's events, Canada won gold in the pentathlon (Diane Jones Konihowski), discus (Carmen Ionesco), several individual swimming and two relay events (Robin Corsiglia, Lisa Borsholt, Wendy Quirk, Carol Klimpel, Cheryl Gibson), in diving (Janet Nutter, Linda Cuthbert), and individual gymnastics (Elfi Schlegel) and the team event, as well as many silver and bronze medals.[68] Throughout the 1980s, the federal government continued to pour money into elite sport by supporting athletes, constructing facilities, and directing policy. By 1989, over 800 athletes, at least half of whom were women, were funded through Sport Canada's Athlete Assistance Program in exchange for the monitoring of their training programs, mandatory training camps, random drug testing, and involvement in non-commercial promotional activities for Sport Canada.[69] Being an elite amateur athlete in Canada was now a full-time job, although most athletes struggled to make ends meet.

In this atmosphere, it is little wonder that many women athletes focussed almost entirely on becoming the very best in their sport, if not world champions. As early as the mid-1970s, articles began to appear questioning whether "Olympic baubles" were worth the effort, especially the expense and long hours of intense training.[70] Only 16 years old, figure skater Elizabeth Manley left home for the first time to train in Lake Placid, NY, in 1982. Depressed and lonely, she gained 20 pounds and developed a nervous condition that caused her to lose most of her hair. She nearly quit, but battled back to win a silver medal at the 1988 Calgary Olympics and then went on to a lucrative professional career with the Ice Capades and her own skating tour.[71]

The late 1970s through the 1980s also saw the rise of the "Caribbean domination" in Canadian track athletics, certainly among women athletes. Canada's ties to Commonwealth countries and a more liberal immigration policy beginning in the 1960s brought thousands of immigrants to its shores, many from countries like Jamaica, Barbados, and Trinidad.[72] Mostly from Toronto's African-Canadian community, athletes like Angela Bailey, Marita Payne, Angella Taylor, Jillian Richardson, Charmaine Crooks, and Molly Killingback were born outside Canada and emigrated with their parents as young children. Most began their athletic careers in the late 1970s, and by 1982 all were members of the Commonwealth Games team competing in Brisbane, Australia. Angella Taylor won four medals, more than any other athlete at the games, and the Australian press called her "sprint empress Angie Taylor"; she was also voted Canada's outstanding female athlete in 1980 and 1982. However, by her own admission, we know now that Taylor (later Issajenko) had been using performance-enhancing drugs since 1979, although in her autobiography she refused to implicate any of her female teammates.[73] Her story, as the book jacket explains, is "about an obsession with being the fastest woman on the planet, the hypocrisy of the written and unwritten rules of international sport, and the bizarre world of elite athletics." African-Canadian female athletes continued to play a major role in Canada's modest success in international track and field especially at the 1983 Pan American Games in Caracas, Venezuela, and at the 1984 Summer Olympics in Los Angeles (the latter boycotted by the Soviet Union and 13 of its allies).

While a few Canadian athletes benefited from lucrative endorsement contracts, most laboured in obscurity only to be publicly recognized every four years when the Olympics rolled around.[74] Laurie Graham, for example, one of Canada's best alpine skiers during the 1980s, was also the best marketed female athlete. By 1988 she was earning roughly $300,000 a year from commercial endorsements (in those days kept in a trust fund, from which she could withdraw money for expenses, so she could retain her amateur status). Her wholesome image graced television commercials for products ranging from McDonald's breakfasts to McCain's orange juice, and other sponsors included the Canadian Imperial Bank of Commerce, Labatts, Kodak, and various ski equipment manufacturers.[75] Throughout her career, Graham won six World Cup races, establishing herself as one of the most consistent racers on the circuit, but an Olympic medal eluded her.

By 1983, trapshooter Susan Nattrass had won six world championships and was the first (and only) woman to compete in Olympic trapshooting in Montreal in 1976. Despite her success, she was virtually unknown in Canada and had nothing in the way of lucrative commercial endorsements; she worked at a variety of jobs in order to train and compete. In 1981 she was awarded the Lou Marsh Trophy, open to both men and women, as Canada's athlete of the year.

Olympic trapshooting was a mixed event until after 1992 when the International Shooting Union banned women from Olympic trap and skeet events, primarily because men did not like being beaten by women. Without asking their advice, women were given a double trap event in which targets are thrown two at a time; for the next five years, Nattrass and others lobbied to have a separate women's single trap event. This happened in Sydney in 2000, and Nattrass competed in her fourth Olympics.[76]

Another successful Canadian woman shooter, a sport pistol specialist, was Ottawa's Linda Thom, who at age 40 won the gold medal at the 1984 Olympics in Los Angeles. Her route to gold was anything but conventional, illustrating patience and perseverence, perhaps a feminist vision without naming it so, of someone who saw a goal and went after it. As a child, Thom and her older brother learned to shoot tin cans with a rifle at the family summer place, but not until university did she join a shooting club and begin competing. She switched to pistol shooting, doing very well in local and Canadian championships (she won the national title between 1970 and 1975). Married in 1972, she continued to compete nationally and internationally until 1975, when she and her husband decided to start a family. For the next seven years, she put away her guns while she had two children and ran a cooking school. After learning that pistol shooting for women was on the 1984 Summer Olympic program, and realizing there was no one competing in Canada of her calibre, she went back into training in 1982 with the gold medal in mind. When asked about the absence of women from Eastern bloc countries in 1984, she was philosophical: "... on any given day there was eight or nine of us who could have won, and if the Russians had been there, there would have been eleven or twelve."[77] Plagued by chronic neck and shoulder problems, Thom retired from competition in 1987.

Many other athletes during this era, deserve to have their stories told: Anne Ottenbrite, the first Canadian woman ever to win an Olympic gold medal in swimming (in 1984); diver Sylvie Bernier, gold medalist in three-metre diving, and Lori Fung, gold medalist in rhythmic gymnastics; synchronized swimmers Carolyn Waldo and Michelle Cameron, gold medal winners in 1988; Christilot Boylen, a dressage rider and member of *seven* Olympic teams between 1964 and 1992; skiers Kathy Kreiner, gold medal (giant slalom) in Innsbruck in 1976, and Karen Percy, bronze medals (downhill and super giant slalom) in 1988; speed skaters Cathy Priestner, Sylvie Daigle, and Eden Donatelli, all medal winners; and rowers Betty Craig, Tricia Smith, and sisters Daniele and Silken Laumann.[78]

Probably the most ambitious woman athlete of this era was Sue Holloway, the only Canadian woman to have competed in two Olympics in the same year.[79] At the 1976 Winter Olympics in Innsbruck, Austria, Holloway competed in cross-country skiing; and later that year in Montreal at the Summer Olympics, she competed in kayaking. Growing up in Ottawa with a younger brother, Holloway spent weekends with her family cross-country skiing at Camp Fortune in the Gatineau Hills. Both her parents were athletic and encouraged her competitiveness. She started ski racing at age 10, and, when as a teenager she started paddling with a club on the Rideau River, she began racing almost immediately. Superbly athletic with a strong build and excellent upper-body strength, Holloway excelled at both sports, soon winning national junior and senior titles. At the 1976 Winter Olympics, skiing in the shadow of the more experienced Firth twins (Sharon and Shirley), Esther Miller, and Joan Groothuysen, her performance was "mediocre." Later that year in Montreal, she and her partner finished eighth in the 500-metre two-person kayak (K2) competition. After the Olympics, and now 21, she decided to focus solely on kayaking, moving to Vancouver to train and attend university. Hard work and good coaching put her in peak condition, and she was devastated when the 1980 Olympic boycott meant the Canadian team did not participate. Her commitment paid off four years later when she won silver in the 500-metre K2 (with Alexandra Barre) and a bronze in the 500-metre K4 (with Barre, Lucy Guay, and Barb Olmstead). As a member of the national paddling team from 1973 to 1985, Holloway was in a unique position to experience many of the changes that took place within the Canadian sport system during that time:

... at the beginning when I first started, they weren't very organized and they didn't have very strict criteria and monitoring of athletes. But then you weren't getting a lot from them either ... but as they started giving us more support, then they demanded more from us. We started having better organization, and more people coming with us to Europe on tours. When I first went, they would have one person, one manager ... then the change from that first couple of years to '84 where we've got a sports medicine doctor, a sport psychologist, an extremely competent manager, a head coach, and specialist coaches — we've got a full complement of experts to give us back-up. They were providing us with all kinds of funding to go everywhere.... The difference as the program progressed and as they were providing us with more opportunities, then they also had more control over us.[80]

Athletes like Sue Holloway, others discussed here, and the many more whose achievements are no less significant, were part of a generation, who made a statement about sexual equality through their hard work, perseverence, and accomplishments, whether or not they actively supported the women's movement. Some were at the vanguard of a new approach to amateur sport in Canada. They became, in fact, employees of the Canadian state, although poorly paid ones, and as a result were monitored, controlled, and to a certain extent professionalized. They committed themselves to full-time training; there were fewer opportunities to pursue an education or career at the same time; they agreed to submit to the demands of their national sport organization; and they were less able to control the events that determined their lives (an Olympic boycott for example). Very few made much money from their sport, and fewer still were able to obtain commercial sponsorship contracts, even if they were Olympic medal winners. Much of this would change in the 1990s, and not necessarily for the better, with the new marketing of women's sports and the making of female sports stars, Canadians included, into commodities.

CHAPTER 7

THE COMMODIFICATION OF
PHYSICALITY: 1990S AND BEYOND

As the century winds down, men have outgrown many of the traditional sports, while women have been growing *into* them.... The
match between today's women and yesterday's men is significant
because it gives us a seat at an unexpected remake of a "golden age"
of athletics, when sport was less about spectacle and entertainment
and more about the game itself.

Jay Teitel, *Saturday Night*, July/August 1997

There is no question that women athletes today experience more competitive
and professional opportunities than ever before. Teitel also argued that
compared to men their exploits on the court or rink or field are more fun and interesting to watch, more like the games of the past, before the days of mass entertainment and spectacle. While men have literally outgrown many of their traditional
sports, like basketball, hockey, golf, and tennis, women have been slowly growing
into them. Male professional athletes, he suggested, have "outstripped in size and
speed the confines of the standard playing spaces that define their games" and their
sports are no longer as exciting or as fun to watch as they once were. Significantly
bigger and stronger than they were before the days of highly commercialized and
commodified professional sport, male athletes just do not seem to fit their spaces
anymore. Women, on the other hand, are rejuvenating sports that men have become
too big to play. They are, wrote Teitel, the "creators of the lost and perfect game."[1]

This is heady praise indeed, but there is also a caveat. Today's women athletes,
when compared to men, are on average still shorter, slower, and weaker. In fact,
they are closer in size to male athletes at the turn of the century, when sport was
purely amateur and played for fun. For example, Teitel showed that nearly every

major track and field record held by women in 1997 was almost identical to the records held by men 70 to 90 years earlier. However, this is what makes women's sport so much more interesting and entertaining to watch compared to men's. Take basketball for instance. Although the manoeuvres of individual female players are not nearly as "awe inspiring" as the male giants of the game, women's basketball relies more on teamwork, finesse, and shooting accuracy, just the way it used to be played by smaller men. Ice hockey is the same. Although less physical (officially no body checking is allowed), the women's game has more passing and flow compared to the stop-start, clutch-grab physicality of the men's, especially in the NHL. Women's tennis generally produces longer rallies, fewer bullet serves, and good net play; professional women golfers, lacking the ability to drive long down the fairway, are often better putters and short-iron players.

As athletes, women are a reflection of the sincerity, sports*man*ship, humility, and love for the game that once was. "In their rudeness," wrote Teitel, "their ego, the unseemly magnitude of their contracts, and their substitution of contempt for sportsmanship, a large percentage of male pro athletes today have become emotional misfits."[2] Robert Lipsyte, a longtime sport commentator in the United States, made much the same observation in a controversial article in the *New York Times Magazine* a few years ago: "Sports no longer reflect the America of our dreams, and the stars of sport are no longer the idealized versions of ourselves." Along the way, he observed, "those manly virtues of self-discipline, responsibility, altruism and dedication seem to have been deleted from the athletic contract with America."[3] In recent years we have witnessed umpires spat on, photographers kicked, female sports reporters harassed, an opponent's ear bitten, a coach nearly strangled to death, and athletes arrested for violence and abuse far from the playing fields.

Following the 1998 Nagano Winter Olympics, where women's ice hockey made its debut, Lipsyte wrote another thought-provoking article, this time about whether women can change sports before it changes them. He asks: "Are women truly the new irresistible force in sports or are they being allowed in to replace what's been lost — morality and passion?"[4] Women play hockey, for instance, with more finesse and less thuggery than do men, but what happens, Lipsyte asks, "when all the women now coming into the arena display the same killer instincts that we thought were exclusive to men?" "Will they recapitulate the male model, and which one?"[5] Envisioning a new North American gladiatorial class that goes beyond gender, social standing, or race, he argued that, like men, women athletes are not immune to the stress and strain of the athletic entertainment industry. Look, for example, at anorexic gymnasts, teenagers burned out by abusive tennis parents, athletes sexually exploited by coaches, and escalating drug use among women athletes.

The 1990s and new millennium have brought some remarkable changes to women's sport, especially in North America. There is clearly a dark side, especially at the highest levels, including cheating, drug use, sexual harassment, and homophobia, as well as unhealthy practices and body abuse. These should not be ignored, and they will be discussed later in this chapter. On the more positive side, there are two changes that stand out the most. One is the valorization of team sports for girls and women, especially at the participatory level, which has increased opportunities for women to make a living playing sport. The other, certainly connected, is the new marketing of women's sport, especially team sports, and the making of female sport stars into commodities. The creation of markets and the commodification of women's sport is not, however, unproblematic, and it is important to understand the many implications of these changes.

First, let us examine several sports in some detail to explore the changes that began in the last decade of the twentieth century and continue today.

VALORIZATION OF TEAM SPORTS

According to the Canadian Hockey Association, 43,421 females were registered to play organized hockey in Canada in 2000, the majority in Ontario and Quebec. The growth since the mid-1980s, when less than 6,000 girls and women were registered, has been steady, which is not the case for males where some years have seen losses. Yet compared to the total number of males (approximately 500,000) playing hockey, there is still a long way to go.[6] Gender inequality persists at every level from ice time to clubs, leagues, championships, and media attention. Still, in the more than 100 years Canadian women have played the game, there has never been the same numbers, resources, programs, administrative structures, and media focus as there is today. Player registration and awareness of the national team soared after Canada won the first Women's World Championship sanctioned by the International Ice Hockey Federation in Ottawa in 1990. Canada won the next six world championships, always beating the United States in the gold medal game. In fact, one of the few times the United States defeated Canada was at the 1998 Nagano Olympics, where six teams competed for the gold medal. Given the disparity in teams from North America compared to those from Europe and Asia, there are some who think that women's hockey does not yet belong in the Olympics; nonetheless, it was again on the program for the 2002 Winter Olympics in Salt Lake City, where Canada won the gold medal.

The National Women's Hockey League (NWHL) made its debut in 1999 as a senior women's league — a professional operation, although the players are not paid. By 2001, there were 10 franchises based mostly in Ontario and Quebec, with one located in Vancouver. The long-term objective of the NWHL is the establishment of a professional league with franchises in major North American cities.

The Women's Television Network (WTN) has broadcast several NWHL league games as well as their national championships. Television audiences for the women's world's championships have also risen steadily since they were first broadcast as a novelty on The Sports Network (TSN). In 1990, for example, numerous print, radio, and TV journalists covered the event, attended by more than 20,000 people. The television audience averaged 450,000 for the first three televised games and about 1.5 million for the gold-medal game.[7] TSN, however, was still very cautious about the viability of televising women's hockey until recently. Commented one network official: "Women's hockey has evolved from a niche sport to a jewel in terms of participants, fans, broadcasters, and advertisers."[8]

Without opportunities for women to play professional hockey in North America, a few still look to the men's professional and semi-professional leagues — for example, goalie Manon Rhéaume. She was selected to play on the women's national team competing at the 1992 world championships in Tampere, Finland, where the Canadians beat the United States 8–0 in the final. As the story goes, Phil Esposito, owner of the NHL Tampa Bay Lightning, was shown a tape of Rhéaume without being told she was female. He was impressed and invited her to the team training camp, where she played in a pre-season game for one period, thus becoming the first (and only) woman to play in an NHL game. In the process she generated substantial media publicity, not all of it positive. The women's hockey community was ambivalent toward Rhéaume, with many thinking her "success" was due more to her attractiveness than to her hockey ability, something confirmed, for example, each time it surfaced that she had been asked to pose nude in *Playboy* magazine (she flatly refused to consider it). On the other hand, the publicity surrounding Rhéaume brought welcome attention to women's hockey and to other women players, confirming their ability to play the game at the highest levels. Regardless, the issues raised illustrate the contemporary struggle to establish the legitimacy of women's sport, especially team sport. It suggests women's sport is inferior, and true success can only be found by playing with men in *their* sport.[9] Meanwhile, Rhéaume signed a professional contract and was sent to Tampa Bay's affiliate team, the Atlanta Knights of the International Hockey League, for more training, although given her media and promotional engagements, there is no question that part of her role was to generate publicity for the team and league. She continued to play for a string of men's professional and semi-professional ice hockey (and roller hockey) teams over the next few years, and at the same time was a member of Canada's women's national team until she retired at age 28 in 2000.[10]

Ringette continued to grow in Canada, but it has not received nearly the same attention and publicity as ice hockey. In fact, there were many who predicted the game would lose out to hockey in popularity. Ringette is a family sport, in which children start at a relatively young age and continue playing until at least their mid-teens. Their fathers and mothers volunteer to coach and run the clubs and associations, making ringette a way of life for many families during the winter months. It is not unusual for women to come back to the sport through their children or to join an adult team after watching their daughters play. The relatively few boys who start the game usually switch to hockey by the time they are 10 or 11. In 1989, player registration was at 28,000, but by 2000 it had grown to 50,000 participants, actually a few more than the numbers in girls and women's ice hockey. Internationally, however, the game is restricted to just a few countries, mostly Finland, Sweden, and the United States.[11]

While Canada is known as a hockey nation, we are not particularly noted for soccer. Yet, among active 5 to 14 year olds, soccer is the game of choice, ranking just behind ice hockey for boys and swimming for girls.[12] Far more Canadian girls play soccer (28 per cent) than they play ice hockey (6 per cent), and the growth during the 1990s has been spectacular. Of the total player registration in 2000, the number of females was 270,145, representing 37 per cent. For the past several years, females have accounted for over one-third of the new registrations each year. The vast majority of players, both male and female, are youths (under 19 years), yet there are nearly 25,000 adult women in Canada playing the game. Ontario, Quebec, British Columbia, and Alberta are the provinces with the largest numbers, although the discrepancy between the numbers of males and females registered is often less in provinces with fewer players.[13]

Like other Canadian sport associations, soccer did not always welcome females, especially if they wanted to play on boys teams, which many had to do before clubs, community centres, schools, and universities began to initiate programs for girls and women. To be fair, many centres encouraged boys and girls playing together, and it was only when a team came under the jurisdiction of a controlling body that problems arose. For example, as late as 1992, the Ontario Soccer Association still believed it could prevent girls from playing with boys. Erin Casselman and Suzanne Ouellet were two Belleville high school students who played on the local boys' team. They had played all during the year, but when their team reached the quarter finals of the Ontario championship, they were told it would be disqualified if they continued to play because they were girls in a boys' competition. A complaint was laid with the Ontario Human Rights Commission, and, after an inquiry, the Ontario Soccer Association was barred from interfering with the right of female players to compete for team positions on the same basis as males.[14]

The remarkable growth of grassroots soccer among female youth during the 1990s has paid off in the development of a women's national team program, first initiated in 1986. For most of the decade the team laboured in obscurity. They did not qualify for the first Women's World Cup in 1991, sanctioned by the

Fédération Internationale de Football Association (FIFA), and, because they came twelfth in the 1995 tournament, they did not qualify for the 1996 Atlanta Olympics, when women's soccer made its debut. Tremendous publicity surrounded the third World Cup, played in seven American cities in the summer of 1999, especially around the team from the United States, led by Mia Hamm.[15] All 32 games were televised live with strong ratings, and thousands attended the matches. The final game, played in the Rose Bowl in Pasadena, California, between the United States (who won) and China, attracted some 90,000 fans, the largest crowd ever to watch a women's sporting event. Unfortunately the Canadians were again not in the top eight, and hence they did not qualify for the 2000 Olympics in Sydney.

The excitement generated in the United States by their team's success in the 1999 World Cup and at the 2000 Olympics contributed to the establishment of an eight-team women's professional soccer league, which began playing in the spring of 2001. The Women's United Soccer Association (WUSA) features top players from the United States as well as the best internationals from 20 different countries. Five Canadian players (Silvana Burtini, Charmaine Hooper, Karen LeBlanc, Sharola Nonen, and Amy Walsh) were signed up to play in the league. According to newspaper reports, top foreign players in the WUSA earn in the neighbourhood of $50,000 US, and mass exposure through television could lead to lucrative endorsements. The main investors in the league are television and cable companies, including Discovery Communications, the parent company of the Discovery Channel and the Learning Channel. CNN/Sports Illustrated will produce a weekly "Inside WUSA Soccer" magazine show, and matches will be broadcast nationally on TNT and CNN/Sports Illustrated, all in the hopes of bringing appealing sports programming to a female demographic in North America.[16]

Softball has been the most enduring of all women's team sports in Canada, yet it also receives the least publicity.[17] Played by thousands of girls and women in communities small and large all across the country, it is still the traditional summer sport of choice for both recreational and higher level competition. Among active females, it is next to swimming and golf in popularity.[18] In the 1970s, girls fought to play on boys' teams because there were insufficient opportunities for them to compete. They won this battle, and at the same time softball organizers worked to provide more competitive experiences for talented females so that Canada could perform better internationally. A senior women's national team was formed, with Canada competing in the 1974 world championship (they came sixth), something they have done every four years since. They usually place fourth or fifth behind the United States, Australia, Japan, or China, and in 1994 they earned a berth at the 1996 Olympics, where women's softball was on the program for the first time. The Canadian team was led by veteran pitcher Lori

Sippel, who had been a member of the national team since 1982. Sippel was also among the first Canadian softball players to be recruited by American universities and awarded full scholarships; in her case she attended the University of Nebraska between 1984 and 1988, after which she was hired as Nebraska's assistant women's softball coach.[19]

The Canadian team came fifth at the 1996 Olympics, but a disappointing eighth at the 2000 Sydney Olympics. On the 2000 Olympic team was Hayley Wickenheiser, all-star member of the women's national hockey team, and one of only three women in Canadian Olympic history to compete in both the Summer and Winter Games.[20] The national senior women's team has also competed at the Pan American Games since the sport was introduced there in 1979, and they usually win a medal. One of the few times they have beaten the United States, the perennial world champions, was at the 1983 Pan-Ams in Caracas, Venezuela. A junior women's national team has also competed at world championships since 1981, although they rarely finish higher than seventh.[21]

Women's basketball in Canada has traditionally been a game played mostly in schools, colleges, and universities. It has a broad participation base; in fact, more active females aged 15 years and older (7.5 per cent) play basketball than they do either soccer (6.0 per cent) or certainly ice hockey (2.1 per cent).[22] Basketball generally in Canada receives little publicity except perhaps in cities where university teams compete. Many top Canadian players obtain scholarships at universities in the United States, where women's basketball both at the college level and as a professional sport thrives. As of 2001, few Canadian players had been drafted into the Women's National Basketball Association (WNBA), launched in 1997 by the men's National Basketball Association (NBA) with eight teams in two conferences; it is now a 16-team league. The WNBA expects to draw 2.5 million fans in its fourth season, with millions more watching games on network television. Point guard Cal Bouchard from Aurora, Ontario, who played for Boston College, was the first Canadian drafted into the WNBA — by the Detroit Shock in the fourth round in 2000; they retained her rights the following year. In the 2001 draft, six-foot-four centre Tammy Sutton-Brown from Markham, Ontario, a player at Rutgers University, was chosen by the Charlotte Sting in the second round. Before the WNBA, as is still the case now, several top Canadian players went to Europe to play professional or semi-professional basketball. Bev Smith of Salmon Arm, BC, undoubtedly the finest female player Canada has ever produced and former head coach of Canada's national women's team, played and coached in the Italian league for 14 years. Women's amateur basketball at the international level is highly competitive, and, although the Canadian team does well, it is not among the top nations.[23]

Advertisers eager to find a way to connect with female consumers, television and Internet producers in need of programming, and a growing pool of professional calibre athletes, all explain the recent boom in women's professional team sports in North America. Canadian athletes, although few in numbers now, will continue to benefit from these growing opportunities. For example, Canada's ice hockey players will be attracted to a women's professional hockey league should that come about, and there is talk of a professional indoor volleyball league in the near future. An 11-team Women's Professional Football League, playing full-contact American football, was launched in 1999 and expects to succeed where others have failed, despite a chaotic first year. According to some experts, men's professional sports will continue to "run the risk of alienating families with skyrocketing salaries and ticket prices, labour problems and players showing up on police blotters," resulting in an increased appetite for women's sports.[24]

Advertisers seeking to access a woefully untapped market are behind the growing number of publications and media properties aimed at women who enjoy sports. Speciality magazines published in the United States — like Time-Warner's *Sports Illustrated for Women* and Condé Nast's *Women's Sports and Fitness* — are generally available in Canada. The Sports Network (TSN) in Canada received approval for a digital cable channel called Women's Sports Network (WTSN) launched in September 2001. It hopes to "cater to the tastes and needs of female sports fans, developed and presented in a way that speaks to women." Mandated to carry at least eight hours of Canadian content a day, WTSN plans to carry coverage of women's tennis, golf, soccer, curling, equestrian, and university sports. Like many television channels, it will use new media by combining content with the latest technology through an interactive "web-zine" on its website. According to press notices, WTSN will also present an opportunity to bring women into sports broadcasting in senior roles. Many skeptics claim there is insufficient interest and too small an audience to make a Canadian women's sports network financially viable.[25] Finally, although this represents only a tiny share of the sports collectibles industry, female athletes are appearing more often on trading cards, sought after by male and female collectors alike.[26]

The commodification of women's sports, and in particular athletes' bodies and physicality, is not without its problems. There has always been a "dark side" to women's sport, just as there is in men's, but it seems magnified now through a marketing lens, which has made the stakes much higher for all concerned. Among the issues and problems are an increased use of performance enhancing drugs among women athletes, the continuing exploitation and abuse of female athletes by male coaches, an often dangerously hostile environment for lesbians in sport, unhealthy practices and body abuse, and the sexualization of female athletes strictly for marketing purposes.

MARKETING WOMEN'S SPORT

Over 60 years ago, the American writer Paul Gallico argued that the simplest explanation for the sudden rise in the popularity of women's swimming in the 1930s was
due mostly to one thing, and that was sex appeal. He was specifically referring to
pictures of attractive young women in revealing bathing suits lined up on the edge
of a pool waiting for the starting gun or caught in mid-air off the end of a diving
board. Daily newspapers regularly published such photographs on the sports pages
to attract (male) readers. "Sport for sport's sake is all right," he wrote, "but even
the most case-hardened athletics enthusiast realizes that it is more than a help when
a couple of the participants look like something off a magazine cover."[27] But,
cautioned Gallico, just being pretty is not enough; they must be winners too.

These comments are as true today as they were then. For example, take the
Russian tennis player Anna Kournikova — youthful, beautiful, sexy — who
garners more attention for her looks than for her ability to win tournaments. Even
the *Globe and Mail* ran an editorial about her, claiming she was discussed on
43,000 websites, making her the most downloaded female athlete in Internet
history — although, warned the *Globe*, "beauty winning makes for a happier
ending."[28] The debates today about whether women athletes can show their
sexual side and still be taken seriously as athletes, or whether it is good to use sex
to sell women's sport at the risk of trivializing their athleticism, certainly go back
a long way. They are not new, but the stakes seem higher now because we are no
longer talking about pretty girls in one-piece bathing suits, but rather nudity and
deliberate posing to titillate, which for some is just another form of soft pornog-
raphy. As women gain more and more inroads into the entertainment industry,
of which sport is a part, the pressure to take off their clothes has never been
stronger. Musical superstars Mariah Carey, Shania Twain, Courtney Love, and
Alanis Morissette, renowned for their artistry and clout in the music business,
have exposed their bodies to gain attention on magazine or album covers or in
videos. Believing firmly in the old adage that sex sells, the women who do this
suggest that, in a highly competitive marketplace, it is possible to be sexy and
smart at the same time. Similarly, Canadian Internet phenomenon NakedNews.com
boasts 6,000,000 viewers monthly (70 per cent male), because female news readers take off their clothes as they read the daily news.[29] Provocative nudity is everywhere, and high profile women athletes are using their bodies to market their
sports and themselves.

It is not surprising that the women's sport community is divided over the use of
nudity and (hetero)sexual attractiveness to sell sport, since in the past decade there
have been several intriguing and controversial episodes, all of which provoked considerable discussion. Figure skater Katerina Witt was paid a great deal of money to pose

semi-nude for *Playboy* magazine (December 1998 issue), but, as she reassured her fans, it was with "purity, naturalness, art and athletics," not at all "sexy and erotic." She argued that the real issue was showing off a beautiful body rather than the size of the pay cheque. Most commentary agreed that since she was no longer competing as an amateur nor aiming for the Olympics, this was fine.[30]

Much more controversial was a decision by international volleyball officials to mandate skin-tight, high-cut uniforms, rather then the traditional shorts and top, for all women players. The rationale was to give the indoor game a more attractive image and make it as popular for spectators and television as outdoor beach volleyball, where female contestants "cannot set foot on the sand court unless they are costumed in backless, scoop-neck, high-cut-leg, body-hugging suits that have no more than six centimetres of fabric at the hip."[31] Canadian volleyball officials would not force their indoor players to wear the new togs, claiming women should not be singled out and the gym was no place for a bathing suit. *Marketing Magazine* published a piece by freelance writer David Menzies, arguing that Volleyball Canada was wrong not to take advantage of the obvious marketing potential for "a little more thigh here and a bit more cleavage there." Angry letters appeared in the next issue stated the obvious — to focus undue attention on women athletes' bodies trivializes their considerable athletic skill, and the sport should be marketed in other ways. This becomes increasingly difficult when for women, the big-money, television-tailored sports are increasingly the ones with the smallest costumes, like tennis, figure skating, and beach volleyball.[32]

Some women athletes and teams see nothing wrong with tastefully exposed skin to garner publicity, indeed financial support, either for themselves or their sports. They willingly participate in the sexualization of their sport, which nowadays produces little controversy, at least outside the sports world. The Canadian women's cross-country ski team sold calendars featuring nude pictures of themselves to raise the profile and funds of their team. Criticism was directed less at their unusual project and more at the sorry state of amateur sport funding in Canada.[33] The Canadian women's water-polo team assistant captain, Waneek Horn-Miller, appeared naked (except for a water-polo ball concealing her breasts) on the cover of *Time*'s preview issue for the 2000 Olympics.[34] These images help send a calculated message that women can be both athletic and feminine, especially in sports that still carry the stigma that women who excel in them are somehow unwomanly. Olympic biathlon gold-medalist Myriam Bédard sued the Wrigley chewing-gum empire over an advertisement she claimed was altered to make her look like a man. "I have always made a point of remaining feminine in a sport that is very demanding and, especially, very masculine," said Bédard, who wanted "to protect her integrity, not only as a woman but also as an athlete."[35] In some situations, women athletes have control over their public images, and in cases like the now retired Bédard, who depend on commercial endorsements for income, they are prepared to safeguard these images through litigation.

New York Times columnist Robert Lipsyte, discussing the connection between sex and sport, stated: "Sexuality may be so intrinsic to sports that unless the audience is sexually comfortable, the game just won't sell." This does not mean, he argued, that players have to be "sexually alluring"; it just means they cannot be threatening. "A lovely lesbian may be bad for business if you are pushing a traditional family package."[36] Lipsyte was referring specifically to the United States women's soccer team (dubbed in the press as "booters with hooters"), who had just won the 1999 women's World Cup. They were marketed as "soccer babes," not sexually available in any sense, but "normal" and proper role models for all the girls who will buy the shoes and gear they endorse. He went even further, making it crystal clear: "For the World Cup team to crack into the male-dominated merchandising mart as a group and as individuals, they must dispel the aura of homosexuality that was hung on women's athleticism as a way of stifling their emerging physical and political power."

Professional women's golf and tennis have spent years feminizing their players to dispel the "aura of homosexuality" while at the same time attracting sponsorship, television deals, and prize money. In the late 1980s, the Ladies Professional Golf Association (LPGA) countered the perception that many of their players were lesbians, euphemistically called their "butch image," by adopting the "old tried-and-true apologetic stance of highlighting femininity" with seductive photo poses of young players modelling revealing swim suits and by hiring an image and fashion consultant. While lesbian players do not keep their sexual identities secret from friends and family, only one player in the 50-year history of the LPGA has made any public revelations. Muffin Spencer-Duffin, a successful veteran player in her 40s, talked openly about being a lesbian in a 1996 *Sports Illustrated* article, but most of her fellow players wished she had kept quiet, keeping the issue hidden as always and preventing the entire tour from being "branded that way."[37]

Probably more of an issue for female professional golfers, certainly those who are married with children, is how to combine working with raising a family. Besides, there is no evidence that the LPGA of the 1990s suffered in terms of prize money, tournaments, sponsor support, or television exposure from Spencer-Duffin's revelation, except that it is still lags far behind the men's PGA. For example in 1999, Lorie Kane of Charlottetown, PEI, Canada's most successful women golfer ever on the LPGA, was fifth in earnings at just over $1 million. Her Canadian contemporary on the PGA, Mike Weir, earned almost $2 million, but was ranked fifteenth. Kane has become the "nation's sweetheart on the strength of a fierce golf swing and one of the sunniest dispositions in sport."[38] Named female athlete of the year in 1997 and 2000, she won three LPGA tournaments in 2000, finishing fifth on the tour, and during her career has earned over $2.5 million in prize money and a good deal more in endorsements.[39]

Some argue that with the increasing commodification of women's sport — the availability of commercial markets for women athletes in advertising, sponsorship, merchandise, and personal appearances — comes a new wave of "dyke bashing."[40] For instance, following the Nagano Olympics in 1998, where Canada won the silver medal, the Canadian Hockey Association (CHA) did not renew coach Shannon Miller's contract, maintaining she was let go because a full-time women's head coach and staff were not a priority after the Olympics. Speculation was rife as to the real reason Miller was dismissed; it was stated bluntly by an irate fan in a letter to the editor of the *Globe and Mail*: "It is my firm belief that Shannon Miller is being let go because she is perceived to be a lesbian."[41] During the build-up to the Olympics, there were unsubstantiated rumours that Miller was romantically involved with one of the players; for example, on the Internet, specifically the CBC Newsworld online forum on hockey at Nagano, there was frank but totally speculative discussion about Miller's sexuality. Only those closely connected to the team know all the facts. Clearly there were team problems, and it seems that homophobia was marshalled to deflect these difficulties.[42]

Back in 1982, Betty Baxter, coach of the national women's volleyball team, was fired without explanation. She was probably among the first "out" lesbians in Canadian high performance sport, and it cost her dearly.[43] Has much changed in the intervening 16 years, or even now? The answer is both yes and no. According to Pat Griffin, author of *Strong Women, Deep Closets: Lesbians and Homophobia in Sport*, the climate for lesbians in sport ranges from dangerously hostile, to conditional tolerance, to being open and inclusive.[44] In the hostile environment, lesbians must conceal their identity from everyone, and certainly from those in authority; athletes and coaches deny their lesbian identity and act in ways that lead others to believe they are heterosexual. Sometimes women are not hired for coaching positions if they are suspected lesbians, whereas men with a history of sexual involvement with their (usually younger) female athletes certainly have been.

In the conditionally permissive athletic climate, lesbians willing to abide by certain rules are tolerated, even welcomed, but these rules require silence. Here, lesbians live in a "glass closet": where their identities are secret, but everyone knows who they are. In her study of the "Blades," a Canadian women's ice hockey team playing at the highest levels, sociologist Nancy Theberge illustrates how the stigma of mannishness, and by extension lesbianism, is challenged through strict dress and behaviour codes reminiscent of the rules that governed players on the All-American Girls Professional Baseball League 50 years ago. Lesbian players on the team experienced a mix of invisibility and inclusion, although the dynamics of homophobia are much less intrusive than they were then. While there was no expectation of lesbian invisibility and lesbian partners were welcome within the Blades community, the emphasis on feminine image and behaviour to counter the stigmatization of mannishness and lesbianism indicates, as Theberge points out, a degree of homophobia.[45] However, in the marketing of women's ice hockey, there is a deliberate effort to distance the athletes from even the suspicion of lesbianism by stressing their femininity and (hetero)sexual attractiveness. Said one longtime women player and coach: "It's kind of a joke amongst the players: grow your hair long or you won't make the national team. It's a joke because there is that pressure to sell the sport and they pick players not always just on talent. There's the image part of it — the being married, having kids sort of thing." And, another former player said it all: "[They] don't want a bunch of dykes representing our country."[46]

In their book, *Stroke: The Inside Story of Olympic Contenders*, Heather Clarke and Susan Gwynne-Timothy talk about Doug Clark, Canada's first professional rowing coach, who coached both Heather and her sisters Tina and Suzanne in the late 1970s. They speak glowingly of Clark: "To pass out, to die, to gain Doug's approval — that would have equalled the opening of heaven's gate to glory."[47] Five years after *Stroke* was published, Suzanne Clarke revealed on national television that as a 17-year-old aspiring rower she had been sexually involved with her coach, Doug Clark, something she had never told her sisters.[48] The CBC program exposed a pattern of secret sexual abuse perpetrated by Clark on other female rowers at the Woodstock club in Ontario, in addition to allegations of inappropriate sexual behaviour levelled at several male coaches in a variety of sports. The program also examined the lack of appropriate mechanisms within the Canadian sport system to deal with this issue. Public reaction to these revelations ranged from shock and astonishment to many athletes and sport officials calling it just the "tip of the iceberg." Also in 1993, an Edmonton track coach was found guilty of sexually assaulting several female athletes and was sent to prison.[49]

Reports of exploitative and abusive relationships between male coaches and female athletes are nothing new. In the early 1980s, for example, while engaged in a study of former Canadian women Olympians, I was struck by the number who told me (in confidence) about their negative, sometimes degrading, experiences with male coaches. Over the years, the general climate in Canada about sexual abuse in other social institutions changed from silence to scrutiny, reconciliation, and punishment, which encouraged researchers to address the problem in sport and journalists to profile known cases and incidents. Helen Lenskyj was one of the first researchers in Canada to address these issues, and journalists Mary Jollimore and Laura Robinson were among those who wrote the earliest stories for national newspapers.[50] The world of men's junior hockey in Canada was stunned by the arrest and eventual conviction of Swift Current Broncos coach Graham James for sexual assault, prompting a serious examination of institutionalized abuse in hockey.[51]

More studies followed, including a 1996 prevalence survey among 1,200 Canadian national team athletes conducted by Sandra Kirby and Lorraine Greaves. Despite the low response rate (approximately 22 per cent), there was evidence of widespread abuse, especially by males in authority over female athletes, throughout the sport system.[52] Canada is not alone in uncovering disturbing facts about exploitation, harassment, and abuse within its amateur sport system; there are now a number of studies conducted in various parts of the world that confirm the magnitude of the problem. Perhaps where Canada leads at present is in the development of programs and strategies to expose and eradicate the abuse, especially sexual abuse.[53]

In the wake of drug scandals involving Chinese women swimmers and revelations about systematic doping of athletes under the former East German regime, the Canadian media smugly suggested our athletes should seek redress over medals lost. Nancy Garapick, for example, "lost" two gold medals to East German swimmers at the Montreal Olympics in 1976; at those Games the East German swimmers won 11 gold medals in 13 events. When evidence of their drug abuse surfaced, demands were made that these medals be taken away and the record books amended.[54] When Irish swimmer Michelle Smith was caught tampering with her urine sample two years after she unexpectedly won one bronze and three gold medals at the 1996 Atlanta Olympics, it confirmed suspicions that she had been taking performance-enhancing drugs all along. In the resulting furore, two Canadian swimmers, Marianne Limpert and Joanne Malar, who came second and fourth respectively in the Atlanta 200-metre individual medley, publicly stated that Smith's medals should be taken away.[55]

The first woman athlete in Canada to admit to drug use was Angella (Taylor) Issajenko, one of the country's best sprinters in the 1980s. A training partner of Ben Johnson, she appeared at the 1989 Commission of Inquiry into the Use of Drugs and Banned Substances Intended to Increase Athletic Performance (commonly known as the Dubin Inquiry), held following Johnson's positive test for steroids at the 1988 Olympics in Seoul. At the inquiry, and subsequently in her book, Issajenko detailed the anabolic steroids, human growth hormones, and other drugs she took throughout a decade of international competition.[56] In his 638-page report, Mr. Justice Dubin attributed blame to the moral character of individual athletes and those around them, rather than challenging and recommending changes to the structural conditions (e.g., media pressure, economic rewards, overemphasis on winning, and government expectations), which causes some athletes to use performance-enhancing drugs.[57] With the pressures on today's athletes even more extreme than they were a decade ago, all that has changed is that the Canadian sport system has more resources and tools to catch the cheaters.

The night before 23-year-old Robin Lyons, the Canadian women's hammer-throw champion from Edmonton, was to leave for the Olympics in Sydney, she was informed that a drug test a month earlier had turned up traces of a perform-ance-enhancing steroid (norandrosterone) in her system. She was immediately suspended from the Olympic team, even though she vehemently denied ever taking banned substances. "I'm no Ben Johnson," she protested, to which an editorial in the *Globe and Mail* replied: "... indeed, she is not. She is a somewhat anonymous athlete in a somewhat anonymous sport that has none of the glam-our of the 100 metres."[58] Lyons was slapped with a four-year suspension and permanent ineligibility for federal government funding in accordance with the *Canadian Policy on Doping in Sport.* She has applied for reinstatement on the basis that her natural levels of norandrosterone were higher than the allowed thresh-old or that she ingested the substance innocently in a contaminated nutritional supplement. Canada's 100-metre sprint champion, Venolyn Clarke, a 34-year-old educational assistant from Oshawa, Ontario, was dismissed from the track team at the 2001 world athletic championships in Edmonton when she tested positive for the anabolic steroid stanozolol. In a statement of denial, Clarke said: "Of course, I am not the first athlete who has been wrongly accused of misconduct and I suspect I won't be the last. There have been many instances where athletes have been accused of similar behaviour — only to be exonerated later."[59] Perhaps Lyons and Clarke will both be vindicated, but sadly these will not be the last cases of a serious doping infraction among Canadian women athletes.

Female athletes seem as willing as males to expose themselves to physical risk, whether it is through taking performance-enhancing substances, disordered eating, or engaging in violent, excessive, and health-compromising sports (e.g., boxing). Researchers report remarkable gender similarities in the attitudes of athletes to phys-ical danger, aggression, and injury. Some argue this is the price of sexual equality in sport; others point to the declining number of women leaders and coaches, whose philosophy may differ from males in similar positions. In either case, it is an issue that needs further attention.

FROM EQUALITY TO EQUITY

It has been over 25 years since the first cases of sex discrimination in sport were brought before provincial human rights commissions, with the result that through time most provinces have dealt with the issue and usually assured girls their right to play on boys' teams, especially when there were no equivalent girls' teams. The majority of sport-related complaints of discrimination involved girls wishing to play on exclusively male soccer, softball, or ice hockey teams. Other complaints were directed at the restriction of women playing at private golf clubs during prime hours; pregnancy testing and the reduction of funding to high-performance athletes because of pregnancy; allowing female reporters in male team locker rooms; and, in one case about employment discrimination, a male physical education teacher wishing to teach girls' physical education. The majority of complaints were resolved without going to a formal board of inquiry (or tribunal), or eventually to the courts. In fact, between 1978 and 1993 there were only about a dozen such "formal" cases altogether.[60]

Risa Saraga, a 14-year-old teenager with a love for basketball, was kicked off her school team just before it was to play in a divisional finals in the spring of 2000. The problem was that Risa was playing on the boys' team, simply because there was no girls' team at her Toronto public school. The school board decided she could not play at all, because they had a rule preventing girls from playing on boys' teams. Justine Blainey-Broker, who more than a decade ago had battled for the right to play on a boys' hockey team, was shocked, as were a good many others. Now a chiropractor in her late 20s, she had this advice: "I'd tell her to keep on going, to keep fighting, to hang in there and to continue following your dreams.... If you want to play in the sport you love, then don't let anybody stand in your way."[61]

The fact that these situations still arise and that girls are prevented from playing the sport of their choice, means that some issues are still unresolved, and girls continue to suffer discrimination. In British Columbia, for example, a young girl named Melanie Merkley fought from 1996 to 1999 to play on a local bantam boys' hockey team. According to Laura Robinson, writer and women's sport activist, the "wait was so long at the BC Human Rights Commission, and the tactics of the local hockey league so dirty, that Ms. Merkley told her parents to get rid of her equipment."[62]

Beginning in the 1990s, and in most areas of organizational life including sport, there has been a subtle shift in the discourse of human rights in Canada and elsewhere from "equality" to "equity." Equality generally meant "equality of opportunity," and women (along with other disadvantaged groups) were identified as target groups. In sport, equal opportunity programs were designed to increase women's overall participation by opening up opportunities for them to enjoy equal access. The shift to equity signalled a more comprehensive view in which the focus was no longer exclusively on women (or any other group) but on a system, in this case sport, which needed to change to accommodate them.[63] As longtime sport activist (and now Dean of the Faculty of Physical Education and Health at the University of Toronto) Bruce Kidd put it: "Equality focuses on creating the same starting line for everyone; equity has the goal of providing everyone with the same finish line."[64] It was stated even more clearly in a report on gender equity from the Department of Athletics and Recreation at the University of Toronto: "An athletics program is gender equitable when the men's program would be pleased to accept as its own the overall participation, opportunities, and resources currently allocated to the women's program and vice versa."[65] "Equity is an issue of quality;

excellence in sport cannot occur without equity," explains Marion Lay, a respected advocate for women's sport both nationally and internationally, who has spent more than 25 years working on behalf of amateur sport in Canada.[66]

The Canadian Association for the Advancement of Women and Sport and Physical Activity (CAAWS) fully endorsed this shift from equality to equity, and from the early 1990s onwards its focus has primarily been on bringing gender equity within the Canadian sport system. When its leaders sought increased funding from the Fitness and Amateur Sport Branch, after its operational budget had been cut from the Secretary of State Women's Program in 1990, it positioned itself as the only group that could work with other national sport organizations to assist them in becoming gender equity organizations (whether they wanted to was a different matter).[67] CAAWS also removed all references to feminism from its mission statements and goals. By 1992, its purpose was "to ensure that girls and women in sport and physical activity have access to a complete range of opportunities and choices and have equity as participants and leaders," and a new vision was portrayed as follows:

> As the leading organization for girls and women in sport and physical activity, CAAWS is inclusive and equitable in its philosophies and practice.
>
> CAAWS provides expert advice, positive solutions and support to Canada's communities. Innovative and responsive attitudes ensure that CAAWS adapts quickly to change. Policies, plans and actions are based upon these attitudes and are supported by a solid foundation of research and information.[68]

By 2001, the language had changed somewhat, but the mission and goals were much the same: "CAAWS is in business to encourage girls and women to get out of the bleachers, off the sidelines, and onto the fields and rinks, into the pools, locker rooms and board rooms of Canada"; and "CAAWS works in partnership with Sport Canada and with Canada's sport and active living communities to achieve gender equity in the sport community."[69]

Throughout the past decade, CAAWS has gained considerable credibility within the amateur sport community in Canada, indeed elsewhere in the world. Like any multi-sport organization, it receives (since 1994) core funding from Sport Canada, which allows it to support an office, executive director, small staff, and volunteer board of directors, as well as to run its programs. Marg McGregor, the organization's energetic executive director from 1992 until 2000, believed that a not-for-profit organization was no different than a business. In other words, it must fill a need, be cost effective, productive, show value, be supported by clientele, and able to market its product.[70]

To this end, CAAWS focussed on building national partnerships with recreation and active living communities, aboriginal sport groups, other multi-sport organizations, the women's health community, and others. On the communications front, it established a well-designed and interesting Internet website and, most importantly, keeps it updated regularly. CAAWS continued to educate sport leaders and organizations about gender equity, especially by working when requested with national sport organizations in reviewing policies and publications and providing resource materials. CAAWS was a major player in a series of national Sport Forums in the early 1990s that led to the formation of the Canadian Sport Council, a now defunct coalition of national and multi-sport organizations, where a serious effort was made to build equity, in particular gender equity, into its structure.[71] CAAWS also contributes to the international women's sport movement by sending representatives to conferences, working with worldwide organizations like the International Working Group and WomenSport International, and helping to organize the third World Conference on Women and Sport Conference to be held in 2002 in Montreal.[72]

Perhaps more controversial was the partnership CAAWS established with Nike Canada Ltd. With the exception of one letter to the CAAWS newsletter, there was little concern expressed over Nike's appropriation of women's issues to suit their entrepreneurial goals (through ad campaigns like "Just Do It" and "If You Let Me Play"), or about the consumption of Nike products at the expense of women in developing countries where these goods are made.[73] The Nike partnership allowed for activities like the Girls@Play Network, a club targeted at girls and young women with a membership package, newsletter, interactive website, on-line chats, and more. Nike also helped sponsor small, weekly grants to deserving young women athletes, as well as a women and sport symposium.

WHERE ARE WE TODAY?

Some 30 years have passed since the first serious efforts were undertaken by individuals, women's groups, government agencies, recreational bodies, educational institutions, and the like to improve gender equity in Canadian physical activity and sport. Where are we now? Despite ample evidence of an increased interest and participation by females in certain sports, as well as renewed exercise and recreational physical activity among sectors of the population, far too few Canadian women (and men) are not active enough to benefit their health. For instance, some 60 per cent of young female adults (age 18 to 24 years), compared to 36 percent of males in the same age group, do not engage in physical activity frequently and intensely enough to develop fitness. As age increases, the level of inactivity also increases such that at the upper age range (65 and over), 78 per cent of women (and 65 per cent of men) are insufficiently active.[74]

Fewer Canadians are active in sports than was the case a decade earlier. This is true for both children and adults, and, as always, fewer girls and women play sport than do boys and men. In 1998, one-third (34 per cent) of the Canadian population age 15 and over participated in sport on a regular basis (at least once a week), down almost 11 percentage points from the 45 per cent reporting participation in 1992. There is an even more noticeable drop in the rate of adult females engaging in sport over this six-year period. In 1992, 38 per cent of Canadian women over 15 years of age were regularly engaged in sport, but by 1998, this figure had dropped to 26 per cent as compared to 43 per cent for males. Women's involvement in physical activity is more likely to take the form of individual fitness activities than organized sports. In 1998, only 19 per cent of Canadians aged 15 and older belonged to a club, a local community league, or other local or regional amateur sport organizations. On the other hand, most women doing sport tended to belong to a club or league. Of the 2.4 million Canadians who were registered members of national and provincial sport organizations, just under 30 per cent were female, despite the growth mentioned earlier in sports like ice hockey and soccer. Finally, every study of sport involvement demonstrates that participation for both genders decreases with age and increases with the level of education and household income.[75]

Children and adolescents with physically active parents tend to be more active than children with inactive parents. In 1998, just over half (54 per cent) of the estimated 4.1 million Canadian children aged five to 14 were regularly active in sport. Girls were less active than boys. While 61 per cent of boys were active in sport, the corresponding figure for girls was 48 per cent.[76] Children of both genders are getting increasingly less exercise as measured by being overweight, even obese. Between 1981 and 1996, the percentage of overweight girls between the ages of seven and 13 went from 15 per cent to 24 per cent (for boys it went from 15 to 29 per cent). Eating habits and long hours of watching television or playing video games, as well as insufficient exercise, all contribute to the growing problem.[77]

Analyses of persistent physical inactivity by girls and women have become more sophisticated and far-reaching during the last decade. Abby Hoffman, who in 1991 left Sport Canada to become Director General of the Women's Health Bureau in the federal government, argues that "real gains will only be achieved if we take account of the social, cultural, economic, and political realities of women's lives beyond sport, and if we endeavour to change those conditions beyond sport that limit sport involvement."[78] Women's increased labour force participation, their domestic and family responsibilities, substantially lower incomes and higher poverty rate all contribute to fatigue, stress, and health-related problems. These are significant factors, although not necessarily causes, contributing to women's lower participation in physical activity and sport. University of British Columbia professor Patricia Vertinsky, who has researched the subject for many years, argues that even today the medical profession assists "not only in rendering women dependent upon the health care system, but also in poisoning their concept of physical self by causing them to perceive their natural processes as deviant and problematic, thus thwarting a vigorous approach to exercise and competitive sport."[79] Menstruation, pregnancy, childbirth, and menopause have become increasingly medicalized, so that much of the professional and popular discourse on female health, exercise, and sport is contaminated by a focus on women's reproductive function. For example, a recent article appearing in the *Edmonton Journal*, with the headline "Bike Riding May Endanger Women's Sexual Health," reported on genital numbness in women from recreational cycling; the fact that males also complained of penile numbness from the same activity was not considered significant.[80] Cultural messages that overstate the negative rather than positive effects of exercise and physical activity on women's health continue to act as a deterrent to women's enjoyment and participation.

Early in adolescence, girls (most often white and middle-class) are socialized in ways that promote body-hating attitudes, which in turn distort their attitudes towards exercise and sport. "It's fair to say," argues sociologist Helen Lenskyj, "that by puberty most girls have learned that others evaluate them first and foremost in terms of their physicality and sexuality."[81] Even though images of today's healthy, beautiful women allow for more muscularity and vigour, young women and girls are still bombarded through fashion magazines, advertisements, and television programs with models and bodies they simply cannot emulate. Some become obsessed with their bodies and view them as segmented objects in need of repair — nose, breasts, face, bottom, legs, whatever — something overindulgent and misguided parents allow with increasing frequency.[82] The pursuit of thinness leads to unhealthy eating at best and disordered eating at worst, sometimes unhealthy patterns of excessive exercise, and at the very least instills little appreciation for the joy of movement and physicality, what Lenskyj calls "physical illiteracy."

It is also important to recognize that we cannot rely on the sameness of girls and women when discussing their bodies, their health, and their exercise and sport participation. For example, the rate of participation among women with disabilities is lower than that of able-bodied women, due to inaccessible facilities, transportation problems, and lack of program information.[83] Aboriginal women, especially those living in rural and remote areas are severely disadvantaged and marginalized. On First Nations reserves with sporting facilities and programs, far fewer girls and women compared to boys and men have access to these resources and opportunities.[84]

For a relatively small minority of women, Canada's top level athletes, opportunities to compete internationally have increased significantly since the beginning of the 1990s. For example, the 1992 Summer Olympics in Barcelona offered 159 events for men, 86 for women, and 12 open to both women and men, which meant that men had double the chances to compete for a medal. The Canadian team reflected this imbalance with 189 men and 125 women (40 per cent). However, with the addition of more sports and events for women at the Olympics — soccer, softball, beach volleyball, water polo, triathlon, mountain biking, modern pentathlon, taekwondo, weightlifting, and others — the percentage of women on the Canadian team for both 1996 and 2000 was 50.2 per cent. Boxing, wrestling, and baseball are the only sports not yet available to women at the Olympic level. Improvement at the Winter Olympics is not quite as dramatic, but the number of women on the Canadian team jumped from 26 per cent in 1992 to 42 per cent in 1998, due mainly to the inclusion of women's curling and ice hockey. Other major games, like the Commonwealth, Pan-American, World Student Games, and Paralympics have also added more women's sports and events, and there are more world championships in a variety of sports for women. Overall in 1998, the representation of women athletes on Canada's national teams was 47 per cent, and, according to a survey, they appear to have equal access to training and competitive environments, as well as to health, medical, and sport science services.[85]

As for the leadership of Canadian sport, the improvement for women has not been nearly as impressive; they are still under-represented, in some cases vastly so, just as they are everywhere else in the sports world. Starting at the top, only 13 of the 123 active members of the International Olympic Committee are women, three of whom are European royalty (as of spring, 2001). Since the first woman was not appointed to the IOC until 1981, 85 years after it was formed, this could be viewed as progress. One woman member is Canadian Charmaine Crooks, an international track athlete who participated in four Olympics and was the Canadian flag bearer at Atlanta in 1996. She is only the second woman, and the first woman of colour, from Canada to sit on the IOC. With the untimely death of Canadian Olympic Association executive Carol Anne Letheren in 2001, unfortunately both the IOC and Canada lost an experienced and respected member.[86] One reason for the lack of female members on the IOC is that so few presidents of international sport federations or national Olympic committees have been (and are) women. There are also very few women involved in the power structure of disability sport: in 2000, for example, there was only one woman on the 22-member executive committee of the International Paralympic Committee.[87]

The Canadian amateur sport system, from the local club right up to national sport organizations, requires volunteers to help run it. Traditionally, many more men have been involved in this capacity than women, but in 1998, there was an equal proportion of males and females, a change from 1992 when nearly twice as many men were sport administrators.[88] Whether the increase in women as volunteer sport administrators means that they will overcome the barriers to their participation on boards of directors and committees of provincial and national sport organizations remains to be seen. In the past, approximately 25 per cent of the volunteer sector in amateur sport was female, as was the case with senior executives and technical directors in paid positions.[89] Similarly, in 1992, the proportion of male referees, officials, and umpires outnumbered females five to one, but the gender gap had decreased to less than two to one by 1998. Fewer women (36 per cent) than men officiate at the international level, even though the numbers of male and female national team athletes is about even. At Canadian universities in 2001, 22 per cent (11 out of 49) of the athletic directors are female.

More women are also coaching in Canadian amateur sport than was the case a few years ago. While approximately 200,000 women (2 per cent of the total) reported coaching in 1992, this figure had more than tripled to 766,000 (6 per cent) by 1998. There is no longer a large difference between the percentage of coaches who are male (56 per cent) and those who are female (44 per cent). However, many of these coaches are young adults between 15 and 24 years; coaching numbers decline substantially with age.[90] Many women coach at the lower levels and with younger children, which is obviously fine, but their numbers become much fewer as the level of competition increases. For example, at the university-level, 15 percent (84 out of 559) of the head coaches are female. There were just over 250 full and part-time coaches in 1998 employed by 37 federally-funded national sport organizations. Of these, 17 per cent were female. Among full-time coaches at the national level, there were 10 times more males than females (70 versus seven). Women coaches were paid less than their male counterparts, even though their qualifications under the National Coaching Certification Program were similar and in some cases higher than the males.[91] For instance, when Melody Davidson (who completed Level V, the highest possible level of certification) was coach of the women's national ice hockey team in 1999, she was paid an $8,000 honorarium, supplementing her income by running a hockey school in Alberta and coaching at a college in the United States. The national men's team had two full-time coaches, paid at least $70,000 each.[92]

Coaching, especially at the higher levels such as university or national teams, is a tough profession requiring commitment, dedication, endurance, late hours, and much travel, to the extent that women with families find it difficult to balance both. As Kathy Shields, a highly successful university-level and former national team basketball coach, pointed out:

> In Canada, coaching is a great life, but it's a tough life if you've got a family.
> I've had the longevity because, one, I love the game, and two, I don't have
> children. I admire so much women coaches who have been able to balance

both. In Canada, to be able to stay in coaching with a family, to me those women are the real heroes in this country.[93]

There now appears to be a concerted effort, particularly among women coaches themselves, to find solutions to high levels of burnout and frustration, and to convince organizations hiring coaches that they cannot abdicate their responsibility in assisting and encouraging women (and men for that matter) who wish to combine career and family, just like everywhere else in the labour market.

Sport organizations have not always seen the need for strategies and programs to train and promote women coaches and to allow them to gain the necessary experience to move up the ranks. This is especially true for sports that have equal numbers of male and female athletes, but have been traditionally run by men. Competitive swimming is a good case in point. Women swim coaches have long been denied the same opportunities to coach at the elite, for example Olympic, level. In preparation for the Sydney Olympics, 26-year-old Shauna Nolden was added to the six men already appointed to the team, the first time a woman was part of the Canadian swimming coaching staff at an Olympic Games. Nolden, whose qualifications were questionable, was appointed without benefit of a selection committee nor criteria established for such appointments. Most coaches were outraged, and many felt that other women deserved the spot ahead of her. Consequently, a very public and messy controversy ensued, with the 900-member Canadian Swimming Coaches Association filing a complaint; her appointment was subsequently voided, but a new selection committee with different criteria re-appointed her, and she went to Sydney. Despite their good intentions, this was a public relations disaster for Swimming Canada, and, according to other women coaches, a giant step backward for women in coaching. Following Canada's lacklustre swimming performance at Sydney (one bronze medal), a positive outcome of the controversy was that women coaches were invited to come forward with recommendations to redefine the role of the female coach at the high-performance level.[94]

HOPE FOR THE FUTURE

Statistics about fitness levels and inactivity among Canadian girls and women and the gender inequities still present in the coaching and leadership ranks, aside from being depressing, do not necessarily tell the whole story. Every day, thousands of girls and women, from the very young to older seniors, can be found engaging in some sort of physical activity, including games on playgrounds, jogging in the streets, riding bicycles, or purposively walking through shopping malls. Special events, especially fundraisers like the Terry Fox Run or those for breast cancer research, bring out hundreds of women of all descriptions, some fit and some not so. Yoga classes are especially popular with women, and they attract a huge variety of individuals, from the more spiritually inclined to older athletes (like myself) desperate to regain some lost flexibility. Women's fitness classes, especially if they are inexpensive, easy to get to, and have built-in childcare, are popular and well-attended. *Chatelaine,* Canada's most popular women's magazine, has recently introduced "Sweat central," a virtual fitness club, where users can obtain useful advice and information — for example, how to hire a personal trainer and the best equipment or gear for your activity. In partnership with CAAWS, *Chatelaine* has launched walking clubs designed to bring like-minded women together to enjoy fitness within a community of friends.[95] In winter, the mountain ski hills buzz with women of all ages, who are fortunate enough to afford an expensive sport. The same is true of golf courses in summer, where opportunities for fun, companionship, competition, and networking are drawing more females to learn the game. For the superbly fit, there are the many marathons and triathlons, some with so many contestants, they have at times become dangerous. More and more women are taking up "extreme" sports, like rock climbing, parachute jumping, bodyboarding, mountain biking, and others, for the same reasons — adventure, thrill, testing themselves — as do men.

Much of this activity goes unrecorded because it is private, sometimes hidden, and certainly not organized. Statistics cannot take account of informal women's sporting groups, like the Beckwith Belles in Edmonton, Alberta. We are a group of mostly middle-aged women (a few, indeed, are seniors) whose passion is horse riding, specifically the ancient and intricate art of dressage. During the summer, some compete at horse shows, but most are simply content to ride every day, even when it is miserably wet or brutally cold, just for the sheer pleasure of being at one with a horse. Naturally, riding and equipping horses is expensive, and all of us are privileged to be able to afford this luxury. Regardless, you will not find a more passionate group of sportswomen anywhere, although our tribulations and accomplishments generally receive little or no public recognition. The stable and its culture provide an emotional support network outside our families; it is clearly *our* time for leisure, fun, and companionship away from the stresses of everyday life. The sports world rarely recognizes these small pockets of women's physical activity, and we are often excluded from the dominant sporting culture. No matter, clubs like this are vitally important to the girls and women who participate in them.

EPILOGUE

As the days of 2000 dwindled down, the print and broadcast media were rife with lists and rankings of the millennium's best athletes and teams, as well as the most memorable sporting events. Grandiosely claiming that few Canadian cities could match Edmonton's rich sporting heritage, the *Edmonton Journal* ran a special series profiling the city's greatest athletes, teams, coaches, and sporting movers and shakers. National newspapers provided similar features, although less parochial in scope, and TSN broadcast a six-part retrospective entitled "100 Years of Canadian Sports" (also available on home video). Based on the names, lists, stories, and photos in these various media, it seemed that for every woman athlete or sporting moment, at least 20 or more male athletes and their events or moments were celebrated. Some might argue that 20-to-1 is a satisfactory ratio given women's "lesser" achievements in sport.

Women's sporting accomplishments should not be compared to those of men, nor should they simply be an addendum to men's achievements. Media sport is a prime site for the ideological construction of gender differences, forcing people to make comparisons between men and women and establishing male performance as the yardstick for *all* sport, including women's. No doubt one of the reasons for these never-ending comparisons and the female athlete's marginalization — what some call "symbolic annihilation" — is the persistent under-representation of women in sports journalism. In an informal survey taken in 1999 of the top 12 daily newspapers in Canada, just over 7 per cent of their sportswriters were women, which probably amounts to less than 20 in the whole country.[1] In their third annual survey of the coverage by Canada's largest daily newspapers (21 in total), CAAWS found the average space devoted to women's sport was a dismal 8.8 per cent, although up from 2.8 per cent in 1991.[2] In television sport, increasingly more women appear in front of the cameras, a few more behind; yet women's sport in Canada, except for curling, and figure skating, and the Olympics every two years, is noticeably absent from the major networks, although it is more prevalent on speciality cable channels and everywhere in the new media, such as the Internet.

The end-of-millennium lists and rankings of the best Canadian teams and athletes over the previous 100 years were entirely predictable. A list of nominees for the Canadian Press and Broadcast News awards, almost all from the last 50 years, was sent to sports editors and directors (not many would be women) at more than 500 newspapers and broadcast outlets in Canada. They were to vote on the top 10 Canadian male athletes, female athletes, and teams. Among the latter, heavily weighted with men's professional sport teams, only one women's team made it — Sandra Schmirler's curling rink from 1993–98. (The Olympic gold medal winner and three-time world champion from Saskatchewan died tragically of cancer at age 36 in 2000.) Further down the list in eleventh position was the Edmonton Grads basketball team, and in fifteenth place, the 1928 Olympic women's "Matchless Six" track team. Skier Nancy Greene was voted the century's top female athlete, followed by rower Silken Laumann, figure skater Barbara Ann Scott, biathlete Myriam Bédard, rower Marnie McBean, all-round athlete Bobbie Rosenfeld, speed skater Catriona Le May Doan, golfer Sandra Post, and swimmers Marilyn Bell and Elaine Tanner.[3] A panel at the *National Post* ranked the 25 most memorable moments in Canadian sports since 1948, only three of which related to women: Barbara Ann Scott's 1948 Olympic win, Nancy Greene's Olympic victories in 1968, and Silken Laumann's return from a devastating leg injury to win an Olympic bronze medal in 1992 at Barcelona. Observant readers pointed out that one glaring omission (among many) was Marilyn Bell's swim of Lake Ontario in 1954.[4]

TSN's "100 Years of Canadian Sports" program did a slightly better job of balancing male and female coverage, although male professional team sports, especially hockey and football, were a major focus. In the segment on "personalities and characters," the only woman mentioned was curler Marilyn Bodogh, who along with her sister Christine, skipped the world-title winning rink in 1986. Her main claim to fame was that she "brought sex appeal" to the game of curling, and her rink lost a "battle of the sexes" match with Eddie "The Wrench" Werenich in 1986, but defeated him 10 years later. In the program about "innovators, movers, and shakers," a tribute to the people who helped build and shape Canada's sport legacy, not a single woman was mentioned. They were, truly, the "boys in the back room." Where were women like Alexandrine Gibb, Irene Wall, Myrtle Cook, Phyllis Griffiths, Ann Clark, Donalda Smith, Helen Gurney, Abby Hoffman, Carol Anne Letheren, Marion Lay, and many others?

What should we make of these millennium rankings and programs aside from the fact that they are produced mostly by male broadcasters and sportswriters? One observation is that memories are short, and the accomplishments and triumphs of Canadian athletes (both women and men) in the first half of the twentieth century have been mostly forgotten. The truly remarkable athletes, like the incomparable Bobbie Rosenfeld, have not been neglected, but there are scores of others, many discussed in this book, whose achievements at the time were equal to those in the second half of the century. Canada's sports halls of fame, who play a strategic role in the public memory and interpretation of sports, have a dearth of women athletes and builders.[5] Among the 419 recognized (as of 2000) in Canada's Sports Hall of Fame, only 63 (15 per cent) are women, and in the Canadian Olympic Hall of Fame there are 94 (27 per cent) women out of 350. A similar pattern exists in the 30 or so formal sports halls of fame and museums across the country.[6] Although it is an excellent resource, Bob Ferguson's *Who's Who in Canadian Sport*, contains fewer than 900 (20 per cent) females among the nearly 4,500 biographies of athletes, coaches, builders, and officials.

There was also an inexcusable lack of recognition of the contributions by female athletes of colour, aboriginal women, and athletes with disabilities among the millennium nominations and awards. Beginning with pioneer athletes of colour like Barbara Howard and Rosella Thorne, to the highly successful track athletes whose parents immigrated to Canada in the 1960s, and finally to the many fine high performance athletes of today in a great variety of sports, their accomplishments and contributions have been outstanding and out of proportion to their numbers in the general population. Admittedly, the recognition of aboriginal athletes is complicated by the fact that many more compete in specifically indigenous sports organizations and competitions than do in so-called mainstream or "white" sport. With regard to the latter, there have been very few top-level aboriginal women athletes in Canada, and only a handful have achieved international success, like cross-country skiers Sharon and Shirley Firth, middle-distance runner Angela Chalmers, and, most recently, water polo player Waneek Horn-Miller. The Aboriginal Sport Circle, Canada's national voice for aboriginal sport, also recognizes outstanding achievement among native athletes.

Although a few female athletes with disabilities train with or compete against able-bodied counterparts, the majority participate in insular, disability-specific clubs, organizations, and competitions, which separate them practically and symbolically from the mainstream of sport. One disabled athlete of the past, whose accomplishments have never been fully appreciated, is Shirley Gordon (later Olafsson) from Vancouver. Born with a deformed left foot, she spent much of her childhood in operating rooms, leg casts, wheelchairs, or on crutches. As a teenager, with the operations complete and the leg brace gone, but still with one leg shorter, an immobile ankle, and little calf muscle, she decided to make up for lost time by participating in a variety of sports, including high jumping. Soon she was winning high school championships and invited to join the Hudson Bay track club, where she came under the tutelage of former British Empire Games star Frank Richard. Due to her handicap, Gordon used the outmoded scissors jump and was forced to take off and land on the same foot. In 1948, she came second at the Canadian championships, made the Olympic qualifying standard, and was named to the team; at the London Olympics she placed a respectable tenth. Referred to in the media as the "crippled girl" who became an Olympic star, Gordon continued to compete for several more years, including at the 1950 British Empire Games in Auckland, New Zealand, where she finished fifth.[7]

Today, even those who perform spectacularly at the international level, such as the Paralympics, do not receive the same acclaim either in the media or popular consciousness as do able-bodied athletes. It is only in the 1990s that major international competitions, such as the Olympics and the Commonwealth Games, have seen the inclusion of selected full medal events for disabled athletes. Elite sportswomen with disabilities, therefore, are "constructed less frequently as *sporting* heroines and more usually as *disabled* sportswomen."[8]

To place too much emphasis on a small group of highly talented athletes, either female or male, is to diminish the accomplishments of the thousands of other athletes, some of whom made it to the podium, but most of whom did not. It also neglects the role played by parents, siblings, teachers, coaches, spouses, friends, and others who supported and encouraged these athletes, sometimes at considerable personal sacrifice over many years. Many of these supporters have been women. In an enlightening book called *Mother's Taxi*, about the work women do that enables others to play sport, New Zealand sport sociologist Shona Thompson points out that ignoring, denying, and undervaluing women and their contributions is yet another way of rendering women invisible. Not surprisingly, she found that sport is maintained and reproduced by women's work through unequal and usually exploitative gender relations: "These relations have at their core divisions of labor by which women are disproportionately responsible for domestic work and child care. Such divisions of labor serve both to maintain and reproduce sport and are further reproduced by sporting structures and practices."[9]

I wrote *The Girl and the Game* partly because no one else had, but also as an opportunity to explore the uncharted story of women's sport in Canada. It remains, however, merely a beginning. As mentioned in the Introduction, my approach has been to paint the broader picture in the hope that others will fill in the missing details through regional and local stories, more specific studies in depth, and tracking down former athletes and competitors. Who now will take up this challenge?

NOTES

PREFACE AND ACKNOWLEDGEMENTS

1   Don Morrow, "Canadian Sport History: A Critical Essay," *Journal of Sport History* 10.1 (1983): 67.

2   Patricia A. Vertinsky, "Gender Relations, Women's History and Sport History: A Decade of Changing Inquiry, 1983–1993," *Journal of Sport History* 21.1 (1994): 23.

3   Catriona M. Parratt, "About Turns: Reflecting on Sport History in the 1990s," *Sport History Review* 29.1 (1998): 4–17.

INTRODUCTION

1   This paragraph and part of the next originally appeared in M. Ann Hall, "Creators of the Lost and Perfect Game?: Gender, History, and Canadian Sport," *Sport and Gender in Canada*, eds. Philip White and Kevin Young (Don Mills: Oxford University Press, 1999) 7.

2   Susan Birrell and Nancy Theberge, "Feminist Resistance and Transformation in Sport," *Women and Sport*, eds. D. Margaret Costa and Sharon R. Guthrie (Champaign: Human Kinetics, 1994).

3   Toby Miller, *Sportsex* (Philadelphia: Temple University Press, 2001) 23–24. The quote cited is from cultural theorist Stuart Hall.

4   Alison Prentice *et al., Canadian Women: A History* (Toronto: Harcourt Brace Jovanovich, 1988) 13.

5   M. Ann Hall *et al., Sport in Canadian Society* (Toronto: McClelland and Stewart, 1991) 13–15.

6   For information about the early games and sports played by aboriginal peoples, especially women, see Alyce Cheska, "Ball Game Participation of North American Indian Women," *Her Story in Sport: A Historical Anthology of Women in Sports*, ed. Reet Howell (West Point: Leisure Press, 1982) 19–34; Stewart Culin, *Games of the North American Indians* (1907; New York: Dover Publications, 1975); Diamond Jenness, *Indians of Canada*, 7th ed. (Toronto: University of Toronto Press, 1977) 158; Morris Mott, "Games and Contests of the First 'Manitobans,'" *Sports in Canada: Historical Readings*, ed. Morris Mott (Toronto: Copp Clark Pitman, 1989) 18–27; and Joseph B. Oxendine, *American Indian Sports Heritage* (Champaign: Human Kinetics, 1988) 22–26, 55–58.

7   W.G. Beers, *Lacrosse* (Montreal: Dawson Bros., 1869) 22.

8   *Kingston Gazette*, 28 April 1812.

9   Cited in Henry Roxborough, *One Hundred-Not Out* (Toronto: Ryerson Press, 1966) 18.

10 R. Wayne Simpson, "The Elite and Sport Club Membership in Toronto 1827–1881," diss.,
    University of Alberta, 1987.

11 *Montreal Gazette*, 24 February 1879. See also reports on 21 and 22 February.

12 *Globe* (Toronto), 28 October 1879.

13 Dahn Shaulis, "Pedestriennes: Newsworthy But Controversial Women in Sporting
    Entertainment," *Journal of Sport History* 26.1 (1999): 30–50. Shaulis mentions a French-
    Canadian pedestrienne named Exilda La Chapelle, who was among the more than 100
    women in 1879 (the peak of the craze) walking for money (39).

14 *Globe*, 17 January 1879: 2. A portion of the editorial was also published in the *New York
    Times*, 19 January 1879: 8.

15 *Globe*, 17 January 1879: 2.

16 Cited in Roxborough 242.

17 *Globe*, 31 October 1879. Originally cited in the *Prescott Telegraph*.

18 "Modern Mannish Maidens," *Blackwood's Magazine* (February 1890): 252–64. A small
    portion was reprinted in the *Globe*, 15 March 1890: 12.

19 Catriona M. Parratt, "About Turns: Reflecting on Sport History in the 1990s," *Sport History
    Review* 29.1 (1998): 8.

20 Jennifer Hargreaves, *Heroines of Sport* (London: Routledge, 2000) 6.

21 Kay Rex, *No Daughter of Mine* (Toronto: Cedar Cave Books, 1995); Marjory Lang, *Women
    Who Made the News* (Montreal and Kingston: McGill-Queen's University Press, 1999).

22 Bruce Kidd, *Improvers, Feminists, Capitalists and Socialists,* diss., University of Toronto,
    1990, 205. Unfortunately, I have located none of Gibb's earlier publications; the first arti-
    cle found with her byline was written on 26 September 1926 for the *Toronto Daily Star*. For
    early descriptions of Gibb as a writer, see "Ontario Basketball Champions," *Edmonton
    Bulletin*, 12 April 1924: 4 and Deacon White, "Sport is My Subject," *Edmonton Bulletin*, 21
    April 1924: 4.

23 Since Gibb averaged 25 columns a month written between 8 May 1928 and 26 November
    1940, and taking account of the periods when she was travelling, on holidays, or ill, I esti-
    mate that she published between 3,300 and 3,400 columns. Gibb also wrote the occasional
    article for the *Toronto Star Weekly* and for national magazines such as *Maclean's*, as well as
    additional articles on women's sport for the *Star*.

24 Bruce Kidd, *The Struggle for Canadian Sport* (Toronto: University of Toronto Press, 1996) 263.

25 Rex 31–32.

CHAPTER I EARLY BEGINNINGS: THE "NEW WOMAN" AND ATHLETICISM

1   Patricia Marks, *Bicycles, Bangs, and Bloomers* (Lexington: The University Press of Kentucky,
    1990) 201.

2   Richard Harmond, "Progress and Flight: An Interpretation of the American Cycle Craze
    of the 1890s," *Journal of Social History* 5.2 (1971–72): 235–57.

3   Tom Sandland, *Something About Bicycling in Newfoundland* (St. John's: Tom Sandland,
    1983) 15.

4   *Athletic Life*, October 1895: 171.

5   *Manitoba Morning Free Press*, 17 July 1896.

6   Harmond 244–45.

7   Charles Whipp and Edward Phelps, *Petrolia 1866–1966* (Petrolia: Advertiser-Topic and the Petrolia Centennial Committee, 1966) 52–53.

8   *Globe*, 4 June 1895: 4.

9   See advertisement in the *Toronto Saturday Night*, 28 March 1896: 12.

10 *Athletic Life*, April 1986: 170.

11 Norah H. Heneley, "Bicycling that Fascinates Fair Women," *Halifax Herald Women's Extra*, 10 August 1895: 3.

12 *Athletic Life*, March 1896: 125.

13 *Athletic Life,* March 1896: 125. See also the advertisement in *Toronto Saturday Night*, 14 March 1896: 5.

14 *Athletic Life*, April 1896: 169–71. Also, see advertisements in *Toronto Saturday Night*, 28 March 1896: 11 and 23 May 1896: 11.

15 Wendy Mitchinson, *The Nature of Their Bodies* (Toronto: University of Toronto Press, 1991) 65. I am indebted to Mitchinson for providing the necessary Canadian references to locate this debate. The medical debates around cycling in Canada were certainly influenced by those in Britain and the United States. For extended discussions of these, see Patricia A. Vertinsky, *The Eternally Wounded Woman* (Manchester: Manchester University Press, 1990) 76–82; and Helen Lenskyj, "The Role of Physical Education in the Socialization of Girls in Ontario, 1890–1930," diss., University of Toronto, 1983, 81–84.

16 *The Dominion Medical Monthly and Ontario Medical Journal* 7.3 (1896): 255.

17 See, for example, *The Dominion Medical Monthly and Ontario Medical Journal* 8.2 (1897): 134–136 and 11.1 (1898): 28–30; *The Canada Medical Record* 24.11 (1896): 552–55.

18 *The Dominion Medical Monthly and Ontario Medical Journal* 7.3 (1896): 256.

19 *Canadian Practitioner* 21.11 (1896): 848–49.

20 P.E. Doolittle, "Cycling for Women," *Canadian Practitioner* 21.5 (1896): 332.

21 See, in particular, *The Canadian Medical Record* 18.2 (1889): 27; *The Canadian Medical Record* 24.11 (1896): 552–55. Clothing manufacturers, however, responded with the "cycling corset," shorter at the front and on the hips, but still boned with "unbreakable Aluminized Steel" (see advertisement in *Toronto Saturday Night*, 11 July 1896: 8). See also Ellen Gruber Garvey's very interesting article about how mainstream magazines in the United States defused the bicycle's threatening aspects through attractive images in advertisements and formulaic fiction reframing its apparent social risks as benefits. "Reframing the Bicycle: Advertising — Supported Magazines and Scorching Women," *American Quarterly* 47.1 (1995): 66–101.

22 Mitchinson in *The Nature of Their Bodies* points out that in the census of 1891 only 76 out of 4,448 doctors listed in Canada were women (29).

23 Elizabeth Mitchell, "The Rise of Athleticism Among Girls and Women," in *Women Workers of Canada: Being a Report of the Proceedings of the Third Annual Meeting and Conference of the National Council of Women of Canada* (Montreal: John Lovell and Sons, 1896) 106–09. See also the "Discussion" that followed on pages 116–18.

24 Lucy M. Hall, "The Tricycle for Women," *The Chautauquan* 12 (October 1890): 90–91.

25 Heneley 3.

26 *New York Times*, 5 July 1896: 12; *Inland Sentinel* (Kamloops, BC), 10 July 1896; Robert A. Smith, *A Social History of the Bicycle* (New York: American Heritage Press, 1972) 75–76.

27 C.S. Clark, *Of Toronto the Good* (1898; Toronto: Coles, 1970) 112.

28 Helen Lenskyj, "Physical Activity for Canadian Women, 1890–1930: Media Views," *From 'Fair Sex' to Feminism,* eds. J.A. Mangan and Roberta J. Park (London: Frank Cass, 1987) 210.

29 Carol Lee Bacchi, *Liberation Deferred?* (Toronto: University of Toronto Press, 1983) 104, 109.

30 Marks 205.

31 James C. Whorton, "The Hygiene of the Wheel: An Episode in Victorian Sanitary Science," *Bulletin of the History of Medicine* 52.1 (1978): 85.

32 Heneley 3. For an alternative view, which downplays the role of the bicycle as a transformative agent in turn-of-the-century Canadian society, see Anita Rush, "The Bicycle Boom of the Gay Nineties: A Reassessment," *Material History Bulletin* 18 (Fall 1983): 1–12. For a selection of wonderful photographs of women cycling, see Glen Norcliffe, *The Ride to Modernity* (Toronto: University of Toronto Press, 2001).

33 Michael Smith, "Graceful Athleticism or Robust Womanhood: The Sporting Culture of Women in Victorian Nova Scotia, 1870–1914," *Journal of Canadian Studies* 23.1–2 (1988): 132.

34 "Modern Mannish Maidens," *Blackwood's Magazine* (February 1890): 252–64. A small portion was reprinted in the *Globe,* 15 March 1890: 12.

35 *Globe,* 22 January 1895.

36 "Modern Mannish Maidens" 260.

37 Martyn Kendrick, *Advantage Canada* (Toronto: McGraw-Hill Ryerson, 1990) 16.

38 See H.G. MacKenzie, "History of Lawn Tennis in Canada," *Athletic Life,* January 1895: 16–21; Kendrick, *Advantage Canada*; Scott Griffin, "Lawn Tennis," *Athletic Life,* June 1895: 241–45.

39 James A. Barclay, *Golf in Canada* (Toronto: McClelland and Stewart, 1992) 170–90.

40 Quoted in Smith, "Graceful Athleticism or Robust Womanhood," 131.

41 Barclay 377.

42 *The Standard,* Canadian Winter Sports Number, February 1909: 8; John. A. Stevenson, *Curling in Ontario 1846–1946* (Toronto: Ontario Curling Association, 1950) 95–96.

43 *Athletic Life,* April 1896: 172.

44 John Kerr, *Curling in Canada and the United States* (Edinburgh: Geo. A. Morton, 1904) 169–70, 190–01, 204–05, 555.

45 Stevenson 123.

46 Helen M. Eckert, "The Development of Organized Recreation and Physical Education in Alberta," MA thesis, University of Alberta, 1953; *Edmonton Daily Bulletin,* 25 February 1914; *Manitoba Free Press,* 14 January 1911, 19 February 1914; Morris Mott and John Allardyce, *Curling Capital* (Winnipeg: University of Manitoba Press, 1989) 29.

47 "It Was Ladies' Day," *Montreal Gazette,* 11 September 1905: 12.

48 *The Canadian Magazine,* February 1894: 490–91; *Montreal Gazette,* 22 February 1890; *Globe,* 19 February 1895; *Halifax Herald,* 2 September 1895.

49 Lynne Marks, *Revivals and Roller Rinks* (Toronto: University of Toronto Press, 1996) 127–30.

50 W. George Beers, *Over the Snow* (Montreal: W. Drysdale and Co., and J. Theo. Robinson, 1883) 18.

51 Don Morrow, "The Knights of the Snowshoe: A Study of the Evolution of Sport in Nineteenth Century Montreal," *Journal of Sport History* 15.1 (1988): 16, 29.

52 David W. Brown, "Social Darwinism, Private Schooling and Sport in Victoria and Edwardian Canada," *Pleasure, Profit, Proselytism,* ed. J.A. Mangan (London: Frank Cass, 1988) 215–30. See also J.A. Mangan, "Discipline in the Dominion: The 'Canuck' and the Cult of Manliness," *The Games Ethic and Imperialism* (New York: Viking, 1986) 142–223.

53 Morris Mott, "The British Protestant Pioneers and the Establishment of Manly Sports in Manitoba, 1870–1886," *Journal of Sport History* 7.3 (1980): 25–36.

54 Colin D. Howell, *Northern Sandlots* (Toronto: University of Toronto Press, 1995) 5.

55 R. Tait McKenzie, "Rugby Football in Canada," *The Dominion Illustrated Monthly* 1.1 (1892): 11–19.

56 *Canadian Standard Efficiency Tests*, 6th ed. (October 1914): 34. Quoted in David Howell and Peter Lindsay, "Social Gospel and the Young Boy Problem," *Canadian Journal of History of Sport* 17.1 (1986): 82.

57 Frank Proctor, *Fox Hunting in Canada and Some Men Who Made It* (Toronto: Macmillan, 1929) 110–11.

58 "Chronique Scientifique: Influence des Sports sur la Beauté Feminine," *Le Devoir*, 19 September 1912: 5. I am grateful to Gilles Janson for finding this article.

59 *Canadian Alpine Journal* 1 (1907): 169–70.

60 PearlAnn Reichwein, "Beyond the Visionary Mountains: The Alpine Club of Canada and the Canadian National Park Idea, 1906 to 1969," diss., Carleton University, 1995, Appendix B.

61 See the excellent thesis by Siri Winona Louie, "Gender in the Alpine Club of Canada, 1906–1940," MA thesis, University of Calgary, 1996.

62 For more information on early Canadian women climbers, see Cyndi Smith, *Off the Beaten Track* (Canmore, AB: Coyote Books, 1989).

63 Jamie Benidickson, *Idleness, Water, and a Canoe* (Toronto: University of Toronto Press, 1997) 78. Since the focus of this book is on organized sport, I do not discuss the history of women and wilderness or activities such as mountaineering, canoe tripping, and camping. For a start, see Benidickson (especially Chapter 6); several essays in *Using Wilderness*, eds. Bruce W. Hodgins and Bernadine Dodge (Peterborough: Trent University, 1992); Patricia Jason, *Wild Things* (Toronto: University of Toronto Press, 1995); and Kristopher L. Churchill, "Character Building and Gender Socialization in Early Private Youth Camps in Ontario," MA thesis, University of Guelph, 1991.

64 Edward Playter, "The Physical Culture of Women," *Woman; Her Character, Culture and Calling*, ed. B.F. Austin (Brantford: The Book and Bible House, 1890) 225.

65 Pauline Olafson, "Sport, Physical Education and the Ideal Girl in Selected Ontario Denominational Schools, 1870–1930," MA thesis, University of Windsor, 1990, 49. Olafson studied six schools: Loretto Abbey (Toronto) and St. Mary's Academy (Windsor), which were Roman Catholic schools; Bishop Strachan and Havergal College, both Anglican and located in Toronto; and two Methodist schools located in small towns, namely, Trafalgar Castle (formerly Ontario Ladies College) in Whitby and Alma College in St. Thomas. For an interesting description of ladies' colleges in Toronto in 1910, including their sports facilities and programs, see Margaret Bell, "The Girls' Colleges of Toronto," *Toronto Star Weekly*, 21 May 1910: 12.

66 Olafson 123–32; Mary Byers, *Havergal: Celebrating a Century 1894–1994* (Toronto: Boston Mills Press, 1994) 39–40.

67 Ellen Knox, *The Girl of the New Day* (Toronto: McClelland and Stewart, 1919) 19–29.

68 Byers 46, 226.

69 Kathleen E. McCrone, *Playing the Game* (Lexington: The University of Kentucky Press, 1988) 89.

70 Olafson 47–48.

71 Helen Lenskyj, "Training for 'True Womanhood': Physical Education for Girls in Ontario Schools, 1890–1920," *Historical Studies in Education* 2.2 (1990): 205–23. See also Helen

Gurney, *Girls' Sports: A Century of Progress in Ontario High Schools* (Don Mills: OFSAA, 1982) 14–15.

72 E.B. Houghton, *Physical Culture* (Toronto: Warwick and Sons, 1886) 220.

73 Don Morrow, "Sport and Physical Education in Schools and Universities," *A Concise History of Sport in Canada,* Don Morrow *et al.* (Toronto: Oxford University Press, 1989) 67–87; Don Morrow, "The Strathcona Trust in Ontario, 1911–1939," *Canadian Journal of History of Sport and Physical Education* 8.1 (1977): 72–90.

74 Strathcona Trust, *Syllabus of Physical Exercises for Schools* (Toronto: Copp, Clark, 1911) 164.

75 Lenskyj, "Training for 'True Womanhood'" 217.

76 *Globe*, 6, 13, 22, 25 June 1900; *Globe*, 13 May 1901; Gurney, *Girls' Sports*, 17–20.

77 James Naismith, *Basketball: Its Origin and Development* (New York: Association Press, 1941). See especially Chapter IX.

78 Reported in Gurney, *Girls' Sports*, 21.

79 Prentice *et al.* 162.

80 A.B. McKillop, "Marching as to War: Elements of Ontario Undergraduate Culture, 1880–1914," *Youth, University and Canadian Society*, eds. Paul Axelrod and John G. Reid (Kingston: McGill-Queen's University Press, 1989) 80. McKillop argues that the appearance of women on campuses in the 1880s prompted an increasing interest in "manly" sports, such as football, rugby, and hockey, among male students concerned about the feminization of campus life.

81 Susan Cahn, *Coming on Strong* (New York: The Free Press, 1994) 18.

82 Margaret Gillett, *We Walked Very Warily* (Montreal: Eden Press, 1981) 104–06.

83 A.E. Marie Parkes, *The Development of Women's Athletics at the University of Toronto* (Toronto: Women's Athletic Association, University of Toronto, 1961) 6.

84 *Old McGill* 11 (1901): 161.

85 Anne Rochon Ford in *A Path Strewn With Roses* (Toronto: Women's Centenary Committee, University of Toronto, 1985, 65–75) tells the depressing story of the 40-year struggle by women students and faculty to gain a building comparable to Hart House. See also Helen Gurney, *A Century to Remember 1893–1993: Women's Sports at the University of Toronto* (Toronto: University of Toronto Women's T-Holders' Association, 1993).

86 Gurney, *A Century to Remember*; M. Ann. Hall, "A History of Women's Sport in Canada Prior to World War I," MA thesis, University of Alberta, 1968.

87 John McBryde, "The Bipartite Development of Men's and Women's Field Hockey in Canada in the Context of Separate International Hockey Federations," MA thesis, University of British Columbia, 1986.

88 *The Gateway*, February 1913.

89 *The Gateway* (February 1913): 225–29; Yvette M. Walton, "The Life and Professional Contributions of Ethel Mary Cartwright, 1880–1955," MA thesis, University of Western Ontario, 1976.

90 Marjory MacMurchy, "Women and the Nation," *The New Era in Canada*, ed. J.O. Miller (London: J.M. Dent and Sons, 1917).

91 Carolyn Strange, *Toronto's Girl Problem* (Toronto: University of Toronto Press, 1995) 217–19; Sharon Myers, "'Not to be Ranked as Women': Female Industrial Workers in Turn-of-the-Century Halifax," *Separate Spheres*, eds. Janet Guildford and Suzanne Morton (Fredericton: Acadiensis Press, 1994) 165–66; Margaret Bell, "Among the People Who Serve," *Toronto Star Weekly*, 7 May 1910: 12.

92 Elsie M. McFarland, *The Development of Public Recreation in Canada* (Canadian Parks/Recreation Association, 1970) 18–39; Strange, endnote 25, 244.

93 Strange 118.

94 Diana Pedersen, "'Building Today for the Womanhood of Tomorrow': Businessmen, Boosters, and the YWCA, 1890–1930," *Urban History Review* 15.3 (1987): 225–42; John Byl, "Directing Physical Education in the Canadian YMCAs: Margaret Eaton School's Influence, 1901–1947," *Sport History Review* 27.2 (1996): 139–54; Mary Quayle Innis, *Unfold the Years* (Toronto: McClelland and Stewart, 1949); Donald G. Wetherell, *Useful Pleasures* (Regina: Canadian Plains Research Centre, 1990) 88.

95 Margaret Bell, "Toronto Girls in Pursuit of Athletics," *Toronto Star Weekly*, 23 April 1910: 12.

96 Ethel M. Chapman, "The Miracle of Physical Training," *Maclean's Magazine*, 1 March 1920: 74, 78.

97 The history of the Margaret Eaton School has been remarkably well researched. See, in particular, the following dissertations: John Byl, "The Margaret Eaton School, 1901–1942: Women's Education in Elocution, Drama and Physical Education," diss., State University of New York at Buffalo, 1992; Anna H. Lathrop, "Elegance and Expression, Sweat and Strength: Body Training, Physical Culture and Female Embodiment in Women's Education at the Margaret Eaton Schools (1901–1941)," diss., University of Toronto, 1997. See also the following pamphlets and articles: John Byl, "Why Physical Educators Should Know About the Margaret Eaton School," *CAHPER Journal* 59.1 (1993): 10–13; Dorothy N.R. Jackson, *A Brief History of Three Schools* (Toronto: University of Toronto, 1953); Anna H. Lathrop, "Elegance and Expression, Sweat and Strength: A Portrait of the Margaret Eaton Schools (1901–1941) through the Life History of Emma Scott Nasmith, Mary G. Hamilton, and Florence A. Somers," *Vitae Scholasticae* 16.1 (1997): 69–92; Heather Murray, "Making the Modern: Twenty-Five Years of the Margaret Eaton School of Literature and Expression," *Essays in Theatre* 10.1 (1991): 39–57.

98 John Byl, "Directing Physical Education in the Canadian YWCAs: Margaret Eaton School's Influence, 1901–1947," *Sport History Review* 27.2 (1996): 139–54.

99 *Globe*, 18 April 1895: 10

100 *Queen's University Journal*, 1 December 1910.

101 "The Herald's Sporting Chat," *Halifax Herald*, 6 January 1910: 5.

102 John Dewar, "Saskatchewan's Basketball Beginnings (1891–1922)," *Saskatchewan History* 41.3 (1988): 99–112.

103 There is, as yet, no book about the Edmonton Grads. Probably the best historical summary to date is Cathy Macdonald, "The Edmonton Grads: Canada's Most Successful Team, A History and Analysis of Their Success," MA thesis, University of Windsor, 1976. See also the archival material listed under Sources.

104 *Ottawa Citizen*, 11 February 1891: front page.

105 *Montreal Gazette*, 24 January 1900; Donald Guay, *L'Histoire du Hockey au Québec* (Montreal: Les Éditions JCL, 1990) 152; Brian McFarlane, *Proud Past, Bright Future: One Hundred Years of Canadian Women's Hockey* (Toronto: Stoddart, 1994) 7–45.

106 Howell, *Northern Sandlots* 76.

107 Howell provides a great deal of information about this particular tour (74–96).

108 *Vancouver Province*, "Bunco and Baseball," 9 July 1900.

109 Barbara Gregorich, *Women at Play* (Orlando: Harcourt Brace, 1993) 6–11.

110 Lewis St. George Stubbs, *Shoestring Glory* (Winnipeg: Turnstone Press, 1996) 28; Earl Drake, *Regina* (Toronto: McClelland and Stewart, 1955) 108–09.

[111] Camille Roy, "La Femme ou Réflexions sur les 'Bloomer Girls," *Propos Canadiens* (Québec: Imprimerie de l'action sociale, 1912) 71–81.

[112] Howell, *Northern Sandlots* 93.

[113] Jenni Mortin, *Safe at Home* (Regina: Softball Saskatchewan, 1997); William Humber, *Diamonds of the North* (Toronto: Oxford, 1995); Wetherell, *Useful Pleasures* 148.

[114] *Toronto Saturday Night*, 20 October 1900: 6.

[115] Barclay 188.

[116] Barclay 187–90.

[117] Barclay 204–06.

[118] Marian I. Pitters-Caswell, "Woman's Participation in Sporting Activities as an Indicator of Femininity and Cultural Evolution in Toronto, 1910 to 1920," MA thesis, University of Windsor, 1975.

[119] Norman R. Raine, "Girls Invade Track and Diamond," *Maclean's Magazine*, 15 August 1925: 13.

CHAPTER 2 ASSUMING CONTROL: WOMEN'S SPORT RUN (ALMOST) BY WOMEN

[1] Gregory Clark, "Bobbed-Headed Athletes Menace Male Supremacy," *Toronto Star Weekly*, 24 April 1926: 21.

[2] Cited in Kidd, *The Struggle for Canadian Sport* 114.

[3] Kidd, *The Struggle for Canadian Sport* 100; "Girls' Sports," *Toronto Evening Telegram*, 28 November 1925: 34; "Girls' Sports," *Toronto Evening Telegram*, 25 January 1928: 35.

[4] "Leader in Girls' Sport Movement," *Toronto Star Weekly*, 31 March 1928.; Kidd, *The Struggle for Canadian Sport* 109.

[5] Susan L. Forbes, "The Influence of the Social Reform Movement and T. Eaton Company's Business Practices on the Leisure of Eaton's Female Employees During the Early Twentieth Century," diss., University of Western Ontario, 1998.

[6] *The Beaver: A Journal of Progress*, October 1920, March 1921, November 1922, December 1924.

[7] Joan Sangster, "The Softball Solution: Female Workers, Male Managers and the Operation of Paternalism at Westclox, 1923–60," *Labour/Le Travail* 32 (Fall 1993): 167–99. For more on the early history of industrial recreation and its relationship to women's sports, see Monys Ann Hagen, "Industrial Harmony Through Sports: The Industrial Recreation Movement and Women's Sports," diss., University of Wisconsin-Madison, 1990.

[8] *Toronto Daily Star*, 25 October 1924: 8.

[9] Fred G. 'Ted' Oke Scrapbook 1901–32, National Archives of Canada, MG 28 I99 Vol. 25 (microfilm); S.F. Wise and Douglas Fisher, *Canada's Sporting Heroes* (Don Mills: General Publishing, 1974) 286–87; Kidd, *The Struggle for Canadian Sport* 109.

[10] *Outdoor Canada*, December 1907: 262.

[11] Louise Mead Tricard, *American Women's Track and Field* (Jefferson: McFarland and Company, 1996), chapters 1–3.

[12] *Halifax Herald*, 17 June 1910.

[13] Lucille E. Hill, ed., *Athletics and Out-door Sports for Women* (New York: Grosset and Dunlap, 1903) 180.

[14] For a list of these and subsequent records prior to World War I, see Tricard 10–16.

15 Bill McNulty and Ted Radcliffe, comp. *Canadian Athletics 1839–1992* (n.p., 1992) 203.

16 See F.A.M. Webster, *Athletics of Today for Women* (London: Frederick Warne, 1930) and George Pallett, *Women's Athletics* (London: The Normal Press, 1955) for detailed descriptions, including competitors, times, records, and photographs of these early international track and field meetings.

17 *Toronto Daily Star*, 30 January 1924: 3.

18 Cited in Kidd, *The Struggle For Canadian Sport* 114.

19 *Globe*, 5 August 1924: 12.

20 Norman R. Raine, "Girls Invade Track and Diamond," *Maclean's Magazine*, 15 August 1925: 12.

21 "Confirms Appointment of Miss 'Alex' Gibb," *Globe*, 9 July 1925: 7.

22 *Globe*, 4 July 1925: 11.

23 Alexandrine Gibb, "Canadian Girls Trained Faithfully," *Toronto Daily Star*, 4 August 1925: 10. Note that this article appeared *after* the competition had taken place. The *Globe*, on the other hand, provided comprehensive reports of the meet.

24 Webster 53. The members of the Canadian team were: Clara Ballard, Grace Conacher, Hazel Conacher, Myrtle Cook, Josie Dyment, Kathleen Flanagan, Jean Godson, Velma Springstead, Mollie Trinnell, and Gertrude Woods.

25 Kidd, *The Struggle for Canadian Sport* 116.

26 The first media reference to "F. Rosenfeldt" found in a Toronto paper was in the *Globe* on 2 March 1922 (10) when she was playing hockey for the Toronto YWCA. Most sources (e.g., Kidd) suggest that the family moved to Toronto in the summer of 1922, which means that either she was in Toronto by herself (perhaps going to school), or the date is wrong. Also, her last name was often spelled as Rosenfeldt, but according to Ethel Berman (her sister), this was a mistake due to poor typing on her birth certificate.

27 *Toronto Daily Star*, 24 August 1925: 8.

28 Bobbie Rosenfeld, "Feminine Sports Reel," *Globe and Mail*, 6 January 1940: 16.

29 "Women's AAU of C Organized by Women," *Toronto Daily Star*, 11 September 1925: 79.

30 Alexandrine Gibb, "Plans Outlined for Women's AAU of C," *Toronto Daily Star*, 26 September 1925: 105.

31 Gibb, "No Man's Land of Sport," *Toronto Daily Star*, 1 May 1937: 17.

32 "Women's Athletic Federation Elects Its New Officers," *Montreal Daily Star*, 8 December 1926.

33 Pallet 36. See the last section of this chapter for more analysis of Dr. Lamb's beliefs regarding athletics for women.

34 Diane Ransom, "'The Saskatoon Lily': A Biography of Ethel Catherwood," *Saskatchewan History* 41.3 (1988): 81–98.

35 *Halifax Herald*, 8 August 1927: 4; 16 August 1927: 8; 17 August 1927: 8.

36 There is some confusion surrounding the Gertrude Phinney case. Sport historian Sandy Young interviewed her in 1982, when she maintained she was selected for the 1928 Olympic team, but her father asked her not to make the trip, promising instead a European trip when she turned 20; see A.J. "Sandy" Young, *Beyond Heroes*, vol. 1 (Hantsport, NS: Lancelot Press, 1988) 77. I also interviewed Gertrude Phinney Beattie (then 91 years of age) by telephone on 28 August 2000 and received the same information. However, at the Olympic trials in Halifax on 2 July 1928, although she did win the 220-yard event, she did not compete in the 100-metres, and she was not named to the Olympic team (see *Halifax Herald*, 3 July 1928:

11). I surmise that her lack of experience and poor starts kept her off the team and that it was the trip to Toronto in 1927 her father asked her to forego, not the trip to Amsterdam.

37   Another athlete who wanted to make the 1928 Olympic team was Lillian Palmer, a runner from Vancouver. Only 15, she was declared ineligible by the WAAF of C to compete at the trials in Halifax. She even wrote to the International Olympic Committee, who at that time did not have an age limit, but since she came under the jurisdiction of the WAAF of C, she could not compete. When I interviewed her at age 87, she was still bitter about this decision (Lillian Palmer Alderson, interview by author, tape recording, Vancouver, BC, 7 September 2000).

38   The best sources are: Alexandrine Gibb, "Canada at the Olympics," *Maclean's Magazine*, 1 October 1928: 16, 46, 48–50; Ron Hotchkiss, "'The Matchless Six': Canadian Women at the Olympics, 1928," *The Beaver* 73.5 (1993): 23–42; *The Matchless Six*, Great North Productions, 1996 (available in VHS format from Film West Associates, 2399 Hayman Road, Kelowna, BC V1Z 1Z7).

39   Gibb, "Canada at the Olympics" 49.

40   Arthur S. Lamb, Report to the Amateur Athletic Union of Canada, December 1928 (National Archives of Canada, MG 30 C 164 Vol. 19 File 7).

41   Gibb, "In No Man's Land of Sport," 10 December 1928: 14.

42   Kidd, *The Struggle for Canadian Sport* 101–02.

43   Phyllis Griffiths, "The Girl and the Game," *Toronto Evening Telegram*, 5 December 1929: 41.

44   Griffiths, "The Girl and the Game," 5 December 1929: 41; Sue Swain, "History of the Ontario Women's Intercollegiate Athletic Association (OWIAA)," *CAHPER Journal* 49.2 (1982): 26–28.

45   *Edmonton Journal*, 1 May 1922; Patricia Page, "Feminine Flashes," *Edmonton Journal*, 30 May 1936: 9.

46   The best accounts of these games are in the *Edmonton Bulletin*, September 1923 and April 1924.

47   Macdonald.

48   Abbie Scott Kennedy, unpublished diary, 19 June–31 August 1924 (photocopy obtained from Alberta Sports Hall of Fame and Museum).

49   J. Anna Norris, "Basketball — Girls' Rules," *Child Health Magazine*, December 1924. Reprinted in Gurney, *Girls' Sports* 37.

50   "Random Notes on Current Sports," *Toronto Daily Star*, 2 April 1925: 12.

51   Mary E. Keyes, "Women's Basketball in Central Canada Revisited 1899–1970," paper presented at the annual meeting of the North American Society for Sport History, Chicago, Illinois, May 1991; Kidd, *The Struggle for Canadian Sport* 121–22.

52   Brenda Zeman, *88 Years of Puck Chasing in Saskatchewan* (Regina: WDS Associates and the Saskatchewan Sports Hall of Fame, 1983) 259–60.

53   Julie A. Stevens, "The Development of Women's Hockey: An Explanation of Structure and Change within the Canadian Hockey System," MA thesis, Queen's University, 1992. McGill University withdrew from the league in 1925 and Queen's in 1935. By 1952, university competition had ceased altogether and was not revived until 1960.

54   Donald Guay, *L'Histoire du Hockey au Québec* (Montreal: Les Éditions JCL, 1990) 153. Edouard "Newsy" Lalonde was a member of the Montreal Canadiens between 1913 and 1922, a four-time scoring champion, and member of two Stanley Cup winning teams. He was also an outstanding lacrosse player.

55   For first-hand accounts of these games, see the *Ottawa Citizen* 31 January; 14, 21, 23, 24, 29 February; and 4, 6, 7 March 1916. Donald Guay makes the point that although the best

two hockey players at this time were French Canadian, women's hockey in Quebec and eastern Ontario was primarily Anglo-Protestant due to religious and social pressures that kept many young women from Catholic, French-speaking families from playing sport.

56 Richard Gruneau and David Whitson, *Hockey Night in Canada* (Toronto: Garamond Press, 1993); Guay, *L'Histoire du Hockey au Québec*.

57 *Globe*, 18 February, 1921: 8.

58 *Toronto Evening Telegram*, 18 December 1922: 27.

59 *Toronto Daily Star*, 8 December 1924: 6; 14 December 1925: 10.

60 Wayne Norton, "'Fair Manipulators of the Twisted Hickory': Women's Hockey in Fernie, 1919–1926," *The Forgotten Side of the Border*, eds. Wayne Norton and Naomi Miller (Kamloops: Plateau Press, 1998) 206–16.

61 Gary W. Zeman, *Alberta on Ice: The History of Hockey in Alberta Since 1893* (Edmonton: Westweb Press, 1985) 251–52; Margaret E. Pruden, interview by author, tape recording, 13 May 1998. Pruden also played softball for the Army and Navy Pats and later took up curling and golf.

62 "Random Notes on Current Sports," *Toronto Daily Star*, 6 March 1922: 9.

63 Quoted in Wise and Fisher 79.

64 Griffiths, "The Girl and the Game," 18 May 1938: 37.

65 Toronto Harbour Commission Archives (THCA), RG 3/3, Box 303 (Folders 19 and 20), Box 304 (Folder 1).

66 Women's Softball Association of Toronto *Constitution*, THCA, RG 3/3, Box 303, Folder 20.

67 *Toronto Daily Star*, 14 November 1925: 10 and 10 March 1926: 10.

68 Mortin.

69 Cahn, *Coming on Strong* 209.

70 Henry H. Roxborough, "Give the Girls a Hand," *Maclean's Magazine*, 15 February 1929: 16.

71 Sheila L. Mitchell, "The Organizational Development of Women's Competitive Sport in Canada in the 1920's," MA thesis, University of Windsor, 1976.

72 Gibb, "In the No Man's Land of Sport," 15 May, 1929: 10.

73 Dorothy G. Bell, "Brain-work Made Her Golf Champion," *Maclean's Magazine*, 1 May, 1926: 66; Mary Lowrey Ross, "Golf Missionary," *Saturday Night*, 27 April 1935: 20.

74 Mitchell, "The Organizational Development of Women's Competitive Sport in Canada in the 1920's," 51.

75 Lamb, Report to the AAU of C.

76 Roxborough, "Give the Girls A Hand," 19.

77 Judith Jenkins George, "The Fad of North American Women's Endurance Swimming During the Post-World I Era," *Canadian Journal of History of Sport* 26.1 (1995): 57.

78 *Globe*, 11 August 1913: 11.

79 "Audrey Griffin Wins Long Swimming Race," *Victoria Daily Colonist*, 13 August 1916: 10; Cleve Dheensaw, *Island of Champions* (Victoria: Orca Book Publishers, 1988) 231–32.

80 A.W. (Bill) Leveridge, *Fair Sport* (Toronto: Canadian National Exhibition, 1978) 4–11; *Globe*, 27, 29, 30 August; 3 September 1927.

81 *Halifax Herald*, 29 August 1927: 1, 7; 30 August 1927: 9.

82 *La Presse*, 17 September 1928: 18.

83 *Halifax Herald*, 2 February 1921: 3. See also Mark Reynolds, "The Great Canadian Foot Race," *The Beaver*, August/September 2000: 30–31.

84 See articles in *La Presse*, 4, 5, 7, 10 October 1929.

85 Gladys Robinson, "How I Trained for Speed Skating — and Won Title," *Maclean's Magazine*, 15 April 1921: 62.

86 *Toronto Star Weekly*, 7 March 1925: 34; David McDonald, *For the Record* (Rexdale: John Wiley and Sons, 1981) 3–6.

87 *Toronto Daily Star*, 29 January 1924: 10.

88 David Young, *The Golden Age of Canadian Figure Skating* (Toronto: Summerhill Press, 1984) 37–58.

89 See, for example, Arabella Kenealy, "Woman As An Athlete," *The Living Age*, May 1899: 363–70; L. Ormiston Chant, "Woman As An Athlete: A Reply to Dr. Arabella Kenealy," *The Living Age*, 24 June 1899: 799–805; Arabella Kenealy, "Woman As An Athlete: A Rejoinder," *The Living Age* 24 June 1899: 201–13. See also Patricia Vertinsky's discussion of Kenealy's ideas in *The Eternally Wounded Woman* 151–53.

90 "Should Feminine Athletes Be Restrained?" *Saturday Night*, 28 May 1921: 36.

91 "Margaret Currie's Chats: The Athletic Girl," *Montreal Star*, 23 July 1921: 18.

92 "Des grand advantages pour la race," *Le Devoir*, 17 October 1918: 6. For more information about the campaign in *Le Devoir*, see Gilles Janson, "Sport et modernité: *Le Devoir*, 1910–1920," *Le Devoir* eds., Robert Comeau and Luc Desrochers (Québec: Presses de l'Université du Québec, 1996) 89–90.

93 "Seance sportive jeudi au Nationale," *La Presse*, 15 March 1922: 6.

94 Quoted in Lenskyj, "The Role of Physical Education in the Socialization of Girls in Ontario" 104. It is from Jesse Williams's 1922 textbook, *Personal Hygiene Applied*.

95 Arthur S. Lamb, "Physical Education for Girls," *Proceedings of the Sixty-Second Annual Convention of the Ontario Educational Association* (Toronto: Clarkson W. James, 1923) 285.

96 *Toronto Evening Telegram*, 2 September 1922: 33. The touring team was the Dick Kerr Ladies' Football Club from Preston. For a history of the team, see Gail J. Newsham, *In A League of Their Own!* (London: Scarlet Press, 1994).

97 Lamb, "Physical Education for Girls" 288.

98 Yvette M. Walton, "The Life and Professional Contributions of Ethel Mary Cartwright, 1880–1955," MA thesis, University of Western Ontario, 1976, 100; see also Diane Ransom, "Ethel Mary Cartwright," *Pioneers and Performers* (Saskatchewan: n.p., 1984) 35–46.

99 Ethel M. Cartwright, "Athletics and Physical Education for Girls," *Proceedings of the Sixty-Second Annual Convention of the Ontario Educational Association* (Toronto: Clarkson W. James, 1923) 281.

CHAPTER 3 GIRLS SHOULDN'T DO IT!: DEBATES OVER COMPETITION AND SEXUALITY

1   There is a good deal of excellent scholarship and analysis about the Women's Division of the NAAF. In particular, see Hagen, Chapter 6; Susan K Cahn, "Coming on Strong: Gender and Sexuality in Women's Sport, 1900–1960," diss., University of Minnesota, 1990, Chapter 3; Cindy L. Himes, "The Female Athlete in American Society: 1860–1940," diss., University of Pennsylvania, 1986, Chapter 4. See also Gurney, *Girls' Sports* 35–36, for reproductions of Women's Division documents. For a highly supportive and contemporary description of their philosophy, see John. R. Tunis, "Women and the Sport Business," *Harper's Monthly Magazine* (July 1929): 211–21.

2   Quoted in Tunis 216.

3   Helen Gurney, interview by author, tape recording, Toronto, ON, 26 July 1996. See also Kidd, *The Struggle for Canadian Sport,* who claims that she "probably achieved greater influence in Canadian physical education during the 1930s then anyone else, male or female" (124).

4   In a book chapter published in 1965, Bryans traces the evolution of the secondary school girls' physical education curriculum, making it clear that the "increase in competition" had brought problems, such as girls' sports being coached by men, and the conflict between girls' and boys' rules, especially in basketball. See Helen Bryans, "Secondary School Curriculum for Girls," *Physical Education in Canada,* ed. M.L. Van Vliet (Scarborough: Prentice-Hall of Canada, 1965).

5   Florence A. Somers, *Principles of Women's Athletics* (New York: A.S. Barnes and Company, 1930) 32, 62.

6   For a different perspective, which argues that most women physical education leaders of this era had to navigate between biological determinism and environmentalism and that their arguments about sex differences were both convoluted and nuanced, see Martha H. Verbrugge, "Recreating the Body: Women's Physical Education and the Science of Sex Differences in America, 1900–1940," *Bulletin of the History of Medicine* 71.2 (1997): 273–304.

7   Somers, *Principles of Women's Athletics* 72–73.

8   Florence A. Somers, "Ideals for Girls' Athletics," *Bulletin of the Canadian Physical Education Association* 3.9 (1936): 10.

9   Some scholars have suggested that whole school boards decided to eliminate interschool competition for girls. This is very unlikely, since Helen Bryan's influence affected individual teachers (especially those she had taught), rather than organizations, and, more importantly, not everyone agreed with her.

10   Gurney, *Girls' Sports* 38.

11   Marian (Henderson) Penney, interview by author, tape recording, Victoria, BC, 5 December 1998.

12   Fanny (Bobby) Rosenfeld, "What's What in Girls' Sport," *Toronto Star Weekly,* 10 October 1931: 10. The column heading uses "Bobby" as opposed to "Bobbie." However, according to Rosenfeld's sister Ethel Berman, Rosenfeld herself preferred "Bobbie."

13   Myrtle Cook, "In the Women's Sportlight," *Montreal Daily Star,* 7 October 1931: 28.

14   Gibb, "No Man's Land of Sport," 7 October 1931: 16.

15   Gibb, "No Man's Land of Sport," 6 May 1939: 14.

16   Gibb, "No Man's Land of Sport," 6 May 1939: 14.

17   Cahn, *Coming on Strong* 74.

18   Blanche M. Trilling, "The Playtime of a Million Girls or an Olympic Victory — Which?" *The Nation's Schools* 4.2 (1929): 54.

19   Doris H. Pieroth, *Their Day in the Sun* (Seattle: University of Washington Press, 1996) 5–6.

20   *Montreal Daily Herald,* 21 May 1930: 9.

21   E.W. Ferguson, "The Gist and Jest of It," *Montreal Daily Herald,* 23 May 1930: 13.

22   *Montreal Daily Herald,* 29 May, 1930: 8.

23   Barbara Schrodt, "Canadian Women at the Commonwealth Games: 1930–1974," *CAHPER Journal* 44.4 (1978): 32.

24   Gibb, "No Man's Land of Sport," 19, 20, 21 August 1930; V.L. ("Pinky") Stewart, "Western Sport Arrives," *Maclean's Magazine,* 15 July 1931.

25 Mary Campbell, interview by author, tape recording, Vancouver, BC, 8 September 2000; Louise Zerba, "The 1930 University of British Columbia Women's Basketball Team: Those Other World Champions," *Her Story in Sport: A Historical Anthology of Women in Sports,* ed. Reet Howell (West Point, NY: Leisure Press, 1982) 548–51; *Toronto Daily Star,* 9 September 1930: 8; Gibb, "No Man's Land of Sport," 11 September 1930: 16; Jim Kearney, *Champions* (Vancouver: Douglas and McIntrye, 1985) 91–92.

26 "Bobbie" Rosenfeld, "Girls are in Sports for Good," *Chatelaine* (July 1933): 29. See also Henry Roxborough, *Canada at the Olympics* (Toronto: Ryerson, 1963) 82.

27 Hotchkiss 42.

28 Since the last names of Mildred Fizzell and Mary Frizzell are remarkably similar, they were often misspelled and made the same. Understandably, some researchers have mistaken them for sisters (e.g., Pieroth 111), when in fact, Mildred Fizzell from Toronto and Mary Frizzell from Vancouver were not related.

29 Gibb, "No Man's Land of Sport," 8 August 1932: 10.

30 H.H. Roxborough, "What Happened at Los Angeles?" *Maclean's Magazine* (1 October 1932).

31 Cook, "In the Women's Sportlight," 13 August 1934.

32 Cook, "In the Women's Sportlight," 18 August, 1934.

33 Gibb, "No Man's Land of Sport," 29 November 1934: 17.

34 Elizabeth Pitt Barron, "Chaperoning the 1936 Winter Olympics," unpublished manuscript.

35 Bruce Kidd, "Canada's Opposition to the 1936 Olympics in Germany," *Canadian Journal of History of Sport and Physical Education* 9.2 (1978): 20–40.

36 For more information, see M. Ann Hall, "Alexandrine Gibb: In 'No Man's Land of Sport,'" *Freeing the Female Body,* eds. J.A. Mangan and Fan Hong (London: Frank Cass, 2001) 149–72.

37 Gibb, "No Man's Land of Sport," 2 November 1935: 12.

38 Eva Dawes insists that she was not associated with the Workers' Sport Association in any way, and that she was surprised by her suspension and the controversy it caused. She also firmly denies any knowledge of the proposed boycott of the 1936 Olympics, claiming that she played no role in it whatsoever. While in London waiting to return home, Dawes met her future husband. She returned to England the following year when she married and has lived there ever since. (Eva Dawes Spinks, interview by Stephanie Daniels and Anita Tedder, tape recording, Thames Ditton, England, 25 October 1999; also, interview by author, tape recording, Thames Ditton, England, 14 November 2000.)

39 Katherine M. Laubman. "A Historical-Ethnographic Account of a Canadian Woman in Sport, 1920–1938: The Story of Margaret (Bell) Gibson," MA thesis, University of British Columbia, 1991.

40 Pat Page, "Feminine Flashes," *Edmonton Journal,* 26 November 1938: 11.

41 Barbara Howard, interview by author, tape recording, Burnaby, BC, 12 September 2000.

42 Phyllis Griffiths, "The Girl and the Game," *Toronto Evening Telegram,* 18 February 1931: 21; "WAAF of C Rejects Motion That Would Bar Sports Writers," *Winnipeg Free Press,* 28 November 1932: 15.

43 For a good description of these regional conflicts, see Kidd, *The Struggle for Canadian Sport* 130–34.

44 Griffiths, "The Girl and the Game," 9 May 1934: 23; "Claim Insult to WAAF By Organizer," *Edmonton Journal,* 9 May 1934: 16.

45 Lou Marsh, "With Pick and Shovel," *Toronto Daily Star,* 8 September 1934: 10. For a history

of the Ontario Athletic Commission, see Bruce Kidd, "Making the Pros Pay for Amateur Sports: The Ontario Athletic Commission, 1920–1947," *Ontario History* 87.2 (1995): 105–28.

46 Gibb, "No Man's Land of Sport," 9 October 1934: 11; "OAC Will Safeguard Feminine Athletics," *Toronto Daily Star*, 9 October 1934: 10.

47 Gibb, "No Man's Land of Sport," 30 October 1934: 12.

48 Cahn, *Coming on Strong* 108.

49 Bobbie Rosenfeld, "Feminine Sports Reel," *Globe and Mail*, 9 July 1938: 17.

50 Gibb, "No Man's Land of Sport," 26 January 1932: 10.

51 Maxwell Stiles of the Los Angeles *Examiner* cited in Roxborough, *Canada at the Olympics* 83.

52 Gibb, "No Man's Land of Sport," 25 and 26 January 1933: 10. See also Andy Lytle, "Sport Rays," *Vancouver Sun*, 20 and 26 January 1933: 12; Andy Lytle, "Girls Shouldn't Do It," *Chatelaine* (May 1933) 12–13.

53 Rosenfeld, "Girls are in Sports for Good" 6.

54 Paul Gallico, "The Texas Babe," *The Thirties: A Time to Remember*, ed. Don Congdon (New York: Simon and Schuster, 1962) 73–78.

55 Susan K. Cahn, "From the 'Muscle Moll' to the 'Butch' Ballplayer: Mannishness, Lesbianism, and Homophobia in U.S. Women's Sport," *Feminist Studies* 19.2 (1993): 347; Susan E. Cayleff, *Babe* (Urbana: University of Illinois Press, 1995) 91. "Muscle moll" is also similar to "gun moll," which means a gunner's mistress.

56 Susan Cayleff's biography of Didrikson (cited above) is a fascinating study in the social construction of femininity, and how her life as it appeared in public was not the life led in private.

57 Since there is no biography of Rosenfeld, it is difficult to know for certain when she stopped competing. I believe it was the summer of 1935, when Phyllis Griffiths reported in her column: "Bobbie Rosenfeld, whose starry athletic career probably ended when she underwent a double hernia operation just at the close of the basketball season, is still using a cane to help her get around. Her recovery has been somewhat slower than anticipated. Miss Rosenfeld thinks it hardly likely that she will go into competitive athletics again — but you can never tell with this young lady. The lure of the game has made her change her 'retiring' mind before this" ("The Girl and the Game," 24 June 1935). However, she continued to coach and manage women's athletic teams.

58 Elmer W. Ferguson, "I Don't Like Amazon Athletes," *Maclean's Magazine* (1 August 1938): 9, 32–33.

59 Roxy Atkins, "Elmer, You're Goofy," *Maclean's Magazine* (15 September 1938): 18, 37–38. Atkins retired from active competition in 1938 at the age of 21 and subsequently became involved with the administration of women's sport. From 1939–42 she was president of the Ontario branch of the WAAF of C. She married and became Roxy Campbell in 1940 or 1941. After the war, she travelled to the United States and married again (Andersen). She has lived in the United States since then, becoming deeply involved in the administration of women's track and field. See Tricard, 317–20; Bob Ferguson, *Who's Who in Canadian Sport*, 3rd ed. (Kanata: Bob Ferguson, 2000) 7.

60 Gibb, "No Man's Land of Sport," 3 February 1932: 13.

61 Jean M. Leiper, "J. Percy Page: An Ordinary Coach with Extraordinary Results," paper presented at the annual meeting of the North American Society for Sport History, Hamilton, Ont., May 1981. Leiper conducted a number of interviews with former Grads.

62 Frederick Griffin, "Sport Enhances Womanhood," *Toronto Star Weekly*, 10 October 1931: 16.

63 Gibb, "No Man's Land of Sport," 13 June 1929: 18.

64 Cook, "In the Women's Sportlight," 26 May 1931.

65 "Hommage aux 'reines,'" *La Presse*, 11 February 1933: 39. This is only one of many articles about "snow queens" found in *La Presse* during the 1930s.

66 "Concours de beauté à l'occasion du marathon en raquettes de Vincent," *La Presse*, 18 November 1930: 23.

67 Cahn, "From the 'Muscle Moll' to the 'Butch' Ballplayer" 344.

68 Gibb, "No Man's Land of Sport," 30 May 1936: 13.

69 "Star Czech Girl Athlete Soon Will Become Man," *Toronto Daily Star*, 3 December 1935: Section 3, 1; "Czech Athlete Changes Sex," *Montreal Daily Star*, 4 December 1935: 26. Others identified by Eric Cowe in his *International Women's Athletics 1890–1940* are Stefanie Pekarova (Czechoslovakia), Ida Ehrl, Dora (Hermann) Ratjen, and Erika Matthes (Germany), Mary (Mark) Weston and Edith (Eddie) Halstead (Great Britain), and Zofia Smetek (Poland).

70 Shelley Page, "Who Is Female and How Do You Know?" *Ottawa Citizen*, 19 July 1992: E1; see also "Ex-athlete seeking justice," *Globe and Mail*, 5 December 1991: A14. Lillian Palmer, who competed in the 1932 Olympics for Canada, expressed a similar view (Lillian Palmer Alderson, interview by author, 7 September 2000). Stella Walsh, on the other hand, lived her entire life as a woman, and there is not sufficient evidence to prove she was a man. She was in all likelihood what today we would call "intersexual."

71 Ann (Mundigel) Meraw, interview by author, tape recording, Vancouver, BC, 6 September 2000. Meraw also swam at the CNE in 1947 when the swims resumed, but soon after switched to solo swimming, establishing speed and endurance records by swimming Okanagan Lake in British Columbia.

72 Quote from Mae Nelson, Mortin 22.

73 Cited in Lois Browne, *Girls of Summer* (Toronto: HarperCollins, 1992) 35.

74 Cited in Laura Robinson, *She Shoots, She Scores* (Toronto: Thompson, 1997) 173.

75 Griffiths, "The Girl and the Game," 4 June 1935: 23.

76 Cook, "In the Women's Sportlight," 15 April 1930; *Globe and Mail*, 9 June 1937: 17.

77 Griffiths, "The Girl and the Game," 15 September 1938: 27; Page, "Feminine Flashes," 2 November 1938: 6; Toronto Harbour Commission Archives, R/G 3/3 Box 304, Folders 5–12.

78 *Toronto Daily Star*, 9 May 1933:12; Griffiths, "The Girl and the Game," 9 May 1933: 21. During the 1932 and 1933 seasons in Montreal, there was substantial controversy over the case of Marge Ellerby, who played in the Montreal Major Ladies Softball League, because she wished to switch teams. In the end, Myrtle Cook, President of the Provincial Women's Softball Union of Quebec, resigned over the issue.

79 Gibb, "No Man's Land of Sport," 11 May, 1931: 8. For more on this controversy, see Kidd, *The Struggle for Canadian Sport*, 135–37.

80 Gibb, "No Man's Land of Sport," 18 October, 1933: 12.

81 Joanna Avery and Julie Stevens, *Too Many Men on the Ice* (Victoria: Polestar, 1997) 66–71. In 1935, the Countess of Bessborough, wife of the Governor General, donated a trophy for the Canadian championship, known since then as the Bessborough Trophy.

82 Gibb, "No Man's Land of Sport," 31 October 1934: 12; Griffiths, "The Girl and the Game," 7 June, 1935, 30 and 23 September, 1938: 38; Jimmy Coo, "Cherchez la Femme," *Winnipeg Free Press*, 10 November 1938: 17 and 19 December 1941: 21.

83 *Globe and Mail,* 12 July 1938: 14.

84 Page, "Feminine Flashes," 27 May 1936: 10; Robert Collins, "The Ferocious Young Ladies from Edmonton," *Maclean's Magazine* (10 December 1955): 72.

85 There is much to be written about the Edmonton Grads, and they deserve a book of their own. For the past 60 years and more, the Grads have played an active role in creating their own history, and the few who are alive today continue to do so. They have maintained a remarkable loyalty to Percy Page (still referred to as *Mr.* Page) and have steadfastly refused to discuss anything that might detract from his image (for a recent example, see Brian Bergman, "When Girls Ruled," *Maclean's* [9 July 2001]: 28–29.) For an interesting analysis of the problem this presents for historians, see Kevin B. Wamsley, "Power and Privilege in Historiography: Constructing Percy Page," *Sport History Review* 28.2 (1997): 146–55.

86 Mary E. Keyes, "The History of the Women's Athletics Committee of the Canadian Association for Health, Physical Education and Recreation, 1940–1973," diss., Ohio State University, 1980, 48.

87 Jill Julius Matthews, "They Had Such a Lot of Fun: The Women's League of Health and Beauty Between the Wars," *History Workshop* 30 (Autumn 1990): 23–54. See also Prunella Stack, *Zest for Life* (London: Peter Owen, 1988).

88 "Miss P. Stack Opens League," *Globe,* 26 September 1935: 10.

89 As with many topics in this book, the story of the Women's League of Health and Beauty in Canada needs to be told. It continues today, although in a very limited form, and some of the original members are still alive.

90 Arthur P. Woollacott, "B.C. Gymnastic Movement May Sweep All Canada," *Saturday Night* (26 August 1939): 20.

91 For more on Pro-Rec, its significance, and eventual demise in 1953, see two articles by Barbara Schrodt: "The Seeds of Destruction: Factors in the Dissolution of British Columbia's Pro-Rec Programme," *Proceedings of the 5th Canadian Symposium on the History of Sport and Physical Education* (Toronto: University of Toronto, 1982) 431–37; and "Federal Programmes of Physical Recreation and Fitness: The Contributions of Ian Eisenhardt and BC's Pro-Rec," *Canadian Journal of History of Sport* 15.2 (1984): 45–61.

92 What Gibb did not reveal was that she had been unwillingly removed from her column by the *Star's* sports editor, Fred Jackson, primarily at the request of Andy Lytle, her old nemesis, who soon succeeded Jackson as sports editor. She and Lytle detested each other, and Lytle made it clear in his own column that he had little empathy for amateur sport. After former sports editor Lou Marsh's early death in 1936, Gibb no longer had the support she needed, and she became something of an outcast in the sports department, although a more respected "member of the gang" in the newsroom. Trent Frayne, another longtime Toronto sportswriter, confirmed that Lytle was a "terrible man" and that the sports staff at the *Star* were "terrified" of him (interview by author, tape recording, Toronto, 22 May 1998).

93 Although Jimmy Coo returned to work for the *Winnipeg Free Press* after the war, writing her women's sport column and another one about skiing, she soon got a job in Washington with External Affairs. She worked for the Canadian government for 10 years, then married and moved to South Africa, where she has lived ever since (Lillian "Jimmy" Coo Price, telephone conversation with author, 5 November 1996).

94 Rosenfeld, "Sports Reel," *Globe and Mail,* 15 May 1944: 16.

95 Rosenfeld, "Sports Reel," 26 May 1944: 17.

96 Cook, "In the Women's Sportlight," 20 June 1940: 28.

97 Griffiths, "The Girl and the Game," 8 December 1941: 23.

98 Barclay 386.

99 Griffiths, "The Girl and the Game," 17 December 1941: 27.

100 Griffiths' columns between 20 January and 2 February 1942 promoted the event.

101 "Athletic Groups Urged To Carry On," *Winnipeg Tribune*, 28 March 1942: 19.

102 Ruth Roach Pierson, *Canadian Women and the Second World War* (Ottawa: Canadian Historical Association, 1983).

103 Helen Carscallen and Hilda Rickett, "Problems of Providing Physical Recreation for Women," *AIM — A Sports World Digest* 4.2 (1945): 52–57.

104 Bob Warren, "Industrial Recreation Canadian Style," *Recreation* (December 1944): 483, 500–01; Sangster, "The Softball Solution," 167–99.

105 Shirley Boulton, "Women in Sport," *Winnipeg Tribune*, 18 April 1942: 20.

CHAPTER 4 Sweetheart Heroines: Athletic and Lovely

1   Cited in Wendy Long, *Celebrating Excellence* (Vancouver: Polestar, 1995), 44. See also Young, *The Golden Age of Canadian Figure Skating*.

2   There is no lack of interesting material about Barbara Ann Scott, including her own book, *Skate With Me*, published in 1950 (Garden City, NY: Doubleday), a combination of biography and advice. See also Douglas How, "Blonde on Blades," *Maclean's Magazine* (15 February 1947): 16, 45–66; Eva-Lis Wuorio, "Backstage With Barbara Ann," *Maclean's Magazine* (15 February 1949): 12–13, 48–49; Barbara Ann Scott, "What It's Like to be a Celebrity," *Maclean's Magazine* (15 January 1951): 6–7, 41–42; Susan Swan, "Barbara Ann — Are You Still Happy?" *Chatelaine* (November 1975): 51, 74–86; Young, *The Golden Age of Canadian Figure Skating*, chapters 7–10; Don Morrow, "Sweetheart Sport: Barbara Ann Scott and the Post World War II Image of the Female Athlete in Canada," *Canadian Journal of History of Sport* 18.1 (1987): 36–54; Stephen R. Wenn, "Give Me the Keys Please: Avery Brundage, Canadian Journalists, and the Barbara Ann Scott Phaeton Affair," *Journal of Sport History* 18.2 (1991): 241–54. Not at all helpful is Cay Moore, *She Skated Into Our Hearts* (Toronto: McClelland and Stewart, 1948), a very silly "fictionalized biography" of Scott. Finally, see the CBC documentary on Scott in its *Life and Times* series, "Queen of the Blades," first shown on television in 1997.

3   "Une étoile canadienne-française," *La Presse*, 31 January 1944: 4; "Mlle Suzanne Thouin remporte le championnat junior du pays," *La Presse*, 31 January 1944: 14.

4   *Globe and Mail*, 17 February 1947: 1.

5   As a result, Brundage was thoroughly savaged in the Canadian press. For an analysis, see Wenn. The Canadian Olympic Association was not in the slightest doubt that Scott's disqualification at the 1948 Olympics would have followed automatically had the incident not been "clarified." Their view was that the people of Canada owed Brundage a "vote of thanks" (*Canada at the Olympic Games 1948*, Official Report of the Canadian Olympic Association 1938 to 1948, 31–32). Barbara Ann Scott agreed: "My gratitude went out to him that he had raised the question when he did" (*Skate With Me*, 65–66).

6   Ray O'Meara, "The Passing Sports Show," *Montreal Daily Star*, 6 February 1948: 28.

7   Swan 51.

8   Matt O'Connell, "Mary Rose Thacker," *Maclean's Magazine* (1 March 1940): 24, 26–27; *Vancouver Sun*, 25 September 1945: 19. Thacker coached for the next 35 years until her death in 1983, passing on her knowledge to thousands of young skaters, including Karen Magnussen, who dominated Canadian women's skating in the late 1960s and early 1970s.

9   *Maclean's Magazine* (15 January 1943): 9, 24–25. McCarthy married fellow skater Michael Kirby in 1944 (*Globe and Mail*, 21 October 1944: 19).

10 Bruce McLeod, "Ice Ballerina," *Maclean's Magazine*, 15 February 1944: 12, 28–30. O'Meara retired in 1946, married the following year, and began to raise a family. She died at 83 years in March 2000 (see obituary in *Globe and Mail*, 25 March 2000: A23).

11 Gordon Sinclair, "Sister Act," *Maclean's Magazine*, 15 December 1943: 13, 52–53.

12 Cook, "In the Women's Sportlight," 7 December 1946: 16.

13 Shirley Boulton, "Women in Sport," *Winnipeg Tribune*, 3 January 1942: 19.

14 *Montreal Daily Star*, 11 December 1946: 25.

15 "Queen of the Blades."

16 Dink Carroll, "Ski Twins," *Maclean's Magazine* (1 February 1944): 27.

17 Ruth Roach Pierson, "Wartime Jitters over Femininity," *"They're Still Women After All"* (Toronto: McClelland and Stewart, 1986) 129–68.

18 In fact, in the early 1940s, one in 20 women worked outside the home; in 1951 that figure had risen to one in ten, only to rise again, to one in five, by 1961. See Joan Sangster, "Doing Two Jobs: The Wage-Earning Mother, 1945–1970," *A Diversity of Women: Ontario, 1945–1980*, ed. Joy Parr (Toronto: University of Toronto Press, 1995) 99–100.

19 Prentice *et al.* 307.

20 Mary Louise Adams, *The Trouble With Normal: Postwar Youth and the Making of Heterosexuality* (Toronto: University of Toronto Press, 1997) 25.

21 Letter, *Canadian Sport Monthly*, October 1950: 31.

22 See, for example, Bobbie Rosenfeld, "Let's Try Winning Olympics," *Saturday Night* (12 January 1952): 7, 19–20.

23 The others were Corine Cooper (Pats Olympic Club), Corliss Taylor, Sybil Jones (Basketball, YWCA), and Beryl White (Swimmer, YWCA). See Cook, "In the Women's Sportlight," 6 November 1945: 19.

24 Thorne married in 1956 and moved to the United States where she has lived ever since. (Rosella Thorne Johnson, telephone conversation with author, 1 August 2000; Cook, "In the Women's Sportlight," 16 March 1949: 31; 5 April 1950: 46; 16 May 1951.)

25 *Globe and Mail*, 22 January 1952: 14.

26 Trent Frayne, "The Champ Still Baby Sits," *Maclean's Magazine*, 1 May, 1952: 16.

27 Frayne, "The Champ Still Baby Sits"; see also Bob Hesketh, "The Bobby-Soxer Who Beat All the Big Girls," *Chatelaine* (November 1951): 26–30; Barclay 515–29.

28 Hillis R. Pickens, "Marlene Stewart's Achievement," *Canadian Sport Monthly* (July 1953): 5.

29 Marlene Stewart Streit continued to play tournament golf as an amateur, racking up numerous victories; she is the only woman amateur golfer to have won the Canadian, British, Australian, and United States championships, and she is still active in senior women's tournament play.

30 Stanley Westall, "How Marilyn Became a Great Swimmer," *Globe and Mail*, 18 September 1954: 19; Ron McAllister, *Swim to Glory* (Toronto: McClelland and Stewart, 1954).

31 June Callwood, "How Marilyn Swam the Lake," *Maclean's Magazine* (1 November 1954): 12–15, 72–78, 80–83.

32 Winnie Roach Leuszler, interview by author, tape recording, Surrey, BC, 6 September 2000.

33 McAllister 122.

34 For extensive coverage of the English Channel swim, see *Toronto Telegram*, 2–4 August 1955. For the Juan de Fuca Strait swims, see *Toronto Star*, 10–11, 23 August 1956.

35 Marilyn Bell is now a grandmother, but there is a renewed interest in her swims through two interesting films: the documentary, "Lady of the Lake," produced by Barna Alper for History Television, but unfortunately not available on video, and the fictional, made-for-television movie, "Heart: The Marilyn Bell Story," first shown on CBC in February 2001.

36 Kaye (McNamee) Neale, interview by author, tape recording, Penticton, BC, 13 September 2000.

37 Helen (Stewart) Hunt, interview by author, tape recording, Vancouver, BC, 11 September 2000. I was also given access to her many scrapbooks. Helen Hunt's second international competitive career was in volleyball (see Chapter 5).

38 Vic Allen, "Canadian Skiing: Past, Present, and Future," *Canadian Sport Monthly*, March 1957: 8; H.P. Douglas, "Development of Ladies Racing," *Canadian Sport Monthly*, January 1950: 10–11, 23.

39 Long 17.

40 *Canadian Sport Monthly*, March 1958: 10; McKenzie Porter, "The 'Royal Family' of the Laurentians," *Maclean's Magazine*, 8 November 1958: 20, 93–95; Jacqueline Moore, "Why Lucile Wheeler Called It Quits," *Weekend Magazine*, 6 December 1958: 20, 23–24.

41 Wise and Fisher 202–03; Long 18–19.

42 *Canadian Sport Monthly*, October 1954: 25.

43 Cahn, *Coming on Strong* 129.

44 *Toronto Telegram*, 14 August 1947: 13; *Globe and Mail*, 2 September 1948: 19; Leuszler interview.

45 *Globe and Mail*, 13–17, 30 August 1951; *Toronto Star*, 16–18, 29 August 1951; Conrad Wennerberg, *Wind, Waves, and Sunburn* (New York: Breakaway Books, 1997); Leuszler interview.

46 *Globe and Mail*, 27 March 1954: 22; *Toronto Telegram*, 19 June 1956; *Toronto Star*, 23 July and 28 August 1956. It is interesting that Winnie Roach Leuszler was written right out of the dramatic television movie about Marilyn Bell, cited above.

47 Doreen Ryan, interview by author, tape recording, Edmonton, AB, 8 June 2000.

48 In 1964, the famous Russian speed skater, Lydia Skoblikova, was the first person to win four gold medals at one Winter Olympic Games.

49 *Globe and Mail*, 4 August 1959: 16.

50 Mary Louise Adams, in her Canadian study of postwar youth and the making of heterosexuality, also confirms that not a single writer in this era mentions the possibility that sissies and tomboys might turn into homosexuals. She writes: "While homosexuality was thought to be the result of (failed) adolescent development, sissyness and tomboyness were presented as conditions that (successful) adolescent development could cure" (see Adams 95–98). See also Kathryn Campbell, "'Deviance, Inversion and Unnatural Love': Lesbians in Canadian Media, 1950–1970," *Atlantis: A Women's Studies Journal* 23.1 (1998): 128–36.

51 Susan Cahn makes this connection far more strongly for the United States in this era (see Cahn, "From the 'Muscle Moll' to the 'Butch' Ballplayer").

52 C.K. Cameron, "The Problem That Is Never Mentioned," *Canadian Home Journal*, November 1951: 12.

53 Bobbie Rosenfeld and Jim Coleman, "Slide, Nellie, Slide," *Maclean's Magazine*, 15 May 1944: 7.

54 Cited in Browne 32.

55 There is a wealth of excellent material about the AAGPBL. In particular, see Browne; Sue Macy, *A Whole New Ball Game* (Henry Holt, 1993); Susan E. Johnson, *When Women Played Hardball* (Seal Press, 1994); Susan K. Cahn, "No Freaks, No Amazons, No Boyish Bobs," *Coming on Strong* and W.C. Madden, *The Women of the All-American Girls Professional Baseball League* (McFarland and Company, 1997). The Browne and Madden books contain good biographical information about some of the Canadian players in the league. There are also two films about the league. One is a 1988 documentary, "A League of Their Own," by Kelly Candaele, whose mother Helen Callaghan Candaele St. Aubin (a native of Vancouver) played in the league, and the other is the 1992 Hollywood film by the same name.

56 Cahn, *Coming on Strong* 148.

57 Twenty-five players came from Saskatchewan, 12 from Manitoba, 10 each from Alberta and Ontario, and six from British Columbia. The player from Quebec was Alice Janowski from Sherbrooke, who played one season in 1951. (Information collected from Madden and the AAGPBL official web site at <www.dlcwest.com/~smudge/index.html.>)

58 Faye (Burnham) Eccleston, interview by author, tape recording, North Vancouver, BC, 11 September 2000.

59 Browne 5.

60 Cahn, *Coming on Strong* 148–53.

61 Cited in Johnson, *When Women Played Hardball* 250–51.

62 Bobbie Rosenfeld, "Women's Fastball Event Created Fine Precedent," *Globe and Mail*, 29 December 1951: 13.

63 See reports in *Toronto Star*, September 1952 and September 1953; also in Leveridge 291–93.

64 Bobbie Rosenfeld, "Girls Softball Reached Zenith at Sunnyside Park," *Globe and Mail*, 14 March 1956.

65 *Toronto Star*, 8 March 1956: 1; Fred McFadden, *Abby Hoffman* (Don Mills: Fitzhenry and Whiteside, 1978) 17–23.

66 Bobbie Rosenfeld, "Sports Reel," *Globe and Mail*, 25 January 1952: 17.

67 McFarlane 114.

68 Rosenfeld, "Sports Reel," 20 April 1955: 21.

69 Barbara Schrodt, "Vancouver's Dynastic Domination of Canadian Senior Women's Basketball: 1942 to 1967," *Canadian Journal of History of Sport* 26.2 (1995): 19–32.

70 Rosenfeld, "Sports Reel," 15 April 1955: 21; *Globe and Mail*, 25 April 1955: 29.

71 Schrodt, "Vancouver's Dynastic Domination."

72 For the record, the team members were Darlene Currie, Pat Lawson, Heather Waddell, Mary MacDonald, Judy Holt, Shirley Topley, Audrey Campbell, Zoe Shephard, Nora McDermott, Lena Fior, and Judy Jenkin. It was coached by Jack Adilman and Bob Stayner (*Canada at the 3rd Pan American Games*, Official Report of Canada's Participation in the 3rd Pan American Games held in Chicago, USA, August 27–September 7 1959, 32–34).

73 Rosenfeld, "Sports Reel," 1 January 1952: 17.

74 Allen Guttmann, *Women's Sports: A History* (New York: Columbia University Press, 1991) 206. It was not until 1966 that the International Amateur Athletic Federation introduced "femininity testing" to establish an individual's eligibility to compete as a woman.

75 Jackie MacDonald, interview by author, tape recording, Ottawa, ON, 19 July 2000; *Toronto Star*, 10 August 1954: 12.

238 / THE GIRL AND THE GAME

76 June Callwood, "She wants to be the World's Strongest Woman, But ...," *Maclean's Magazine* (16 April 1955): 22.

77 MacDonald interview. See also Jock Carroll, "The Glamour Girl of the Canadian Olympic Trials: Jackie MacDonald," *Weekend Magazine,* 25 August 1956: 32–34. The notion of a "feminine apologetic" was first discussed by Jan Felshin in "The Dialectics of Woman and Sport," *The American Woman in Sport,* ed. Ellen W. Gerber *et al.* (Reading, PA: Addison-Wesley, 1974) 179–210.

78 Cahn, *Coming on Strong* 224.

79 Catherine Williamson, "Swimming Pools, Movie Stars: The Celebrity Body in the Postwar Marketplace," *camera obscura* 38 (May 1996): 9–10.

80 Gladys Bean, ed. *The History of Synchronized Swimming in Canada* (Ottawa: Canadian Amateur Swimming Association, 1975); Laurene Clark, *Synchronized Swimming: 60 Years to Celebrate* (Ottawa: Canadian Amateur Synchronized Swimming Association, 1985).

81 Williamson 9. See also Laura M. Thomas, "Local and Global Mermaids: The Politics of 'Pretty Swimming,'" MA thesis, University of British Columbia (2001) for an analysis of the impact of Esther Williams and her films on the growth of synchronized swimming, especially in British Columbia.

82 As far as I know, the actress Norma Shearer was not related to Margaret (Peggy) Shearer Seller mentioned earlier. Norma Shearer was born in Montreal in 1900 or 1902, and Margaret Shearer in Edinburgh in 1905. In 1925, with her movie career in full swing, Norma Shearer accepted the honorary presidency of the Montreal Amateur Athletic Association Ladies Swimming Club (*Montreal Daily Star*, 26 November 1925).

83 See Bean, *The History of Synchronized Swimming in Canada.*

84 See Thomas, for a description and analysis of this event. She argues it was a significant catalyst for the growth of synchronized swimming in British Columbia.

85 Jane Hughes, "Get in the Swim," *Maclean's Magazine* (1 August 1945): 34.

86 Clark, *Synchronized Swimming.* The members of the 1955 Pan-American team were Giselle Poulin, Eila Lindell, Louise Genereaux, Diane Baker, and Beverely McKnight.

87 Kidd, *The Struggle for Canadian Sport* 143–44.

88 Kidd, "The Struggle for Canadian Sport," *Globe and Mail,* 22 March 1954: 27.

89 "Constitution and Track & Field Rules & Regulations of the Women's Amateur Athletic Federation of Canada," revised January 1938 (National Archives of Canada, MG 30 C 164, Vol. 35, File 16).

90 Iveagh Munro, "Dorothy N.R. Jackson: In Memoriam," *Journal of CAHPER* 33.6 (1967): 20–21.

91 Keyes, "The History of the Women's Athletics Committee." Keyes points out that, although Jackson operated as if the WAC existed, the CPEA did not formally acknowledge it until 1948.

92 "Dix années d'une oeuvre d'éducation," *La Presse,* 16 June 1949: 4, 15.

93 For a history of IAPESGW, see M. Ann Hall and Gertrud Pfister, *Honoring the Legacy* (Northhampton, MA: Smith College, 1999).

CHAPTER 5 SERIOUS ATHLETES OR "ODDBALLS"?: TRANSITIONAL YEARS

1 For a complete analysis, see M. Ann Hall and Dorothy A. Richardson, *Fair Ball* (Ottawa: Canadian Advisory Council on the Status of Women, 1982) 37–48.

2 Jim Coleman, "Canadian Women at the Forefront," *Edmonton Journal*, 27 March 1974: 57.

3 Lionel Wilson, "The Brainwash That Sold Us On the Sport of Slobs," *Maclean's*, October 1970: 13.

4 See, for example, Trent Frayne, "The Human Body Is Better Than Anyone Thought," *Maclean's*, 16 December 1961: 18, 65–67.

5 John Gillanders, "National Meet or Rural Sports-Day?" *Canadian Sport Monthly*, July 1961: 8–9, 25.

6 Donald Macintosh, *Sport and Politics in Canada* (Kingston and Montreal: McGill-Queen's University Press) 10–23.

7 *House of Commons Debates*, 21 November 1960: 39–40

8 For a comprehensive analysis of the origins of Bill C-131 and its early impact, see Macintosh, *Sport and Politics in Canada* 10–41.

9 Bruce Kidd, "Reflections on the 8th Commonwealth Games," *Journal of the Canadian Association for Health, Physical Education, and Recreation* 33.1 (1966): 11–12. See also Macintosh, *Sport and Politics in Canada*, Chapter Three.

10 Nancy Greene (with Jack Batten), *Nancy Greene* (Don Mills: General Publishing, 1968) vii.

11 Greene; see also Linda Crutchfield Bocock, "Reflections of a Racer," *Canadian Sport Monthly*, January 1965: Pt. 1, 6–7; February 1965: Pt. 2, 22–27.

12 Macintosh, *Sport and Politics in Canada* 57–76.

13 Keyes, "The History of the Women's Athletics Committee" 49–59, also Appendix B and C; Mary Jo Festle, *Playing Nice* (New York: Columbia University Press, 1996) 82; Marilyn Pomfret, interview by author, tape recording, Vancouver, BC, 4 December 1998.

14 Keyes, "The History of the Women's Athletics Committee" 73–80; Helen Gurney, interview by author, tape recording, Toronto, ON, 26 July 1996.

15 Sue Hilton, "National Intercollegiate Competition for Women," *Journal of CAHPER* 33.6 (1967): 4; Mary E. Keyes, "The Administration of the Canadian Women's Intercollegiate Athletic Union," *CAHPER Journal* 40.6 (1974): 21–23, 32–33; Pomfret interview. The CIAU is now officially known as Canadian Interuniversity Sport.

16 Peter Gzowski, "Young and Fast," *Maclean's*, 17 November 1962: 28.

17 McFadden.

18 In the three decades following the 1968 Olympics, Elaine Tanner has had a tough life. See James Christie, "Olympic Pressure Takes Personal Toll: Loser Label Sticks 24 Years," *Globe and Mail*, 23 July 1992; Long 88–90.

19 Alan Edmonds, "The Pressure on Nancy Garapick," *Canadian Magazine*, 6 September 1975: 10.

20 Nancy Garapick, interview by author, tape recording, Halifax, NS, 22 August 1985.

21 It is now known that the swimmers from the former East Germany who beat Garapick were steroid users.

22 Garapick interview. Garapick was a member of the national swimming team between 1974 and 1983; her career came to an end after a serious cycling accident.

23 Edmonds, "The Pressure on Nancy Garapick" 12.

24 Frayne, "The Human Body Is Better Than Anyone Thought" 18.

25 Gzowski, "Young and Fast" 34.

26 Cook, "In Women's Sportlight," 10 February 1960: 56; 19 February 1960: 28.

27 Greene 121.

28 Hilles Pickens, "A Visit With Our Gals Abroad," *Canadian Sport Monthly*, November 1963: 16.

29 Robert Fulford, *Best Seat in the House: Memoirs of a Lucky Man* (Toronto: Collins, 1988), 31–3; conversation with author via E-mail, 20 December 1996.

30 Marjorie Harris, "Blotchface!" *Quest: Canada's Urban Magazine*, February 1977: Toronto Section, T4.

31 Nora McCabe, telephone interview with author, 30 August 2001. McCabe became a free-lance writer in 1984 and subsequently published several in-depth profiles of women athletes in a variety of magazines. She also published *Laurie Graham*, a book about the skier, for a young reader series (Don Mills, ON: Fitzhenry and Whiteside, 1990).

32 Jane O'Hara, telephone interview with author, 21 August 2001. O'Hara is now back at *Maclean's* as a senior writer and contributing editor.

33 Alison Gordon, *Foul Balls: Five Years in the American League* (Toronto: McClelland and Stewart, 1984) 10, 130.

34 Jack Batten, "Up From the Depths," *Maclean's*, August 1973: 30.

35 Jack Batten, "Our Beautiful Chance in Tokyo," *Maclean's*, 3 October 1964: 15. At the 1964 Olympics, Wingerson came thirteenth in the pentathlon; Gerace came fifteenth in the pentathlon and fifth in the high jump. Wingerson competed again in the 1968 Olympics and came eleventh.

36 Paul Grescoe, "I'm Just This Little Kid From Canada," *Canadian Magazine*, 19 August 1972: 25. Van Kiekebelt won a gold medal in the pentathlon at the 1971 Pan American Games and came fifteenth in the same event at the 1972 Olympics.

37 Debbie Brill (with James Lawton), *Jump* (Vancouver/Toronto: Douglas and McIntyre, 1986) 27–28.

38 Ladies Professional Golf Association. "The Ladies Professional Golf Association: 50 Years of Growth, Tradition and Excellence," <www.lpga.com/history/index.cfm>, 2001; see also Todd W. Crosset, *Outsiders in the Clubhouse: The World of Women's Professional Golf* (New York: SUNY Press, 1995) 39–54.

39 Post was not, however, Canada's first woman professional golfer. That distinction belongs to Verena Newton, who in 1932 took over the professional's duties at Lakeside Golf Club in the Muskokas. See Barclay 534–35.

40 Lorne Rubenstein, "Post Remains Only Canadian With a Major," *Globe and Mail*, 25 June 2001: S3.

41 Alan Edmonds, "And Sandra Post Makes Three," *Maclean's*, September 1968: 39.

42 After her initial success on the LPGA Tour, Post had numerous personal difficulties until 1974 when she again resumed her winning form. She played until 1984 with eight LPGA victories to her credit. See Barclay 530–36, and Long 199–200.

43 Jack Batten, "The Ecstasy of Long Drives," *Maclean's*, July 1973: 44, 46.

44 Marci McDonald, "Out of the Rough," *Maclean's*, June 1975: 46.

45 Barclay 536–41; Long 199.

46 Batten, "The Ecstasy of Long Drives" 35.

47 Barclay 536–37.

48 Batten, "Up from the Depths" 64.

49 Bev Boys, interview by author, tape recording, Vancouver, BC, 10 July 1985; Long 111–12.

50 Peter Gzowski, "Sports," *Saturday Night*, March 1966: 50–51.

51 "What the Girls Are Doing," *Homemaker's Magazine,* September 1973.

52 Jack Batten, "Something to Cheer About," *Homemaker's Magazine,* September 1973: 9–10.

53 Batten, "Something to Cheer About" 10.

54 Batten, "Something to Cheer About" 11.

55 "National Honors on Line Here Today," *Montreal Star,* 21 April 1962: 17.

56 Helen (Stewart) Hunt, interview by author, tape recording, Vancouver, BC, 11 September 2000; *Fifth Pan-American Games, July 22–August 7, 1967, Winnipeg, Canada* (Winnipeg: MacFarlane Communication Services, 1969); Robert D. Bratton, *Canadian Volleyball* (Ottawa: Canadian Volleyball Association, 1972) 40–41.

57 Paul Grescoe, "Volleyball is Hell," *Canadian Magazine,* 28 April 1978: 13.

58 Hunt interview.

59 Ferguson, *Who's Who in Canadian Sport* 349; "The Great Canadian Athlete Nobody Knows," *Star Weekly,* 1 April 1961: 14.

60 "Martha Benjamin: She Skis Like a Pro, When She Isn't Shooting Caribou," *Maclean's,* 14 December 1963: 66.

61 Brenda Zeman, *To Run With Longboat* (Edmonton: GMS² Ventures, 1988) 101–19; Sharon Firth, interview by author, tape recording, Edmonton, AB, 2 June 1985.

62 Vicky Paraschak, "An Examination of Sport for Aboriginal Females of the Six Nations Reserve, Ontario from 1968 to 1980," *Women of the First Nations,* eds. Christine Miller and Patricia Chuchryk (Winnipeg: University of Manitoba Press, 1996) 92–93; William Humber, *Diamonds of the North* (Toronto: Oxford, 1995) 60.

63 Mortin 115.

64 Information obtained from the (Ontario) Provincial Women's Softball Association website at <www.ontariopwsa.com>.

65 Mortin 115–21.

66 Helen Eckert, "Women and Competitive Basketball," *Journal of CAHPER* 26.6 (1960): 5–8.

67 Schrodt, "Vancouver's Dynastic Domination."

68 *La Presse,* 12 April 1967: 58.

69 McFarlane 121–28; Elizabeth Etue and Megan K. Williams, *On the Edge* (Toronto: Second Story Press, 1996) 69–70; Jean-Claude Trait, "Enceinte de 3 mois, elle score," *La Presse,* 12 November 1974: E3.

70 Etue and Williams 43–44. See also Ringette Canada, "The History of Ringette," <www.ringette.ca/history.html>, 2001.

71 Etue and Williams 48.

72 Alan Edmonds, "Go Git a Piece of Her, Debbie," *Canadian Magazine,* 8 February 1975: 24–26. Edmond's article is a reasonably sympathetic portrayal of players on the Point Edward women's hockey team from Sarnia, Ontario.

73 McFarlane 133–35.

74 "Judo Tightening Grip on Canada," *Maclean's Magazine,* 13 February 1960: n.p.

75 Carolyn Chisholm, "Women Take on the Daring New Sports," *Chatelaine,* April 1970: 44.

76 Alan Edmonds, "Go Kill Me a Tiger, Darling," *Maclean's,* 17 September 1966: 17.

77 Ford 73.

78 Sandra Peredo, "They're Canada's Only Ladies' Professional Football Team," *Canadian Magazine,* 29 August 1970: 6–7.

79 Tom Alderman, "Atta Girl Francine. Kill 'em! Murder 'em! Slaughter 'em!" *Canadian Magazine*, 27 February 1971: 8–11.

80 See note 69 in Chapter 3 for examples of female athletes in the 1930s who later changed their sex designation to male. After the war, when international competition resumed, there were several more cases reported, although the information was often anecdotal. In 1948, the IAAF issued a ruling that all women contestants in IAAF-sanctioned meets must have a medical certificate signed by a doctor as proof they were female. As well, proof of sex (for women only) was required any time a world record was claimed (see *Montreal Daily Star*, 10 August 1948: 15). The IAAF eventually decided that on-the-spot testing was necessary to be completely sure that all competitors were female.

81 "Sex Test Disqualifies Athlete," *New York Times*, 16 September 1967: 28.

82 There is a volume of literature on the subject of sex testing, but in the context of women's athletics, Laura A. Wackwitz, "Sex Testing In International Women's Athletics: A History of Silence," *Women and Sport and Physical Activity Journal* 5.1 (1996): 51–68 provides an excellent summary of the historical background.

83 *Canadian Skier Magazine,* March 1968: 26; for a reproduction of Abby Hoffman's certificate, see Jean Cochrane *et al.*, *Women in Canadian Life* (Toronto: Fitzhenry and Whiteside, 1977) 83.

84 Jennifer Hargreaves, *Sporting Females: Critical Issues in the History and Sociology of Women's Sports* (London: Routledge, 1994) 220; Guttmann 204–05.

85 Statistics supplied by the Canadian Olympic Association.

86 Gail Vines, "Last Olympics for the Sex Test?" *New Scientist* (4 July 1992): 39–42. Finally bowing to pressure after years of protest, the IAAF eliminated genetic sex testing in 1995; the IOC suspended "gender verification" at the 2000 Sydney Olympics, but only as an experiment with no guarantee it would not be brought back.

87 Renate Wilson, "What Turns Women to Lesbianism?" *Chatelaine,* October 1966: 134.

88 See also Campbell 128–36.

89 Grescoe, "Volleyball is Hell" 13.

90 Cahn, "From the 'Muscle Moll' to the 'Butch' Ballplayer" 353.

91 Elizabeth Halsey, *Women in Physical Education* (New York: G.P. Putnam's Sons, 1961) 47–48.

CHAPTER 6 FEMINIST ACTIVISM: INCHING TOWARDS GENDER EQUITY

1 Abby Hoffman, "Running for Gold," *Maclean's*, February 1975: 33; see also "Super-Jock in Decline: Liberating Sport from Sexist Stereotypes," *Canadian Dimension*, August 1971: 41–42.

2 There are now many accounts of the origins of second-wave feminism in Canada, but one of the best general sources is Prentice *et al.* 343–66; see also Naomi Black, "The Canadian Women's Movement: The Second Wave," in *Changing Patterns*, 2nd ed., eds. Sandra Burt *et al.*, (Toronto: McClelland and Stewart, 1993) 151–75.

3 Prentice *et al.* 349.

4 For further analysis of these issues, see Hall and Richardson 15–17. Title IX has been in effect for 30 years, and it remains a controversial piece of legislation. For a statistical assessment of Title IX's effect (not always positive) on women in intercollegiate sport over this period, see R. Vivian Acosta and Linda Jean Carpenter, "Women in Intercollegiate Sport," unpublished paper, 2000.

5 The original study was Carol Kirsh, Brian Dixon, and Michael Bond, *A Leisure Study — Canada 1972* (Ottawa: Arts and Culture Branch, Department of Secretary of State,

Government of Canada, 1973). For further analysis, see M. Ann Hall, "Sport and Physical Activity in the Lives of Canadian Women," *Canadian Sport: Sociological Perspectives*, eds. Richard S. Gruneau and John G. Albinson (Don Mills: Addison-Wesley, 1976) 170–99. See also James E. Curtis and Brian G. Milton, "Social Status and the 'Active Society': National Data on Correlates of Leisure-Time Physical and Sport Activities," 302–29 in the same volume.

6   Michael J. Heit and Don Malpass, *Do Women Have Equal Play?*, report prepared for the Sports and Fitness Division, Ontario Ministry of Culture and Recreation, 1975.

7   *Mayor's Task Force on the Status of Women in Toronto Final Report*. "A Study of Services and Facilities Offered to the Women of Toronto by the Department of Parks and Recreation" (January 1976). Recreation directors in Ontario had traditionally been male: in 1949, only two out of 56 were female, and in 1961, the ratio was four out of 86. For an interesting history of gender and the politics of recreation in postwar Ontario, see Shirley Tillotson, *The Public at Play* (Toronto: University of Toronto Press, 2000).

8   "Girls Fight for a Turn at Bat," *Toronto Sun*, 12 July 1977: 5.

9   Donald Macintosh, "Inequalities in Sport and Physical Activity Programs in Ontario Schools," *Interchange* 12.1 (1981–82): 61–68.

10   Joan N. Vickers and Barbara J. Gosling, *The Changing Participation of Men and Women in the Canadian Interuniversity Athletic Union (1978–1982)*, report prepared for the Women's Representative Committee of the Canadian Interuniversity Athletic Union, 1984.

11   Naomi Mallovy, "Women in Sports," *Homemaker's Magazine*, November 1975: 82.

12   Hall and Richardson 75–81.

13   Hall and Richardson 81. For a more extensive critique of psychological research proving that sport competition does not masculinize female participants, see M. Ann Hall, *Feminism and Sporting Bodies* (Champaign: Human Kinetics, 1996) 18–25.

14   Nancy E. Spencer, "Reading Between the Lines: A Discursive Analysis of the Billie Jean King vs. Bobby Riggs 'Battle of the Sexes,'" *Sociology of Sport Journal* 17.4 (2000): 386–402.

15   *Recommendation 77*: We recommend that the provinces and territories (a) review their policies and practices to ensure that school programmes provide girls with equal opportunities with boys to participate in athletic and sports activities, and (b) establish policies and practices that will motivate and encourage girls to engage in athletic and sport activities. *Recommendation 78*: We recommend that, pursuant to section 3(d) of the federal Fitness and Amateur Sport Act, a research project be undertaken to (a) determine why fewer girls than boys participate in sport programmes at the school level and (b) recommend remedial action. *Report of the Royal Commission on the Status of Women* (Ottawa: Information Canada, 1970) 185–87.

16   Canadian Advisory Council on the Status of Women, *What's Been Done? Assessment of the Federal Government's Implementation of the Recommendations of the Royal Commission on the Status of Women* (March 1974): 15.

17   *Report of the National Conference on Women and Sport*, Toronto, 24–26 May 1974 (Ottawa: Fitness and Amateur Sport Branch) 11.

18   For example, see Marion Lay and M. Ann Hall, "Proposed Women's Program Within the Fitness and Amateur Sport Branch," unpublished document, July 1974 (Sport Canada File No. 7865–5).

19   Pamela J. Lewis, "Fitness and Amateur Sport Branch Policies as They Pertain to Women in Sport in Canada from 1974 to 1979," MA thesis, University of Western Ontario, 1980, 80.

20   Macintosh, *Sport and Politics in Canada* 80.

21   Lewis 62.

22 Earl McRae and Roy MacGregor, "Executive Sweat: Gentlemen, Players and Other People Who Make Sport," *The Canadian,* 29 January 1977: 4–9.

23 Mary E. Keyes, "Feminist Lobbying and Decision-Making Power in Fitness and Amateur Sport National Policies, Programs and Services: the Case of Canada," *Sport: The Third Millennium,* eds. Fernand Landry *et al.* (Sainte-Foy: Les Presses de l'Université Laval, 1991) 424.

24 Macintosh, *Sport and Politics in Canada* 143; Pamela L. Ponic, "Herstory: The Structuring of the Fitness and Amateur Sport Branch's Women's Program: 1970–1988," MA thesis, University of Windsor, 1994, 41.

25 Sue Vail, "What the Federal Government Is Doing to Promote Women's Sport," *Canadian Woman Studies/les cahiers de la femme* 4.3 (1983): 76.

26 Fitness and Amateur Sport, *Women in Sport Leadership: Summary of National Survey,* 1982.

27 Donald Macintosh and A.J.C. King, *The Role of Interschool Sports Programs in Ontario Secondary Schools* (Toronto: Ministry of Education, 1977); Vickers and Gosling; "Fitness and Amateur Sport," *Women in Sport Leadership.*

28 Vickers and Gosling; Douglas Sagi, "Cheer for the Losers, Men," *Canadian Magazine,* 27 January 1973: 27.

29 For example, see David Whitson and Donald Macintosh, "Gender and Power: Explanations of Gender Inequality in Canadian National Sport Organizations," *International Review for the Sociology of Sport* 24.2 (1989):137–50; M. Ann Hall *et al.,* "Organizational Elites Reproducing Themselves," *Quest* 41 (1989): 28–45; M. Ann Hall *et al.,* "Gender Structure of National Sport Organizations," *Sport Canada Occasional Papers* 2.1 (December 1990); Annelies Knoppers, "Explaining Male Dominance and Sex Segregation in Coaching: Three Approaches," *Quest* 44 (1992): 210–27; Suzanne Laberge, "Employment Situation of High Performance Coaches in Canada," *Sport Canada Occasional Papers* 3.1 (1992); Nancy Theberge, "The Construction of Gender in Sport: Women, Coaching, and the Naturalization of Difference," *Social Problems* 40.3 (1993): 401–13.

30 See "Women in Rowing," special issue of *Catch* (Summer 1984). This is a publication of the Canadian Amateur Rowing Association.

31 Hall *et al.,* "The Gender Structure of National Sport Organizations" 21–26.

32 FAS, *Sport Canada Policy on Women in Sport* (1986): 14.

33 David Whitson and Donald Macintosh, "Equity vs. High Performance Canadian Amateur Sport: Policy Tensions," *CAHPER Journal* (May/June 1990): 27–30; Donald Macintosh and David Whitson, *The Game Planners* (Montreal and Kingston: McGill-Queen's University Press, 1990) 87–91; Ponic 55–60.

34 Whitson and Macintosh, "Equity vs. High Performance."

35 M. Ann Hall, "Feminist Activism in Sport: A Comparative Study of Women's Sport Advocacy Organizations," *Gender, Sport and Leisure: Continuities and Challenges,* ed. Alan Tomlinson (University of Brighton: Chelsea School Research Centre, 1995) 217–50.

36 Ann Popma , ed., *The Female Athlete: Proceedings of a National Conference About Women in Sports and Recreation* (Burnaby: Simon Fraser University, 1980) 185.

37 The original acronym was CAAW&S to emphasize the "women *and* sport," but it was later shortened to CAAWS. Also, in 1988 the words "and Physical Activity" were added, so that the official name for the organization is the Canadian Association for the Advancement of Women and Sport and Physical Activity, but the acronym has remained the same.

38 I was a delegate at the workshop, but for this section, I have relied on Nancy Theberge's account in "Feminism and Sport: Linking the Two Through A New Organization," *Canadian Woman Studies/les cahiers de la femme* 4.3 (1983): 79–81.

39 Theberge, "Feminism and Sport" 80.

40 CAAWS Annual General Meeting Kit, 1982.

41 Jill Vickers, "The Intellectual Origins of the Women's Movement in Canada," *Challenging Times: The Women's Movement in Canada and the United States*, eds. Constance Backhouse and David H. Flaherty (Montreal and Kingston: McGill-Queen's University Press, 1992) 44–45.

42 Helen Lenskyj, "Good Sports: Feminists Organizing on Sport Issues in the 1970s and 1980s," *Resources for Feminist research/Documentation sur la recherche féministe* 20.3/4 (1991): 130–35; Ponic.

43 Lenskyj, "Good Sports"; Hall, *Feminism and Sporting Bodies* 90–2.

44 Lenskyj, "Good Sports."

45 See Lenskyj, "Good Sports"; Helen Lenskyj, "Combating Homophobia in Sport and Physical Education," *Sociology of Sport Journal* 8.1 (1991): 61–69; Janis Lawrence-Harper, "The Herstory of the Canadian Association for the Advancement of Women and Sport," unpublished document, November 1991; Janis Lawrence-Harper, "Change in a Feminist Organization: The Canadian Association for the Advancement of Women and Sport and Physical Activity 1981–1991," master's thesis, University of Alberta, 1993.

46 *The Starting Line,* CAAWS/ACAFS Newsletter, Spring 1988: 18.

47 Lawrence-Harper, "The Herstory of the Canadian Association for the Advancement of Women and Sport" 85.

48 Some of the material in this section originally appeared in Hall and Richardson 18–28.

49 *Bannerman v. Ontario Rural Softball Association,* unpublished decision, Ontario Human Rights Commission Board of Inquiry, 1979.

50 *Bannerman v. Ontario Rural Softball Association.*

51 *Re Bannerman v. Ontario Rural Softball Association (1979),* Supreme Court of Ontario Court of Appeal, 26 O.R. (2d) 134.

52 *Re Cummings and Ontario Minor Hockey Association,* Ontario Human Rights Commission Board of Inquiry (1978) 29 R.F.L. 259.

53 Judy Steed, "The New Amazons," *The Canadian,* 28 October 1978: 8.

54 Judy Steed, "Cummings Continues to Chase Sports Dream," *Toronto Star,* 8 August 1993: E16.

55 *Re Forbes and Yarmouth Minor Hockey Association (1978),* decision of the Nova Scotia Human Rights Commission Board of Inquiry; *La Commission des droits de la personne contre la Fédération québécoise de hockey sur glace inc. et autres* (1978) C.S. 1076.

56 John Aitken, "She Shoots, She Scores," *Weekend Magazine,* 12 February 1977: 10.

57 Manon Rhéaume (with Chantal Gilbert), *Manon* (Toronto: HarperCollins, 1993) 46.

58 John Sopinka, *Can I Play,* report of the Task Force on Equal Opportunity in Athletics. vol. 1 and 2 (Toronto: Task Force on Equal Opportunity in Athletics, 1983, 1984).

59 Jennifer Hunter, "Playing By Discrimination," *Globe and Mail,* 30 March 1985.

60 See, for example, Judy Steed, "Girls Winning the War Against Shutouts," *Globe and Mail,* 31 August 1985: 10; James Davidson, "Girls Just Want to Play Hockey," *Globe and Mail,* 2 November 1985: D1, D3; James Davidson, "Split Decision," *Globe and Mail,* 21 December 1985; "Moving Against Discrimination," editorial, *Toronto Star,* 12 May 1986: A10.

61 Gwen Brodsky, "Justine Blainey and the Ontario Hockey Association: An Overview," *Newsletter of the Canadian Association for the Advancement of Women and Sport*, Fall 1986: 17.

62 Nancy Theberge, *Higher Goals* (Albany: State University of New York Press, 2000) 150–52.

63 Helen Lenskyj, "A Discussion Paper: Female Participation in Sport," report prepared for CAAWS and Sport Canada Joint Steering Committee, April 1984.

64 "Integrated Sports: A Question of Fair Play," *Chatelaine*, February 1988: 38, 41.

65 Rhéaume.

66 Brill 161.

67 Macintosh, *Sport and Politics in Canada* 106–07.

68 For a complete list of all Canadian women medal winners at the 1978 Commonwealth Games, see Long 238.

69 M. Ann Hall *et al.*, *Sport in Canadian Society* (Toronto: McClelland and Stewart, 1991) 94–96.

70 Mary Trueman, "Are Olympic Baubles Worth Training Effort," *Globe and Mail*, 26 February 1975: 31. The article profiled diver Cindy Shatto, runner Abby Hoffman, high jumper Louise Walker, and gymnast Jennifer Diachun.

71 Elizabeth Manley *Thumbs Up!* (Toronto Macmillan, 1990); see also Nora McCabe, "Chatelaine's Woman of the Year: Elizabeth Manley," *Chatelaine*, January 1989: 39–43, 93; Mary Jollimore, "Manley Finally Gets Life In Order," *Globe and Mail*, 20 February 1992: A13.

72 Laura Robinson, "Put Race Back Into Racing," *Globe and Mail*, 11 August 2000: A13.

73 Angella Issajenko, *Running Risks* (Toronto: Macmillan, 1990).

74 Mary Jollimore, "No Gold For Olympic Heroes," *Globe and Mail*, 25 July 1992: D1, D4.

75 Brian D. Johnson, "A Woman of Steel," *Maclean's*, February 1988: 52–56.

76 Judy Steed, "The Fastest Gun in the World," *Globe and Mail*, 3 July 1982: 10; Allan M. Gould, "Susan Nattrass: Canada's Shooting Star," *Chatelaine*, December 1983: 52, 110–12; Beverley Smith, "Nattrass Goes Great Guns," *Globe and Mail*, 23 August 2000: S3.

77 Linda Thom, interview by author, tape recording, Ottawa, ON, 28 December 1985.

78 A complete list of all medal winners, as well as profiles of many of these athletes, can be found in Long.

79 Two other Canadian woman athletes have competed in both the Summer and Winter Olympics, but not in the same year: Hayley Wickenheiser (hockey in 1998 and softball in 2000) and Clara Hughes (cycling in 1996, 2000 and speed skating in 2002). See also note 20 in Chapter 7.

80 Susan Holloway, interviews by author, tape recordings, Calgary, AB, 25 March 1985 and Ward's Island, Toronto, 23 April 1985. Today, Holloway is married to former Olympic high jumper Greg Joy, has two children, and works for the Canadian Olympic Association.

CHAPTER 7 THE COMMODIFICATION OF PHYSICALITY: 1990S AND BEYOND

1 Jay Teitel, "Shorter, Slower, Weaker," *Saturday Night*, July/August 1997: 61.

2 Teitel 63; see also, Allan Maki, "Today's Pro Athletes Taking All the Fun, Games Out of Sport," *Globe and Mail*, 25 March 2000: S4.

3 Robert Lipsyte, "The Emasculation of Sports," *New York Times Magazine*, 2 April 1995: 56, 52.

4 Robert Lipsyte, "Nagano's Legacy: Female Gladiators," *New York Times*, 22 February 1998: 13.

5 Lipsyte, "The Emasculation of Sports" 55; Lipsyte, "Nagano's Legacy" 13.

6   James Christie, "Women's Hockey is Different," *Globe and Mail*, 8 April 2000: S1; Nancy Theberge, *Higher Goals* (Albany: State University of New York Press, 2000) 8; Etue and Williams 63.

7   Etue and Williams 210.

8   Christie, "Women's Hockey is Different."

9   For an interesting analysis of these issues, see Nancy Theberge, "Playing With the Boys: Manon Rhéaume, Women's Hockey and the Struggle for Legitimacy," *Canadian Woman Studies/les cahiers de la femme*, 15 (4), 1995, 37–41. See also: Rhéaume; Mary Jollimore, "All Rhéaume Wanted Was a Chance to Play," *Globe and Mail*, 28 September 1992: A13; articles by Marlene Habib, Wendy Long, and Michael Farber in *Vancouver Sun*, 25 September 1992: A3, D20; Etue and Williams 222–30.

10   At the time of writing, Rhéaume works with USA-based Mission Hockey as head of global marketing for women's hockey, although she continues to play hockey (as a forward) for the Montreal Wingstars of the National Women's Hockey League. She is married to a hockey player and has one child.

11   See articles in the *Edmonton Journal* at the time of the 18th Annual Silver Ring Tournament in Edmonton, 4, 5, 6 February 2000; Ringette Canada, "The History of Ringette," <www.ringette.ca/history.html>, 2001.

12   Sport Canada, *Sport Participation in Canada: 1998 Report* (Ottawa: Minister of Public Works and Government Services Canada, 2000) 25.

13   Canadian Soccer Association, "2000 Demographics: Player Registrations," <www.canadasoccer.com/eng/docs/index.asp>, 2001.

14   "Girls Win Soccer Tussle," *Globe and Mail*, 2 November 1993: A1.

15   Most daily newspapers in Canada covered the event extensively. See, for example, the special section in the *Edmonton Journal* between 10 June and 11 July 1999. See also, David Leeder, "Suddenly, Women's Soccer Is Hot," *Globe and Mail*, 19 June 1999: A30.

16   Peter Mallett, "Hooper Endorses Women's Pro Loop," *Globe and Mail*, 13 April 2001: S4; Thomas Heath, "To Market, To Market," *Washington Post*, 1 April 2001: D3; see also the WUSA website at <www.wusa.com>. For a profile of Charmaine Hooper, see Joe O'Connor, "Lightning Striker," *Saturday Night*, 18 August 2001: 30–5.

17   Softball refers to both the slow pitch and fastball versions of the game. Many girls and young women also play baseball (same game as the major leagues), although this is much more recent. The Central Ontario Girls Baseball League, for example, was established in 1996 and includes a peewee division (ages 11–13), a bantam division (ages 14–16), and a junior (women's) division (ages 17–25). Players from this league are also members of Team Canada, which competes in the Women's World Series (against the United States, Japan, and Australia). For an interesting film about women's baseball and softball, although unfortunately with little Canadian content, see *Baseball Girls* (National Film Board of Canada, 1996).

18   *Sport Participation in Canada* 23.

19   Mary Jollimore, "Spark Still There for Veteran Pitcher," *Globe and Mail*, 4 July 1995: E4.

20   The others are Sue Holloway and Clara Hughes. Hughes is the first Canadian and only the fourth Olympian in history to win medals in *both* the Summer and Winter Olympics (two bronze cycling medals in 1996 and a bronze in speed skating in 2002).

21   Based on statistics and information found on the Softball Canada website at <www.softball.ca>.

22   *Sport Participation in Canada* 23.

23 "Canadian Taken in WNBA Draft," *Edmonton Journal*, 21 April 2001: D6; Women's National Basketball Association website at <www.wnba.com>; information about the Canadian women's national team at <www.eteamz.com/canadabasketball>. Another player in the WNBA from Canada is Kelly Schumacher, who although born in the United States, grew up in Canada and played basketball at John Abbott College near Montreal. She plays for the University of Connecticut and was drafted to the Indiana Fever of the WNBA.

24 Michael Grange, "Future Looks Rosy for Women's Pro Sports," *Globe and Mail*, 17 February 2000: S1. Women's Professional Football League information at <www. womensprofootball.com>; see also Barry Bortnick, "Pursuing a Dream," *Edmonton Journal*, 27 December 2000: D5.

25 "Rick Brace Comments on New Women's Sports Network (WSN)," Canada NewsWire, 24 November 2000 <www.newswire.ca/releases/November2000/24/C7907.html>; "Truth and Rumours," *Globe and Mail*, 28 and 30 November 2000: S3 and S5.

26 Lisa and Richard Scott, "Women Finally Making Sports Card Breakthroughs," *Canadian Sportscard Collector*, November 1999: 80.

27 Paul Gallico, "S.A.," *Farewell to Sport* (New York: Alfred A. Knopf, 1938) 245.

28 "Truth As/Is Beauty," *Globe and Mail*, 16 August 2000: A16. See also Sarah Sands, "Is Anna Good for Tennis?" *National Post*, 1 July 2000: A20.

29 Jere Longman, "'Booters with Hooters' Are Showing Women Can Be Athletic and Feminine," *National Post*, 8 July 1999: B10 (originally published in *The New York Times*); Steve Knopper, "Barenaked Ladies," *Globe and Mail*, 7 November 1998: C1; Sarah Hampson, "And Now, the Nudes," *Globe and Mail*, 25 January 2001: R1, 4.

30 Beverley Smith, "Leaving Nothing to the Imagination," *Globe and Mail*, 20 November 1998: A25; Phil Hersh, "Witt Courts Controversy Posing Nude," *Edmonton Journal*, 29 October 1998: D5.

31 Sally Armstrong, "Olympia's Secret," *Chatelaine*, September 2000: 85–92.

32 James Christie, "Sexy Togs Irritate Volleyballers," *Globe and Mail*, 4 November 1998: A19; David Menzies, "Scoring With a Little T&A," *Marketing Magazine*, 4 January 1999: 8; "Letters," *Marketing Magazine*, 1 February 1999; Allan Casey, "The Wide World of Sexy Sports," *Ottawa Citizen*, 3 April 1999. For an interesting take on women's pole vaulting, see Allan Maki and James Christie, "Pole Vaulting Fashion is all T and A: Technology and Advancement," *Globe and Mail*, 11 August 2001: L4.

33 Carol Harrington, "Skiers Bear Brunt of Some Criticism," *Globe and Mail*, 7 September 2000: S3.

34 *Time*, Canadian edition, 11 September 2000.

35 Ingrid Peritz, "Athlete to Sue Over Ad For Gum," *Globe and Mail*, 15 January 2000: A3.

36 Robert Lipsyte, "Sports and Sex Are Always Together," *New York Times*, 11 July 1999: SP13.

37 Shauna Richer, "LPGA Players Build Bonds Off Greens," *Globe and Mail*, 2 August 1997: A14.

38 Shauna Richer, "Final Round Leaves Kane Crestfallen," *Globe and Mail*, 14 August 2000: S1.

39 Neil Davidson, "Kane Scores Another Win," *Globe and Mail*, 28 December 2000: S2; Margaret Webb, "2nd to None," *Saturday Night*, 4 August 2001: 19–23.

40 Miller 113.

41 *Globe and Mail*, 27 March 1998: A22; see also, Allan Maki, "Miller's Contract With National Team Expiring in April," *Globe and Mail*, 25 March 1998: A21 and James Monsees, "Shannon Miller's Firing Is Just Fine," *Edmonton Sports Scene*, April 1998: 5. A few weeks

later, Miller was named head coach of the women's hockey program at the University of Minnesota-Duluth.

42 I am grateful to Nancy Theberge for this insight.

43 Mary Ormsby, "Fired National Volleyball Coach Fighting Back," *Toronto Star*, 22 August 1992: B3.

44 Pat Griffin, *Strong Women, Deep Closets: Lesbians and Homophobia in Sport* (Champaign, IL: Human Kinetics, 1998).

45 Theberge, *Higher Goals* 87–99.

46 Both quotes cited in Etue and Williams 217–18.

47 Heather Clarke and Susan Gwynne-Timothy, *Stroke* (Toronto: James Lorimer, 1988) 23.

48 "Crossing the Line," CBC, *The Fifth Estate*, 2 November 1993. For a partial transcript of this program, see Sandra Kirby *et al.*, *The Dome of Silence* (Halifax: Fernwood, 2000) 22–24.

49 Mary Jollimore, "Women Athletes Face Sexual Harassment, Too," *Globe and Mail*, 8 February 1993: A13; "Report on Harassment Said to Be 'Tip of Iceberg,'" *Globe and Mail*, 6 November 1993: A19; "A Gross Betrayal of Coach's Trust," *Globe and Mail*, 3 January 1994: A16.

50 See previous endnote. See also Helen Lenskyj, "Unsafe at Home Base: Women's Experiences of Sexual Harassment in University Sport and Physical Education," *Women in Sport and Physical Activity Journal* 1.1 (1992): 19–33; relevant articles in Robinson, *She Shoots, She Scores*.

51 Laura Robinson, *Crossing the Line* (Toronto: McClelland and Stewart, 1998).

52 Sandra Kirby and Lorraine Greaves, "Foul Play: Sexual Harassment in Sport," report to Sport Canada, June 1996; see also Kirby *et al.* 33–97.

53 See Kirby *et al.*, especially 124–68.

54 "Olympic Dross," *Globe and Mail*, 10 August 1998: A12.

55 See articles by James Christie in the *Globe and Mail* on 7 August 1998: A1, S1.

56 Issajenko.

57 Hall *et al.*, *Sport in Canadian Society* 223–27.

58 "Sports and Drugs: Just Say 'Payback Time,'" *Globe and Mail*, 7 September 2000: A16. See also stories about Robin Lyons in the *Edmonton Journal* on 30 June 2000: D4; 28 August 2000: D8: 2 February 2001: D4: and in the *Globe and Mail* on 6, 7, and 21 September 2000.

59 "The Venolyn Clarke Affair," *National Post*, 18 August 2001: A17. See also coverage in the *Globe and Mail* on 8 August 2001: S1; 17 August 2001: S3; 18 August 2001: S1, S4.

60 See Cathy Meade, "The Efficacy of Canadian Human Rights Legislation in Dealing with Sex Discrimination and Gender Inequality in Sport," unpublished document, University of Alberta, September 1993.

61 Nicolaas van Rijn, "A Champ's Advice: 'Hang In There,'" *Toronto Star*, 12 March 2000; "School Board Bounces Girl From Boys' Team," *Edmonton Journal*, 13 March 2000: A1.

62 Laura Robinson, "The Jock-strap Ceiling," *Globe and Mail*, 15 March 2000: A15.

63 Hargreaves, *Sporting Females* 237–42; *Women and Sport: Policy and Frameworks for Action* (London: The Sports Council, 1993).

64 Bruce Kidd in *Towards Gender Equity for Women in Sport: A Handbook for National Sport Organizations* (Ottawa: Canadian Association for the Advancement of Women and Sport and Physical Activity, 1993) 4.

65 *Task Force on Gender Equity*, Final Report to the Council of the Department of Athletics and Recreation, University of Toronto, December 31, 1993. The actual statement was from *Athletics Administration*, April 1993: 22.

66 Cited in Sandra Kirby, "Gender Equity in the Canadian Sport Council: The New Voice for the Sport Community," *Feminist Success Stories/ Célébrons nos réussites féministes*, eds. Karen A. Blackford *et al.* (Ottawa: University of Ottawa Press, 1999) 57.

67 "CAAWS Priorities for 1991," *Action: The Newsmagazine of Women in Sport and Physical Activity*, Spring 1991: 2–4.

68 "CAAWS Activities in 1992–93," *Action*, October 1992. The same statements also appear in *Action*, 21, 1999: 8–9.

69 Statements found on the CAAWS web site, April 2001 <www.caaws.ca/english>.

70 "Marg a Top 40 Under 40 Winner!" *Action*, Spring 1996: 11.

71 Kirby 57–69. CAAWS is now part of the "Sport Matters Working Group," a voluntary collective of national and provincial multi-sport and major games organizations <www.sportmatters.ca>.

72 For a useful, critical analysis of the international women's sport movement, see Hargreaves, *Heroines of Sport* 215–33.

73 The letter appeared in *Action*, Number 23, 1999: 25. For an analysis of the Nike situation, see Mélisse R. Lafrance, "Colonizing the Feminine: Nike's Intersections of Postfeminism and Hyperconsumption," *Sport and Postmodern Times*, ed. Geneviève Rail (New York: SUNY Press, 1998) 117–39; see also Shari L. Dworkin and Michael A. Messner, "Just Do ... What?: Sport, Bodies, Gender," *Revisioning Gender*, eds. Myra Marx Ferree *et al.* (Thousand Oaks: Sage, 1999) 341–61; Shelley Lucas, "Nike's Commercial Solution: Girls, Sneakers, and Salvation," *International Review for the Sociology of Sport* 35.2 (2000): 149–64.

74 Canadian Fitness and Lifestyle Research Institute, 1998 and 1999 Physical Activity Monitor available through their web site <www.cflri.ca>.

75 Sport Canada, *Sport Participation in Canada* (Ottawa: Minister of Public Works and Government Services Canada, 2000) 9–18, 28–29.

76 Sport Canada, *Sport Participation in Canada*, 24–28; see also Frances Kremarik, "A Family Affair: Children's Participation in Sports," *Canadian Social Trends*, Autumn 2000: 20–24.

77 *Globe and Mail*, 28 November 2000: A1, A11, A18.

78 Abby Hoffman, "Women's Access to Sport and Physical Activity," *Avante* 1.1 (1995): 85.

79 Patricia Vertinsky, "Physical Activity, Sport and Health for Girls and Women: Issues and Perspectives," *Bulletin of the International Association of Physical Education and Sport for Girls and Women* 7.1 (1997): 3.

80 *Edmonton Journal*, 31 May 1999: B4.

81 Helen Lenskyj, "What's Sport Got to Do With It?" *Canadian Woman Studies/les cahiers de la femme* 15.4 (1995): 6.

82 Louise Humbert, "Behind the Smiles," *Action*, Winter 1995: 2.

83 E. Jane Watkinson and Karen Calzonetti, "Physical Activity Patterns of Physically Disabled Women in Canada," *CAHPER Journal* 55.6 (1989): 21–26; Lisa M. Olenik *et al.*, "Women, Disability and Sport: Unheard Voices," *Canadian Woman Studies/les cahiers de la femme* 15.4 (1995): 54–57; Jennifer Hoyle and Philip White, "Physical Activity in the Lives of Women with Disabilities," *Sport and Gender in Canada*, eds. Philip White and Kevin Young (Don Mills, ON: Oxford University Press) 254–68.

84 Vicky Paraschak, "Invisible But Not Absent: Aboriginal Women in Sport and Recreation," *Canadian Woman Studies/les cahiers de la femme* 15.4 (1995): 71–2; Hargreaves, *Heroines of Sport* 78–128.

85 Statistics supplied by the Canadian Olympic Association. See also Sport Canada, "Sport Gender Snap Shot 1997–1998: Survey Results Report," May 1999, <www.pch.gc.ca/sportcanada/SC_E/snapshot.htm>, 2001.

86 See article and obituary by James Christie in *Globe and Mail*, 3 February 2001: A14 and S1.

87 Hargreaves, *Heroines of Sport* 207.

88 Sport Canada, *Sport Participation in Canada* 44–5.

89 Canadian Association for the Advancement of Women and Sport, *Towards Gender Equity for Women in Sport* (Ottawa: CAAWS and Women's Program Sport Canada, March 1993) 38; M. Ann Hall *et al.*, "The Gender Structure of National Sport Organizations," *Sport Canada Occasional Papers* 2.1 (December 1990): 1–2.

90 Sport Canada, *Sport Participation in Canada* 39–41.

91 Sport Canada, "Sport Gender Snap Shot 1997–1998: Survey Results Report," 25–30. The percentage of national coaches who are female has varied considerably over the years. There have been so few that small changes up or down produce large percentage points.

92 Laura Robinson, "Games Boys Play," *Canadian Forum*, October 1999: 18–21.

93 Sheila Robertson, "In Their Own Voices: Women Coaches Raising a Family," *Canadian Journal for Women in Coaching Online* 1.2 (2000) <www.coach.ca/women/e/journal>. This is an interesting and informative article that tells the personal stories of seventeen Canadian women coaches with families. See also Rose Mercier's article in the same issue for an analysis of what the stories tell us.

94 See stories in the *Globe and Mail* mostly by James Christie on 10, 13, 15, 17 and 27 June, 6 and 26 July, 5 and 6 August, and 2 November 2000.

95 The website can be found at <http://sweatcentral.chatelaine.com>.

EPILOGUE

1 Christina Bergstrom, "Jocks and Jills," *The Langara Journalism Review*, 1999 (online journal at <www.langara.bc.ca/ljr/bergstrom.html>); Amanda Smith, "Back-Page Bylines: Newspapers, Women, and Sport," *Sportcult*, eds. Randy Martin and Toby Miller (Minneapolis: University of Minnesota Press, 1999) 261.

2 "Expanded Survey Reveals a Modest Upsurge in Coverage of Women's Sports," CAAWS News Release, February 8, 1994. The survey covered a two-week period from November 22 to December 6, 1993, and is, therefore, a reflection of the coverage of winter sports.

3 Neil Davidson, "Summit Series Winners Named Team of the Century," 16 November 1999 <www.canoe.ca/CANOE2000/sports_2.html>, 2001; Neil Davidson, "Greene Female Athlete of the Century," *Globe and Mail*, 23 November 1999: S1.

4 Dave Feschuk, "Our Panel Ranks the Most Significant Events Since 1948," *National Post*, 4 January 1999: B6–7.

5 Bruce Kidd, "Missing: Women from Sports Halls of Fame," *Action*, Winter 1994: 4–5.

6 For a list of female inductees in several Canadian sports halls of fame, see Long 246–48.

7 Shirley (Gordon) Olafsson, interview by author, tape recording, Vancouver, BC, 8 September 2000. After retiring from competition, Olafsson continued to contribute to women's sport as a volunteer coach and administrator.

8 Hargreaves, *Heroines of Sport* 202–03. Among those in particular who should be recognized are wheelchair athletes Marni Abbott, Chantal Benoit, Colette Bourgonje, Elaine Ell, Linda Hamilton, Chantal Petitclerc, and Diane Rakiecki; swimmers Rebeccah Bornemann and

Marie-Claire Ross; shot put and discus specialist Ljiljana Ljubusic; skier Lana Spreeman; and power lifter Lee Ann Dalling. For a list of Canadian women Paralympic medalists between 1984 and 1992, as well as useful profiles, see Long. For additional profiles see Ian Gregson, *Irresistible Force* (Victoria: Polestar Books, 1999) and Robert Steadward and Cynthia Peterson, *Paralympics* (Edmonton: Alberta Northern Lights Wheelchair Basketball Society, 1997).

9   Shona M. Thompson, *Mother's Taxi* (Albany: State University of New York Press, 1999) 6.

SOURCES

BOOKS, ARTICLES, REPORTS, UNPUBLISHED WORK

Adams, Mary Louise. *The Trouble With Normal: Postwar Youth and the Making of Heterosexuality*. Toronto: University of Toronto Press, 1997.

Acosta, R. Vivian, and Linda Jean Carpenter. "Women in Intercollegiate Sport: A Longitudinal Study—Twenty-Three Year Update." Unpublished paper, 2000. Available from P.O. Box 42, West Brookfield, MA 01585.

Aitken, John. "She Shoots, She Scores." *Weekend Magazine* 12 February 1977, 10.

Alderman, Tom. "Atta Girl Francine. Kill 'em! Murder 'em! Slaughter 'em!" *Canadian Magazine* 27 February 1971: 8–11.

Allen, Vic. "Canadian Skiing: Past, Present, and Future." *Canadian Sport Monthly* March 1957: 8.

Armstrong, Sally. "Olympia's Secret." *Chatelaine* September 2000: 85–92.

Atkins, Roxy. "Elmer, You're Goofy." *Maclean's Magazine* 15 September 1938: 18, 37–8.

Avery, Joanna, and Julie Stevens. *Too Many Men on the Ice: Women's Hockey in North America*. Victoria: Polestar, 1997.

Bacchi, Carol Lee. *Liberation Deferred?: The Ideas of the English-Canadian Suffragists, 1877–1918*. Toronto: University of Toronto Press, 1983.

Bannerman v. Ontario Rural Softball Association. Unpublished decision. Ontario Human Rights Commission Board of Inquiry, 1979.

Barclay, James A. *Golf in Canada: A History*. Toronto: McClelland and Stewart, 1992.

Barron, Elizabeth Pitt. "Chaperoning the 1936 Winter Olympics." Unpublished manuscript transcribed by John Byl.

Batten, Jack. "The Ecstasy of Long Drives." *Maclean's* July 1973: 35, 44, 46, 48, 50.

——. "Our Beautiful Chance in Tokyo." *Maclean's* 3 October 1964: 14–17.

——. "Something to Cheer About." *Homemaker's Magazine* September 1973: 9–11, 14, 17.

——. "Up From the Depths." *Maclean's* August 1973: 30–31, 62–64.

——, ed. *Canada at the Olympics: The First Hundred Years*. Toronto: INFACT Publishing, 1996.

Bean, Gladys, ed. *The History of Synchronized Swimming in Canada*. Ottawa: Canadian Amateur Swimming Association, 1975.

——. "Looking Back." *A Fair Shake: Autobiographical Essays by McGill Women.* Ed. Margaret Gillett and Kay Sibbald. Montreal: Eden Press, 1984. 329–43.

Beers, W.G. *Lacrosse: The National Game of Canada.* Montreal: Dawson Bros., 1869.

——. *Over the Snow.* Montreal: W. Drysdale and Co., and J. Theo. Robinson, 1883.

Bell, Dorothy G. "Brain-work Made Her Golf Champion." *Maclean's Magazine* 1 May 1926: 22, 65–66.

Bell, Margaret. "Among the People Who Serve." *Toronto Star Weekly* 7 May 1910: 12.

——. "The Girls' Colleges of Toronto." *Toronto Star Weekly* 21 May 1910: 12.

——. "Toronto Girls in Pursuit of Athletics." *Toronto Star Weekly* 23 April 1910: 12.

Benedickson, Jamie. *Idleness, Water, and a Canoe: Reflections on Paddling for Pleasure.* Toronto: University of Toronto Press, 1997.

Bergman, Brian. "When Girls Ruled" *Maclean's*, 9 July 2001: 28–29.

Bergstrom, Christina. "Jocks and Jills." *The Langara Journalism Review*, 1999. Online journal at <www.langara.bc.ca/ljr/bergstrom.html>.

Birrell, Susan, and Nancy Theberge. "Feminist Resistance and Transformation in Sport." *Women and Sport: Interdisciplinary Perspectives.* Ed. D. Margaret Costa and Sharon R. Guthrie. Champaign: Human Kinetics, 1994. 361–76

Black, Naomi. "The Canadian Women's Movement: The Second Wave." *Changing Patterns: Women in Canada.* Ed. Sandra Burt, Lorraine Code, and Lindsay Dorney. 2nd ed. Toronto: McClelland and Stewart, 1993. 151–75.

Bocock, Linda Crutchfield. "Reflections of a Racer." *Canadian Sport Monthly*, January 1965: Part 1, 6–7 and February, 1965: Part 2, 22–27.

Bratton, Robert D. *Canadian Volleyball: A History to 1967.* Ottawa: Canadian Volleyball Association, 1972.

Brill, Debbie (with James Lawton). *Jump.* Vancouver and Toronto: Douglas and McIntyre, 1986.

Brodsky, Gwen. "Justine Blainey and the Ontario Hockey Association: An Overview," *Newsletter of the Canadian Association for the Advancement of Women and Sport*, Fall 1986: 17.

Brown, David W. "Social Darwinism, Private Schooling and Sport in Victorian and Edwardian Canada." *Pleasure, Profit, Proselytism: British Culture and Sport at Home and Abroad 1700–1914.* Ed. J.A. Mangan. London: Frank Cass, 1988. 215–30.

Browne, Lois. *Girls of Summer: In Their Own League.* Toronto: HarperCollins, 1992.

Bruce, Harry. "Martha Benjamin: She Skis Like a Pro, When She Isn't Shooting Caribou." *Maclean's* 14 December 1963: 66.

Bryans, Helen. "Secondary School Curriculum for Girls." *Physical Education in Canada.* Ed. M.L. Van Vliet. Scarborough: Prentice-Hall of Canada, 1965. 124–39.

Bryden, Wendy. *Canada at the Olympic Winter Games: The Official Sports History and Record Book.* Edmonton: Hurtig, 1987.

Burstyn, Varda. *The Rites of Men: Manhood, Politics, and the Culture of Sport.* Toronto: University of Toronto Press, 1999.

Byers, Mary. *Havergal: Celebrating a Century 1894–1994.* Toronto: Boston Mills Press, 1994.

Byl, John. "Directing Physical Education in the Canadian YWCAs: Margaret Eaton School's Influence, 1901–1947," *Sport History Review*, 27 (2): 139–54 (1996).

——. "The Margaret Eaton School, 1901–1942: Women's Education in Elocution, Drama and Physical Education." Diss. State University of New York at Buffalo, 1992.

——."Why Physical Educators Should Know About the Margaret Eaton School." *CAHPER Journal* 59.1 (1993): 10–13.

Cahn, Susan K. "Coming on Strong: Gender and Sexuality in Women's Sport, 1900–1960." Diss. University of Minnesota, 1990.

——. *Coming on Strong: Gender and Sexuality in Twentieth-Century Women's Sport.* New York: The Free Press, 1994.

——. "From the 'Muscle Moll' to the 'Butch' Ballplayer: Mannishness, Lesbianism, and Homophobia in U.S. Women's Sport," *Feminist Studies* 19.2 (1993): 343–68.

Callwood, June. "How Marilyn Swam the Lake." *Maclean's Magazine* 1 November 1954: 12–15, 72–78, 80–83.

——. "She wants to be the World's Strongest Woman, But ..." *Maclean's Magazine* 16 April 1955: 22–25, 50–54.

Cameron, C.K. "The Problem That Is Never Mentioned" *Canadian Home Journal* November 1951: 12, 103–6.

Campbell, Kathryn. "'Deviance, Inversion and Unnatural Love': Lesbians in Canadian Media, 1950–1970." *Atlantis: A Women's Studies Journal* 23.1 (1998): 128–36.

Canada at the 3rd Pan American Games. Official Report of Canada's Participation in the 3rd Pan American Games held in Chicago, U.S.A., August 27th to September 7th 1959.

Canada Competes at the Olympic Games 1948. Official Report of the Canadian Olympic Association, 1938 to 1948.

Canada Competes at the Olympic Games 1952. Official Report of the Canadian Olympic Association, 1948 to 1952.

Canada Competes at the Olympic Games 1956. Official Report of the Canadian Olympic Association.

Canada Competes at the Olympic Games 1964. Official Report of the Canadian Olympic Association, 1961 to 1964.

Canada's Part in the 1958 British Empire and Commonwealth Games. Official Report of the British Empire and Commonwealth Games Association of Canada, 1954–1958.

Canada's Part in the 1962 British Empire and Commonwealth Games. Official Report of the British Empire and Commonwealth Games Association of Canada, 1958–1962.

Canada's Part in the 1970 British Commonwealth Games. Official Report of the British Empire and Commonwealth Games Association of Canada, 1966–70.

Canadian Advisory Council on the Status of Women, *What's Been Done? Assessment of the Federal Government's Implementation of the Recommendations of the Royal Commission on the Status of Women,* March 1974.

Canadian Association for the Advancement of Women and Sport, *Towards Gender Equity for Women in Sport: A Handbook for National Sport Organizations.* Ottawa: CAAWS and Women's Program Sport Canada, March 1993.

Carroll, Dink. "Ski Twins." *Maclean's Magazine* 1 February 1944: 18, 27.

Carroll, Jock. "The Glamour Girl of the Canadian Olympic Trials: Jackie MacDonald." *Weekend Magazine* 25 August 1956: 32–34.

Carscallen, Helen, and Hilda Rickett. "Problems of Providing Physical Recreation for Women." *AIM—A Sports World Digest* 4.2 (1945): 52–57.

Cartwright, Ethel M. "Athletics and Physical Education for Girls." *Proceedings of the Sixty-Second Annual Convention of the Ontario Educational Association.* Toronto: Clarkson W. James, 1923. 274–81.

———. "Physical Education and the Strathcona Trust." *The School* 4 (January, 1916): 306–10.

———. "The Place of Physical Education in the School and Home Curriculum." *Proceedings of the Sixty-Second Annual Convention of the Ontario Educational Association,*. Toronto: Clarkson W. James, 1923. 291–300.

Cayleff, Susan E. *Babe: The Life and Legend of Babe Didrikson Zaharias.* Urbana and Chicago: The University of Chicago Press, 1995.

Chant, L. Ormiston. "Woman As An Athlete: A Reply to Dr. Arabella Kenealy." *The Living Age* 24 June 1899: 799–805.

Chapman, Currie (with Randy Starkman). *On the Edge: The Inside Story of the Canadian Women's Ski Team.* Toronto: McGraw-Hill Ryerson, 1988.

Chapman, Ethel M. "The Miracle of Physical Training." *Maclean's Magazine* 1 March 1920: 74, 78.

Cheska, Alyce. "Ball Game Participation of North American Indian Women." *Her Story in Sport: A Historical Anthology of Women in Sports.* Ed. Reet Howell. West Point: Leisure Press, 1982. 19–34.

Chisholm, Carolyn. "Women Take on the Daring New Sports." *Chatelaine* April 1970: 44–45.

Churchill, Kristopher L. "Character Building and Gender Socialization in Early Private Youth Camps in Ontario." MA thesis. University of Guelph, 1991.

Clark, C.S. *Of Toronto the Good.* 1898. Toronto: Coles, 1970.

Clark, Gregory. "Bobbed-Headed Athletes Menace Male Supremacy." *Toronto Star Weekly* 24 April 1926: 21.

Clark, Laurene. *Synchronized Swimming: 60 Years to Celebrate.* Ottawa: Canadian Amateur Synchronized Swimming Association, 1985.

Clark, S.D. *The Social Development of Canada.* Toronto: The University of Toronto Press, 1942.

Clarke, Heather, and Susan Gwynne-Timothy. *Stroke: The Inside Story of Olympic Contenders.* Toronto: James Lorimer, 1988.

Cochrane, Jean, Abby Hoffman, and Pat Kincaid. *Women in Canadian Life: Sports.* Toronto: Fitzhenry and Whiteside, 1977.

Collins, Robert. "The Ferocious Young Ladies from Edmonton" *Maclean's Magazine,* 10 December 1955: 36–37, 66–73.

Collins, Winston. "Rebel With A Cause." *Saturday Night* July 1981: 57–58.

La Commission des droits de la personne contre la Fédération québécoise de hockey sur glace inc. et autres, 1978.

Conrad, Peter C. *In the Winning Lane: A History of Competitive Swimming in Saskatchewan.* Regina: Swim Saskatchewan, 1990.

Cowe, Eric L., comp. *International Women's Athletics 1890–1940: A Statistical History.* Bingley, UK: Eric L. Cowe, 1985.

Crosset, Todd W. *Outsiders in the Clubhouse: The World of Women's Professional Golf.* New York: SUNY Press, 1995.

Culin, Stewart. *Games of the North American Indians.* 1907. New York: Dover Publications, 1975.

Curtis, James E., and Brian G. Milton, "Social Status and the 'Active Society': National Data on Correlates of Leisure-Time Physical and Sport Activities." *Canadian Sport: Sociological Perspectives.* Ed. Richard S. Gruneau and John G. Albinson. Don Mills: Addison-Wesley, 1976. 302–29.

Deacon, James. "Leagues of Their Own." *Maclean's* 7 April 1997: 62–70.

Denison, Grace E. "The Evolution of the Lady Cyclist." *Massey's Magazine* April 1897: 281–84.

Dewar, John. "Saskatchewan's Basketball Beginnings (1891–1922)." *Saskatchewan History* 41.3 (1988): 99–112.

Dheensaw, Cleve. *The Commonwealth Games: The First 60 Years 1930–1990.* Victoria: Orca Book Publishers, 1994.

———. *Island of Champions: A Sporting History of Vancouver Island.* Victoria: Orca Book Publishers, 1988.

Doolittle, P.E. "Cycling for Women." *Canadian Practitioner* 21.5 (1896): 329–32.

Douglas, H.P. "Development of Ladies Racing." *Canadian Sport Monthly* January 1950: 10–11, 23.

Drake, Earl. *Regina: The Queen City.* Toronto: McClelland and Stewart, 1955.

Dworkin, Shari L., and Michael A. Messner, "Just Do ... What?: Sport, Bodies, Gender." *Revisioning Gender.* Ed. Myra Marx Ferree, Judith Lorber, and Beth B. Hess. Thousand Oaks, CA: Sage, 1999. 341–61.

Eaton, John D. "The Life and Professional Contributions of Arthur Stanley Lamb, M.D., to Physical Education in Canada. Diss. Ohio State University, 1964.

Eckert, Helen M. "The Development of Organized Recreation and Physical Education in Alberta." MA thesis. University of Alberta, 1953.

———. "Women and Competitive Basketball." *Journal of CAHPER* 26.6 (1960): 5–8.

Edmonds, Alan. "And Sandra Post Makes Three." *Maclean's* September 1968: 38–39, 65–66, 68.

———. "Go Kill Me a Tiger, Darling." *Maclean's* 17 September 1966: 16–19.

———. "The Pressure on Nancy Garapick." *Canadian Magazine* 6 September 1975: 10, 12.

Etue, Elizabeth, and Megan K. Williams. *On the Edge: Women Making Hockey History.* Toronto: Second Story Press, 1996.

Felshin, Jan. "The Dialectics of Woman and Sport." *The American Woman in Sport.* Ed. Ellen W. Gerber, Jan Felshin, Pearl Berlin, and Waneen Wyrick. Reading: Addison-Wesley, 1974. 179–210.

Ferguson, Bob. *Who's Who in Canadian Sport.* 3rd Edition. Kanata: Bob Ferguson, 2000.

Ferguson, Elmer W. "I Don't Like Amazon Athletes." *Maclean's Magazine* 1 August 1938: 9, 32–3.

Festle, Mary Jo. *Playing Nice: Politics and Apologies in Women's Sports.* New York: Columbia University Press, 1996.

Fifth Pan-American Games, July 22–August 7, 1967, Winnipeg, Canada. Winnipeg: MacFarlane Communication Services, 1969.

Fitness and Amateur Sport, *Women in Sport Leadership: Summary of National Survey,* 1982.

Fitness and Amateur Sport, *Changing Times: Women and Physical Activity,* October 1984.

Fitness and Amateur Sport, *Sport Canada Policy on Women in Sport,* 1986.

Forbes, Susan L. "The Influence of the Social Reform Movement and T. Eaton Company's Business Practices on the Leisure of Eaton's Female Employees During the Early Twentieth Century." Diss. University of Western Ontario, 1998.

Ford, Anne Rochon. *A Path Strewn With Roses: One Hundred Years of Women at the University of Toronto 1884–1984.* Toronto: Women's Centenary Committee, University of Toronto, 1985.

Frayne, Trent. "The Champ Still Baby Sits." *Maclean's Magazine* 1 May 1952: 16–17, 43.

——. "The Human Body Is Better Than Anyone Thought." *Maclean's* 16 December 1961: 18, 65–67.

Fulford, Robert. *Best Seat in the House: Memoirs of a Lucky Man.* Toronto: Collins, 1988.

Gallico, Paul. *Farewell to Sport.* New York: Alfred A. Knopf, 1938.

——. "The Texas Babe." *The Thirties: A Time to Remember.* Ed. Don Congdon New York: Simon and Schuster, 1962. 73–78. Rpt. *Vanity Fair* October 1932: 36, 71.

Garvey, Ellen Gruber. "Reframing the Bicycle: Advertising-Supported Magazines and Scorching Women." *American Quarterly* 47.1 (1995): 66–101.

George, Judith Jenkins. "The Fad of North American Women's Endurance Swimming During the Post-World I Era." *Canadian Journal of History of Sport* 26.1 (1995): 52–72.

Gibb, Alexandrine. "Canada at the Olympics." *Maclean's Magazine* 1 October 1928: 16, 46, 48–50.

Gillanders, John. "National Meet or Rural Sports-Day?" *Canadian Sport Monthly* July 1961: 8–9, 25.

Gillett, Margaret. *We Walked Very Warily: A History of Women at McGill.* Montreal: Eden Press, 1981.

Gordon, Alison. *Foul Balls: Five Years in the American League.* Toronto: McClelland and Stewart, 1984.

Gould, Allan M. "Susan Nattrass: Canada's Shooting Star." *Chatelaine* December 1983: 52, 110–12

Greene, Nancy (with Jack Batten). *Nancy Greene: An Autobiography.* Don Mills: General Publishing, 1968.

Gregorich, Barbara. *Women at Play: The Story of Women in Baseball.* Orlando: Harcourt Brace, 1993.

Gregson, Ian. *Irresistible Force: Disability Sport in Canada.* Victoria: Polestar Books, 1999.

Grescoe, Paul. "I'm Just This Little Kid From Canada." *Canadian Magazine* 19 August 1972: 25–26.

——. "Volleyball is Hell." *Canadian Magazine* 28 April 1978: 12–15.

Griffin, Frederick. "Sport Enhances Womanhood." *Toronto Star Weekly* 10 October 1931: 16.

Griffin, Pat. *Strong Women, Deep Closets: Lesbians and Homophobia in Sport.* Champaign: Human Kinetics, 1998.

Griffin, Scott. "Lawn Tennis." *Athletic Life* June 1895: 241–45.

Guay, Donald. *Introduction à l'histoire des sports au Québec.* Montréal: VLB Éditeur, 1987.

——. *La conquête du sport: Le sport et la société québécoise au XIXe siècle.* Outremont: Lanctôt Éditeur, 1997.

——. *L'Histoire du Hockey au Québec.* Montréal: Les Éditions JCL, 1990.

Gurney, Helen. *A Century to Remember 1893–1993: Women's Sports at the University of Toronto.* Toronto: University of Toronto Women's T-Holders' Association, 1993.

——. *Girls' Sports: A Century of Progress in Ontario High Schools.* Toronto: Ontario Federation of School Athletic Associations, 1982.

Guttmann, Allen. *Women's Sports: A History.* New York: Columbia University Press, 1991.

Gzowski, Peter. "Sports." *Saturday Night* March 1966: 50–51.

——. "Young and Fast." *Maclean's* 17 November 1962: 25–29, 34, 36–38.

Hagen, Monys Ann. "Industrial Harmony Through Sports: The Industrial Recreation Movement and Women's Sports." Diss. University of Wisconsin-Madison, 1990.

Hall, Lucy M. "The Tricycle for Women." *The Chautauquan* October 1890: 90–91.

Hall, M. Ann. "Alexandrine Gibb: In 'No Man's Land of Sport.'" *Freeing the Female Body: Inspirational Icons.* Ed. J.A. Mangan and Fan Hong. London: Frank Cass, 2001. 149–172.

——. "Creators of the Lost and Perfect Game?: Gender, History, and Canadian Sport." *Sport and Gender in Canada.* Ed. Philip White and Kevin Young. Don Mills: Oxford University Press, 1999. 5–23.

——. *Feminism and Sporting Bodies: Essays on Theory and Practice.* Champaign: Human Kinetics, 1996.

——. "Feminist Activism in Sport: A Comparative Study of Women's Sport Advocacy Organizations." *Gender, Sport and Leisure: Continuities and Challenges.* Ed. Alan Tomlinson. University of Brighton: Chelsea School Research Centre, 1995. 217–250.

——. "A History of Women's Sport in Canada Prior to World War I." MA thesis. University of Alberta, 1968.

——. "Sport and Physical Activity in the Lives of Canadian Women." *Canadian Sport: Sociological Perspectives.* Ed. Richard S. Gruneau and John G. Albinson. Don Mills: Addison-Wesley, 1976. 170–99.

Hall, M. Ann, Dallas Cullen, and Trevor Slack. "The Gender Structure of National Sport Organizations." *Sport Canada Occasional Papers* 2.1, December 1990.

——. "Organizational Elites Recreating Themselves: The Gender Structure of National Sport Organizations." *Quest* 41: 28–45 (1989).

Hall, M. Ann, and Dorothy A. Richardson. *Fair Ball: Towards Sex Equality in Canadian Sport.* Ottawa: Canadian Advisory Council on the Status of Women, 1982.

Hall, M. Ann, Trevor Slack, Garry Smith, and David Whitson. *Sport in Canadian Society.* Toronto: McClelland and Stewart, 1991.

Hall, M. Ann and Gertrud Pfister. *Honoring the Legacy: Fifty Years of the International Association of Physical Education and Sport for Girls and Women.* Northhampton, MA: Smith College, 1999.

Halsey, Elizabeth. *Women in Physical Education: Their Role in Work, Home, and History.* New York: G.P. Putnam's Sons, 1961.

Hargreaves, Jennifer. *Heroines of Sport: The Politics of Difference and Identity.* London: Routledge, 2000.

——. *Sporting Females: Critical Issues in the History and Sociology of Women's Sports.* London: Routledge, 1994.

Harmond, Richard. "Progress and Flight: An Interpretation of the American Cycle Craze of the 1890s." *Journal of Social History* 5.2 (1971–72): 235–57.

Harris, Marjorie. "Blotchface!" *Quest: Canada's Urban Magazine* February 1977: Toronto Section, T2–4, 6–9.

Heit, Michael J., and Don Malpass. *Do Women Have Equal Play?* Report prepared for the Sports and Fitness Division, Ontario Ministry of Culture and Recreation, 1975.

Hesketh, Bob. "The Bobby-Soxer Who Beat All the Big Girls." *Chatelaine* November 1951: 26–30.

Hill, Lucille E., ed. *Athletics and Out-door Sports for Women.* New York: Grosset and Dunlap, 1903.

Hilton, Sue. "National Intercollegiate Competition for Women." *Journal of CAHPER* 33.6 (1967): 4.

Himes, Cindy L. "The Female Athlete in American Society: 1860–1940." Diss. University of Pennsylvania, 1986.

Hodgins, Bruce W., and Bernadine Dodge, eds. *Using Wilderness: Essays on the Evolution of Youth Camping in Ontario.* Peterborough, ON: Trent University, 1992.

Hoffman, Abby. "Running for Gold." *Maclean's* February 1975: 31–33.

——. "Super-Jock in Decline: Liberating Sport from Sexist Stereotypes." *Canadian Dimension* August 1971: 41–2. Rpt. in *The New Feminist* January 1972: 7–9.

——. "Towards Equality for Women in Sport ... A Canadian Perspective." *Momentum* 4.2 (1979): 1–15 .

——. "Women's Access to Sport and Physical Activity." *Avante* 1.1 (1995): 77–92.

Hotchkiss, Ron. "'The Matchless Six': Canadian Women at the Olympics, 1928." *The Beaver* 73.5 (1993): 23–42.

Houghton, E.B. *Physical Culture.* Toronto: Warwick and Sons, 1886.

How, Douglas. "Blonde on Blades." *Maclean's Magazine,* 15 February 1947: 16, 45–46.

Howell, Colin D. *Blood, Sweat, and Cheers: Sport and the Making of Modern Canada.* Toronto: University of Toronto Press, 2001.

——. *Northern Sandlots: A Social History of Maritime Baseball.* Toronto: University of Toronto Press, 1995.

Howell, David, and Peter Lindsay. "Social Gospel and the Young Boy Problem." *Canadian Journal of History of Sport* 17.1 (1986): 75–87.

Hoyle, Jennifer, and Philip White. "Physical Activity in the Lives of Women with Disabilities." *Sport and Gender in Canada.* Eds. Philip White and Kevin Young. Don Mills, ON: Oxford University Press. 254–68.

Hughes, Jane. "Get in the Swim." *Maclean's Magazine* 1 August 1945: 18–20, 34–36.

Humber, William. *Diamonds of the North: A Concise History of Baseball in Canada.* Toronto: Oxford, 1995.

Humbert, Louise. "Behind the Smiles." *Action/ CAAWS.ACAFS* Winter 1995: 1–3, 20–21.

Innis, Mary Quayle. *Unfold the Years: A History of the Young Women's Christian Association in Canada.* Toronto: McClelland and Stewart, 1949.

"Integrated Sports: A Question of Fair Play." *Chatelaine* February 1988: 38, 41.

Issajenko, Angella (as told to Martin O'Malley and Karen O'Reilly). *Running Risks.* Toronto: Macmillan, 1990.

Jackson, Dorothy N.R. *A Brief History of Three Schools.* Toronto: University of Toronto, 1953.

Janson, Gilles. *Emparons-nous du sport: Les Canadiens français et le sport au XIXe siècle.* Montréal: Guérin, 1995.

——. "Sport et modernité: *Le Devoir*, 1910–1920." *Le Devoir: Un journal indépendant (1910–1995).* Ed. Robert Comeau and Luc Desrochers. Québec: Presses de l'Université du Québec, 1996. 80–92.

Jason, Patricia. *Wild Things: Nature, Culture, and Tourism in Ontario 1790–1914.* Toronto: University of Toronto Press, 1995.

Jenness, Diamond. *Indians of Canada.* 7th ed. Toronto: University of Toronto Press, 1977.

Johnson, Brian D. "A Woman of Steel." *Maclean's* February 1988: 52–6.

Johnson, Susan E. *When Women Played Hardball.* Seattle: Seal Press, 1994.

Kearney, Jim. *Champions: A British Columbia Sports Album.* Vancouver: Douglas and McIntrye, 1985.

Kenealy, Arabella. *Feminism and Sex Extinction.* London: T. Fisher Unwin, 1920.

——. "Woman As An Athlete." *The Living Age* May 1899: 363–70.

——. "Woman As An Athlete: A Rejoinder." *The Living Age* 24 June 1899: 201–13.

Kendrick, Martyn. *Advantage Canada: A Tennis Centenary.* Toronto: McGraw-Hill Ryerson, 1990.

Kennedy, Abbie Scott. Unpublished diary. 19 June-31 August 1924 (photocopy obtained from Alberta Sports Hall of Fame and Museum).

Kerr, John. *Curling in Canada and the United States: A Record of the Tour of the Scottish Team, 1902–03, and of the Game in the Dominion and the Republic.* Edinburgh: Geo. A. Morton, 1904.

Keyes, Mary E. "The Administration of the Canadian Women's Intercollegiate Athletic Union." *CAHPER Journal* 40.6 (1974): 21–23, 32–33.

——. "Feminist Lobbying and Decision-Making Power in Fitness and Amateur Sport National Policies, Programs and Services: the Case of Canada." *Sport: The Third Millennium.* Ed. Fernand Landry, Marc Landry, and Magdeleine Yerlès. Sainte-Foy, QC: Les Presses de l'Université Laval, 1991. 419–30.

——. "The History of the Women's Athletics Committee of the Canadian Association for Health, Physical Education and Recreation, 1940–1973." Diss. Ohio State University, 1980.

——. "Women's Basketball in Central Canada Revisited 1899–1970." Paper presented at the annual meeting of the North American Society for Sport History, Chicago, Illinois, May 1991.

Kidd, Bruce. "Canada's Opposition to the 1936 Olympics in Germany." *Canadian Journal of History of Sport and Physical Education* 9.2 (1978): 20–40.

——. "Improvers, Feminists, Capitalists and Socialists: Shaping Canadian Sport in the 1920s and 1930s." Diss. York University, 1990.

——. "Making the Pros Pay for Amateur Sports: The Ontario Athletic Commission, 1920–1947." *Ontario History* 87.2 (1995): 105–28.

——. "Missing: Women from Sports Halls of Fame." *Action CAAWS/ACAFS* Winter 1994: 4–5.

——. "Reflections on the 8th Commonwealth Games." *Journal of the Canadian Association for Health, Physical Education, and Recreation* 33.1 (1966) : 11–12.

——. *The Struggle for Canadian Sport.* Toronto: University of Toronto Press, 1996.

Kirby, Sandra. "Gender Equity in the Canadian Sport Council: The New Voice for the Sport Community." *Feminist Success Stories/ Célébrons nos réussites féministes.* Ed. Karen A. Blackford, Marie-Luce Garceau, and Sandra Kirby. Ottawa: University of Ottawa Press, 1999. 57–69.

Kirby, Sandra, and Lorraine Greaves, "Foul Play: Sexual Harassment in Sport." Report to Sport Canada, June 1996.

Kirby, Sandra, Lorraine Greaves, and Olena Hankivsky. *The Dome of Silence: Sexual Harassment and Abuse in Sport.* Halifax: Fernwood, 2000.

Kirsh, Carol, Brian Dixon, and Michael Bond. *A Leisure Study –Canada 1972.* Arts and Culture Branch, Department of Secretary of State, Government of Canada, 1973.

Knoppers, Annelies. "Explaining Male Dominance and Sex Segregation in Coaching: Three Approaches." *Quest* 44 (1992): 210–27.

Knox, Ellen. *The Girl of the New Day.* Toronto: McClelland and Stewart, 1919.

Kremarik, Frances. "A Family Affair: Children's Participation in Sports." *Canadian Social Trends* Autumn 2000: 20–24.

Laberge, Suzanne. "Employment Situation of High Performance Coaches in Canada," *Sport Canada Occasional Papers,* 3.1, March 1992.

Ladies Professional Golf Association. "The Ladies Professional Golf Association: 50 Years of Growth, Tradition and Excellence." <www.lpga.com/history/index.cfm>, 2001.

Lafrance, Mélisse R. "Colonizing the Feminine: Nike's Intersections of Postfeminism and Hyperconsumption." *Sport and Postmodern Times.* Ed. Geneviève Rail. New York: SUNY Press, 1998. 117–139.

Lamb, Arthur S. "Physical Education for Girls." *Proceedings of the Sixty-Second Annual Convention of the Ontario Educational Association.* Toronto: Clarkson W. James, 1923. 285–90.

Lang, Marjory. *Women Who Made the News: Female Journalists in Canada, 1880–1945.* Montreal and Kingston: McGill-Queen's University Press, 1999.

Lathrop, Anna H. "Elegance and Expression, Sweat and Strength: Body Training, Physical Culture and Female Embodiment in Women's Education at the Margaret Eaton Schools (1901–1941)." Diss. University of Toronto, 1997.

——. "Elegance and Expression, Sweat and Strength: A Portrait of the Margaret Eaton Schools (1901–1941) through the Life History of Emma Scott Nasmith, Mary G. Hamilton, and Florence A. Somers." *Vitae Scholasticae* 16.1 (1997): 69–92.

Laubman, Katherine M. "A Historical-Ethnographic Account of a Canadian Woman in Sport, 1920–1938: The Story of Margaret (Bell) Gibson." MA thesis. University of British Columbia, 1991.

Lawrence-Harper, Janis. "Change in a Feminist Organization: The Canadian Association for the Advancement of Women and Sport and Physical Activity 1981–1991." MA thesis. University of Alberta, 1993.

——. "The Herstory of the Canadian Association for the Advancement of Women and Sport." Unpublished document, November 1991.

Lay, Marion, and Ann Hall. "Proposed Women's Program Within the Fitness and Amateur Sport Branch." Unpublished document, July 1974 (Sport Canada File No. 7865–5).

Leigh, Mary H., and Thérèse M. Bonin, "The Pioneering Role of Madame Alice Milliat and the FSFI in Establishing International Track and Field Competition for Women." *Journal of Sport History* 4.1 (1977) : 72–83.

Leiper, Jean M. "J. Percy Page: An Ordinary Coach with Extraordinary Results." Paper presented at the annual meeting of the North American Society for Sport History, Hamilton, Ontario, May 1981.

Lenskyj, Helen. "Combating Homophobia in Sport and Physical Education." *Sociology of Sport Journal* 8.1 (1991): 61–69.

——. *A Discussion Paper: Female Participation in Sport.* Report prepared for CAAWS and Sport Canada Joint Steering Committee, April 1984.

——. "Good Sports: Feminists Organizing on Sport Issues in the 1970s and 1980s." *Resources for Feminist research/Documentation sur la recherche féministe* 20.3/4 (1991): 130–35.

——. *Out of Bounds: Women, Sport and Sexuality.* Toronto: The Women's Press, 1986.

——. "Physical Activity for Canadian Women, 1890–1930: Media Views." *From 'Fair Sex' to Feminism: Sport and the Socialization of Women in the Industrial and Post-industrial Eras.* Ed. J.A. Mangan and Roberta J. Park. London: Frank Cass, 1987. 208–31.

——. "The Role of Physical Education in the Socialization of Girls in Ontario, 1890–1930." Diss. University of Toronto, 1983.

——. "Training for 'True Womanhood': Physical Education for Girls in Ontario Schools, 1890–1920." *Historical Studies in Education* 2.2 (1990): 205–23.

——. "Unsafe at Home Base: Women's Experiences of Sexual Harassment in University Sport and Physical Education." *Women in Sport and Physical Activity Journal* 1.1 (1992): 19–33.

——. "What's Sport Got to Do With It?" *Canadian Woman Studies/les cahiers de la femme* 15.4 (1995): 6–10.

——. *Women, Sport and Physical Activity: Research and Bibliography.* Ottawa: Minister of Supply and Services Canada, 1988.

——. *Women, Sport and Physical Activity: Research and Bibliography.* 2nd ed. Ottawa: Minister of Supply and Services Canada, 1991.

——. *Women, Sport and Physical Activity: Selected Research Themes.* Ottawa: Minister of Supply and Services Canada, 1994.

Leveridge, A.W. (Bill). *Fair Sport: The History of Sport at the Canadian National Exhibition, 1879–1977 Inclusive.* Toronto: Canadian National Exhibition, 1978.

Lévesque, Andrée. *Making and Breaking the Rules: Women in Quebec, 1919–1939.* Trans. Yvonne M. Klein. Toronto: McClelland and Stewart, 1994.

Lewis, Pamela J. "Fitness and Amateur Sport Branch Policies as They Pertain to Women in Sport in Canada from 1974 to 1979." MA thesis. University of Western Ontario, 1980.

Lipsyte, Robert. "The Emasculation of Sports." *New York Times Magazine* 2 April 1995: 51–7.

Ljungqvist, Arne, and Joe Leigh Simpson. "Medical Examination for Health of All Athletes Replacing the need for Gender Verification in International Sports." *Journal of the American Medical Association* 267.6 (12 February 1992): 850–52.

Long, Wendy. *Celebrating Excellence: Canadian Woman Athletes.* Vancouver: Polestar, 1995.

Louie, Siri Winona. "Gender in the Alpine Club of Canada, 1906–1940." MA thesis. University of Calgary, 1996.

Lucas, Shelley. "Nike's Commercial Solution: Girls, Sneakers, and Salvation." *International Review for the Sociology of Sport* 35.2 (2000): 149–64.

Lytle, Andy. "Girls Shouldn't Do It!" *Chatelaine* May 1933: 12–13.

Macdonald, Cathy. "The Edmonton Grads: Canada's Most Successful Team, A History and Analysis of Their Success." MA thesis. University of Windsor, 1976.

Macintosh, Donald, "Inequalities in Sport and Physical Activity Programs in Ontario Schools." *Interchange* 12.1 (1981–82): 61–8.

Macintosh, Donald, and A.J.C. King. *The Role of Interschool Sports Programs in Ontario Secondary Schools.* Toronto: Ministry of Education, 1977.

Macintosh, Donald, with Tom Bedecki and C.E.S. Franks. *Sport and Politics in Canada: Federal Government Involvement Since 1961.* Kingston and Montreal: McGill-Queen's University Press, 1987.

Macintosh, Donald, and David Whitson. *The Game Planners: Transforming Canada's Sport System.* Montreal and Kingston: McGill-Queen's University Press, 1990.

MacKenzie, H.G. "History of Lawn Tennis in Canada." *Athletic Life,* January 1895: 16–21.

MacMurchy, Marjory. "Women and the Nation." *The New Era in Canada.* Ed. J.O. Miller. London: J.M. Dent and Sons, 1917. 211–26.

Macy, Sue. *A Whole New Ball Game: The Story of the All-American Girls Professional Baseball League.* New York: Henry Holt, 1993.

Madden, W.C. *The Women of the All-American Girls Professional Baseball League: A Biographical Dictionary.* Jefferson: McFarland and Company, 1997.

Mallovy, Naomi. "Women in Sports." *Homemaker's Magazine* November 1975: 75–84.

Mangan, J.A. "Discipline in the Dominion: The 'Canuck' and the Cult of Manliness." *The Games Ethic and Imperialism: Aspects of the Diffusion of an Ideal.* New York: Viking, 1986.

Manley, Elizabeth (as told to Elva Clairmont Oglanby). *Thumbs Up!: The Elizabeth Manley Story.* Toronto: Macmillan, 1990.

Marks, Lynne. *Revivals and Roller Rinks: Religion, Leisure, and Identity in Late-Nineteenth-Century Small-Town Ontario.* Toronto: University of Toronto Press, 1996.

Marks, Patricia. *Bicycles, Bangs, and Bloomers: The New Woman in the Popular Press.* Lexington, KY: The University Press of Kentucky, 1990.

Matthews, Jill Julius. "They Had Such a Lot of Fun: The Women's League of Health and Beauty Between the Wars." *History Workshop: A Journal of Socialist and Feminist Historians* 30 (Autumn 1990): 23–54.

Mayor's Task Force on the Status of Women in Toronto Final Report. "A Study of Services and Facilities Offered to the Women of Toronto by the Department of Parks and Recreation." January 1976.

McAllister, Ron. *Swim to Glory: The Story of Marilyn Bell and the Lakeshore Swimming Club.* Toronto: McClelland and Stewart, 1954.

McBryde, John. "The Bipartite Development of Men's and Women's Field Hockey in Canada in the Context of Separate International Hockey Federations." MA thesis. University of British Columbia, 1986.

McCabe, Nora. "Chatelaine's Woman of the Year: Elizabeth Manley." *Chatelaine* January 1989: 39–43, 93.

———. *Laurie Graham.* Don Mills, ON: Fitzhenry and Whiteside, 1990.

McCrone, Kathleen E. *Playing the Game: Sport and the Physical Emancipation of English Women, 1870–1914.* Lexington, KY: The University of Kentucky Press, 1988.

McDonald, David. *For the Record: Canada's Greatest Women Athletes.* Rexdale: John Wiley and Sons, 1981.

McDonald, Marci. "Out of the Rough." *Maclean's* June 1975: 46, 48–50.

McFadden, Fred. *Abby Hoffman.* Don Mills: Fitzhenry and Whiteside, 1978.

McFarland, Elsie M. *The Development of Public Recreation in Canada.* Canadian Parks/Recreation Association, 1970.

McFarlane, Brian. *Proud Past, Bright Future: One Hundred Years of Canadian Women's Hockey.* Toronto: Stoddart, 1994.

McKay, Jim. *Managing Gender: Affirmative Action and Organizational Power in Australian, Canadian, and New Zealand Sport.* Albany, NY: State University of New York Press, 1997.

McKenzie, R. Tait. "Rugby Football in Canada." *The Dominion Illustrated Monthly* 1.1 (1892): 11–19 .

McKillop, A.B. "Marching as to War: Elements of Ontario Undergraduate Culture, 1880–1914." *Youth, University and Canadian Society: Essays in the Social History of Higher Education.* Ed. Paul Axelrod and John G. Reid. Kingston: McGill-Queen's University Press, 1989. 75–93.

McLeod, Bruce. "Ice Ballerina." *Maclean's Magazine* 15 February 1944: 12, 28–30.

McNulty, Bill, and Ted Radcliffe, comp. *Canadian Athletics 1839–1992.* N.p., 1992.

McRae, Earl, and Roy MacGregor. "Executive Sweat: Gentlemen, Players and Other People Who Make Sport." *The Canadian* 29 January 1977: 4–9.

Meade, Cathy. "The Efficacy of Canadian Human Rights Legislation in Dealing with Sex Discrimination and Gender Inequality in Sport." Unpublished document, University of Alberta, September 1993.

Miller, Toby. *Sportsex.* Philadelphia: Temple University Press, 2001.

Mitchell, Elizabeth. "The Rise of Athleticism Among Girls and Women." *Women Workers of Canada: Being a Report of the Proceedings of the Third Annual Meeting and Conference of the National Council of Women of Canada.* Montreal: John Lovell and Sons, 1896.

Mitchell, Sheila L. "The Organizational Development of Women's Competitive Sport in Canada in the 1920s." MA thesis. University of Windsor, 1976.

Mitchinson, Wendy. *The Nature of Their Bodies: Women and Their Doctors in Victorian Canada.* Toronto: University of Toronto Press, 1991.

Moodie, Susanna. *Roughing It In the Bush*. 1853. Toronto: McClelland and Stewart, 1962.

Moore, Cay. *She Skated Into Our Hearts*. Toronto: McClelland and Stewart, 1948.

Moore, Jacqueline. "Why Lucile Wheeler Called It Quits." *Weekend Magazine* 6 December 1958: 20, 23–24.

Morrow, Don. "Canadian Sport History: A Critical Essay." *Journal of Sport History* 10.1 (1983): 67–79.

———. "The Knights of the Snowshoe: A Study of the Evolution of Sport in Nineteenth Century Montreal." *Journal of Sport History* 15.1 (1988): 5–40.

———. *A Sporting Evolution: The Montreal Amateur Athletic Association 1881–1981*. Montreal: Amateur Athletic Association, 1981.

———. "The Strathcona Trust in Ontario, 1911–1939." *Canadian Journal of History of Sport and Physical Education* 8.1 (1977): 72–90.

———. "Sweetheart Sport: Barbara Ann Scott and the Post World War II Image of the Female Athlete in Canada." *Canadian Journal of History of Sport* 18.1 (1987): 36–54.

Morrow, Don, Mary Keyes, Wayne Simpson, Frank Cosentino, and Ron Lappage. *A Concise History of Sport in Canada*. Toronto: Oxford University Press, 1989.

Mortin, Jenni. *Safe at Home: A History of Softball in Saskatchewan*. Regina: Softball Saskatchewan, 1997.

Mott, Morris. "The British Protestant Pioneers and the Establishment of Manly Sports in Manitoba, 1870–1886." *Journal of Sport History* 7.3 (1980): 25–36.

———. "Games and Contests of the First 'Manitobans.'" *Sports in Canada: Historical Readings*. Ed. Morris Mott. Toronto: Copp Clark Pitman, 1989. 18–27.

Mott, Morris, and John Allardyce. *Curling Capital: Winnipeg and the Roarin' Game, 1876 to 1988*. Winnipeg: University of Manitoba Press, 1989.

Munro, Iveagh. "Challenging Years." *A Fair Shake: Autobiographical Essays by McGill Women*. Ed. Margaret Gillett and Kay Sibbald. Montreal: Eden Press, 1984. 321–28.

———. "Dorothy N.R. Jackson: In Memoriam." *Journal of CAHPER* 33.6 (1967): 20–21.

Murray, Heather. "Making the Modern: Twenty-Five Years of the Margaret Eaton School of Literature and Expression." *Essays in Theatre* 10.1 (1991): 39–57.

Myers, Sharon. "'Not to be Ranked as Women': Female Industrial Workers in Turn-of the-Century Halifax." *Separate Spheres: Women's Worlds in the 19th-Century Maritimes*. Ed. Janet Guildford and Suzanne Morton. Fredericton: Acadiensis Press, 1994. 161–83.

Naismith, James. *Basketball: Its Origin and Development*. New York: Association Press, 1941.

Newsham, Gail J. *In A League of Their Own!: The Dick Kerr Ladies' Football Club*. London: Scarlet Press, 1994.

Norcliffe, Glen. *The Ride to Modernity: The Bicycle in Canada, 1869–1900*. Toronto: University of Toronto Press, 2001.

Norton, Wayne. "'Fair Manipulators of the Twisted Hickory': Women's Hockey in Fernie, 1919–1926." *The Forgotten Side of the Border: British Columbia's Elk Valley and Crowsnest Pass*. Ed. Wayne Norton and Naomi Miller. Kamloops: Plateau Press, 1998. 206–16.

O'Connell, Matt. "Mary Rose Thacker." *Maclean's Magazine* 1 March 1940: 24, 26–27.

O'Connor, Joe. "Lightning Striker." *Saturday Night* 18 August 2001: 30–35.

Official Report of Canada's Participation in the 3rd Pan American Games held in Chicago, U.S.A., August 27th to September 7th 1959. Pan American Games Committee of Canada.

Olafson, Pauline. "Sport, Physical Education and the Ideal Girl in Selected Ontario Denominational Schools, 1870–1930." MA thesis. University of Windsor, 1990.

Olenik, Lisa M., Joan M. Matthews, and Robert D. Steadward. "Women, Disability and Sport: Unheard Voices." *Canadian Woman Studies/les cahiers de la femme* 15.4 (1995): 54–57.

Oxendine, Joseph B. *American Indian Sports Heritage.* Champaign: Human Kinetics, 1988.

Pallett, George. *Women's Athletics.* London: The Normal Press, 1955.

Paraschak, Vicky. "An Examination of Sport for Aboriginal Females of the Six Nations Reserve, Ontario from 1968 to 1980." *Women of the First Nations: Power, Wisdom, and Strength.* Ed. Christine Miller and Patricia Chuchryk. Winnipeg: University of Manitoba Press, 1996. 83–96.

——. "Invisible But Not Absent: Aboriginal Women in Sport and Recreation." *Canadian Woman Studies/les cahiers de la femme* 15.4 (1995): 71–2.

——. "Native Sports History: Pitfalls and Promise." *Canadian Journal of History of Sport* 20.1 (1989): 57–64.

——. "Organized Sport for Native Females on the Six Nations Reserve, Ontario from 1968 to 1980: A Comparison of Dominant and Emergent Sport Systems." *Canadian Journal of History of Sport* 21.2 (1990): 70–80.

——. "Variations in Race Relations: Sporting Events for Native Peoples in Canada." *Sociology of Sport Journal* 14.1 (1997): 1–21.

Parkes, A.E. Marie. *The Development of Women's Athletics at the University of Toronto.* Toronto: Women's Athletic Association, University of Toronto, 1961.

Parratt, Catriona M. "About Turns: Reflecting on Sport History in the 1990s." *Sport History Review* 29.1 (1998): 4–17.

Pedersen, Diana. "'Building Today for the Womanhood of Tomorrow': Businessmen, Boosters, and the YWCA, 1890–1930." *Urban History Review* 15.3 (1987): 225–42.

Peredo, Sandra. "They're Canada's Only Ladies' Professional Football Team." *Canadian Magazine* 29 August 1970: 6–7.

Pickens, Hillis R. "Marlene Stewart's Achievement." *Canadian Sport Monthly* July 1953: 5.

——. "A Visit With Our Gals Abroad." *Canadian Sport Monthly* November 1963: 16, 19.

Pieroth, Doris H. *Their Day in the Sun: Women of the 1932 Olympics.* Seattle: University of Washington Press, 1996.

Pierson, Ruth Roach. *Canadian Women and the Second World War.* Ottawa: Canadian Historical Association, 1983.

——. *"They're Still Women After All": The Second World War and Canadian Womanhood.* Toronto: McClelland and Stewart, 1986.

Pitters-Caswell, Marian I. "Woman's Participation in Sporting Activities as an Indicator of Femininity and Cultural Evolution in Toronto, 1910 to 1920." MA thesis. University of Windsor, 1975.

Playter, Edward. "The Physical Culture of Women." *Woman; Her Character, Culture and Calling.* Ed. B.F. Austin. Brantford: The Book and Bible House, 1890. 211–33.

Ponic, Pamela L. "Herstory: The Structuring of the Fitness and Amateur Sport Branch's Women's Program: 1970–1988." MA thesis. University of Windsor, 1994.

Popma, Ann, ed. *The Female Athlete: Proceedings of a National Conference About Women in Sports and Recreation.* Burnaby: Simon Fraser University, 1980.

Porter, McKenzie. "The 'Royal Family' of the Laurentians." *Maclean's Magazine* 8 November 1958: 20, 93–95.

Prentice, Alison, Paula Bourne, Gail Cuthbert Brandt, Beth Light, Wendy Mitchinson, and Noami Black. *Canadian Women: A History.* Toronto: Harcourt Brace Jovanovich, 1988.

Proctor, Frank. *Fox Hunting in Canada and Some Men Who Made It.* Toronto: Macmillan, 1929.

Raine, Norman R. "Girls Invade Track and Diamond." *Maclean's Magazine* 15 August 1925: 12–14.

Ransom, Diane. *Pioneers and Performers.* Saskatchewan: S.n., 1984.

——. "'The Saskatoon Lily': A Biography of Ethel Catherwood." *Saskatchewan History* 41.3 (1988): 81–98.

Re Bannerman v. Ontario Rural Softball Association. The Supreme Court of Ontario Court of Appeal, 1979.

Re Cummings and Ontario Minor Hockey Association. Ontario Human Rights Commission Board of Inquiry, 1978.

Re Forbes and Yarmouth Minor Hockey Association. Decision of the Nova Scotia Human Rights Commission Board of Inquiry, 1978.

Reichwein, PearlAnn. "Beyond the Visionary Mountains: The Alpine Club of Canada and the Canadian National Park Idea, 1906 to 1969." Diss. Carleton University, 1995.

Reid, John E. "Sports and Games in Alberta Prior to 1900." MA thesis. University of Alberta, 1969.

Report of the National Conference on Women and Sport, Toronto, 24–26 May 1974. Ottawa: Fitness and Amateur Sport Branch, 1974.

Report of the Royal Commission on the Status of Women. Ottawa: Information Canada, 1970.

Reynolds, Mark. "The Great Canadian Foot Race." *The Beaver* August/September 2000: 30–31.

Rex, Kay. *No Daughter of Mine: The Women and History of the Canadian Women's Press Club 1904–1971.* Toronto: Cedar Cave Books, 1995.

Rhéaume, Manon (with Chantal Gilbert). *Manon: Alone in Front of the Net.* Toronto: HarperCollins, 1993.

Robertson, Sheila. "In Their Own Voices: Women Coaches Raising a Family." *Canadian Journal for Women in Coaching Online* 1.2 (2000) <www.coach.ca/women/e/journal>.

Robinson, Gladys. "How I Trained for Speed Skating—and Won Title." *Maclean's Magazine* 15 April 1921: 62.

Robinson, Laura. *Crossing the Line: Violence and Sexual Assault in Canada's National Sport.* Toronto: McClelland & Stewart, 1998.

——. "Games Boys Play." *Canadian Forum*. October 1999: 18–21.

——. *She Shoots, She Scores: Canadian Perspectives on Women and Sport*. Toronto: Thompson Educational Publishing , 1997.

Rosenfeld, Bobbie. "Girls are in Sports for Good." *Chatelaine* July 1933: 6–7, 29.

——. "Let's Try Winning Olympics." *Saturday Night* 12 January 1952: 7, 19–20.

Rosenfeld, Bobbie and Jim Coleman, "Slide, Nellie, Slide." *Maclean's Magazine* 15 May 1944: 7, 64–5.

Ross, Mary Lowrey. "Golf Missionary." *Saturday Night* 27 April 1935: 20.

Roxborough, Henry H. *Canada at the Olympics*. Toronto: Ryerson Press, 1963.

——. "Give the Girls a Hand." *Maclean's Magazine* 15 February 1929: 16, 48, 50.

——. *One Hundred-Not Out: The Story of Nineteenth-Century Canadian Sport*. Toronto: Ryerson Press, 1966.

——. "Speed Is Their Game." *Maclean's Magazine* 1 March 1929: 13, 58.

——. "What Happened at Los Angeles?" *Maclean's Magazine* 1 October 1932: 19, 52–54.

Roy, Camille. "La Femme ou Réflexions sur les 'Bloomer Girls.'" *Propos Canadiens*. Québec: Imprimerie de l'action sociale, 1912. 71–81.

Rubinstein, David. "Cycling in the 1890s." *Victorian Studies* 21.1 (1977): 47–71.

Rush, Anita. "The Bicycle Boom of the Gay Nineties: A Reassessment." *Material History Bulletin* 18 (Fall 1983): 1–12.

Sagi, Douglas. "Cheer for the Losers, Men." *Canadian Magazine* 27 January 1973: 27.

Sandland, Tom. *Something About Bicycling in Newfoundland*. St. John's: Tom Sandland, 1983.

Sangster, Joan. "Doing Two Jobs: The Wage-Earning Mother, 1945–1970." *A Diversity of Women: Ontario, 1945–1980*. Ed. Joy Parr. Toronto: University of Toronto Press, 1995. 98–134.

——. "The Softball Solution: Female Workers, Male Managers and the Operation of Paternalism at Westclox, 1923–60." *Labour/Le Travail* 32 (Fall 1993): 167–99.

Schrodt, Barbara. "Canadian Women at the Commonwealth Games: 1930–1974." *CAHPER Journal* 44.4 (1978): 30–37.

——. "Federal Programmes of Physical Recreation and Fitness: The Contributions of Ian Eisenhardt and BC's Pro-Rec." *Canadian Journal of History of Sport* 15.2 (1984): 45–61.

——. "The Seeds of Destruction: Factors in the Dissolution of British Columbia's Pro-Rec Programme." *Proceedings of the 5th Canadian Symposium on the History of Sport and Physical Education*. Toronto: University of Toronto, 1982. 431–37.

——. "Vancouver's Dynastic Domination of Canadian Senior Women's Basketball: 1942 to 1967." *Canadian Journal of History of Sport* 26.2 (1995): 19–32.

Scott, Barbara Ann. *Skate With Me*. Garden City, NJ: Doubleday and Company, 1950.

——. "What It's Like to be a Celebrity." *Maclean's Magazine* 15 January 1951: 6–7, 41–2.

Scott, Lisa, and Richard Scott. "Women Finally Making Sports Card Breakthroughs." *Canadian Sportscard Collector* November 1999: 80.

Shaulis, Dahn. "Pedestriennes: Newsworthy But Controversial Women in Sporting Entertainment." *Journal of Sport History* 26.1 (1999): 30–50.

Simpson, R. Wayne. "The Elite and Sport Club Membership in Toronto, 1827–1881." Diss. University of Alberta, 1987.

Sinclair, Gordon. "Sister Act." *Maclean's Magazine* 15 December 1943: 13, 52–53.

Smith, Amanda. "Back-Page Bylines: Newspapers, Women, and Sport." *Sportcult.* Ed. Randy Martin and Toby Miller. Minneapolis: University of Minnesota Press, 1999. 253–61.

Smith, Cyndi. *Off the Beaten Track: Women Adventurers and Mountaineers in Western Canada.* Canmore, Alberta: Coyote Books, 1989.

Smith, Michael. "Graceful Athleticism or Robust Womanhood: The Sporting Culture of Women in Victorian Nova Scotia, 1870–1914." *Journal of Canadian Studies* 23.1/2 (1988): 120–37.

Smith, Robert A. *A Social History of the Bicycle.* New York: American Heritage Press, 1972.

Somers, Florence A. "Ideals for Girls' Athletics." *Bulletin of the Canadian Physical Education Association* 3.9 (1936): 9–10.

——. *Principles of Women's Athletics.* New York: A.S. Barnes and Company, 1930.

Sopinka, John. *Can I Play,* Report of the Task Force on Equal Opportunity in Athletics. Vol. 1 and 2. Toronto: Task Force on Equal Opportunity in Athletics, 1983, 1984.

Spencer, Nancy E. "Reading Between the Lines: A Discursive Analysis of the Billie Jean King vs. Bobby Riggs 'Battle of the Sexes.'" *Sociology of Sport Journal* 17.4 (2000): 386–402.

Sport Canada, *Sport Participation in Canada: 1998 Report.* Minister of Public Works and Government Services Canada, 2000.

Sport Canada, "Sport Gender Snap Shot 1997–1998: Survey Results Report," May 1999 <www.pch.gc.ca/sportcanada/SC_E/snapshot.htm>, 2001.

Sport Canada Women's Program. *Women in Sport Leadership: An Issue for Sport.* 1988.

Stack, Prunella. *Zest for Life: Mary Bagot Stack and the League of Health and Beauty.* London: Peter Owen, 1988.

Steadward, Robert, and Cynthia Peterson. *Paralympics: Where Heroes Come.* Edmonton: Alberta Northern Lights Wheelchair Basketball Society, 1997.

Steed, Judy. "The New Amazons." *The Canadian* 28 October 1978: 5–9.

Stell, Marion K. *Half the Race: A History of Australian Women in Sport.* Sydney: Angus and Robertson, 1991.

Stevens, Julie A. "The Development of Women's Hockey: An Explanation of Structure and Change within the Canadian Hockey System." MA thesis. Queen's University, 1992.

Stevenson, John. A. *Curling in Ontario 1846–1946.* Toronto: Ontario Curling Association, 1950.

Stewart, V.L. ("Pinky"). "Western Sport Arrives." *Maclean's Magazine* 15 July 1931: 14, 48.

Strathcona Trust, *Syllabus of Physical Exercises for Schools.* Toronto: Copp, Clark, 1911.

Strange, Carolyn. *Toronto's Girl Problem: The Perils and Pleasures of the City, 1880–1930.* Toronto: University of Toronto Press, 1995.

Stubbs, Lewis St. George. *Shoestring Glory: A Prairie History of Semi-Pro Ball.* Winnipeg: Turnstone Press, 1996.

Swain, Sue. "History of the Ontario Women's Intercollegiate Athletic Association (OWIAA)." *CAHPER Journal* 49.2 (1982): 26–28.

Swan, Susan. "Barbara Ann—Are You Still Happy?" *Chatelaine* November 1975: 51, 74–86.

Task Force on Gender Equity. Final Report to the Council of the Department of Athletics and Recreation, University of Toronto, December 31, 1993.

Teitel, Jay. "Shorter, Slower, Weaker." *Saturday Night* July/August 1997: 61–63.

Theberge, Nancy. "The Construction of Gender in Sport: Women, Coaching, and the Naturalization of Difference." *Social Problems* 40.3 (1993): 401–13.

———. "Feminism and Sport: Linking the Two Through A New Organization." *Canadian Woman Studies/les cahiers de la femme* 4.3 (1983): 79–81.

———. *Higher Goals: Women's Ice Hockey and the Politics of Gender*. Albany: State University of New York Press, 2000.

———. "Playing With the Boys: Manon Rhéaume, Women's Hockey and the Struggle for Legitimacy." *Canadian Woman Studies/les cahiers de la femme* 15.4 (1995): 37–41.

Thomas, Laura M., "Local and Global Mermaids: The Politics of 'Pretty Swimming.'" MA thesis. University of British Columbia, 2001.

Thompson, Shona M. *Mother's Taxi: Sport and Women's Labor*. Albany, NY: State University of New York Press, 1999.

Tillotson, Shirley. *The Public at Play: Gender and the Politics of Recreation in Post-War Ontario*. Toronto: University of Toronto Press, 2000.

Todd, Jan. *Physical Culture and the Body Beautiful: Purposive Exercise in the Lives of American Women 1800–1875*. Macon, GA: Mercer University Press, 1998.

Towards Gender Equity for Women in Sport: A Handbook for National Sport Organizations. Ottawa: Canadian Association for the Advancement of Women and Sport and Physical Activity, 1993.

Tricard, Louise Mead. *American Women's Track and Field: A History, 1895 through 1980*. Jefferson: McFarland and Company, 1996.

Trilling, Blanche M. "The Playtime of a Million Girls or an Olympic Victory—Which?" *The Nation's Schools* 4.2 (1929): 51–54.

Tunis, John. R. "Women and the Sport Business" *Harper's Monthly Magazine* July 1929: 211–21.

Vail, Sue. "What the Federal Government Is Doing to Promote Women's Sport." *Canadian Woman Studies/les cahiers de la femme* 4.3 (1983): 75–76.

Verbrugge, Martha H. "Recreating the Body: Women's Physical Education and the Science of Sex Differences in America, 1900–1940." *Bulletin of the History of Medicine* 71.2 (1997): 273–304.

Vertinsky, Patricia A. *The Eternally Wounded Woman: Women, Exercise and Doctors in the Late Nineteenth Century*. Manchester: Manchester University Press, 1990.

———. "Gender Relations, Women's History and Sport History: A Decade of Changing Inquiry, 1983–1993." *Journal of Sport History* 21.1 (1994): 1–25.

———. "Physical Activity, Sport and Health for Girls and Women: Issues and Perspectives." *Bulletin of the International Association of Physical Education and Sport for Girls and Women* 7.1 (1997): 1–15.

Vickers, Jill. "The Intellectual Origins of the Women's Movement in Canada." *Challenging Times: The Women's Movement in Canada and the United States*. Ed.

Constance Backhouse and David H. Flaherty. Montreal and Kingston: McGill-Queen's University Press, 1992. 39–60.

Vickers, Joan N., and Barbara J. Gosling, *The Changing Participation of Men and Women in the Canadian Interuniversity Athletic Union (1978–1982)*. Report prepared for the Women's Representative Committee of the Canadian Interuniversity Athletic Union, 1984.

Vines, Gail. "Last Olympics for the Sex Test?" *New Scientist* 4 July 1992: 39–42.

Wackwitz, Laura A. "Sex Testing In International Women's Athletics: A History of Silence." *Women and Sport and Physical Activity Journal* 5.1 (1996): 51–68.

Walton, Yvette M. "The Life and Professional Contributions of Ethel Mary Cartwright, 1880–1955." MA thesis. University of Western Ontario, 1976.

Wamsley, Kevin B. "Power and Privilege in Historiography: Constructing Percy Page." *Sport History Review* 28.2 (1997): 146–55.

Warren, Bob. "Industrial Recreation Canadian Style." *Recreation* December 1944: 483, 500–01.

Watkinson, E. Jane, and Karen Calzonetti. "Physical Activity Patterns of Physically Disabled Women in Canada." *CAHPER Journal* 55.6 (1989): 21–26.

Watts, Heather. *Silent Steeds: Cycling in Nova Scotia to 1900*. Halifax: Nova Scotia Museum, 1985.

Webb, Margaret. "2nd to None." *Saturday Night* 4 August 2001: 19–23.

Webster, F.A.M. *Athletics of Today for Women: History, Development and Training*. London: Frederick Warne, 1930.

Wenn, Stephen R. "Give Me the Keys Please: Avery Brundage, Canadian Journalists, and the Barbara Ann Scott Phaeton Affair." *Journal of Sport History* 18.2 (1991): 241–54.

Wennerberg, Conrad. *Wind, Waves, and Sunburn: A Brief History of Marathon Swimming*. New York: Breakaway Books, 1997.

Wetherell, Donald G., with Irene Kmet. *Useful Pleasures: The Shaping of Leisure in Alberta 1896–1945*. Regina: Canadian Plains Research Center, 1990.

Whipp, Charles, and Edward Phelps. *Petrolia 1866–1966*. Petrolia: Advertiser-Topic and the Petrolia Centennial Committee, 1966.

Whitson, David, and Donald Macintosh. "Equity vs. High Performance Canadian Amateur Sport: Policy Tensions." *CAHPER Journal* (May/June 1990): 27–30.

———. "Gender and Power: Explanations of Gender Inequalities in Canadian National Sport Organizations." *International Review for the Sociology of Sport* 24.2 (1989): 137–50.

Whorton, James C. "The Hygiene of the Wheel: An Episode in Victorian Sanitary Science." *Bulletin of the History of Medicine* 52.1 (1978): 61–88.

Williamson, Catherine. "Swimming Pools, Movie Stars: The Celebrity Body in the Post-War Marketplace." *camera obscura* 38 (May 1996): 4–29.

Wilson, Lionel. "The Brainwash That Sold Us On the Sport of Slobs." *Maclean's* October 1970: 13.

Wilson, Renate. "What Turns Women to Lesbianism?" *Chatelaine* October 1966: 33, 130–34.

Wise, S.F., and Douglas Fisher, *Canada's Sporting Heroes*. Don Mills: General Publishing, 1974.

Women and Sport: Policy and Frameworks for Action. London: The Sports Council, 1993.

"Women in Rowing." Special issue of *Catch*, Summer 1984 (Canadian Amateur Rowing Association publication).

Woollacott, Arthur P. "BC Gymnastic Movement May Sweep All Canada." *Saturday Night* 26 (August 1939): 13, 20.

Wuorio, Eva-Lis, "Backstage With Barbara Ann." *Maclean's Magazine* 15 February 1949: 12–13, 48–49.

Young, A.J. "Sandy." *Beyond Heroes: A Sport History of Nova Scotia.* Vol. 1 and 2. Hantsport, NS: Lancelot Press, 1988.

Young, David. *The Golden Age of Canadian Figure Skating.* Toronto: Summerhill Press, 1984.

Zerba, Louise. "The 1930 University of British Columbia Women's Basketball Team: Those Other World Champions." *Her Story in Sport: A Historical Anthology of Women in Sports.* Ed. Reet Howell. West Point: Leisure Press, 1982. 548–51.

Zeman, Brenda. *88 Years of Puck Chasing in Saskatchewan.* Regina: WDS Associates and the Saskatchewan Sports Hall of Fame, 1983.

———. *To Run With Longboat: Twelve Stories of Indian Athletes in Canada.* Edmonton: GMS² Ventures, 1988.

Zeman, Gary W. *Alberta on Ice: The History of Hockey in Alberta Since 1893.* Edmonton: Westweb Press, 1985.

Newspapers

Calgary Herald

Edmonton *Bulletin*

Edmonton Journal

Halifax Herald

Halifax Mail

La Presse

Montreal *Gazette*

Montreal Daily Herald

Montreal Star

Ottawa Citizen

Toronto *Globe* (*Globe and Mail* after 1936)

Toronto Star

Toronto *Telegram*

Toronto World

Vancouver *Province*

Vancouver Sun

Winnipeg Free Press

Winnipeg Tribune

MAGAZINES

Athletic Life
Canadian Home Journal
Canadian Magazine
Canadian Sport Monthly
Champion
Chatelaine
Maclean's (*Maclean's Magazine* before 1930; *Maclean's Magazine* until 1961)
Saturday Night
Toronto Star Weekly
Weekend Magazine

MANUSCRIPT COLLECTIONS

Archives of Ontario
       John Fisher
       Young Women's Christian Association
City of Edmonton Archives
       Edmonton Grads
National Archives of Canada
       Lela Brooks
       Canadian Ladies Curling Association
       Canadian Ladies Golf Association
       Major John W. "Jack" Davies
       Fred G. "Ted" Oke
       Royal Caledonian Curling Club
Provincial Archives of Alberta
       Edmonton Grads
Toronto Harbour Commission Archives (now Toronto Port Authority Archives)
       Sunnyside Softball Leagues

INDEX

aboriginal. *See* native women in sports
Adams, Lynda, 83, 86
African-Canadian women in sports, 11–12, 85–86, 113, 184–85, 208, 214. *See also* race and ethnicity
  first woman of colour in international competition, 85–86
  first woman of colour on International Olympic Committee, 208
All-American Girls Professional Baseball League, 94, 124–25
Allen, Janet, 50
Allen, Roseann, 153–54
Amateur Athletic Union of Canada (AAU of C), 42–43, 47–48, 133
amateurism, 95, 105, 129, 184
archery, 7, 158
Archibald, Joan and Nancy, 85
associations. *See* control of sports by women; names of associations; names of sports
athletic facilities and gymnasiums. *See also* names of sports
  early history, 28–33
Atkins, Roxy, 90, 93, 102
Austin, Patricia, 140

badminton
  history of, 21, 44–45, 102–3, 109, 112, 119, 163
  media coverage, 111, 151, 153
Bailey, Angela, 184
Baker, Mary "Bonnie," 125

Bannerman v. Ontario Rural Softball Association, 177
Barber, Sara, 117
Barre, Alexandra, 186
baseball. *See also* softball
  All-American Girls Professional Baseball League, 94, 124–25
  history of, 7, 21, 25, 37–39, 146
  organizations, 41, 43, 49
  softball and, 39, 61–62
basketball. *See also* "Grads" (Edmonton Commercial Graduates) basketball team; Page, J. Percy
  in 1930s and before, 3, 28–29, 32–33, 35–36, 41–45, 54–57, 72, 76–77
  in 1940s and 1950s, 102–3, 112–13, 127–28, 134
  in 1960s and 1970s, 139–41, 155
  in 1980s and after, 176, 194–95, 203
  femininity and athleticism, 109–10, 155
  first women's championship, 41–42
  first women's intercollegiate match, 54
  first women's team, 30–31
  first women's world title, 55
  funding and sponsorships, 95, 128, 139, 155
  intercollegiate, 54, 56, 155, 195
  media coverage, 112–13, 141, 153, 194–95
  Olympics, 81, 98
  organizations, 43–44, 50, 98, 127–28, 141, 176, 194
  professional, 194

  regions and regionalism, 36, 50, 98, 127–28, 141, 155
  rules problem, 55–56, 77, 81, 98, 128, 134, 139–40, 155
  sex discrimination legal challenges, 203
  social class, 43, 90
  sportswear and uniforms, 41–42, 57
  Vancouver Eilers, 127–28, 155
Baxter, Betty, 176, 199
Bazso, Debbie, 177–78
Bean, Gladys, 134
Beaver, Bev, 154
Bédard, Myriam, 197–98, 213
Bedingfield, Wendy, 176
Bell, Jane, 52–53, 82
Bell, Margaret, 85, 90
Bell, Marilyn, 111–12, 114–16, 141, 213
Benjamin, Martha, 153
Benoit, Denise and Francine, 108
Bernier, Sylvie, 186
Bertram, Louise, 83
bicycles. *See* cycling
Bill C-131, Fitness and Amateur Sport Act, 138–39, 166
biological determinism, 75–76
biological differences and sport. *See* medical discourse
Bishop, Carole, 159
Bishop Strachan School, Toronto, 28–29
Black athletes. *See* African-Canadian women in sports
Blainey-Broker, Justine, 180–83, 203
Blatchford, Christie, 145–46, 168
bloomers, 15, 17, 19, 35

Bodogh, Marilyn and Christine, 213
body-building, 2
Bomberry, Phyllis, 154
Borsholt, Lisa, 184
Boulton, Shirley, 13, 103
Bourassa, Jocelyne, 149–51
bowling, 44–45, 163
boxing, 42–43
Boylen, Christilot, 186
Boys, Bev, 149–51
Bradshaw, Marjorie, 132
Brill, Debbie, 135, 147, 183
British Empire Games, 80–83, 85–87, 93, 113, 129, 158, 215. See also Commonwealth Games
Brookshaw, Dorothy, 85
Brooks (Potter), Lela, 67, 81
Brown, May, 134
Bryans, Helen, 74–76
Burka, Petra, 135
Burnham, Faye, 125
Burtini, Silvana, 193
business sponsorships. See company and corporate sponsorships; names of sports
Butler, Lois, 83–84

Caley, Dorothy and Hazel, 106, 108
Callow, Eleanor "Squirt," 124
Cameron, Hilda, 85
Cameron, Michelle, 186
Campagnola, Iona, 167–68
Campbell, Florence, 39
Campbell, Mary, 81
camping, 27
Canada Games, 138
Canadian Advisory Council on the Status of Women, 165
Canadian Association for Health, Physical Education and Recreation (CAHPER), 139–40. See also Women's Athletic Committee of the Canadian Physical Education Association (WAC)
Canadian Association for the Advancement of Women and Sport and Physical Activity (CAAWS), 172–77, 181, 204–5, 212
Canadian Interuniversity Athletic Union (CIAU), 141, 164

Canadian Olympic Committee, 51–52
Canadian Women's Intercollegiate Athletic Union (CWIAU), 140–41
canoeing and canoe-tripping, 5–7, 9, 27
Cartwright, Ethel Mary, 33–34, 54, 71–72
Cartwright, Katherine "Cookie," 156–57
Catherwood, Ethel, 51–53, 57, 81–82, 147
Catherwood, Genevra "Ginger," 57
Chadwick, Florence, 115–16
Chalmers, Angela, 214
Chanier, Edwina, 83–84
character-building and sport in 1920s, views on, 72
early private schools, 28–33
Charter of Rights and Freedoms, 180–81
Clark, Ann, 85, 87, 133, 213
Clark, Ruth, 54
Clarke, Heather, Tina and Suzanne, 200
Clarke, Venolyn, 202
Cliff, Leslie, 135, 151
climbing, 21, 26–27, 72
Alpine Club of Canada, 26–27
first woman to climb Mt. Robson, 27
clubs. See control of sports by women; names of clubs; names of sports
CNE swimming marathons, 65–66, 93, 115, 120–21
coaching
coaching programs, 169, 172, 176, 209
gender equality and equity, 78, 169, 209–10
Cochu, Francine, 157
Cole, Betty Stanhope, 114
colleges. See intercollegiate sports; universities and colleges
commercialization and commodification. See also Bell, Marilyn; industrial leagues and recreation; names of sports; Scott, Barbara Ann
first woman athlete as commodity, 109

marketing women's sports, 196–202
team sports, 190–95
Commonwealth Games, 138, 142, 153, 183–84. See also British Empire Games
company and corporate sponsorships, 44–45, 93–95, 205. See also industrial leagues and recreation; names of sports
Conacher, Grace, 47
control of sports by women. See also Canadian Association for the Advancement of Women and Sport and Physical Activity (CAAWS); gender equality and equity; names of sports; Sport Canada; Women's Amateur Athletic Federation of Canada (WAAF of C)
first all-women's multi-sports club in Canada, 45
first sport controlled by women: golf, 39
first women's organization: ice hockey, 58
history, before WWII, 3, 42–44, 63–64, 71–72, 77
history, after WWII, 3, 132–34, 137, 140–41, 166–72, 186–87
male hegemony, 1–2, 14
national survey of sport leadership, 169
organizations, 49, 73–74, 208
ratio male/female in amateur sport system, 208–9
Coo, Lillian "Jimmy," 13, 100
Cook (McGowan), Myrtle, 13, 47, 52–53, 77–78, 82–83, 91, 96–97, 101, 113, 119, 144–45, 161, 213
corporate sponsorships. See company and corporate sponsorships; names of sports
Corsiglia, Robin, 184
Corson, Marilyn, 135
Coughlan, Angela, 135
Court, Joyce, 116
Craig, Betty, 186
Crawford, Judy, 151
cricket, 5, 7, 21, 25, 29
Crooks, Charmaine, 104, 208
croquet, 15, 41
cross-country skiing. See skiing, cross-country

Crutchfield, Linda, 144
Cummings and Ontario Minor Hockey Association (Gail Cummings), 178–79
curling, 7, 23–25, 43, 119, 163, 212–13
  first curling bonspiels in Western Canada, 24
  first women's curling club, 23
  Montreal Ladies' Curling Club, 23
Cuthbert, Linda, 184
cycling
  emancipation and, 10, 15–21
  first "lady cyclist," 16
  first two-wheeler bicycles, 15–16
  medical attitudes, 18–19, 207
  Olympics, 208
  organizations and participation, 163–64, 171

Dafoe, Frances, 112
Daigle, Sylvie, 186
Dalhousie University, 32
dance, 5, 33, 35, 44, 72, 99
Darling, Judy, 114
darts, 102–3
Davidson, Mabel, 24
Davidson, Melody, 209
Dawes, Eva, 52, 82, 84–85
Dearnley, Audrey, 82
Depression and women's sports, 82–83, 87, 93–95, 99, 122
Dewar, Phyllis, 83, 85–86
Didrikson Zaharias, Mildred "Babe," 82, 89–90, 148
dieting, 150, 207
Dill, Jennie, 66
disabilities and sport, 11–12, 174, 207–8, 214–15
diving
  first diving gold medal in British Empire Games (Commonwealth Games), 80
  history of, 34, 72, 80–82, 86, 90, 112, 117, 130, 150–51, 186
  Olympics and British Empire Games, 80–83, 86, 150
Doan, Catriona Le May, 213
Dokka, Karen, 144
Dolson, Jeanette, 85–86
Donatelli, Eden, 186
drug use and testing, 184–85, 201–2

Duthie, Carol Anne, 112

Eaton's sports sponsorships, 44
Ederle, Gertrude, 64
Edmonton Commercial Graduates ("Grads") basketball team. *See* "Grads" (Edmonton Commercial Graduates) basketball team; Page, J. Percy
educational institutions. *See* names of schools; physical education; universities and colleges
Empire Games. *See* British Empire Games
equality. *See* gender equality and equity
equestrian sports, 5, 8, 15, 21, 26, 44, 72, 103, 186, 211
ethnicity. *See* race and ethnicity
eugenics, 69–70
extreme sports, 211

family. *See* heterosexual marriage, family and sports
FAS. *See* Fitness and Amateur Sport Branch (FAS); Women's Program, Fitness and Amateur Sport Branch (FAS)
federal government. *See* government and sports
Fédération sportive féminine internationale (FSFI), 47, 51–53, 55, 57, 80–81, 83, 93, 142
female reproduction. *See* medical discourse
femininity, beauty and athleticism. *See also* heterosexual marriage, family and sports; names of sports; Scott, Barbara Ann
  in 1920s and before, 6, 20–21, 62–69, 71–72
  in 1930s and 1940s, 73, 88–93, 104–6, 125–26, 129–32
  femininity and athleticism, 88–93, 207
  gender roles, 62–64, 109–11, 157, 165
  golf, 148–50
  media coverage, 88–89, 129–30, 146–48, 157
  in post-WWII, 3, 109–13
  sexually explicit descriptions, 146–48, 196–98

womanliness as Victorian ideal, 25–26, 42, 64
feminism, second-wave
  1960s and 1970s, 3–4, 11, 151, 162
  1980s and 1990s, 172–77
fencing
  history of, 31–32, 42–44, 141
  Olympics, 80–81, 85
field days. *See* sports and play days
field hockey, 21, 32, 72, 112–13, 153
figure skating. *See also* Scott, Barbara Ann
  femininity, beauty and sexualization, 21, 103–6, 109, 130, 197
  first commodification of a Canadian woman athlete, 109
  first French-Canadian junior singles champion, 105
  first Olympic Canadian woman competitor, 67–68
  first Olympic singles gold medal, 104–5
  first pairs figure skaters, 68
  first world champion singles figure skater, 104–5
  first world figure skating medal, 68
  history of, 7–8, 24, 67–68, 83, 103–9, 112, 141, 151, 184, 197, 212
  media and marketing, 197, 212
  Olympics, 67–68, 81, 84, 104, 184
  pairs, male/female and female, 68, 107–8
  professional companies, 107–9, 111, 184, 187
  social class, 24, 90, 106, 109, 112
First Nations. *See* native women in sports
firsts for Canadian sport. *See* names of sports
Firth, Sharon and Shirley, 153–54, 186, 214
Fisher, Lenore, 117
Fitness and Amateur Sport Act (Bill C-131), 138–39, 166
Fitness and Amateur Sport Branch (FAS), 165–68, 174, 204. *See also* Women's Program, Fitness and Amateur Sport (FAS)

fitness and exercise
Fitness Canada, 168
  history of, 29–30, 98–100,
    134, 163, 205–6, 211
Fizzell, Mildred, 82
football, 10, 21, 157, 164, 195
*Forbes and Yarmouth Minor
  Hockey Association,* 177
French-Canadian sports
  figure skating, 105, 108
  first French-Canadian junior
    singles figure skating
    Canadian champion, 105
  history of, 5, 53, 66, 70, 92,
    134, 179–80
  ice hockey, 37, 60
  La Palestre Nationale, 70
  snowshoeing, 9, 24–25, 66, 92
Frizzell, Mary, 82, 85
FSFI. *See* Fédération sportive
  féminine internationale (FSFI)
funding. *See* company and
  corporate sponsorships;
  government and sports
Fung, Lori, 186

Garapick, Nancy, 142–43, 201
gender and gender roles. *See*
  control of sports by women;
  femininity, beauty and
  athleticism; gender equality
  and equity
gender equality and equity. *See
  also* Canadian Association for
  the Advancement of Women
  and Sport and Physical Activity
  (CAAWS); control of sports by
  women; sex discrimination in
  recreation and sports
  amateur sports system, 206,
    208–10
  definitions, 203
  millennium-end lists, 212–15
  University of Toronto report,
    203–4
George, Gene, 125
Gerace, Diane, 147
Gibb, Alexandrine
  athlete and administrator, 43,
    48, 53, 55, 82, 88, 90, 213
  sports advocate, 78, 81–82,
    86–88
  sportswriter, 12–13, 45, 63, 78,
    83–84, 88, 91–92, 97, 100, 161
Gibson, Cheryl, 184

Gilfoy, Doris, 66
Golden, Thelma, 125
golf
  Canadian Ladies Golf Union
    (CLGU), 39–40, 43, 63, 101
  company sponsorships and
    professionalism, 44, 102–3,
    136, 148–50, 198–99
  first golf tournament, 22
  first national golf
    championship, 22
  first outstanding woman
    golfer, 22
  first sport where women
    sought control, 39
  first televised women's
    tournament, 148
  first woman to play on LPGA
    Tour, 148
  first women's clubs, 22
  gender issues, 111, 119, 148–50,
    198–99
  history, before WWI, 7, 15,
    21–23, 29
  history, after WWI, 39–40,
    43, 63, 101, 111–14, 119, 136,
    148–51, 198–99
  Ladies Professional Golf
    Association (LPGA),
    148–50, 198–99
  media, 111–12, 148, 151, 198
  organizations, 22, 39–40, 43,
    63, 101, 148–50, 198–99
  social class, 43, 90, 112
Gordon, Alison, 146
Gordon (Olafsson), Shirley, 214–15
government and sports. *See also*
  human rights commissions;
  Sport Canada; Women's
  Program, Fitness and Amateur
  Sport Branch (FAS)
  in 1930s and 1940s, 99–100, 102
  in 1960s and 1970s, 136–39, 153
  in 1980s and 1990s, 162–68,
    173–77
  first national survey of leisure
    activities, 163–64
  Fitness and Amateur Sport Act
    (Bill C-131), 138–39, 166
  Fitness and Amateur Sport
    Branch (FAS), 165–68, 174,
    204
  funding, 87, 173, 176–77,
    186–87, 202–3
  Olympics, 82–83

Royal Commission on the
    Status of Women, 162, 166,
    168
"Grads" (Edmonton Commercial
  Graduates) basketball team. *See
  also* Page, J. Percy
  feminine athleticism, 42, 91, 155
  first women's basketball
    championship, 41–42
  first women's world
    basketball title, 55
  history of, 36–37, 54–57, 81,
    85, 97–98, 100, 213
Graham, Laurie, 185
Grant, Kae Otten, 119
Grant, Virginia, 117
grass hockey. *See* field hockey
Greene, Elizabeth, 143–44
Greene (Raine), Nancy, 135, 139,
  143–44, 148, 213
Grénier, Cecile, 134
Griffin, Audrey, 65
Griffiths, Phyllis, 12–13, 45, 94,
  100–101, 161, 213
Groothuysen, Joan, 186
Grosse (O'Neill), Rosa, 47–48, 91
ground hockey. *See* field hockey
Guay, Lucy, 186
Gurney, Helen, 134, 140, 213
Gurr, Donna-Marie, 135, 151
Gwynne-Timothy, Susan, 200
gymnasiums and sports facilities.
  See names of sports
gymnastics
  history of, 28, 33, 42–44, 109,
    112, 130, 134, 141, 186
  Olympics, 184
  Pro-Rec physical recreation,
    99–100
  Swedish, 28, 30, 99, 134

Halifax Ladies College, 32–33, 46
handball, 42–43
Harvey, Florence, 39–40
Harvey, Gail, 114
Haslam, Phyllis, 83
Havergal College, 28
Hedin, Edith, 65
hegemony, male, 1–2, 14
Heggtveit, Anne, 111–12, 119, 135,
  141, 144
Herriott, Jessie, 74–75, 77
heterosexual marriage, family
  and sports. *See also* medical
  discourse

combining family and sports,
90–91, 119–23, 170–71,
198–99, 209–10, 215
femininity and, 90–92,
109–14, 119–23
fitness and health, 19–20,
206–7
rules about married athletes,
90–91
Hewson, Joanne, 119
Higgins, Robina, 86
Hitchens, Gayle, 114
hockey. See field hockey; ice
hockey
Hodgkins, Anne, 77
Hoffman, Abby, 127, 135,
142–43, 151–52, 157, 161,
167–68, 171, 206
Holland, Janet, 119
Holland, Nancy, 119, 144
Holloway, Sue, 186–87
homophobia, 175, 199–200. See
also lesbians and lesbianism
Hooper, Charmaine, 193
Horn-Miller, Waneek, 197, 208,
214
Howard, Barbara, 85–86, 113, 214
Hudson's Bay Company, 44
Hughes, Clara, 247n20
Hughes-Hallett, Kathleen, 85
human rights commissions. See
also government and sports
government and
organizational support,
163–64, 175
sport-related sex
discrimination cases,
177–81, 192–93, 202–3
Humble, Florence, 83
Hunt, Helen Stewart, 117–18,
141–42, 151–53
hunting, 7–8
Hutton, Margaret, 83
Hyde, Ernest, 36

ice hockey
before WWI, 7–8, 21, 31–32,
37
in 1920s and 1930s, 3, 42, 45,
57–59, 96–97, 127
in 1940s and 1950s, 3, 127
in 1960s, 1970s, and 1980s,
153, 155–57, 177–82
in 1990s and beyond, 195,
199–200, 202–3

equipment and sportswear,
58, 97, 155, 157
femininity and athleticism,
72, 109–10, 112–13, 156
first women's hockey
association, 57
first women's hockey game
played in Montreal, 37
first women's hockey
tournament, 155
first women's ice hockey
teams, 37
funding, 95, 97
industrial sponsorships and
commercialism, 45, 57–59,
102–3, 127
intercollegiate competitions,
57, 127, 156
media coverage, 109–10,
112–13, 153, 155, 195
Olympics, 157, 182
organizations and teams, 32,
37, 43, 49, 58–59, 96–97, 195
Preston Rivulettes, 97
professional, 190–91
regions and regionalism, 37,
50, 57–58, 96–97, 127,
155–57
ringette and, 156
rules, 58–59, 181–82
sex discrimination legal
challenges, 178–82, 202–3
social class, 43, 57–58, 90
ice skating. See figure skating;
speed skating
Indian-club exercises, 29–31, 33,
35, 54
industrial leagues and recreation,
44–45, 78–79, 102–3. See also
names of sports
intercollegiate sports, 32–33,
140–41, 164. See also names of
sports; universities and colleges
International Amateur Athletic
Federation (IAAF), 47, 51, 53,
80, 158
International Association of
Physical Education and Sport
for Girls and Women
(IAPESGW), 134
international competitions. See
also British Empire Games;
Commonwealth Games;
Fédération sportive féminine
internationale (FSFI);

Olympics; Pan-American
Games; Paralympics
first women to travel to
another country to compete
in organized sport, 22
Ionesco, Carmen, 183
Issajenko, Angella Taylor, 184,
201

Jackson, Dorothy, 98, 133–34
Jackson, Patricia, 170
Jelinek, Marie, 112
Johnson, Dorothy and Daisy,
41–42
Jones (Konihowski), Diane, 148,
183
journalists. See sportswriters
judo
first woman's judo black belt,
157

Kane, Lorie, 198–99
kayaking, 158, 186–87
Kenealy, Arabella, 69
Kerr, Barbara Simpson, 151
Kidd, Bruce, 84, 179, 203
Killingback, Molly, 184
King, Billie Jean, 166, 172–73
King, Vivian, 116
Klimpel, Carol, 184
Knox, Ellen, 28
Konihowski, Diane Jones, 148, 183
Kreiner, Kathy, 186
Kruger, Carlyn, 119

"la belle neige," 92
lacrosse, 4–7, 21, 72, 156, 179
Ladies Professional Golf
Association (LPGA), 148–49,
198–99
Lamb, Dr. Arthur S., 51, 53, 61,
63–64, 70–71, 74, 80
Langlais, Monique, 119
Lapensée, Albertine, 57
Laumann, Daniele, 186
Laumann, Silken, 186, 213
lawn bowling, 7, 100
Lawrence, Mary, 128–29
Lay, Marion, 135, 166–68, 204,
213
LeBlanc, Karen, 193
legal challenges. See human
rights commissions; sex
discrimination in recreation
and sports

Lennox, Diana Gordon, 83–84
Lenskyj, Helen, 182, 200, 207
lesbians and lesbianism
    CAAWS advocacy, 174–75
    history in sport, 92, 123,
        159–60, 165, 195
    media discourse, 92–93, 123,
        159–60, 198–200
Letheren, Carol Anne, 208, 213
Leuszler, Winnie Roach, 64, 112,
    115–16, 120–23
Limpert, Marianne, 201
Lindell, Eila, 132
Linton, Marjorie, 80
Little, Olive "Ollie" (Bend), 125
Lovett, Claire, 112
Lowe, Jean, 113
Lyons, Robin, 201–2

MacDonald, Irene, 112, 117
MacDonald, Jackie, 111, 129–30
MacKenzie, Ada, 63, 119
Magnussen, Karen, 135, 151
Malar, Joanne, 201
male hegemony, 1–2, 14
Malenfant, Barbara, 132
Manley, Elizabeth, 184
manliness as Victorian ideal,
    25–26, 63–64
marathons. See swimming,
    marathon; track and field
Margaret Eaton School, 35, 44,
    75, 133–34
marriage. See heterosexual
    marriage, family and sports
martial arts, 2
Martin, Andrée, 151
Martin, Winnie, 41–42
"Matchless Six," 52–53, 82, 213
McBean, Marnie, 213
McCabe, Nora, 146
McCarthy, Norah, 106–7
McCredie, Nancy, 135
McCrossan, Elaine, 157
McGill University, 31–33, 54, 57,
    134, 156
McGowan, Myrtle Cook. See
    Cook (McGowan), Myrtle
McGregor, Marg, 204
McKenzie, Violet, 113
McKinley, Nancy, 151
McMaster University, 156
McNamee, Kaye, 116–17
Meagher, Aileen, 82, 85–86, 90

media coverage and discourse.
    See also femininity, beauty and
    athleticism; names of
    sportswriters; sportswriters
    in 1910s and before, 9, 12–14,
        20–21, 24
    in 1920s through 1950s, 3,
        61–62, 69, 89, 92–93,
        111–13, 115–16, 196
    in 1960s and 1970s, 135–36,
        141–52, 158–60
    in 1980s and later, 194–97,
        211–15
    adolescents, treatment of,
        142–44
    first woman photo editor of
        Canadian newspaper, 100
    individual/team sports
        differences, 153
    language and metaphors,
        61–62
    legal challenges, 203–4
    mannish stereotypes, 20–21,
        24, 89, 92–93, 158–60
    marathon swimming, 115–16
    millenium-end sports lists,
        212–15
    sexually explicit, 146–48,
        196–97
    television and media
        convergence, 137–38, 195,
        211–12
medical discourse
    biological determinism,
        75–76, 165
    cycling controversy, 18–19,
        207
    fertility rates, 91, 155
    motherhood and
        competition, 119–21, 123,
        165, 202–3
    negative messages, 207
    reproductive damage, 18–19,
        75–76, 91, 119, 123, 165
    rules modifications for
        females, 71, 155
    susceptible to injuries, 18–19,
        69–70, 165
Meraw, Ann (Mundigel), 93
military school programs,
    29–30, 54
military sport carnivals, 102
millenium-end sports lists,
    212–15
Miller, Esther, 186

Miller, Marjory, 83
Miller, Shannon, 199
Monaghan, Barbara, 132
Monaghan, Claire, 119
Montgomery, Violet, 86
Montreal, Quebec
    1910s and before, 7–9, 22–23,
        25, 34, 37, 57
    1920s and 1930s, 50, 53, 60,
        66, 70, 74, 77, 80, 82,
        85–86, 88, 92, 95–96, 99
    1940s and 1950s, 113, 117
    1960s and 1970s, 149, 152, 157,
        179
    first hockey championship, 37
    first provincial swimming
        competition, 130
    first women's hockey game, 37
    first women's ski club, 118
    Montreal Amateur Athletic
        Association, 130–31
    Olympics, Summer 1976, 142,
        150, 152–53, 161, 183, 185–86,
        201
    physical education, 74, 77,
        80, 134, 141
Morrow, Suzanne, 112
Moss, Judith, 83
motherhood. See heterosexual
    marriage, family and sports;
    medical discourse
mountaineering. See climbing
Mount Allison University, New
    Brunswick, 31
Mountifield, Eleanor, 42
multi-sports centres, 70, 95
    first all-women's multi-sports
        club, 45
Munday, Phyllis, 27
Munro Iveagh, 134
Murray, Ella, 63

native women in sports. See also
    race and ethnicity
    as concern in sports history,
        11–12, 214
    discrimination, 207, 214
    early beginnings, 4–7, 186
    first female recipient of Tom
        Longboat Award, 154
    first native women at
        Olympic Games, 153–54
    organizations and
        competitions, 214
    softball, 94, 154

Nattrass, Susan, 185
Nelson, Helen (Sandiford), 125
Nelson, Maud, 38
Nesukaitis, Violetta, 151
netball, 167
newspapers. *See* media
Nichol, Dorothy, 134
Nolden, Shauna, 210
Nonen, Sharola, 193
Nutter, Janet, 184

Ogilvie, Doris, 82–83
O'Hara, Jane, 146
Oke, Fred G. "Teddy," 45, 52, 67
Olmstead, Barb, 186
Olympics
  Canadian Olympic
    Association directors, 170
  first Canadian woman at
    Olympic Games, 67–68
  International Olympic
    Committee (IOC), 47,
    79–80, 208
  political protests and
    cancellations, 84–85,
    100–101, 107
  ratio male/females, 135, 151,
    158
  social class, 90, 112
Olympics, Summer 1920s and
  1930s, 13, 51, 55, 57, 79–81
Olympics, Summer 1936, Berlin,
  84–85, 89–90, 98
Olympics, Summer 1948,
  London, 116, 120, 132
Olympics, Summer 1950s and
  1960s, 55, 113, 117, 129–30, 132,
  135, 137, 142, 147, 158
Olympics, Summer 1970s and
  1980s, 135, 151, 158, 183, 185–86,
  201
Olympics, Summer 1976,
  Montreal, 142, 150, 152–53, 161,
  183, 185–86, 201
Olympics, Summer 1990s and
  2000s, 193–94
Olympics, Winter 1920s and
  1930s, 68, 81, 83
Olympics, Winter 1950s and
  1960s, 135, 137, 144, 153
Olympics, Winter 1970s and
  1980s, 135, 151, 153, 184, 186
Olympics, Winter 1998,
  Nagano, 199
O'Meara, Eleanor, 106–8

Ontario Athletic Commission, 87
Ontario Rural Softball
  Association, *Bannerman v.,* 177
organizations. *See also* control of
  sports by women; names of
  organizations; names of sports
  first all-male sports club, 6
  first national conference on
    women and sport, 166
  first woman appointed to
    Ontario Athletic
    Commission, 87
Orser, Joan, 132
Ottenbrite, Anne, 186

Page, J. Percy, 13, 36, 41–42, 55,
  91, 97–98
Page (Hollingsworth), Patricia, 13
Palmer, Lillian, 81–82, 85
Pan-American Games, 117,
  128–29, 132, 142, 152, 155
"paper chases," 31, 46
parachute jumping, 157
Paralympics, 208, 215
Parkes, Doris, 97
Parkes, Marie, 50, 53–54
parks associations, 34
Payne, Marita, 184
pedestrianism and walking
  matches, 8–9, 21, 45–46, 66, 211
Penney, Marian, 76–77
pentathlon, 147, 183
Percival, Lloyd, 129
Percy, Karen, 186
Perry, Nellie, 41–42
Phinney, Gertrude, 52
physical culture, 4, 19, 33–35, 98.
  See also physical education
physical education. *See also*
  names of sports; physical
  culture
  in 1910s and earlier, 27–33, 35,
    54
  in 1920s and 1930s, 54, 57,
    68–79, 130
  in 1940s and 1950s, 131–34
  in 1960s and 1970s, 138, 160,
    164
  in 1980s and 1990s, 169
Pike, Shelagh, 144
Pirie, Irene, 80, 83
pistol shooting, 185–86
Pitt, Faye, 119
play and sports days, 33, 39, 46,
  62, 74, 76–77

playground associations, 34
Plewes, Doris, 134
Policy on Women's Sport, 171
Post, Sandra, 148–49, 151, 213
Potter, Lela Brooks, 67, 81
pregnancy and sports. *See*
  medical discourse
Priestly, Gladys, 117
Priestner, Cathy, 186
Prior, Dorothy, 52
professional sport. *See also*
  Ladies Professional Golf
  Association (LPGA)
  basketball, 194
  hockey, 190–91
  soccer, 193
Pro-Rec physical recreation,
  99–100
provincial governments. *See*
  government and sports;
  human rights commissions
Pruden, Margaret "Prudie," 59

Queen's University, 31–32, 36, 54,
  57, 156
Quirk, Wendy, 184
quoits, 44

race and ethnicity. *See also*
  African-Canadian women in
  sports; native women in sports
  as concern in sports history,
    11–12, 14, 214–15
  organizations and, 113, 165, 174
Raff, Emma Scott, 35
Raine, Nancy Greene, 135, 139,
  143–44, 148, 213
Ray, Mabel, 43, 61, 86, 96
records and record-keeping,
  46–47
recreation. *See* names of sports
regions and regionalism. *See*
  names of sports
Reiser, Glenda, 151
*Report of the Royal Commission
  on the Status of Women in
  Canada,* 162, 166
reproduction, female. *See*
  medical discourse
Rhéaume, Manon, 179–80, 182,
  191
rhythmic exercises, 99
Richardson, Jillian, 184
ringette, 156, 167, 182
Robinson, Gladys, 66–67

roller skating, 8, 24, 157
Rosenfeld, Fanny "Bobbie"
  athlete and coach, 13, 47–49,
    52–53, 56, 59–61, 82, 87–89,
    95–96, 127–28, 145–46, 161,
    213
  sportswriter, 77, 88–89, 95,
    100, 127, 145, 161
Ross, Marion, 134
rowing
  control by women, 171
  history of, 5–7, 9–10, 21, 24,
    72, 200
Royal Commission on the
  Status of Women in Canada,
  162, 166, 168
rugby football, 2, 21, 25
rules modifications, 55–56, 71,
  88, 125–26. See also basketball
Russell, Ernestine, 112
Rutledge, Vicki, 144
Ruys de Perez, Stephane, 157
Ryan, Doreen, 120, 122–23

sailing, 44
Sallis, Victoria, 86
Samuel, Constance (Wilson), 81,
  106–7
Sander, Helen, 153
Schlegel, Elfi, 184
Schmirler, Sandra, 213
Schutz, Rosemarie, 119
Scott, Abbie, 55
Scott, Barbara Ann, 103–6, 109,
  111–12, 147, 213
scuba diving, 157
second-wave feminism. See
  feminism, second-wave
Seller, Peg (formerly Margaret
  Shearer), 130
Sequin, Gigi, 119
sex discrimination in recreation
  and sports. See also Canadian
  Association for the
  Advancement of Women and
  Sport and Physical Activity
  (CAAWS); human rights
  commissions
  legal challenges, 163, 177–82,
    192–93, 202–3
  structural inequities as
    sexism, 165, 173
  surveys of activity, 163–64
sex testing, 92–93, 158–60
sexual abuse of athletes, 200–201

sexuality. See femininity, beauty
  and athleticism; media
  coverage and discourse;
  medical discourse
sexualization, 196–98
sexual preference. See
  heterosexual marriage, family
  and sports; lesbians and
  lesbianism
Shatto, Cindy, 151
Shaw, Daisy King, 66
Shearer, Norma, 131
Shedd, Marjory, 112, 153
Shields, Kathy, 209–10
Simon Fraser University, 168
Sippel, Lori, 193–94
skating. See figure skating; roller
  skating; speed skating
skiing, cross-country, 153, 185–86
  first women to compete in
    Olympic cross-country
    skiing, 153
skiing, downhill
  in 1950s and before, 72,
    83–84, 102–3, 109, 112,
    118–19
  in 1960s and 1970s, 139, 141,
    143–44, 151
  athletes and competitions,
    186
  first Olympic skiing gold
    medal, 144
  first women's ski club, 118
  industrial leagues and
    recreation, 102–3
  media, 111, 151
  Nancy Greene Raine, 143–44,
    148, 213
  Olympics, 83–84, 118–19,
    143–44, 186
  social class, 118–19
Smith, Bev, 194
Smith, Cecil Eustace and
  Maude, 67–68
Smith, Connie, 41–42
Smith, Donalda, 213
Smith, Donald (Lord
  Strathcona), 30–31
Smith, Tricia, 186
Smith (Stewart), Ethel, 52–53, 82
snowshoeing, 5, 9, 24–25, 66, 72
soccer, 2, 5, 21, 25, 192–93, 198,
  202, 208
social class. See also names of
  sports

CAAWS aims, 174
company and corporate
  sponsorships, 44, 64–65
as concern in sports history,
  11–12, 214–15
Olympics, 90, 112
sports history and, 3, 5–7, 10,
  33, 44, 64, 78–79, 90, 110,
  112, 139, 206
social Darwinism, 25, 29
softball. See also baseball
  in 1930s and before, 3, 39,
    43–45, 50, 60–62, 90–91,
    94–96
  in 1940s and 1950s, 100, 102–3,
    109–10, 112–13, 124–26
  in 1960s and 1970s, 153–54,
    193–94
  in 1990s, 193–94, 202, 208
  baseball and, 61–62
  equipment and uniforms, 62,
    94, 96, 100, 126
  fastball, 154
  femininity, 109–10
  first women's softball
    championship, 126
  industrial sponsorships and
    commercialism, 44–45,
    60–62, 102–3, 124–25
  media coverage, 112–13,
    153–54, 193
  Olympics, 193–94, 208
  organizations and teams,
    43–44, 49, 60–62, 91, 95–96
  regions and regionalism, 50,
    61–62, 94–96, 124, 154
  rules modifications, 125–26
  sex-discrimination legal
    challenges, 202
  slow-pitch, 154
  social class, 43, 78–79, 90
  Sunnyside (Toronto), 60–61,
    95–96, 126
Somers, Florence, 75–76
speed skating, 66–67, 81, 112,
  122–23, 186
sport, defined, 4
Sport Canada, 168, 171–72, 177,
  184, 204, 206
sport queen ("la belle neige"), 92
sports and play days, 33, 39, 46,
  62, 74, 76–77
sports car racers, 157
sports facilities. See also names of
  sports

early history, 28–33
sports lists, millenium-end, 212–15
sportswear. *See also* bloomers;
  names of sports
  first sportswear for women, 8
  first uniforms for women, 48
sportswriters. *See also* Cook
  (McGowan), Myrtle; Gibb,
  Alexandrine; Griffiths, Phyllis;
  Rosenfeld, Fanny "Bobbie"
  in 1920s and 1930s, 45, 62
  in 1940s and 1950s, 86–87
  in 1960s and 1970s, 144–48
  contributions to sports
    history, 3, 12–14, 45
  eligibility as volunteer
    administrators, 86–87
  underrepresentation of
    women, 212
Stephens, Helen, 89–90
steroids, anabolic, 201–2
Stewart, Mary, 135, 142–43
Stewart (Hunt), Helen, 111,
  117–18, 141–42, 151–53
Stewart (Streit), Marlene, 111–16,
  141
Stoneham, Pearl, 80
Stott, Ann, 13
Strathcona Trust, 30–31
Stratten, Merrily, 146
Strike, Hilda, 82, 93
Strong, Irene, 116–17
Sunnyside (Toronto), 60–61,
  95–96, 126
surveys
  first national survey of leisure
    activities, 163–64
  first national survey of
    women in sport leadership,
    169
Sutton-Brown, Tammy, 194
Swedish gymnastics. *See*
  gymnastics
swimming. *See also* swimming,
  marathon; swimming,
  synchronized
  in 1910s and earlier, 8, 29, 32,
    34, 50, 52, 65, 72
  in 1920s and 1930s, 82–83,
    85–86, 102–3, 131
  in 1940s and 1950s, 111–12,
    116–19, 131
  in 1960s and after, 138,
    141–42, 151, 184, 186, 196,
    201, 210

British Empire Games, 80,
  83, 85–86
coaching and gender equity,
  210
drug use and testing, 201
first Olympic female
  swimming coach, 210
first Olympic swimming gold
  medal, 186
first outstanding female
  swimmer in international
  competition, 83
first provincial swimming
  competition, 130
first sportswear for women, 8
media coverage, 151, 196
Olympics, 52, 80, 82, 85,
  116–17, 142–43, 184, 201
Pan-American Games, 117–18
regions and regionalism, 50,
  65, 117
social class, 90, 112
sportswear, 8, 82
swimming, marathon, 64–66,
  93, 114–16, 120–21. *See also*
  Bell, Marilyn; Leuszler,
  Winnie Roach
  first Canadian to swim the
    English Channel, 121
  first woman to swim English
    Channel, 64
  youngest person to swim
    English Channel, 116
swimming, synchronized, 109,
  112, 130–32, 141, 186
  first international
    synchronized swimming
    champion, 132
  first provincial synchronized
    swimming competition, 130

table tennis, 151
taekwondo, 208
Take, Marilyn Ruth, 112
Tanner, Elaine, 135, 138, 142, 148,
  213
Taylor, Betty, 85, 90
Taylor (Issajenko), Angella, 184,
  201
tennis
  first women's tennis
    tournament, 22
  history of, 21–22, 28–29, 31–33,
    44, 63, 72, 102–3, 136, 151
  media, 111, 151, 196–97

social class, 22, 43, 90, 112
Thacker, Mary Rose, 106–7
Thom, Linda, 185–86
Thomas, Aileen, 85
Thompson, Jean, 52, 82
Thomson, Mabel, 22, 39
Thorne, Rosella, 113, 214
Thouin, Suzanne, 105
Title IX, 163
tobogganing, 8
tomboys and tomboyism, 89,
  106, 114, 123, 143, 149, 159–60
Toronto Ladies Athletic Club,
  43–47, 60
  first all-women's multi-sports
    club in Canada, 45
  first Ontario track and field
    championships for women,
    49
track and field
  in 1910s and before, 6, 8–9,
    21, 31
  in 1920s and 1930s, 3, 43–53,
    79–82, 86, 92–93, 95
  in 1940s and 1950s, 109–13,
    128–30
  in 1960s and 1970s, 141,
    146–48, 151, 158–60
  in 1980s and after, 197,
    200–202, 208
  Canadian championships, 49,
    51–52
  discus, 51, 53, 82, 111, 128–29,
    183
  drug use and testing, 184–85,
    201–2
  early women's organizations,
    43–44
  femininity and athleticism,
    109–10, 119, 129, 146–48
  first Olympic track and field
    team, 51
  first track and field
    championships, 49, 51
  funding and sponsorships,
    44, 95, 129
  hammer throw, 201–2
  high jump, 51–52, 81–82, 183
  hurdles, 53, 82, 113
  international competitions,
    47–48, 142
  javelin, 53, 81–82, 86, 128–29
  media coverage, 146–48, 151
  Olympics, 47, 51, 79–82, 142,
    147

"paper chases," 31, 46
pedestrianism and walking
    matches, 8–9, 21, 45–46,
    66, 211
records and record-keeping,
    46–47, 51–52
regions and regionalism, 48,
    51–52, 81
relays, 47–48, 51, 82, 86, 113
shot put, 111, 129–30
social class, 43, 90, 112
sportswear and uniforms,
    8–9, 48–50
trapshooting
    first woman trapshooter in
    Olympics, 185
Trueman, Mary, 146
Turbide, Françoise, 179

uniforms. See names of sports
universities and colleges. See also
    intercollegiate sports; names of
    universities and colleges
    adminstrators and coaches,
    170, 209
    behaviour and dress codes,
    160
    first university to grant a
    degree to a woman, 31
    pre-WWI, 31–33
    scholarships for athletes, 163
    social class, 43, 58, 79
University of Alberta, 32, 57
University of British Columbia,
    57, 81
University of Guelph, 156
University of Manitoba, 57
University of Saskatchewan, 57,
    71, 170
University of Toronto, 31–33, 54,
    57, 97, 134, 203–4. See also
    Margaret Eaton School
University of Western Ontario,
    54, 156
University Women's Physical
    Education Committee
    (UPEC), 140

Vail, Sue, 168
Van Kiekebelt, Debbie, 147–48,
    151
Vauthier, Agnés, 57
volleyball
    history, 44, 76, 102–3, 141,
    152–53, 176, 195, 199

international competitions,
    152–53, 208
media coverage, 112–13, 153, 197

Wagner, Barbara, 112, 135
Waldo, Carolyn, 186
Wales, Freda, 134
Walker, Dorothy, 134
walking matches and
    pedestrianism, 8–9, 21, 45–46,
    66, 211
Wall, Irene, 133
Walsh, Amy, 193
Walsh, Stella (formerly
    Stanislawa Walasiewicz),
    92–93, 102
water polo, 34, 130, 197, 208
water skiing, 112
Wawryshyn, Evelyn "Evie," 126
weightlifting, 2, 208
Westclox (Western Clock
    Company), 44–45, 103
Wheeler, Lucile, 111–12, 118–19,
    141
Whitall, Beth, 117
White, Betty, 82
Wickenheiser, Hayley, 194
Wilkes, Debbi, 135
Wilson, Alda, 82
Wilson, Dorothy, 94
Wilson, Jean, 81
Wilson, Ruth, 13, 128
Wingerson (Meldrum), Jenny, 147
womanliness. See also femininity,
    beauty and athleticism
    as Victorian ideal, 25–26, 42,
    64
Women's Amateur Athletic
    Federation of Canada (WAAF
    of C), 50–54, 63–64, 80,
    86–88, 95, 101–2, 132–34
Women's Athletic Committee of
    the Canadian Physical
    Education Association (WAC),
    133–34, 139–40, 169
Women's Division, National
    Amateur Athletic Federation
    (USA), 73–74, 88, 133–34
Women's League of Health and
    Beauty, 98–99
women's movement. See
    feminism, second-wave
Women's Program, Fitness and
    Amateur Sport Branch (FAS),
    165, 168–69, 172–74, 204

Women's Sports Foundation,
    172–73
Workers' Sport Association of
    Canada, 84–85
World War I and women's
    sports, 40, 63, 93
World War II and women's
    sports, 3, 100–103, 106, 108–13,
    127, 133–34
wrestling, 42–43, 164
Wurtele, Rhona and Rhoda, 112,
    118

yachting, 24
yoga, 211
Young Women's Christian
    Association (YWCA), 34, 36